THE
GENERALS

THE
GENERALS

THE
GENERALS

American Military Command
from World War II to Today

THOMAS E. RICKS

THE PENGUIN PRESS

New York | 2012

THE PENGUIN PRESS
Published by the Penguin Group
Penguin Group (USA) Inc., 375 Hudson Street, New York, New York 10014, U.S.A. •
Penguin Group (Canada), 90 Eglinton Avenue East, Suite 700, Toronto, Ontario,
Canada M4P 2Y3 (a division of Pearson Penguin Canada Inc.) • Penguin Books Ltd,
80 Strand, London WC2R 0RL, England • Penguin Ireland, 25 St. Stephen's Green,
Dublin 2, Ireland (a division of Penguin Books Ltd) • Penguin Group (Australia),
707 Collins Street, Melbourne, Victoria 3008, Australia (a division of Pearson
Australia Group Pty Ltd) • Penguin Books India Pvt Ltd, 11 Community Centre,
Panchsheel Park, New Delhi–110 017, India • Penguin Group (NZ), 67 Apollo Drive,
Rosedale, Auckland 0632, New Zealand (a division of Pearson New Zealand Ltd) • Penguin
Books, Rosebank Office Park, 181 Jan Smuts Avenue, Parktown North 2193, South Africa •
Penguin China, B7 Jaiming Center, 27 East Third Ring Road North, Chaoyang
District, Beijing 100020, China

Penguin Books Ltd, Registered Offices:
80 Strand, London WC2R 0RL, England

First published in 2012 by The Penguin Press,
a member of Penguin Group (USA) Inc.

Photograph credits appear on pages 557–58.

Library of Congress Cataloging-in-Publication Data
Ricks, Thomas E.
The generals : American military command from World War II to today / Thomas E. Ricks.
p. cm.
Includes bibliographical references and index.
ISBN 978-1-59420-404-3
1. Generals—United States—History—20th century.   2. United States—
History, Military—20th century—Case studies.   3. Command of troops—
History—20th century—Case studies.   I. Title.
E745.R53 2012
355.0092'2—dc23
[B]
2012015110

Printed in the United States of America
5 7 9 10 8 6

DESIGNED BY MARYSARAH QUINN

ALWAYS LEARNING   PEARSON

For those who died following poor leaders

There are no bad soldiers, only bad generals.

—Saying attributed to Napoleon

CONTENTS

THE
GENERALS

PROLOGUE

Captain William DePuy and the 90th Division
in Normandy, summer 1944

Captain William DePuy of the 90th Division saw it all in north-western France in the summer of 1944.

On June 13, 1944, a few days after the 90th Infantry Division went into action against the Germans in Normandy, Lt. Gen. J. Lawton Collins, to whom the division reported, went on foot to check on his men. "We could locate no regimental or battalion headquarters," he recalled with dismay. "No shelling was going on, nor any fighting that we could observe." This was an ominous sign, as the Battle of Normandy was far from decided, and the Wehrmacht was still trying to push the Americans, British, and Canadians, who had landed a week earlier, back into the sea.

The 90th's assistant division commander, Brig. Gen. "Hanging Sam" Williams, also was looking for the leader of his green division. He found the division commander, Brig. Gen. Jay MacKelvie, sheltered from enemy fire, huddling in a drainage ditch along the base of a hedgerow. "Goddammit, General, you can't lead this division hiding in that goddamn hole," Williams shouted. "Go back to the CP. Get the hell out of that hole and go to your vehicle. Walk to it, or you'll have this goddamn division wading in the

English Channel." The message did not take. Within just a few days the division was bogged down and veering close to passivity. "Orders may have been issued to attack, but no attacks took place," remembered DePuy. "Nothing really happened. Infantry leaders were totally exhausted and in a daze. There was a pervasive feeling of hopelessness."

In June 1944, DePuy was fighting to stay alive—no small feat in the bloody, World War I–like combat of that summer. One infantry company in the 90th began the day with 142 men and finished it with 32. Its battalion commander walked around babbling, "I killed K Company, I killed K Company." Later that summer in Normandy, one of the 90th's battalions, with 265 soldiers, surrendered to a German patrol of fifty men and two tanks. In six weeks of small advances, the division would use up all its infantrymen, requesting replacements totaling 100 percent. The average term of service for a 90th Division lieutenant leading a platoon in combat was two weeks. The 90th Division in Normandy, DePuy would remember bitterly, was "a killing machine—of our own troops."

Gen. Collins relieved MacKelvie. In the relief order, Gen. Collins wrote that the division's enemy opposition had been "relatively light," probably less than a regimental combat team—a blistering aside. Collins instructed the 90th's new commander, Maj. Gen. Eugene Landrum, to fire the commanders of two of the division's three regiments. DePuy considered one of those two, West Point graduate Col. P. D. Ginder, "a horse's ass of the worst order. Goddamned fool . . . he was a disaster." DePuy was hardly alone in his estimate of Ginder: Another officer, Lt. Max Kocour, a mortar forward observer, remembered that the regimental commander "almost constantly made the wrong decisions." Indeed, even after being relieved, the excitable Ginder continued to issue orders, at one point sending troops forward into an artillery target area without seeking permission or coordinating the movement, an action for which he was placed under arrest and sent back to division headquarters under armed escort. Ginder had been in command of the regiment for less than a month. His successor, Col. John Sheehy, was killed in an ambush after two days in command.

Col. George Barth took command of Ginder's regiment after Sheehy's death. One day he saw a long column of perhaps eight hundred men and asked DePuy which battalion they were. That was no battalion, DePuy replied—it was the day's incoming replacements for the division's casualties. Barth later confessed that, before taking over the regiment, he "had never before experienced 'zero morale.'"

MacKelvie's successor, Landrum, was given a few weeks to prove he was an able commander, but by midsummer he also was judged to be wanting. Gen. Omar Bradley, the senior American general in France at the time, decided to replace Landrum with Brig. Gen. Theodore Roosevelt Jr., the son of the former president, whom he had sacked a year earlier as assistant commander of the 1st Infantry Division under Maj. Gen. Terry Allen. But the night before he was given the job, Roosevelt died of a heart attack. Landrum was eventually removed as the commander of the 90th, though before he left, he fired the assistant division commander he had inherited, Brig. Gen. Sam Williams, with whom he had clashed. "I feel that a general officer of a more optimistic and calming attitude would be more beneficial to this division at this time," Landrum wrote. Bradley concurred and topped off the dismissal by demoting Williams to colonel.

The swift reliefs of World War II were not an instrument of precision, and, while often effective in leading to more capable commanders, they were sometimes clearly the wrong move. Other officers watched and assessed the fairness of such firings. In the case of the 90th Division, the consensus was that the removal of

MacKelvie was fully justified but that Ginder and Landrum probably deserved better, and that Williams certainly did. This peer judgment resulted in Ginder, Landrum, and Williams being given second chances. Ginder was assigned to the 2nd Division later that year as a spare commander and redeemed himself with a strong battlefield performance on Elsenborn Ridge, key terrain during the Battle of the Bulge. He was awarded the Distinguished Service Cross for his acts during the grinding Battle of Hürtgen Forest and was given command of the 2nd Division's 9th Infantry Regiment. During the Korean War, he would rise to command the 45th Infantry Division and make news by giving a battlefield tour in his helicopter to the pop singer Eddie Fisher, who had been drafted but was continuing to pump out hits. Even a commander escorted from the battlefield under arrest could recover. In 1963, Ginder retired as a major general.

Landrum was sent back to the United States and put in command of a division in training, but Dwight Eisenhower, the top American commander in Europe, declined to let him bring the division overseas. In 1950, Landrum served in Korea as a colonel, acting as chief of staff to Lt. Gen. Walton Walker, commander of the Eighth Army, during the difficult first year of that war. He was allowed to retire the following year as a major general.

It was the removal of Hanging Sam Williams—the nickname came from his eagerness to impose capital punishment during a peacetime Army court-martial—that especially caught the attention of members of the division, and the Army at large. "They got the wrong man," DePuy would argue, with feeling, decades later. He had seen Williams out and about, pushing officers and encouraging troops, while Landrum was usually found back at his headquarters. "Hanging Sam Williams was the assistant division commander and he was with us all the time. He was very helpful and a very brave and powerful man."

Williams abided, living with his demotion for seven years. He was promoted back to brigadier general in 1951 and a year later won command of the 25th Infantry Division in Korea. Ironically, but in keeping with his Old Army ways, Williams acquired a reputation in the Korean War for ruthlessly relieving officers he perceived to be incompetent. When he asked a briefer how certain troops would get to "Red Beach" in an amphibious landing, the officer said they would be transported by the Navy but conceded that the plan had not been coordinated with that service. "You are fired," Williams responded. Williams's blunt manner would catch up with him later, in Vietnam. In 1955, not long after the French disaster at Dien Bien Phu, he was made the top American military adviser in Vietnam, where he routinely engaged in shouting matches with the U.S. ambassador. (In an interesting coincidence, Creighton Abrams, the future American commander in Vietnam and Army chief of staff, would be assigned in the 1950s to work first for Williams and then for Ginder. He liked Williams but detested Ginder, who continued to display a remarkable mix of pomposity and incompetence.) Williams eventually retired as a three-star lieutenant general.

Later in the summer of '44, Bradley sent Brig. Gen. Raymond McLain, whom he had brought from Italy to England to have on tap as a replacement when someone was fired, to take over the 90th Division. "We're going to make that division go if we've got to can every senior officer in it," Bradley vowed. McLain kept him to his word, two days later giving him a list of sixteen field-grade officers he wanted out of the division. It would not be surprising if DePuy, despite his youth, had helped compile that list, given his growing influence in the turbulent division's operations. DePuy believed that the division had been remiss in not removing several officers before going into combat.

DePuy's own World War II experience illustrates how the swift relief of some officers cleared the way for others with more competence. He began the war as a "green lieutenant" from the ROTC program at South Dakota State College. He finished it having commanded a battalion at age twenty-five and then been operations officer for a division. During the war he was awarded the Distinguished Service Cross and three Silver Stars.

The 90th Division also improved radically, going from a problem division that First Army staff wanted to break up and use to send replacements to other units to being considered, as Bradley wrote later, "one of the most outstanding in the European Theater." Retired Army Col. Henry Gole, in his analysis of the 90th Division and DePuy's command style, directly credits the policy of fast relief:

> Because incompetent commanders were fired and replaced by quality men at division and regiment, and because the junior officers of 1944 good at war, including DePuy, rose to command battalions in a Darwinian process, the division became an effective fighting force. DePuy was 25 years old. His regimental commander was 27. The other two battalion commanders were 28 and 26.

DePuy would be haunted for decades by the bloody, grinding fighting of the summer of 1944 and by the incompetent leadership he witnessed in Normandy. "The brutality and stupidity of those days have affected me all the rest of my professional life," he said. His experience shaped DePuy's approach to fighting in Vietnam, where he would command the 1st Infantry Division twenty-two years later. He then would go on to play a central role in shaping the post-Vietnam Army that fought in Kuwait in 1991. "DePuy is one of the very small handful of very great soldiers that this country had produced in this [20th] century," said another general, Donn Starry. "The Army owes him a great debt, an enormous debt. He set it on the path for the 21st century."

Three aspects of the experience of the 90th Division stand out, even seven decades later. First, that generalship in combat is extraordinarily difficult, and many seasoned officers fail at it. Second, that personalities matter—the 90th floundered under its first two commanders in the summer of 1944 but thrived under McLain's leadership. Third, and most significant for understanding American history, that American generals were managed very differently in World War II than they were in subsequent wars. During World War II, senior American commanders generally were given a few months in which to succeed, be killed or wounded, or be replaced. Sixteen Army division commanders were relieved for cause, out of a total of 155 officers who commanded Army divisions in combat during the war. At least five corps commanders also were removed for cause. Corps and division command, wrote Secretary of War Henry Stimson, "was the critical level of professional competence" during the war.

I first learned about the standards to which American generals were held during World War II when, taking a break from covering the Iraq war, I joined a "staff ride"—that is, a study of a military campaign in which one walks battlefields and recounts the decisions of commanders and the information available to them at the time. The staff ride group, selected mainly from students in the strategy course of the School of Advanced International Studies at Johns Hopkins University, was studying the Allied invasion of Sicily during World War II. We were gathered on the highest point in central Sicily, looking north across the razored ridges of that extraordinary mid-Mediterranean island, when one student recounted how Maj. Gen. Terry de la Mesa Allen, one of the most successful American generals of 1943, had been relieved after winning the last major battle of the Sicily campaign.

I was stunned. How could this be? I still had the dust of Iraq on my walking shoes, and my mind was still focused on that war, where even abject failure did not get a general fired. Relief in the U.S. military had become so rare that, as Lt. Col. Paul Yingling noted during some of the darkest days of the Iraq war, a private who lost his rifle was now punished more than a general who lost his part of a war.

That question haunted me on the flight home from Sicily to Washington, D.C.: Why do we treat our generals differently today, and what does that mean for the conduct of our wars—and for our nation? Trying to find the answer launched me on four years of research about American generalship from the beginning of World War II to the present. It eventually led me to the story of DePuy and the 90th Division, which in turn led me to write this book. What I found was a part of American military culture that has now been lost. During World War II, top officials *expected* some generals to fail in combat and were prepared to remove them when that happened. The personalities of these generals mattered enormously, and the chief of staff of the Army, George C. Marshall, devoted much effort to finding the right men for the jobs at hand. When some did not work out, they were removed quickly—but often given another chance in a different job.

This is a story about a remarkable group of men, the Army general officers of the past three-quarters of a century, and the wars they fought. Each of these men was given powers we accord to few: responsibilities for saving lives and for taking lives; power over promotion and demotion; the responsibility to advise presidents on our most fundamental national issues; and—perhaps most valued by these Army general officers—the responsibility and the privilege of shaping their own institution by deciding how to train, select, and sometimes discard their peers.

George Marshall. Dwight Eisenhower. Terry Allen. Douglas MacArthur. Matthew Ridgway. Maxwell Taylor. William Westmoreland. William DePuy. William "Ray" Peers. Colin Powell. Norman Schwarzkopf. Tommy Franks. Ricardo Sanchez. George Casey. David Petraeus. It is evident that each and every one of these men loved the Army—and, even more than with most institutions, derived their personal as well as professional identities from it. Despite being shaped by the institution, all of them remained recognizable individuals, some of them extraordinary. "Personality plays a tremendous part in war," George Patton once observed, and that certainly is true of the modern American armed forces, Patton himself being a primary example.

Generals are born, and generals are made. The promotion from colonel to brigadier (or one-star) general is one of the largest psychological leaps an officer can take. It is richly symbolic: The promoted officer removes from his or her collar the insignia of an Army branch (the crossed rifles of infantry, for example, or the tiny triple-turreted castle of engineers) and puts on a single star. As brigadier generals, the newly promoted officers are instructed in a special course—they no longer represent a part of the Army, but now are the stewards of the entire service. As members of the Army's select few, they are expected to control and coordinate different branches, such as artillery, cavalry, and engineers—that is, to become generalists.

It is difficult to speak with much authority about that process of promotion to brigadier general, which remains largely the realm of rumor and speculation. The deliberations of promotion boards remain the holy of U.S. military holies, more closely held than the secrets of the nation's nuclear arsenal. But it is possible to look at who was selected, and what sorts of officers rose during different periods. It also is possible to look in detail at the training and education of general officers and at how different personalities struggled to change those processes in decadelong internal fights that did much to shape the future of the Army. From that examination we can see how the institutional choices of the past have shaped the conduct of our wars today.

Most of all, we can study how generals performed in combat command. Different traits are required for different tasks. George Marshall had the military insight to know that at the top of the Allied military in Europe, overseeing the largest armed force in history, he would need an indefatigable team player with balanced judgment. He also had the skill to find the officer who could fit that bill, plucking Dwight Eisenhower from his post as executive officer of an infantry regiment to groom him for that unprecedented task, in which Ike eventually would wear five stars. Eisenhower, in turn, recognized that George Patton could excel in the battlefield task of pursuing the Germans across northwestern Europe. Had the two generals been reversed in their roles, as their relative seniority in service would have dictated, the history of World War II likely would be different.

The qualities that are valued change, partly because the circumstances of war change, partly because tastes change. The Army at various times has screened out certain qualities and decided that other qualities are indispensable. For example, George Marshall and his senior subordinates valued aggressiveness and cooperation—but Marshall was more inclined, on balance, to favor the aggressive officer, such as Terry Allen, while the senior subordinates, especially Bradley and Eisenhower, increasingly wanted cooperative generals who could be part of a larger team. During the 1950s, the Army especially seemed to value conformists. In the late 1980s and the 1990s, Army leaders talked incessantly about "warfighters." In fact, that turned out to be a misnomer, because they produced a generation of tacticians who knew how to fight battles but who apparently lacked the strategic ability to fight and conclude wars.

Despite these changes, there are traits that all generals must possess. These are characteristics often found in the outlines of the Marshall system, the characteristics he prized. They are still visible in today's generals. The same sorts of people—energetic, determined team players—tend to be chosen to lead the military, for what they do is essentially the same. Being a general usually involves being able to impose one's will on a large organization engaged in the most stressful of human activities. It is almost always driven by the twofold ability first to anticipate problems and devise solutions and then to get people to execute the resulting plans.

Yet the way in which the generals themselves are managed has fundamentally shifted since World War II. Marshall saw relief as a natural part of generalship. Firing, like hiring, was simply one of the basic tasks of the senior managers. It was inevitable when selecting human beings for extraordinarily complex and difficult jobs that some percentage would fail. But he did not see it, usually, as disgraceful. On his watch, relief usually was not a discharge from the service but a reassignment.

The politics of relief are complex. In World War II, two senior generals who arguably might have been relieved were kept in place, at least partly for political reasons: Douglas MacArthur and Bernard Law Montgomery. Similarly, it would prove more difficult to relieve generals in small, unpopular wars. So in the latter part of the Korean War and in our wars in Vietnam, Afghanistan, and Iraq, relief of generals by other generals became all but extinct. To a large degree, this has made the Marshall system far less effective: Without the accountability that the prospect of relief brings, the Marshallian approach to leadership did not work nearly as well, as we were to see in Vietnam and Iraq. So while in World War II the firing of a general was seen as a sign that the system was working as planned, now, in the rare instances when it does occur, it tends to be seen, especially inside the Army, as a sign that the system somehow has failed.

The Army's shift away from swift dismissal in our recent wars has gone all but unnoticed, and so major questions about our military have been neglected: How and why did we lose the long-standing practice of relieving generals for failure? Why has accountability declined? And is it connected to the decline in the operational competence of American generals? That is, how did we go from a tough-minded thinker like George Marshall, who made his reputation in part by speaking truth to power, to eminently pliable chairmen of the Joint Chiefs of Staff such as Air Force Gen. Richard Myers, chairman from 2001 to 2005, and his successor, Marine Gen. Peter Pace, who was chairman for two years after him?

Answering these questions promises a way to better understand why our recent wars in Vietnam, Afghanistan, and Iraq have been so long and frustrating.

While touching on other services, this book focuses most on the handling of Army generals, mainly but not exclusively during wartime. Moreover, in discussing World War II, this study disproportionately dwells on the U.S. Army in Europe, because it was the incubator of the postwar Army, the theater of combat service for the six Army chiefs who ran the service from 1945 to 1960, as well as for the generals who oversaw the Vietnam War.

Of all the nation's armed forces, the Army arguably is the dominant service, the one around which the national defense still is constructed. Over the past decade, for example, more Army troops have been sent to Iraq and Afghanistan than troops from the Navy, Air Force, and Marine Corps combined. In addition, there is less to say about the history of leadership in the other services. The Navy follows an entirely different, seafaring custom in handling commanders, and the Marines tend to act within that nautical tradition. The Air Force, having been established in 1947, is too young to have developed many distinct, long-lasting traditions. It had one period of being dominated by bomber pilots, then a second of being overseen by fighter pilots. Now it appears to be at the beginning of a new, indeterminate period, in which its current leader, Gen. Norton Schwartz, is a former C-130 Special Operations aircraft pilot, and it faces the proliferation of drone aircraft, remotely piloted vehicles that could radically change the Air Force's young culture in unpredictable ways.

When it moves beyond World War II, this book looks less at relief, because there was less of it going on, and instead focuses on how the Army tried to compensate for that lack in several ways, but primarily with additional supervision—often referred to by those under supervision as "micromanagement." The second half of the book, covering the era when the Army all but stopped relieving generals, also shows the next step: When the military does not relieve senior generals, civilian officials will. The vicissitudes of the relationship between generals and their civilian overseers are a secondary theme of the book, because the quality of civil-military discourse is often a sign of whether a war is being conducted effectively, one of the few available leading indicators. When presidents and generals speak clearly to one another, in an atmosphere of candor and trust, wars tend to be fought more effectively than when officials mislead one another or simply do not deal among themselves in a straightforward manner that surfaces and examines differences and assumptions. The foremost example of this is the distrustful relationship that existed between Lyndon Johnson and the Joint Chiefs of Staff during the Vietnam War.

When, after the debacle of Vietnam, the Army began rebuilding, it had to rely more on two other critical tools of management: training and education. In the absence of relief as a tool, these became hugely important in shaping the United States Army, which is one of our nation's largest, most interesting, and most important institutions. When we understand the Army, and especially the changes in its generals, we will better understand where we are as a nation and why we have fought our wars the way we have in the era of the American superpower, from Sicily and Normandy to Saigon, Baghdad, and Kabul.

PART I
WORLD WAR II

The Army of 1939 was a small, weak force of 197,000 men, "not even a third-rate military power," as Gen. George Marshall later put it in an official Pentagon report. The Army had introduced a new semi-automatic rifle, the M1 Garand, but most soldiers still were issued the 1903 Springfield. Of the nine infantry divisions the Army had on paper, only three had divisional strengths, while six were actually weak brigades. By September 1944 the Army would number almost eight million and would have forty divisions in Europe and the Mediterranean and twenty-one in the Pacific.

CHAPTER 1
General George C. Marshall
The leader

It is not mentioned much nowadays that for the United States, World War II began with a series of dismissals across the top ranks of the military. Less than two weeks after the attack on Pearl Harbor in December 1941, Adm. Husband Kimmel and Army Lt. Gen. Walter Short were jettisoned from their posts atop the American military establishment in the Pacific, along with Maj. Gen. Frederick Martin, Short's air commander. Even less remembered is that Kimmel, who once had been an aide to Assistant Secretary of the Navy Franklin D. Roosevelt, held the post only because his predecessor, Adm. James Richardson, had been fired by the president a year earlier. The following year, the commander of one of the first Army divisions to fight the Japanese, the 32nd Division's Maj. Gen. Edwin Harding, was relieved by Gen. Douglas MacArthur, along with many of his regimental and battalion commanders. When Lt. Gen. George Kenney arrived to take over the air operation in the Pacific in mid-1942, his first act was to remove five generals he deemed to be "deadwood," along with forty colonels and lieutenant colonels. Adm. Harold Stark, the Navy's top officer, was ousted from his post in March 1942. He was hardly alone:

One-third of the Navy's submarine captains were relieved during the first year of the war. On the North African front, where American soldiers first fought the Germans, the senior tactical commander of those forces, Maj. Gen. Lloyd Fredendall, was fired.

The officer presiding over this dynamic and ruthless system of personnel management was Gen. George C. Marshall, who back in Washington was winnowing the ranks of the Army, forcing dozens of generals into retirement because he believed they were too old and lacking in energy to lead soldiers in combat.

"I hate to think that fifty years from now practically nobody will know who George Marshall was," President Franklin Delano Roosevelt remarked to Gen. Dwight Eisenhower one day in Tunisia during World War II. FDR was correct. Though rarely memorialized by the public today, George Marshall not only was the senior American general of World War II; he was, effectively, the founding father of the modern American armed forces. Under him, the United States for the first time developed a superpower military, a status it has retained for the past seven decades. Far more than George Patton, Douglas MacArthur, or even Dwight Eisenhower, this "coolly impersonal" man (as his subordinate Albert Wedemeyer called him) shaped the military of his time so profoundly that his work lives on into the twenty-first century, sometimes evident in the way Army leaders have operated in Iraq and Afghanistan. Specifically, Marshall's unusual and very American concept of what sort of person constitutes a good general still influences the promotions today's leaders bestow on younger officers. It would be difficult to understand today's Army without knowledge of Marshall's career—and especially his powerful sense of duty and honor.

Marshall formally became chief of staff of the U.S. Army on September 1, 1939, the day Germany invaded Poland. "Things look very disturbing in the world this morning," he wrote in a thank-you note to George Patton's wife. Such understatement reflected the man. It is not unfair to call Marshall colorless. He might have taken it as a compliment, as an implicit recognition that he did his duty even at the cost of personal advancement. He intentionally left no memoir of his service leading the military during the nation's greatest war. There is no weapon or installation named for him, as there is a Bradley Fighting Vehicle and an Abrams tank. Indeed, in the snowy reaches of remote northern New York, there is even a Fort Drum, honoring Gen. Hugh Drum, the "stubborn, pompous, occasionally ignorant" officer who inexplicably had been Marshall's leading rival for the Army's top slot. There is no Fort Marshall.

George Marshall was born in Uniontown, Pennsylvania, fifteen years after the end of the Civil War. In 1901, he graduated from the Virginia Military Institute, where he marched before Stonewall Jackson's widow. He soon joined the Army, which then was recovering from its low ebb of the 1890s, the decade when the frontier officially closed and the last of the Indian wars ended. The Army expanded rapidly in the wake of the Spanish–American War of 1898, almost quadrupling in size to 100,000. As part of that growth, George Marshall received his commission. In this newly energized force, he stood out as a young officer. Marshall was temporarily posted to Fort Douglas, Utah—originally placed on a hillside overlooking Salt Lake City to keep an eye on Brigham Young's nascent and hostile Mormon empire. One of his commanders there was Lt. Col. Johnson Hagood. When asked in an evaluation form if he would like to have Marshall serve under him, Hagood, who himself would rise to major general, wrote in December 1916, "Yes, but I would prefer to serve under *his* command."

Marshall and the Great War

The formative event of Marshall's life would be World War I. Several years after that conflict began, the United States sent into it a constabulary military whose sole experience with large-scale industrial-era combat had been the Civil War, a conflict the Europeans—correctly or not—perceived as a generally amateurish domestic brawl. The U.S. Army was unprepared at the outset of the Great War and was not much better at its close, when, as historian Conrad Crane put it, "foreign leaders still considered the American Expeditionary Forces poorly organized and ignorant of modern warfare."

The United States declared war in April 1917, when the war had been under way for more than thirty months, and the first large groups of draftees reported for duty only in September of that year. The initial American casualties came in November, and it took many more months after that first foray to get large numbers of American troops into combat. The American buildup may have been key to the outcome of the war, because it encouraged the Allies to hold on, but the first solely American offensive was not launched until September 1918. The armistice was declared just eight weeks later. For the Army as a whole, the war was too brief a venture to be transformative, but it was a life-changing experience for some officers in the middle of it, notably George Marshall.

Marshall's first memorable encounter of the war in France came in October 1917. It was not the Germans he confronted, but rather the man who would become his mentor, Gen. John "Blackjack" Pershing, the senior American commander in the war. Reviewing American soldiers training in France for trench warfare, Pershing blew up at what he perceived to be a shambles of an operation, with ill-trained soldiers and leaders apparently ignorant of how to train effectively or even how to follow Army directives. In front of a group of officers, Pershing chastised Maj. Gen. William Sibert, the commanding general, as well as Sibert's chief of staff, who had arrived only two days earlier. "He didn't give General Sibert a chance to talk at all," Marshall recalled.

Marshall walked up to Pershing in an attempt to explain the situation. The irate commanding general shrugged and turned away. Marshall, a mere captain, then did something that could have cost him his promising career, laying his hand on Pershing's arm and insisting that he be heard out. "General Pershing, there's something to be said here, and I think I should say it because I've been here longer," he said. He then let go with a torrent of facts about the hurdles the division had faced in training its soldiers. Confronting the commander of the U.S. Army in France was a risky move, but it also showed moral courage. After Pershing departed, several comrades consoled Marshall in the belief that he had just destroyed his military career. Pershing's opinion of Sibert remained unchanged—the next day Sibert's name headed a list of eleven generals Pershing sent to Washington, D.C., describing the group as ineffectual. By the end of the year, Sibert, the first commander of an American division ever sent overseas, had been relieved.

Sibert's successor, Maj. Gen. Robert Bullard, began his command by emphasizing to subordinates that the dismissals did not necessarily end with Sibert's departure, "telling them they'd be 'relieved' without any hesitation upon the part of General Pershing if they did not 'deliver the goods'; they must succeed or lose their commands." Bullard noted in his diary that Pershing was "looking for results. He intends to have them. He will sacrifice any man who does not bring them." This was not an idle observation, as Bullard, Marshall, and others would see. Maj. Gen. Clarence Edwards, the commander of the 26th ("Yankee") Division, composed of National Guard units from New England, was popular with his men but considered irascible by others, and he was removed from his command by Pershing.

Pershing often used a two-step process to remove generals, first shunting them off to a minor post in France and then, after a short interval, shipping them home. In this way he ousted two division commanders on the same day. On October 16, 1918, he removed the 5th Division's Maj. Gen. John McMahon and the 3rd Division's wonderfully named Maj. Gen. Beaumont Bonaparte Buck. One possible reason for the removal of Buck was a rumor that he intended to lead a bayonet charge. Buck apparently did not lead that attack; he survived the war and did not die until 1950, at the age of ninety, after doing a "vigorous foxtrot" on a dance floor with his thirty-four-year-old wife. All told, Pershing relieved at least six division commanders and two corps commanders during World War I. Lower-ranking officers were also judged severely, with some fourteen hundred removed from combat positions and sent to the U.S. Army officers' casual depot at Blois, France. (American soldiers often pronounced the town's name "Blooey," giving rise to the slang expression, popular in the 1920s, of "going blooey"—falling apart.)

In his policy of swift relief, Pershing was perhaps more sweeping than some other commanders in American wars, but he was well within American military tradition, as demonstrated as far back as the Revolution and the Civil War, when relief of generals was common. During the War for American Independence, Maj. Gen. Philip Schuyler was relieved after the fall of Fort Ticonderoga, New York, in July 1777, and was accused of dereliction of duty by Maj. Gen. Horatio Gates. An inquiry cleared Schuyler of the charge, but he resigned from the Army and went home. Gates himself went on to disastrous defeat near Camden, South Carolina, which then led to his own relief. During the Civil War, Stonewall Jackson famously fired a brigade commander who told him something could not be done. President Lincoln also relieved a series of commanders of the Army of the Potomac—Irvin McDowell, George McClellan, John Pope, McClellan again, Ambrose Burnside, Joseph Hooker, and George Meade. Pershing was also acting consistently with his French allies: In the first weeks of the war, Marshal Joseph Joffre, the French commander, relieved two army commanders, nine of twenty-one corps commanders, thirty-three of seventy-two infantry division commanders, and five of ten cavalry division commanders. "These changes weeded out the higher commands and rejuvenated the list of general officers," Joffre wrote.

Marshall was one of the younger men who rose swiftly during the war. After their first confrontation, Pershing kept an eye on Marshall. Marshall impressed his fellow officers with the central role he played in organizing U.S. military operations in the war, simultaneously planning the two great American offensives: in Saint-Mihiel on September 12, 1918, and, beginning two weeks later, in the Meuse-Argonne sector, which involved moving 200,000 troops out of the front line and 600,000 fresh troops into it. Marshall also played a key role in the formation of the first division ever fielded by the American Army in Europe. Initially, it was simply called "the combat division," because at that time it was the only one of its kind. That unit later became the 1st Infantry Division, also known as the "Big Red One." "Colonel Marshall's greatest attribute was his ability to reduce complex problems to their fundamentals," remembered Benjamin Caffey, who served under him as a young staff officer and would later become a general himself. James Van Fleet, another World War I soldier who went on to become a general, simply remembered that Marshall emerged from that war with a reputation as a "brilliant planner." After the war ended, Pershing asked Marshall to become his aide, a post the younger man filled for five years, the longest tour of duty he would have in his Army career until he became chief of staff himself.

Perhaps the key lesson of World War I for Marshall came from observing Pershing in March 1918, when the outcome of the conflict was still much in doubt. The French army appeared near collapse after the previous year's mutinies. The British were in shock after seeing a generation of young men lost in the mud of Belgium and northeastern France. The Germans were resurgent after the Russian collapse had enabled them to transfer some fifty infantry divisions to the Western Front, and they were pushing deeper into France. "The French and British had no reserves," Marshall remembered in a lecture he gave six months after the war ended. American firepower had not yet been brought to bear, and many doubted how an American force experienced mainly in chasing Indians and bandits on the Mexican border would perform when fighting among the armies of the great powers of Europe. Amid the resulting mood of imminent disaster, Pershing stood out as calm, cheerful, and determined. "In the midst of a profound depression he radiated determination and the will to win," Marshall wrote in his little-known memoir of World War I. That lesson would become key to how Marshall thought of generalship and especially how he selected senior leaders. In observing Pershing, Marshall learned to one day look for an Eisenhower.

Marshall's list

Scholars disagree over whether or not Marshall actually maintained a "little black book" of promising young officers to keep in mind for future promotions or whether that is just an Army myth. No such booklet or list has ever been found, nor even documents indicating that it existed.

Yet Marshall did have a very clear sense of the qualities he looked for in promoting officers. His ideas about what makes a good leader would go a long way toward determining who would become a general in World War II—and toward determining how the Army would think about generalship for decades afterward. In a letter he wrote in November 1920, not long after he became aide-de-camp to Pershing, he listed the qualities of the successful leader, in the following order:

- "good common sense"
- "have studied your profession"
- "physically strong"
- "cheerful and optimistic"
- "display marked energy"
- "extreme loyalty"
- "determined"

At first glance, this list might seem unexceptional, even Boy Scoutish. Yet it merits closer examination. Heeding a lesson of World War I, Marshall placed a premium on vigor, implicitly excluding the older officer from promotion, especially the "château general" who rarely left the comforts of his headquarters to fight in the trenches with his troops. Marshall instead valued the man who wanted to be in the middle of things.

Marshall's list emphasizes character over intellect. He did so consciously, tailoring his template to fit the particular circumstances of the United States. The quiet pessimist might be effective in other militaries, he argued, but not in a democratic nation that, protected by the world's two great oceans, tended always to pursue a "policy of unpreparedness" for war. Given that tendency, which inevitably meant leading ill-trained and poorly equipped units into demoralizing battles, he decided that the American military needed the

optimistic and resourceful type, quick to estimate, with relentless determination, and who possessed in addition a fund of sound common sense, which operated to prevent gross errors due to rapidity of decision and action.

The opposite sort of leader, the man prone to looking at the negative side, must be excised promptly. The units led by these "calamity howlers," he wrote with evident distaste, were "quickly infected with the same spirit and grew ineffective unless a more suitable commander was given charge."

Marshall also was solidly in the American tradition in valuing effectiveness over appearance. He was a reserved man, but not a fussy one. During a 1933 inspection tour, he walked into one Army post and found the commander and another officer asleep. He then went into a supply room and surprised a lieutenant who was working in his undershirt. "You may not be in proper uniform," Marshall reassured the embarrassed man, "but you are the only officer I found working here."

Marshall's list is significant for what it omits. He was ambivalent about the brawler and the adventurous cavalryman. He wanted generals who would fight, but not men who would command recklessly or discredit the military with their personal behavior. "You can sometimes win a great victory by a very dashing action," he once said. "But often, or most frequently, the very dashing action exposes you to a very fatal result if it is not successful. And you hazard everything in that way." He trusted even less the outlier, the individualist, the eccentric, and the dreamer—all well represented in the nineteenth-century American military, especially by heroes of the Union such as Ulysses S. Grant and William T. Sherman, and more so by those of the Confederacy, such as J. E. B. Stuart and Thomas "Stonewall" Jackson, whom Marshall had studied "religiously," according to his official biographer.

In contrast to those two latter-day cavaliers, Marshall called for steady, levelheaded team players. He wanted both competence and cooperativeness. The biggest difference between American commanders in World War I and World War II would be that in the latter war, they were adept at coordinating the efforts of the infantry, artillery, armor, and aviation branches, especially in breaking through enemy lines and then exploiting that penetration. As German field marshal Gerd von Rundstedt put it after being captured in 1945, "We cannot understand the difference in your leadership in the last war and in this. We could understand it if you had produced one superior corps commander, but now we find all of your corps commanders good and of equal superiority."

Yet Marshall was not looking for conformists. He believed in the respectful, confidential expression of dissent, as he had demonstrated by bluntly confronting Gen. Pershing during World War I.

Marshall and President Roosevelt

Marshall's willingness to be blunt with President Franklin Roosevelt about military matters was a major reason he eventually was chosen to be chief of staff of the Army. On the afternoon of November 14, 1938, well before he had become chief of staff, Marshall and eleven other senior government officials gathered at the White House. It was two months after British prime minister Neville Chamberlain's meetings with Adolf Hitler in Munich and just five days after Kristallnacht, in which Nazi mobs launched nationwide attacks on the Jews of Germany and on their shops and synagogues. The issue at hand at the White House meeting was whether to commission the construction of ten thousand warplanes. That was a heady number, given that at the time the Army Air Corps possessed about 160 fighter aircraft and just 50 bombers. In Marshall's view, the proposed program was wildly unbalanced, overemphasizing machines without properly considering everything else that must be done in order to create a modern air force, such as the time and the huge amount of funding required to recruit and train aircrews, to build and staff the bases they would need, and to manufacture the ammunition and bombs they must have if war came. But no one else at the White House meeting seemed concerned. When Roosevelt polled the room, Marshall later recalled, the others present were agreeable and "very soothing." Marshall said nothing until he was asked.

"Don't you think so, George?" Roosevelt inquired, in what may have been the sole instance of his using Marshall's given name. (Marshall took offense at the usage, thinking that it misrepresented their relationship. He would find ways to make it clear that he preferred to be addressed as "General Marshall.")

"I am sorry, Mr. President, but I don't agree with that at all," Marshall responded. He recalled that "the president gave me a very startled look." Roosevelt likely thought that Marshall, who had been pushing for military readiness, would be pleased with the move. But Marshall wanted balanced preparation, not an aircraft construction program he saw as likely to cause huge problems. He may also have suspected that Roosevelt privately intended to manufacture the aircraft and ship them to the British and the French instead of building up the American force. Marshall's approach to generalship was to speak truth to power. His relationship with Roosevelt was not intimate, but FDR was learning that Marshall would tell him what he thought.

At this time, Roosevelt viewed military mobilization from two distinct perspectives. He would say later that he felt he had been walking a tightrope between keeping American isolationists in the camp of his New Deal happy while he tried to counter the rise of foreign fascism. His public statements showed no inclination to go to war. On September 3, 1939, three days after the Nazis invaded Poland, he pledged in a "fireside chat" that the United States would remain neutral in the new European war. He remained wary of rapid expansion of the military, especially as the 1940 election approached. Seeking an unprecedented third term during that year's presidential campaign, he promised not to send American boys into foreign wars.

On May 13, 1940, Marshall would again have occasion to confront the president. This time it was in a tense meeting on whether to rapidly expand the size of the Army. It was three days after the Germans had ended the "Phony War" period by invading France, Belgium, Luxembourg, and the Netherlands. Just that morning, the Luftwaffe had conducted the largest air strike in history, carpet-bombing French units near Sedan and enabling three Panzer divisions, led by Heinz Guderian and Erwin Rommel, to punch a hole through the French line. French troops were running from the battlefield, and their commanders were paralyzed and panicky. On the same day, Queen Wilhelmina and the Dutch government had fled to London, where Neville Chamberlain had resigned as prime minister three days earlier, a victim of his own failed policy of appeasement. His successor, Winston Churchill, in his first speech as the new prime minister, told the British people, "I have nothing to offer you but blood, toil, tears, and sweat."

Marshall spent the morning with Treasury Secretary Henry Morgenthau Jr., explaining the nature and rationale of a major increase in the size of the military. Then, joined by War Department officials, the two walked over to the White House to see the president, who made it clear to Marshall and Morgenthau that he "was not desirous of seeing us," as Marshall recalled. Roosevelt disliked the Army expansion proposal and tried to quell dissent by calling an end to the session prematurely. Morgenthau said he supported the manpower increase, but "the president was exceedingly short with him," Marshall said. When Morgenthau finished, FDR shrugged him off: "Well, you filed your protest."

Morgenthau asked if the president would hear out Marshall. Roosevelt responded that he didn't need to listen to the new Army chief, because, he said airily, "I know exactly what he would say.

There is no necessity for me to hear him at all." Marshall's two civilian overseers—Secretary of War Harry Woodring and Assistant Secretary Louis Johnson—sat mutely, offering Marshall no support. For Marshall, that dismissal was almost a repeat of his confrontation with Gen. Pershing decades earlier. But this time the stakes were infinitely higher—this involved not just the reputations and careers of a few officers, but possibly the future of the nation and, indeed, of the world.

Roosevelt ended the meeting. Marshall stood, but instead of leaving the room he walked over to the president and looked down on him. "Mr. President, may I have three minutes?" he asked.

"Of course, General Marshall," Roosevelt said. He did not invite Marshall to sit back down. When the president started to say something else, Marshall interrupted him, fearing that otherwise he would never get another word in. Marshall spoke in a torrent, spewing out facts about military requirements, organization, and costs. "If you don't do something . . . and do it right away, I don't know what is going to happen to this country," he told Roosevelt. "You have got to do something, and you've got to do it today."

He finally had the president's attention. "We are in a situation now where it's desperate," Marshall continued. "I am using the word very accurately, where it's desperate. We have literally nothing, nothing, and unless something is done immediately, and even then it takes a long, long time to get any return on it, we are caught in a dreadful position of unpreparedness. And with everything being threatened the way it has been, I feel that I must tell you just as frankly and vehemently as I can what our necessities are."

Morgenthau wrote in his diary that Marshall "stood right up to the president." It worked. The next day the president asked Marshall to draw up as soon as possible a list of what the military needed. Marshall would later recall this meeting as a turning point in FDR's military policy.

Marshall's attitude toward his dealings with Roosevelt provided a model of civil-military discourse. It was, most of all, frank—at least on Marshall's side. Yet it was not close. As chief of staff, Marshall would insist on remaining socially and emotionally distant from the president, seeing it as necessary to maintaining a professional relationship. Nowadays, most senior officers would leap at the chance to spend time with the commander in chief during his more relaxed moments. For example, before the Iraq war, Gen. Tommy R. Franks, then chief of the U.S. Central Command, overseeing the Middle East, visited President George W. Bush at the latter's ranch in Crawford, Texas, as Marine Gen. Peter Pace would do later as chairman of the Joint Chiefs of Staff. Marshall was wary of such intimacies. "I found informal conversation with the president would get you into trouble," he later explained. "He would talk over something informally at the dinner table and you had trouble disagreeing without creating embarrassment. So I never went." He refused even to laugh at the president's jokes. The first time he ever visited Roosevelt's home at Hyde Park, New York, was for the president's funeral. But he and the president were perhaps the best wartime civil-military team the nation has ever had.

Marshall prepares for war

Even before he became chief of the Army, Marshall was thinking about how to oust the nonperformers in the Army's senior ranks. In the spring of 1939, war was on the horizon. Marshall had been told he would be the next Army chief, but he had not yet taken that office. He embarked on a sensitive mission to South America to secure agreements to freely move American forces by air and sea across the South Atlantic. The trip was spurred by American worry about growing pro-German sentiment within the Brazilian military, most notably evidenced by a German invitation to the chief of the Brazilian army, Gen. Pedro Aurélio de Góis Monteiro, to lead Nazi troops on a parade in Berlin. Accompanying Marshall was Col. Matthew Ridgway, a rising young officer.

It is difficult to imagine nowadays, but for ten days during the voyage to Rio de Janeiro aboard the USS *Nashville,* Ridgway and Marshall sat on the forward deck of the light cruiser and simply talked. More or less cut off from the world, they discussed the future of the Army, about which Marshall held two great concerns. The first was the need to get more money out of Congress to expand, equip, and train the military. The second was how to find and promote good officers to lead that growing force. "He knew from his own experience in WWI and from his extensive reading of our military history of the political and other pressures which had resulted in the appointment to high command in past wars of so many mediocre and even incompetent officers," Ridgway recalled.

The South American mission was a success, with landing and port rights secured, even though Gen. Góis Monteiro went on to accept the Grand Cross of the Order of the German Eagle the following year. For a spell during World War II, the American air base that was established at Natal, in northeastern Brazil, would become one of the busiest airports in the world, used as a ferrying point into Africa, whose coast was about eighteen hundred miles to the east, and also for antisubmarine patrols over the mid-Atlantic.

Marshall returned to Washington with a battle plan for rapid change in the ranks of the Army's senior officers. "The present general officers of the line are for the most part too old to command troops in battle under the terrific pressure of modern war," Marshall said in October 1939, a month after being sworn in as chief of the Army, in an off-the-record comment to a journalist. "Most of them have their minds set in outmoded patterns, and can't change to meet the new conditions they may face if we become involved in the war that's started in Europe." At Marshall's behest, in the summer and fall of 1941, 31 colonels, 117 lieutenant colonels, 31 majors, and 16 captains were forced into retirement or discharged from the active-duty force. In addition, some 269 National Guard and Army Reserve officers were let go. All told, Marshall estimated that, as chief of staff, he forced out at least 600 officers before the United States entered World War II. "I was accused right away by the service papers of getting rid of all the brains of the army," he said. "I couldn't reply that I was eliminating considerable arteriosclerosis."

Marshall removed officers in part to convey a sense of urgency. When the commandant at Leavenworth, Brig. Gen. Charles Bundel, told him that updating the complete set of Army training manuals would take eighteen months, Marshall offered him three months to do the job. No, it can't be done, Bundel responded. Marshall then offered four months. Bundel again said it was impossible. Marshall asked him to reconsider that statement. "You be very careful about that," Marshall warned.

"No, it can't be done," Bundel insisted.

"I'm sorry, then you are relieved," Marshall informed him, in an exchange that evoked Stonewall Jackson's relief of a colonel in the Shenandoah Valley campaign, an episode Marshall almost certainly knew about. (While on the march in the Shenandoah, Jackson had ordered a colonel to pull together his brigade, which had divided into two or three parts. "It's impossible, General; I can't do it," the officer said. Jackson responded, "Turn your command over to the next officer. If he can't do it, I'll find someone who can.") Marshall replaced Bundel with Brig. Gen. Lesley McNair, who went on to play a major role during the war, overseeing all Army training until he was killed by an Army Air Force fragmentation bomb that fell six miles short in Saint-Lô, France, in July 1944.

Marshall rarely let slip his fierce temper, but he did so when politicians questioned his efforts to get new men into the leadership of National Guard divisions. At one meeting at which his judgment about moving a general was questioned, he gave members of Congress an ultimatum: "I am not going to leave him in command of that division. So I will put it to you this way: If he stays, I go, and if I stay, he goes." When Justice Felix Frankfurter passed along a criticism he had heard from a friend in the Army Reserve about the relief of Guard officers, Marshall tartly replied that "most of our senior officers on such duty are deadwood and should be eliminated from the service as rapidly as possible."

The United States had not yet entered World War II, but Marshall had determined that most of the top generals in the Army were too aged for combat, and that just below them were many officers who were also far past their prime. Eisenhower stated in his memoirs that one of the beneficial side effects of the big Louisiana Maneuvers, staged in August and September 1941 with several hundred thousand troops in two opposing forces, was their demonstration that "some officers . . . had of necessity to be relieved from command." Only eleven of the forty-two generals who commanded a division, a corps, or an army in those maneuvers would go on to command in combat. Just one of the prewar Army's senior generals, Walter Krueger, would be given top command in World War II. Decades later, Eisenhower said that those removals had been key steps to victory in World War II. In his old age, he listed the names of a series of officers who, because they were discarded, are now forgotten by history: "a whole group of people . . . There was Marley, Charley Thompson—what's his name—McKieffer, Daily, Benedict . . . By God, he [Marshall] just took them and threw them out of the room. . . . He got them out of the way, and I think as a whole he was right." The corollary to swift relief is, of course, rapid advancement of others, usually younger officers. "I was the youngest of the people that he pushed up into very high places," Eisenhower continued.

Today's officers sometimes fret about "personnel turbulence," but their lives look unruffled compared with the first two years of Marshall's leadership. He took over an Army of just 197,000 people, a number that included the infant Air Force. Under Marshall, the Army grew in just two years to 1.4 million in the summer of 1941, and two years after that it had reached nearly 7 million, finally peaking in 1945 at 8.3 million. The newcomers were overseen by a new generation of commanders who were being pushed hard. Once those new leaders were in place, Marshall told military journalist George Fielding Eliot, he would put them through their paces to gauge who among them was really capable. He elaborated:

> I'm going to put these men to the severest tests which I can devise in time of peace. I'm going to start shifting them into jobs of greater responsibility than those they hold now. . . . Then I'm going to change them, suddenly, without warning, to jobs even more burdensome and difficult. . . . Those who stand up under the punishment will be pushed ahead. *Those who fail are out at the first sign of faltering.*

Those who passed the tests moved quickly. At one point Marshall, irked by the erratic quality of staff work in the Army Air Force and wanting to reward talent and maturity when he saw it, promoted a major directly to brigadier general, skipping altogether the ranks of lieutenant colonel and colonel.

The nature of the force was changing rapidly. The U.S. Army not only leaped into the front ranks of the world's armed forces but in just a few years would be transformed into the premier mechanized military on the planet. The unprecedented mobility that the Americans developed carried deep implications for personnel policies. Most notably, the speed at which the Army could move would make mental flexibility in leadership even more valuable. As manpower ran short, this suppleness enabled the American military to get by with far fewer divisions than had been planned. As military historian Russell Weigley explained, "If there was a justification for the risk of raising only 89 divisions, much of the justification must be that divisions could be shifted wherever they were needed with a promptness that no other army could match. In combat, too, they could move with unparalleled rapidity."

Marshall's inclination to remove unsuccessful officers intensified once the United States had entered the war. At one point he ordered a general to France immediately but was informed that the man had declined to leave so quickly, because his wife was away and his household furniture was not packed. Astounded, Marshall called the general, whom he had known as a good friend for years. "Was that a fact?" Marshall recalled asking.

"Yes, I can't leave here now," the general responded.

"Well, my God, man, we are at war and you are a general," said a puzzled Marshall.

"Well, I'm sorry," the officer said.

"I'm sorry too," Marshall concluded, "but you will be retired tomorrow."

This take-no-prisoners attitude was instilled in subordinates. To understand just how wide and broad the cuts were, consider the swift decline of the career of Maj. Gen. James Chaney, Eisenhower's forgotten predecessor in Britain. A veteran pilot, Chaney had been sent to England as an observer of the Battle of Britain. When the United States entered the war, he was named the commander of American forces in the British Isles.

Eisenhower, visiting England, found Chaney "completely at a loss" in understanding the state of the war. Chaney and his staff were working peacetime hours, and British officials did not seem to know what the American general was supposed to be doing in their country. Eisenhower reported back to Marshall, who soon informed Chaney that he was being replaced. "I deem it of urgent importance," Marshall told him, "that the commanding general in England be an officer who is completely familiar with all our military plans and affairs and who has taken a leading part in the military developments since December 7." Hence, Marshall informed Chaney, "I am assigning Eisenhower to the post." Marshall's cold-bloodedness was evident when Chaney returned to the United States and Marshall declined to meet with him. In May 1943, less than a year after his removal from London, Chaney was stuck overseeing a boot camp outside Wichita Falls, Texas. Chaney's aide in England, Charles Bolte, received a similarly brisk dismissal. One day, Ike said, "Well, you better go along, too."

Though Marshall and his commanders were quick to punish incompetence, they believed in second chances. The system of relief during Word War II could be forgiving. Bolte, for example, recovered from his earlier setback. During the war, he commanded a division in Italy and eventually rose to four-star rank. Indeed, at least five Army generals of World War II—Orlando Ward, Terry Allen, Leroy Watson, Albert Brown, and, in the South Pacific, Frederick Irving—were removed from combat command and later given another division to lead in combat.

Teamwork was a core value for Marshall. Simply failing to show a spirit of cooperation was, for him, reason enough to remove a senior officer. Early in the war, he seriously considered relieving Brig. Gen. Simon Bolivar Buckner Jr. as the Army commander in Alaska for failing to get along with his Navy counterpart. Buckner was the son of the Confederate general of the same name, who was most noted for surrendering Fort Donelson to Brig. Gen. Ulysses S. Grant in February 1862. He was sent to Alaska in 1940 as an aging colonel. When a new Navy admiral, Robert "Fuzzy" Theobald, showed up a few years later, the two soon clashed. In August 1942, Buckner unaccountably chose to read aloud to his hot-tempered counterpart a poem mocking the Navy's fears of operating in the wild Bering Sea. The performance provoked a wave of naval indignation that soon reached Marshall. (Marshall was long familiar with Buckner's tendency to shoot off his mouth, having cautioned retired Marine Maj. Gen. John Lejeune a decade earlier against hiring Buckner as commandant of the Virginia Military Institute for "fear . . . that his habit of talking a great deal might involve him in difficulties.") Perhaps because he had expected such behavior, Marshall ultimately decided against relieving Buckner from the Alaska post. However, the Navy sacked Theobald early in 1943, relegating him to running a Boston shipyard.

In 1944, ironically, Buckner would go on to lead a board that looked into the most controversial combat relief of the war: the firing on Saipan of Maj. Gen. Ralph Smith, commander of the Army's sluggish 27th Division, by Marine Lt. Gen. Holland M. "Howlin' Mad" Smith. ("The interesting question," observed retired Army Lt. Col. Wade Markel, "is not why Holland Smith relieved Ralph Smith, but why it took him so long.") Marshall later dispatched Buckner to Okinawa, where at the front line in June 1945 he waved off a Marine officer's warning to remove his helmet because its three shiny stars were likely to provoke Japanese artillerymen. Minutes later, as Buckner stood arms akimbo, a Japanese shell exploded next to him, making him the highest-ranking American officer to be killed by enemy fire during World War II.

Perhaps the most significant point about Marshall's approach to generalship in World War II was that it tended to create an incentive system that encouraged prudent risk taking. "A flexible system of personnel management that rapidly identified proven leaders and placed them in appropriate positions of responsibility helped accelerate the process of change during World War II," concluded Markel, a specialist in personnel policy. "The temporary promotion system and its accompanying culture . . . offered unlimited advancement to those who could produce success, and summary dismissal to those who couldn't. Confronted with these stark options . . . the capable found a way to succeed and were accordingly rewarded; the incapable were, of course, replaced by the capable."

In other words, while sometimes mistaken and occasionally brutal to individual officers, the Marshall system generally achieved its goal of producing military effectiveness. To understand how, the best place to begin is with Dwight D. Eisenhower, who just a year before the start of World War II was still a lieutenant colonel, not even in command of a regiment, let alone the armies of millions he would oversee a few years later.

CHAPTER 2
Dwight Eisenhower
How the Marshall system worked

On December 12, 1941, five days after the Japanese attack on Pearl Harbor, Dwight D. Eisenhower sat in his office at Fort Sam Houston, the Army base on the scrubby outskirts of San Antonio. He had been promoted to brigadier general ten weeks earlier. His telephone rang. "Is that you, Ike?" he heard someone say over the line. Eisenhower recognized Col. Bedell Smith's voice.

"Yes," Eisenhower replied. Smith worked in the War Department, in Washington, D.C. He had a message for the young brigadier general: George Marshall wanted Eisenhower to come to the capital immediately.

Whether facing a single battle, an extended campaign, or an entire war, generals often do their most significant work before the major fighting begins. That was the case with Marshall, who made his most important personnel decision of World War II on that Friday, December 12, 1941. Marshall's genius in selecting Dwight Eisenhower was to recognize the potential match between Ike's qualities and the unique challenges of being the supreme commander of a multinational force in a globe-spanning war.

Marshall had witnessed friction and strife between the United

States and its British and French allies in World War I, and he had thought for decades about how to avoid a repetition. He knew he needed someone who could lead a team and enforce its rules. He also calculated that, because the United States was secure on its own continent, when it went to war it would do so overseas, and that necessarily would mean working closely with the militaries and governments of other nations whose aims and interests would not necessarily jibe with those of the United States. Whoever led American forces would need to be able to function well within a coalition framework, and probably also lead it. Out of hundreds of possible candidates, he eventually picked Eisenhower as the man for the job.

When that phone call came through, Ike's heart sank. He knew that Bedell Smith's call could mean only one thing. "The chief says for you to hop a plane and get up here right away," Smith said. "Tell your boss the formal orders will come through later."

"How long?" asked Ike.

"I don't know," Smith said. "Just come along."

Ike hurried home to collect the suitcase that his wife had packed for him, not knowing that he was embarking on a journey that would lead him to become the Allied commander in Europe and then, a decade later, president of the United States. It was not inevitable that Eisenhower would be chosen for top command. "Had Drum or another officer become chief of staff instead of Marshall, the roster of World War II generals would have looked very different," commented historian D. K. R. Crosswell.

Marshall did not know Eisenhower well. The young officer had spent much of the previous decade working as the top aide to Douglas MacArthur, who was perhaps Marshall's opposite in temperament, and indeed might have tried to sidetrack Marshall's career in the early 1930s. Marshall might have considered Eisenhower in the camp of the petulant former Army chief, but he nevertheless picked Eisenhower from relative obscurity, tested him, and then groomed him for supreme command. At the time Eisenhower was tapped, he was writing to George Patton, pleading for a position of command. "I suppose it's too much to hope that I could have a regiment in your division," Ike implored his old friend. "But I think I could do a damn good job of commanding a regiment."

In some ways Eisenhower did not fit the Marshall template. Most notably, he did not have a reputation for being aggressive, and he lacked combat experience. But in other categories he more than compensated. It is easy to forget now, as we try to peer past World War II and President Eisenhower, what it was about Ike the prewar Army officer that caught Marshall's eye. Marshall knew something that is now forgotten: that Eisenhower was a surprisingly sophisticated man, well read and well traveled. During World War II, his public relations aide depicted him as a normal fellow who liked to relax with a Western dime-store novel. Eisenhower allowed this to happen, and likely encouraged it, but in his last volume of memoirs he went out of his way to note that as an officer in the interwar period, he had prepared diligently for his profession, for example reading Clausewitz's *On War* three times. Once, after World War I, a friend asked him why he was reading so many books about Belgium, Luxembourg, and the Netherlands. Ike responded that he was doing so because that was where the next big war would be fought.

Ike also was cosmopolitan, having lived between the wars in Panama, the Philippines, and France, as well as near Washington, D.C. Behind his grinning farm-boy persona there existed an innovative military thinker, as well as fierceness in both ambition and temper. During the interwar period, he worked with Patton, exploring how to use tanks as more than protection for infantry. His work got him in hot water with his own leaders, so much so that after an article by him appeared in the November 1920 issue of *Infantry Journal,* he was called before the chief of the infantry branch and ordered to desist or face a court-martial. "Particularly, I was not to publish anything incompatible with solid infantry doctrine," which maintained that tanks needed to move only as fast as a soldier could walk, as the Army held that the combat task of the tank was to escort the foot soldiers.

British generals in the war tended to treat Eisenhower as a strategic lightweight, and many historians have followed their lead. But there is ample evidence that if he was not a strategic designer himself, he brought to his post a solid understanding of strategy, especially in the key task of translating broad strategic concepts into feasible operational orders. Marshall understood that Eisenhower had a talent for implementing strategy. And that job, Marshall believed, was more difficult than designing it. "There's nothing so profound in the logic of the thing," he said years later, discussing his own role in winning approval for the Marshall Plan. "But the execution of it, that's another matter." In other words, successful generalship involves first figuring out what to do, then getting people to do it. It has one foot in the intellectual realm of critical thinking and the other in the human world of management and leadership. It is thinking *and* doing.

The opening for Eisenhower to be called to Washington was created by trouble on the staff of the Army during the dizzying days after Pearl Harbor. Frank McCarthy, Marshall's junior aide (and decades later the producer of the movie *Patton*), remembered that on the day of the attack, Brig. Gen. Leonard Gerow, the chief of the War Plans Division, which oversaw military operations, "was nervous as a girl, terribly disturbed and concerned, and he didn't seem to be making good decisions. He didn't radiate confidence, let's put it that way." In the wake of that performance, Marshall had one comment, McCarthy said: "Get that fellow Eisenhower." Ironically, Ike had been Gerow's study partner at Command and General Staff College.

As he hurried to leave San Antonio for Washington on that Friday afternoon in December 1941, Eisenhower was far from pleased. "This message [of summons from Marshall's office] was a hard blow," he would remember. Ike already had missed combat in one world war, having been assigned to a stateside training job. Now it looked as if he would be sidetracked into another staff job. "I hoped in any new war to stay with troops," Eisenhower later explained. "Being ordered to a city where I had already served a total of eight years would mean, I thought, a virtual repetition of my experience in World War I."

But this would prove to be perhaps the most momentous weekend of Eisenhower's life, the beginning of both his climb to the top of the military and his subsequent political career. He had missed the last passenger train heading east that day from San Antonio, so he had an Army cargo aircraft fly him along the treetops through stormy weather to Dallas, where he caught up with the eastbound Blue Bonnet Express.

Finding all the train's seats taken, he sat on his suitcase in an aisle. William Kittrell, a Texas lawyer he knew, came across him perched there. "General, I've got a drawing room back there; would you like to come back and sit?" he said. Kittrell was an attorney for Sid Richardson, the oil tycoon, who was relaxing in his own special railcar. Eisenhower accepted the invitation, and the three talked and played poker for much of their ride to Washington, D.C. Early on Sunday, December 14, Eisenhower detrained at the capital's Union Station, where he was met by his brother Milton. Eleven years later, Richardson, the card-playing oilman, would become a major financial backer of Eisenhower's presidential campaign—opposing a more conservative group of Texas oil-men backing Ike's old boss, Gen. Douglas MacArthur.

A few hours after arriving in Washington, Eisenhower entered the office of Gen. Marshall, with whom he would have an encounter even more fateful than the one on the train. He didn't know the Army chief well, having met him only twice and having spoken to him for only about two minutes each time. Marshall clearly had heard good reports about the newly minted brigadier general, as he had invited him to come teach at the Infantry School at Fort Benning. But on this first Sunday following Pearl Harbor, when Ike came into his office in the Munitions Building, Marshall got right to the point. "I walked into his office and within ten seconds he was telling me the problem he wanted me to attack. . . . He just said, 'Look, there are two things we have got to do. We have got to do our best in the Pacific and we've got to win this whole war. Now, how are we going to do it? Now, that is going to be your problem.'" In summary, the question was, Marshall said, "What should be our general line of action?" Both knew what that meant: *Where do we draw the line and begin to fight? And do we abandon our men in the Philippines?* This was the kind of trial Marshall had in mind when he shared with George Fielding Eliot his thoughts about testing rising officers.

"Give me a few hours," Eisenhower requested. It was a difficult assignment, but the kind that Ike particularly relished. He would write decades later that "I loved to do that kind of work. . . . Practical problems have always been my equivalent of crossword puzzles."

"All right," the Army chief agreed, turning away and then leaving the office to make Sunday calls on Gen. Pershing and Secretary of War Henry Stimson.

Eisenhower sat quietly in a nearby office in the Munitions Building, which would be torn down in the 1960s and eventually replaced by, among other things, the Vietnam Veterans Memorial.

"The question before me was almost unlimited in its applications," Eisenhower later wrote. When Marshall returned that afternoon from his round of visits, Eisenhower gave him a three-page typed memo that laid out what he thought the American approach to World War II should be. The Philippines, Ike wrote, were beyond hope. *Don't be sentimental. Give up the islands, and leave American and Filipino friends there to their fate, while giving them what small aid we can. Fall back and regroup.* Nor should the Army heed the panicky calls of West Coast politicians for military protection for their cities, which would divert desperately needed troops and gear. Rather, the initial focus of American military operations against Japan should concentrate on faraway Australia, which would have to be the launching platform for the counteroffensive. Thus, the top military priority in the Pacific would be to keep open the air and sea lanes to it, which meant holding Hawaii, Fiji, New Zealand, and the other islands along the route, as well as Australia itself. That task was essential, and to carry it out successfully was worth almost any risk and expenditure.

Marshall read the memo, then looked up. "I agree with you," he told the young brigadier. Eisenhower had passed his first major test. It was not a test of national strategic planning, but almost certainly one of personality and intellect. That is, Eisenhower in his memo simply elaborated on strategic decisions that the American military establishment had been mulling for the previous decade, when it was all but ignored by the public during the depths of the Depression. In the early 1920s, the Navy's War Plan Orange, written for a conflict with Japan, had called for aggressively defending Manila, but by the early 1930s the plan had been revised in a cautious manner and called for forfeiting the entire Philippine archipelago. In 1939, Maj. Gen. John DeWitt, commandant of the Army War College, emphatically stated in an internal discussion of war plans that "we cannot, even as conditions are today, reinforce the Philippines.

We are going to lose them right away. We are 9,000 miles away; the Japanese [are] next door." This conclusion was made policy in a series of secret discussions between the American military and the British military starting in January 1941. The Navy's "Rainbow 5" global war plan stated in May 1941 that "no Army reinforcements will be sent to the Philippine Coastal Frontier."

So, rather than looking for strategic guidance, Marshall was more likely seeing if Ike had sufficient ice in his veins to recommend that thousands of his old friends and comrades in the Philippines be abandoned, condemning them to death or a war spent as prisoners of the Japanese. Marshall also probably wanted to gauge how much of a hold Gen. MacArthur still had on Ike. It is not clear whether Marshall knew that, in 1938, MacArthur had put aside Ike as his senior staff member and replaced him with the sycophantic Richard Sutherland, who would serve MacArthur throughout World War II—faithfully, except for repeatedly disobeying orders to get rid of the mistress he kept nearby. Ike found out about his demotion only when he returned from leave. When he protested, MacArthur coldly told him he was free to seek another assignment.

At any rate, Eisenhower passed Marshall's first test. Marshall looked up from the memo and immediately gave the brigadier another one: *Tell me how to implement this.* Ike later would recall how Marshall concluded the conversation on that grim Sunday in December 1941. "Eisenhower," Marshall said, "the department is filled with able men who analyze their problems but feel compelled always to bring them to me for final solution. I must have assistants who will solve their own problems and tell me later what they have done." Ike thought to himself that as Marshall spoke, his eyes were "awfully cold."

Prioritizing tends to be a forgotten aspect of strategy. The art of strategy is foremost not about *how* to do something but about *what* to do. In other words, the first problem is to determine what the real problem is. There are many aspects to any given problem, but the strategist must sort through them and determine its essence, for there lies the key to its solution. Eisenhower clearly understood the need to separate the essential from the merely important. In March 1942, he and an aide drafted a long memo for Marshall that differentiated primary war aims from lesser ones. The three primary goals, they wrote, had to be "the security of England, the retention of Russia in the war as an active war ally, and the defense of the Middle East." (Holding the Mideast prevented the possible linkup on land of German and Japanese forces in, perhaps, Iran and also kept open the supply line to Russia, at a time when keeping Russia in the war was indeed essential.) Everything else was secondary, they noted, in a classic summary of the nature of strategic decision making: "All other operations must be considered highly desirable rather than in the mandatory class." The implication of that conclusion, they continued, meant that victory in Europe had to take precedence over winning in the Pacific. Again, this was not original thinking. If anything, it made explicit the Army's version of a quiet understanding that already existed with the British. But it showed a clear grasp of how to implement that understanding.

Eisenhower himself also could be coldly calculating about risk. In his memoirs, he recalled making the decision to put fourteen thousand soldiers aboard the *Queen Mary* and send it through submarine-infested waters, knowing that its lifeboats and rafts could hold only eight thousand. He had calculated that, while it lacked armed escort, the ocean liner was fast enough to outrun German submarines—but not if it encountered one by chance. He had experienced some anxiety when the ship put into a Brazilian port and an Italian radio transmission was intercepted reporting its presence and, later, the direction in which it sailed.

Six months later, in October 1942, Eisenhower would write to Marshall from London, laying out a fairly clear plan for the remainder of the war. Looking forward through the fog and chaos of war is never easy, but Eisenhower, having settled into his new post as U.S. commander for operations in Europe, made it look so when he confidently wrote—even before U.S. forces were engaged against the Germans in North Africa in "Operation Torch"—that he could envision "launching a decisive blow in the spring of '44." In this scenario, "the summer of '43 would be used for building up the necessary forces in Great Britain, firmly establishing ourselves in favorable positions in the Southwest Pacific and exploiting TORCH." That, of course, would prove to be a prescient sentence.

Marshall knew that he could tutor the bright, ambitious Eisenhower in strategic planning in part because Ike already embodied Marshall's insistence on a team spirit in his senior leaders. Military historians tend to dwell on Eisenhower's personal cooperativeness, and indeed he was cooperative, unusually so—with other branches of the military, with civilian American officials, and with representatives of other nations. It was a quality not shared by many of his Army peers, some of whom seemed to revel in distrusting the British. It may have been Ike's most important personal asset. "Some men reach the top through a tremendous intellect, a ruthless disposition, a burning ambition, or an utter disregard for the feelings of others," wrote Maj. Gen. Sir Francis de Guingand, chief of staff through most of World War II to Gen. Bernard Montgomery, who certainly excelled at disregarding the feelings of others. But this was not the case with Eisenhower, de Guingand continued:

I think his success was largely due to his great human qualities: his sense of humor, his common sense and his essential honesty and integrity. He inspired love and unfailing loyalty; he had a magic touch when dealing with conflicting issues or clashes of personalities; and he knew how to find a solution along the lines of compromise, without surrendering a principle. He is, in fact, a great democrat.

Ike's British subordinates also found him very American. "Here was somebody who seemed eager to cast aside conventions and get on with the job" was the first impression he gave to Maj. Gen. Sir Kenneth Strong, his intelligence chief for most of the war. "He seemed to represent a new and interesting world." (Interestingly, one of the officers on his staff Strong deemed "most able" was Enoch Powell, who before the war was a brilliant professor of Greek, during the war turned sharply anti-American, and after the war would become prominent as an anti-immigration politician in the British Parliament. Powell's edition of Thucydides' *Peloponnesian War* is still studied and respected.) The sort of man who became a general in the American military was different from the British mold of minor aristocrats and country gentlemen. One officer who shot to prominence, J. Lawton Collins, was the offspring of Irish immigrants. Maurice Rose was the son of a rabbi. Several other senior generals, such as Clarence Huebner, Courtney Hodges, Ben Lear, Walter Krueger, and Troy Middleton, had risen from the enlisted ranks. An armor general, Ernest Harmon, was an orphan. One of the fastest risers in the Army of World War II, the paratrooper James Gavin, had been adopted out of an orphanage by a Pennsylvania coal-mining family and, not wanting to become a miner himself, had run away from home as a teenager to join the Army.

Marshall and Ike mature

Both Marshall and Eisenhower made several major mistakes during the war. Most notably, Marshall repeatedly advocated invading

Europe earlier than the British wanted to. Had the Allies landed in France in 1943, as he advised, they would have been pitting less experienced troops against a veteran German army that still enjoyed adequate air support, which would have made the Normandy landings a far riskier proposition than they were a year later. He and Eisenhower also opposed Operation Torch, the U.S.-led foray into North Africa in late 1942, which in retrospect probably was essential as a shakedown campaign for the green American forces and their untried commanders. Marshall also seemed to have a tin ear on issues of race and perhaps could have done far more to integrate the armed forces during World War II than he did.

Many of these mistakes were made in 1942 as Marshall and Eisenhower settled into their roles atop the U.S. military in a global war. Eisenhower's letters to Marshall that year have little of the confidence and certainty he would show by the end of the war, when he would address Marshall almost as a peer. In late 1942, after the Operation Torch landings in North Africa and the difficulties over Eisenhower's awkward political embrace of Adm. François Darlan, who had collaborated with the Nazis, followed by the shock of fighting the Germans in Tunisia, Eisenhower even wondered whether he might be replaced. This was probably the most vulnerable point he experienced during the entire war. "At any moment, it is possible that a necessity might arise for my relief and consequent demotion," he told his son. "If so, you are not to worry about it. . . . If it becomes expedient to reduce me, I would be the first to recommend it."

Marshall and Ike also were shaky—and perhaps not completely candid with each other—in one of their first major personnel decisions, the selection of a frontline American commander for the Torch campaign in Africa. When Marshall suggested Lloyd Fredendall to Eisenhower as the field commander, Ike expressed a bit of doubt. "He was not one of those in whom I had instinctive confidence," he wrote, somewhat too delicately, to the Army chief. Yet Fredendall was Marshall's top pick, as of course Eisenhower had been. By December 1942 Eisenhower had warmed to Fredendall, telling Harry Butcher, the Navy reservist who was Eisenhower's personal aide and confidant during the war, that he considered him and Patton his two most competent subordinate commanders. "Patton I think comes closest to meeting every requirement made on a commander," he dictated to Butcher. "Just after him I would at present rate Fredendall, although I do not believe the latter has the imagination in foreseeing and preparing for possible jobs of the future that Patton possesses." On February 4, 1943, Eisenhower even recommended that Fredendall be promoted to lieutenant general, along with two other men. That day he also sent a letter to Fredendall urging him to make sure his subordinate commanders were not staying too close to their command posts. "Generals are expendable just as is any other item in an army," he advised.

So it was all the more shocking to Ike a few days later when he visited Fredendall at his headquarters to see how the corps commander was situated. "It was a long way from the battle front," some seventy miles in the rear, he later wrote, in "a deep and almost inaccessible ravine." Two hundred Army engineers who should have been helping vulnerable combat units dig in and establish defensive positions instead were tunneling into hillsides to provide secure quarters for Fredendall's staff. Eisenhower's contempt for Fredendall's overcautiousness was clear in a line from his memoirs: "It was the only time, during the war, that I ever saw a divisional or higher headquarters so concerned over its own safety that it dug itself underground shelters." This comment is especially striking in the context of the book in which it appears. Aside from that sentence, Eisenhower is unfailingly courteous in discussing his former subordinates.

Motoring on to the front, Ike was shaken by the lackadaisical attitude of American troops facing the Germans. He inspected frontline troops who had been in Tunisia's Faid Pass for two days and was astonished to see that they had not set out a minefield or otherwise prepared their defenses. He told them to do so at first light and left at 3 A.M. Two hours later, before the sun rose, the entire unit was captured by attacking Germans. That event, he noted, was the beginning of the humiliating battle that came to be known as Kasserine Pass, the worst defeat of American ground forces in Europe or Africa during World War II. In about a week, Allied losses, most of them American, amounted to three hundred killed, three thousand wounded, and nearly four thousand missing, most of them taken prisoner. Some two hundred tanks also were lost. "The proud and cocky Americans today stand humiliated by one of the greatest defeats in our history," Ike's aide Butcher recorded in his diary. "This is particularly embarrassing to us with the British." One of the few bright spots at Kasserine was the performance of a 9th Infantry Division artillery battalion, commanded by one Lt. Col. William Westmoreland, that wheeled into place and opened fire in time to blunt a German armored attack.

Eisenhower emerged from the Kasserine episode sobered, with relief on his mind. "Our people from the very highest to the very lowest have learned that this is not a child's game," he wrote in a chastened letter to Marshall. American troops emerged from the fighting, he said after the war, "bedraggled ... tired ... down." The defeat at Kasserine Pass was especially painful to Eisenhower because it added to a string of Allied losses—Dunkirk, Bataan, Hong Kong, Singapore, Surabaya, and Tobruk—that he termed in his memoirs "the black reminders."

Eisenhower decided to make some changes. On February 24, as the Kasserine fight was ending, he wrote to his old friend Leonard "Gee" Gerow, then commanding the 29th Division, about the need to "ruthlessly" weed out "the lazy, the slothful, the indifferent or the complacent. Get rid of them. . . . For God's sake don't keep anybody around that you say to yourself, 'He may get by'— He won't. Throw him out." His first major personnel move was to fire Brig. Eric Mockler-Ferryman, his G-2, or intelligence chief. This was a controversial choice, because Mockler-Ferryman was British. Indeed, Ike's intelligence officer had to be British, because the Allies were relying on the U.K.'s "Ultra" intercepts of secret German communications. The firing came at a time when there was already much muttering among the British about the poor quality of the Americans' training and leadership. Gen. Montgomery commented in his diary that the American forces were "complete amateurs"—a harsh but not entirely unfair assessment of the undertrained, ill-equipped units he observed. Lt. Gen. Sir John Crocker, the British commander in the area, wrote in a letter to his wife, "Believe me, the British have nothing to learn from them." Crocker shared his views with reporters, criticizing the American 34th Infantry Division, a National Guard unit that had been federalized in February 1941. This was noticed by the Americans: "The s.o.b. publicly called our troops cowards," Patton wrote in his diary. British officers might have rightly wondered whether Ike would be as tough on his American subordinates as he had been on his British staffer.

Eisenhower told Marshall that he was thinking of relieving Fredendall, having detected in him a "peculiar apathy." He already had received internal reports that during a battle in late February, Fredendall had been found asleep at eleven in the morning two days in a row. The same day, he was told that, contrary to what he had believed, the British were not impressed with Fredendall and were especially unhappy with the quality of planning done by his staff. Eisenhower added a postscript to the letter. "My own real worry," he wrote, "is his apparent inability to develop a team." That word meant so much to Marshall. The report of

Allied concern might have been the deciding factor. If the British did not want Fredendall either, it was not only easy but necessary to move him out. Two days later, Eisenhower removed Fredendall, and by March 11 the ousted general was headed back to the United States, where he was given a meaningless promotion and the oblivion of a training command.

Eisenhower turned over Fredendall's command to Patton and gave him two clear orders. The first came from knowing Patton well. *Don't be personally reckless,* he told his old friend. The second was a lesson Eisenhower himself was mulling. He told Patton "to be cold-blooded about removal of inefficient officers. If a man fails, send him back to General Ike and let him worry about it." When Ike met the British intelligence officer who would replace the one he had fired, he instructed him that "if I thought any-one was not making the grade or was creating difficulties I was fully empowered to sack him on the spot. 'Hire and fire' was the slogan."

Patton made an impression on the frontline troops. It was hard not to notice him. Lt. Col. Westmoreland, leading his artil-lery battalion, was struck that "Patton would parade around with his boots, yellow britches, his Ike jacket, two pearl-handled revolv-ers, and a shiny helmet with three stars all over it. His jeep looked like a motorized Christmas tree sprinkled with stars." Another ris-ing officer, Col. James Polk, would describe Patton later in the war as resembling "a Wild West cowboy ready to go fox hunting."

The night he succeeded Fredendall, Patton noted in his diary, "I think Fredendall is either a little nuts or badly scared." It was a devastating epitaph for a career. Patton also cast a skeptical eye on one of his division commanders, Orlando Ward, writing not long after taking command that "Ward lacks force. . . . The division has lost its nerve and is jumpy." On the other side of the Atlantic, Gen. Marshall had gotten wind of Ward's naysaying, prompting him to write a letter to the general, who had served under him in the high-profile position of secretary of the Army's general staff, warning that he was giving "the impression of a degree of pessimism which was disturbing to me. . . . Naturally I am deeply interested in you and your career, but I am much more interested, through necessity, in the development of the fighting spirit in our Army." But Patton did not act against Ward until he heard from British Gen. Harold Alexander, who wrote to him, "In my opinion General Ward is not the best man to command the American First Armoured Division." It was the final blow. In his memoirs, Eisenhower presents the removals of Fredendall and Ward as necessary for improving the morale of American forces: After the Kasserine defeat, "the troops had to be picked up quickly."

Like Gen. Chaney, who had preceded Ike in London, Ward was sent back to the United States. But unlike Chaney, Ward was permitted to see Marshall, perhaps because Marshall had a message for him: *Stop talking about how the Germans are more effective than the Allies.* Ward was forgiven his indiscretion, in part because he had been speaking the truth but probably also because he had been relatively close to Marshall before the war, often walking home with him after work along Washington, D.C.'s Connecticut Avenue. Ward was sent to train troops in Texas and then made commandant of the artillery school at Fort Sill, Oklahoma. By the end of the war he was commanding another combat division in Europe, the 20th Armored. After the war he briefly commanded V Corps.

Ernest Harmon was instructed by Patton to head east and replace Ward as commander of the 2nd Armored. "Fine," he said. "Do you want me to attack or defend?"

Patton replied in a typically brusque fashion, according to Harmon's account. "What have you come for, asking me a lot of goddamned stupid questions?"

"I didn't think it was stupid," Harmon said, holding his ground—always important in dealing with Patton. "I simply asked a very fundamental question: whether I am to attack or defend."

Patton wouldn't tell him, so he decided on his own to attack, which was almost always the right attitude in World War II.

The victory in Tunisia, site of ancient Carthage, in May 1943 was the first win for the Allies in the west. It carried additional meaning for Eisenhower, who as a boy had read extensively about the heroes of the worlds of ancient Rome and Greece, and especially about the Carthaginians. "Among all the figures of antiquity, Hannibal was my favorite," he remembered. Meditating on his triumph in Tunis, Eisenhower came to a conclusion that may seem odd in today's context:

> Immediate and continuous loyalty to the concept of unity and to allied commanders is basic to victory. The instant such commanders lose the confidence of either government or of the majority of their principal subordinates, they must be relieved.

He seems to be saying here, between the lines, that Fredendall and Ward were sacrificed for the larger goal of preserving Allied unity. Driving home the point, Eisenhower added, "This was the great Allied lesson of Tunisia." In other words, in coalition warfare, generals must be relieved not just when they lose the confidence of their own leaders, but before that, if they lose the backing of allied leaders.

Not long after the firings of Fredendall and Ward, Gen. Marshall released his second report on the state of the U.S. military, the first issued since the United States had entered the war. In an appendix, he used the opportunity to discuss what he looked for in a general:

> . . . men who have measured up to the highest standards of military skill, who have demonstrated a comprehensive understanding

of modern standards of warfare and who possess the physical stamina, moral courage, strength of character and flexibility of mind necessary to carry the burdens which modern combat conditions impose.

This description, which came after the initial wave of reliefs—Short in the Pacific, Fredendall in Africa, and senior officers on the Army General Staff at the Pentagon—was similar to the list he had drawn up after World War I, except that here Marshall had added "flexibility of mind" as a requirement. The setbacks of 1941 through early 1943 had refined his formula for managing generals. They would adapt and succeed—or be replaced. But they would not be micromanaged, at least not by Marshall and Eisenhower. As Ike put it, "if results obtained by the field commander become unsatisfactory the proper procedure is not to advise, admonish, and harass him, but to replace him by another commander."

The risk of relief is the price senior officers pay in order not to be oversupervised. This is somewhat counterintuitive—nothing is more intrusive than removing a commander—but subsequent history indicates that it makes sense. In the 1950s and 1960s, as the U.S. Army started turning away from the practice of relief, meddling by superiors would increase notably. The tradition would die altogether in the Vietnam War—where, not coincidentally, one of the enduring images of the conflict would be that of lieutenants and captains looking up to see their battalion, brigade, and even division commanders hovering above them in helicopters.

CHAPTER 3

George Patton

The specialist

The Marshall template for generalship was not a rigid mold. It made room for exceptions, especially at higher levels of command. Marshall would put up with George Patton and some other outliers because their combat effectiveness made them irreplaceable.

Even now, more than six decades after his death, Patton remains one of our most remarkable generals. "You have no balance at all," Marshall's wife once scolded the young Patton, correctly, years before World War II. Maj. Gen. Ernest Harmon, one of his peers, wrote that he was "strange, brilliant, moody." The blustery Patton behaved in ways that would have gotten other officers relieved, but he was kept on because he was seen, accurately, as a man of unusual flaws and exceptional strengths. Marshall concluded that Patton was both a buffoon and a natural and skillful fighter. Ike cast himself as Patton's defender, writing to Marshall early in the war that "General Patton has . . . approached all his work in a very businesslike, sane but enthusiastic attitude." It is hardly usual to go out of one's way to reassure a superior that a subordinate is "sane."

The closest Patton came to disgrace was in mid-1943, as the Sicily campaign wound down, when he mistreated two hospitalized privates, one of them recovering from battle fatigue (what is now called post-traumatic stress disorder, or PTSD). On August 3, 1943, Patton walked into the tent of the 15th Evacuation Hospital and asked Pvt. Charles Kuhl of the 1st Infantry Division what his ailment was. "I guess I can't take it," responded Kuhl. Then, according to a report filed at the time by Lt. Col. Perrin Long, a Medical Corps officer, "The General immediately flared up, cursed the soldier, called him all types of a coward, then slapped him across the face with his gloves and finally grabbed the soldier by the scruff of his neck and kicked him out of the tent. The soldier was immediately picked up by corpsmen and taken to a ward tent." Kuhl ultimately was diagnosed as suffering from chronic dysentery and malaria. It was a display of extreme indiscipline by an officer who was expected to set an example. It also was flatly un-American.

On August 10, Patton subjected Pvt. Paul Bennett to similar harsh treatment. Bennett actually had been evacuated against his wishes and had asked to return to his artillery unit, even though he was "huddled and shivering." Patton asked him what he was suffering from. "It's my nerves," Bennett said.

"Your nerves, hell, you are just a goddamned coward," Patton shouted. He then slapped Bennett and said, "Shut up the goddamned crying. I won't have these brave men here who have been shot at seeing a yellow bastard sitting here crying." He then slapped him again, Long recounted, so hard that the private's helmet liner was knocked into the next tent. Patton ordered a hospital officer to discharge Bennett back to the front. "You're going to fight," he told Bennett. "If you don't, I'll stand you up against a wall and have a firing squad kill you on purpose." Patton then reached for his pistol and said, "I ought to shoot you myself, you goddamned whimpering coward."

There was little question about the facts of the matter. Patton had proudly recorded both incidents in his diary, writing of Pvt. Bennett that "I may have saved his soul, if he had one."

Patton's obtuseness about striking soldiers might be better understood if we recall that both he and Eisenhower had observed the exploits of Douglas MacArthur. Both men had been present in July 1932 when MacArthur, then the Army chief of staff, presided over something far harsher than a slap: the teargassing and routing of "Bonus Marchers," Depression-stricken World War I veterans who came to Washington by the thousands to demonstrate in favor of early payment of a cash bonus not due until 1945. MacArthur exceeded or perhaps ignored his orders, not only clearing out the marchers but burning their encampment, not far from the U.S. Capitol. MacArthur would contend that "not more than one in ten" was a veteran, and those who were tended to be "hardcore" Communists, drunks, and criminals. For his part, Eisenhower said that he had advised MacArthur against getting involved. He also said that when he informed MacArthur at the time that orders had arrived from President Hoover instructing MacArthur not to cross the Anacostia River to the marchers' camp, MacArthur responded, "I don't want to hear them and I don't want to see them," and then crossed over the bridge.

Eisenhower went out of his way in 1943 to save Patton, though there were ample grounds for his relief. In addition to the slapping incidents, Patton had violated Marshall's insistence on teamwork with the Allies in Sicily by shooting out ahead of his orders and launching a questionable drive through the western end of the island when the German foe was concentrated in the eastern end. Despite these blunders, Eisenhower hoped to sidestep Patton's removal. He wrote a harsh letter to Patton instead, demanding that he apologize to his troops. Ike pocketed the contrite letter Patton wrote to him in response and also persuaded three reporters who knew about these incidents not to file stories about them. Just a few days later, Eisenhower was lobbying Marshall to promote Patton to the permanent rank of major general, which was approved. "George Patton continues to exhibit some of those unfortunate personal traits of which you and I have always known and which during this campaign caused me some most uncomfortable days," he wrote to Marshall. "His habit of impulsive bawling out of subordinates, extending even to personal abuse of individuals, was noted in at least two specific cases. I have had to take the most drastic steps; and if he is not cured now, there is no hope for him. Personally, I believe that he is cured."

Months later, in November 1943, news of the slapping incidents leaked. In a war being fought in the name of democracy, it was devastating to have an American general behaving like a barroom bully. Eisenhower had recognized this when he ordered Patton to apologize to his enlisted men and to tell them that he "respected their positions as fighting soldiers of a democratic nation."

Despite Ike's hopes, Patton was not cured. In the spring of 1944, with the slapping controversy barely past, Patton again made headlines, wisecracking at a public event in Knutsford, England, that it was "the evident destiny of the British and Americans to rule the world." In the wake of that outburst and the headlines it provoked, Ike commented to Marshall of Patton that "apparently he is unable to use reasonably good sense in all those matters where senior commanders must appreciate the effect of their own actions upon public opinion." Ike made it clear to Patton that he was on the thinnest of ice, informing his old friend, "I am thoroughly weary of your failure to control your tongue and have begun to doubt your all-round judgment, so essential in high military position." He wrote to Marshall that "frankly I am exceedingly weary of his habit of getting everybody into hot water."

But again, Ike did not remove Patton, explaining to Marshall that he found his colleague "admittedly unbalanced but nevertheless aggressive," and so useful to the cause. James Gavin, who knew Patton and served under him in Sicily, concluded that Eisenhower probably would have been justified in relieving Patton, "but he couldn't spare him. Generalship in that high echelon is a rare commodity, and Georgie had it. Patton had it."

There also was an oddly personal element in Eisenhower's handling of Patton. Ike seemed to take a certain pride in protecting the old cavalryman. Part of this was due to their long-standing friendship, and no doubt a sense of obligation. When the war began, it had been Patton who looked out for Eisenhower. As Ike's colleague Wedemeyer reportedly said to Eisenhower during an argument about what to do with Patton, "Hell, get on to yourself, Ike—you didn't make him, he made you." Patton also told Eisenhower early in 1942, "You are about my oldest friend," and a year later Eisenhower used the same phrase in return. But Gavin was correct: Most of all, Ike knew he needed Patton as a matter of military effectiveness.

Ike's appreciation of his old friend would always be far more limited than that of German officers, who reportedly saw Patton as one of the best overall Allied generals. "He is the most modern general and the best commander of armored and infantry combined," a German prisoner of war, Lt. Col. Freiherr von Wangenheim, told his captors.

Eisenhower's final word on Patton would come more than two decades later, in his last memoir, *At Ease*. There he repeatedly praised Patton as "a master of fast and overwhelming pursuit" and "the finest leader in military pursuit that the United States Army has known." It is a revealing superlative, at once lofty and limited. That is, he calls Patton the best, but at something that is described narrowly. He doesn't call Patton the best general or the best combat leader, nor even the best at waging offensive warfare; he makes it clear that in his view Patton excelled at the single task of hounding a retreating enemy. Narrow as that mission is, it was precisely the job the American military faced in Europe in late 1944 and early 1945, and that is likely the primary reason Patton was never sent home in disgrace. On balance, Eisenhower was right to keep him. And the modern American military probably is worse for not having a few senior commanders with a dose of Patton's dynamism and color in them.

CHAPTER 4
Mark Clark
The man in the middle

Like Patton, Lt. Gen. Mark Clark was close to Eisenhower, but he was far less effective on the battlefield. Clark was also a difficult man to like. "It makes my flesh creep to be with him," Patton once wrote in his diary. Ten months later Patton noted that "anyone who serves under Clark is always in danger." As the American commander in the secondary theater of Italy in 1943 and 1944, Clark fired two corps commanders—that is, generals overseeing groups of divisions. A strong case can be made that, if someone had to go, it was Clark who should have been relieved rather than his two subordinates. He was, perhaps, never quite bad enough to relieve but not quite good enough to admire.

Patton was not always a reliable reporter, but his wariness of Clark was borne out in Italy in the fall of 1943 and the following winter. Following the Sicily campaign, American and British forces, on September 9, 1943, landed at Salerno, on the Italian mainland about thirty miles southeast of Naples. It was Clark's first battle command of the war, and, by his own account, the assault was a "near disaster." By the standards of the German army, the counterattack was not particularly fierce. Nonetheless, by September 12 it had driven Clark toward panic. He feared his men might be pushed back to the sea and contemplated ordering the destruction of the mountains of food, vehicles, gasoline, ammunition, and other supplies that had been landed on the beach.

Others were less shaken. When Clark told Maj. Gen. Troy Middleton, the doughty commander of the 45th Division, that he was considering pulling out, Middleton gave him a stiffening response: "Mark, leave enough ammunition and supplies [for my division]. The Forty-fifth is staying." Upon getting wind of Clark's panicky thoughts, British Gen. Harold Alexander, his British superior, cracked his uniform pants with his swagger stick and said, "Never do, never do." He ordered, "There will be no evacuation. Now we'll proceed from there." That put an end to Clark's dalliance with withdrawal.

But Clark needed to settle blame. He called Maj. Gen. Ernest "Mike" Dawley, commander of Clark's VI Corps, who had set up a headquarters in a tobacco barn. Dawley told him that German forces had broken through his lines and were fanning out across the American rear, an extremely dangerous situation.

"What are you going to do about it?" Clark asked.

"Nothing," replied Dawley, according to Clark's account. "I have no reserves. All I have got is a prayer."

Clark was disturbed by that response, he wrote later, but put it aside for about a week, until the situation stabilized. Clark's own memoir of World War II is one of the least informative to emerge from the war, tending to be more notable for its omissions than for its few revelations. His account of this incident is consistent with that pattern. He leaves out a key development: that his own superior, Alexander, said to him about Dawley, "I do not want to interfere with your business, but I have some ten years' experience in this game of sizing up commanders. I can tell you definitely that you have a broken reed on your hands and I suggest you replace him immediately."

Eisenhower, who was Clark's foremost supporter, was even blunter about Dawley's character, asking during a battlefield visit, "For God's sake, Mike, how did you manage to get your troops so fucked up?" It is possible that Ike spoke so sharply in order to make it clear to others present that if anyone was to be blamed, it would not be Clark. Maj. Gen. Fred Walker, commander of the 36th Division, who earlier in his career had been a friend and mentor to Clark, believed that Dawley had "handled his job as well as or better than Clark handled his." Eisenhower supported Clark's decision to relieve Dawley and explained his thoughts to Marshall in a letter. "It seems that when the going is really tough he ceases to function as a commander," Eisenhower wrote. He added that he wanted permission to demote the dismissed general. When Dawley returned to the United States, he went to see Marshall, with whom he had served in France in World War I. At first Marshall had some "misgivings" about the relief, according to Army historians' notes of an interview with him, but Marshall "told Dawley that after listening to his story he had decided he should have been relieved sooner than he was." Dawley had failed as a combat commander. But so had Clark.

The best officers to serve under Clark came away with doubts about his ability to lead in combat. They noted especially that he lacked the ability to sense battlefield developments, an almost mysterious skill that is essential to generalship. "His concern for personal publicity was his greatest weakness," wrote Lucian Truscott, one of the best American generals of World War II and an old polo pal of Patton's. "I have sometimes thought it may have prevented him from acquiring that 'feel of battle' that marks all top-flight battle leaders." Another high-profile general of World War II, James Gavin, came to a remarkably similar conclusion, telling Matthew Ridgway in a letter decades later, "I always had a feeling that . . . Mark Clark really didn't have a true feel for what soldiers could and could not do and how much power it took to accomplish a mission." To his opponents, the two corps under Clark's command appeared to be experience "independent and almost unconnected leadership"—the scathing critique, by captured German intelligence officers, of Clark, who was, after all, the point of connection and coordination.

Clark replaced Dawley as commander of VI Corps with Maj. Gen. John Lucas, who would fare no better. Lucas was an odd choice. He left the impression, wrote one historian, of being "a sensitive and compassionate man, with a faintly old-maidish quality." His behavior in the first two months of 1944 resembled that of the tired, aging, pessimistic generals of World War I, the men Marshall had spent years trying to eliminate or, if they remained in the Army, to keep away from combat command. It is not clear how Lucas slipped through Marshall's net, but it was likely because Marshall's attention shifted away from Italy as planning for the D-Day landings intensified.

In January 1944, the Allies tried to flank German resistance in southern Italy by leapfrogging up the Italian coast to Anzio, just south of Rome. Lucas confided in his diary that he had a deep ambivalence about the enterprise. After a conference with his superiors, he recorded that "I felt like a lamb being led to the slaughter." The same month, he noted, "I will do what I am ordered to do but these 'Battles of Little Big Horn' aren't much fun and a failure now would ruin Clark, kill many of my men, and certainly prolong the war." This was not a good frame of mind in which to take on the Germans. Believing his force to be undermanned, Lucas operated cautiously. Despite achieving complete surprise and managing a virtually unopposed amphibious landing, Lucas chose not to push from the beach toward the inland hills, where he would have held the high ground. His view was that he might have been able to take the hills before him, but he would not have been able to hold them. Instead he began digging in and bringing in supplies. "The strain of a thing like this is a terrible burden," Lucas wrote in his diary. "Who the hell wants to be a general."

Anzio proved to be an even worse mess than Salerno. It was a bloody stalemate that, Eisenhower later wrote, was as close as Allied forces would come in World War II to the "draining sore" of Gallipoli in the First World War. Marshall privately believed that the British forces at Anzio were worn out and demoralized, telling Army historians years later that they "simply had no punch." This was, he added, a curious reversal from two years earlier in North Africa, where the British had been so contemptuous of the Americans. "But in Italy the situation was quite the other way," he told the historians. "The American troops had learned, and the British divisions were exhausted; they had no fight left in them. The situation was now flowing the other way with American divisions improving and British deteriorating."

Clark's approach in a crisis tended to be to blame everyone but himself. Confronted with the mess at Anzio, he remained true to form, advising Lucas to be cautious, then faulting him for taking that advice. At a meeting in late January 1944, with the attack bogged down, Clark denounced his division commanders for making poor planning decisions. Lucas stepped up and said that as corps commander Clark had approved those plans and that he should take the blame. Clark ignored Lucas and next attacked Col. William Darby and Maj. Gen. Lucian Truscott for their handling of a Ranger battalion that had been wiped out while trying to break through German lines. Truscott tartly responded that he had organized the original Ranger battalion and that he and Darby probably understood Ranger capabilities better than anyone else in the Army. "That ended the matter," Truscott remembered.

If Clark would not take responsibility for the failed assault, someone else would have to. On February 22, one month after the landing, Lucas received a message from Clark. "He arrives today with eight generals," Lucas wrote in the last entry in his combat diary. "What the hell." Clark was coming to dump him and replace him with Truscott.

It was not clear that Lucas would have succeeded had he pushed inland, but his relief was seen by his peers as justified simply because he had not tried. However, there is no evidence that Clark encouraged him to move inland, and much evidence that Clark counseled against it. Perhaps reflecting some embarrassment at scapegoating Lucas, Clark made no mention of the firing in his own diary. "In one paragraph the commander of VI Corps had been John Lucas, in the next it is Lucian Truscott," British historian Lloyd Clark noted archly. Gen. Clark later wrote that he fired Lucas at the behest of the British, but added that he agreed with the move. "My own feeling was that Johnny Lucas was ill—tired physically and mentally," he wrote. Truscott would write that seeing his old friend Lucas ejected "was one of my saddest experiences of the war."

British Maj. Gen. Julian Thompson, author of one of the most illuminating modern studies of Lucas at Anzio, concluded that the firing of Lucas was unfair yet also the right thing to do. That is, he explained, given how fundamentally the Anzio operation was misconceived and manned, it was unlikely that another commander would have done much better. Yet, he continued, given Lucas's uninspiring command style, "his removal was both necessary and timely, not for what had gone before, but for what was to come: three months of defensive battles, followed by hard fighting to break out." Given all that, Thompson, who led a commando brigade in the Falklands War in the spring of 1982, still came to the conclusion that Anzio, while poorly conceived and executed as a tactical operation, was nonetheless a strategic success, because it forced the Germans to shift troops from France to central Italy. Five months later, when the Allies invaded north-western France, this made a difference.

Whatever Clark's motivation, his removal of Lucas soon was justified by the results. Truscott quickly proved to be a far more dynamic commander than his predecessor. He got out and about, visited frontline units, and rebuilt British trust in American command. "Unlike Lucas, who had not often ventured out of his vaulted wine-cellar headquarters and who even on his infrequent visits to the troops had failed to project an image of confidence and optimism, Truscott produced the required emotional response," wrote historian Martin Blumenson. Even so, it would take another three months for the Allies to drive the forty miles to Rome.

Disliked and distrusted by subordinates and superiors alike, the querulous Clark should have been removed from his position. But British officers were reluctant to move against him without American support, and American officers were wary of doing so because of Clark's close relationship with Ike. Also, there was no obvious replacement available for Clark. "He thinks he is God Almighty," one American general, Jacob Devers, told a British colleague. "He's a headache to me and I would relieve him if I could, but I can't." Clark, the untouchable mediocrity, seems to represent a flaw in the Marshall system, in which politics and personal relationships combined to stymie moves that should have been made.

The one general who seemed to like having Clark around was his foe in Italy, Field Marshal Albert Kesselring, who early on detected Clark's aversion to risk and would use that understanding to his advantage for months. The irony of this was that, of the two generals who most enjoyed Ike's protection, one was Patton, whom the Germans feared most of all the Americans facing them, and the other was Clark, whom they welcomed as their opposition.

Unlike some generals, Clark has a reputation that has not

improved with the passage of time. "Clark proved one of the more disappointing U.S. commanders of the war," concluded Williamson Murray and Allan Millett, two leading American military historians, who found him "ambitious, ruthless with subordinates, profligate with the lives of his soldiers, unsympathetic to the difficulties of other Allied armies, and more impressed with style than substance." It was a worrisome sign for the future of the U.S. Army that in a war in which dozens of generals were fired, Clark was not. There is much more of Clark than there is of Patton in today's generals.

CHAPTER 5
"Terrible Terry" Allen
Conflict between Marshall and his protégés

The case of Maj. Gen. Terry de la Mesa Allen represented another challenge to the Marshall system. In this situation, Marshall disagreed with his top men in Europe, Eisenhower and Bradley, over the nature of generalship in the military of the nascent American superpower. The point of disagreement was what to do about Gen. Allen.

"Terrible Terry" Allen was as Old Army as they came, a tough, rumpled, hard-driving, hard-drinking cavalryman who had ridden the dusty trails of the American West. As a young lieutenant in 1913, he led six soldiers on a ride against thirty border-crossing Mexican cattle rustlers and captured or killed all of them. In World War I he achieved some notoriety in the Army for refusing to be medically evacuated after being shot in the face. In 1920, he represented the Army in a three-hundred-mile "cowboy vs. cavalryman" horse race across central Texas, which he won in 101 hours and 56 minutes of riding. Allen was in the same class as Eisenhower at Fort Leavenworth's Command and General Staff School, but while Eisenhower was ranked first, Allen was a bottom-dweller, placing at 221 out of 241 students. Eisenhower didn't mind taking a drink—he had made bathtub gin at Fort Meade, Maryland, during Prohibition, and while with the 15th Infantry Regiment at Fort Lewis, Washington, before the war, he had declared "Beer Barrel Polka" to be the regiment's official marching song. But Ike did not consume alcohol like Allen, who could become so staggering drunk that an aide remembered that after one party he "couldn't get into his jeep under his own power."

Marshall was aware of Allen's excesses but believed that his ability as a combat leader was more important. In a prewar letter, he described Allen as one of the few officers he knew who were "of that unusual type who enthuse all of their subordinates and carry through almost impossible tasks." This was a trait that Marshall knew was likely to be especially helpful in the early phases of a war, as an unprepared America sent green troops into battle. In October 1940, Marshall made Allen a brigadier general despite the opposition of several subordinates. "Terry Allen, nobody wanted to give a star to and the General [Marshall] insisted on it," recalled Merrill Pasco, a Marshall aide during World War II. "Terry Allen is one of those I recall General Marshall pushed along over the objection of G-1," the chief of personnel. Lt. Col. Allen was being chewed out by the commanding colonel of the 7th Cavalry Regiment, and perhaps facing a court-martial, when a telegram arrived notifying Allen that he had been jumped to brigadier general—and so immediately outranked the officer berating him.

Marshall kept a protective eye on Allen. Two years later, while in the midst of overseeing the American entrance into a global war, he took the time to send a personal note to Allen expressing concern about his consumption of alcohol. "I must explain to you that there had come to me from several different sources an indication that you had been drinking," Marshall wrote. "I don't mean you were appearing under the influence of liquor, but I do mean drinking in the daytime." Yet he left Allen in command of the 1st Infantry Division, which Allen loved leading. "It is the most honorable place in the most honorable Army in the world, the commander of the First Division," he had once told a group of soldiers new to the division.

Marshall's instincts were correct on both counts. Allen was a rascal, irritating his superiors, but he also would be one of the best combat leaders the U.S. Army had in its first year of operations in Africa and Europe. Early on the morning of March 17, 1943, not long after taking over from the ousted Fredendall, Lt. Gen. George Patton arrived at a frontline position to watch Allen's 1st Infantry Division launch an attack on the Germans in Tunisia. Seeing no troop movement or other signs of imminent attack, Patton stormed off to find Allen. "What the hell is this?" Patton snarled at him, believing that the lack of perceivable movement meant the assault was proceeding hesitantly. To the contrary, Allen replied to Patton: He had decided to attack earlier than planned. His troops were not only moving out; they already were standing on their first set of objectives. Allen had out-Pattoned Patton and was in the vanguard of the war's first clear American-led victory over the Germans.

Yet Allen found it difficult to get along with the new Army way of operating. He tried to toe the Marshall-Eisenhower line about being a team player, but his heart was not in it. "I think the division has done fairly well today," he began in an impromptu post-battle press conference under a Tunisian almond tree. He started by saying the right things: "I want to stress the idea that whatever it did was due to teamwork. Everybody in the division deserves credit. The artillery deserves credit, and so do the engineers, the tank destroyers, and the Ranger battalion—and don't forget the medics and the birds who drive the trucks." But he could keep this up for only so long, and soon he veered into finger-pointing sarcasm. "I don't want anybody to think I'm sore about air support. I guess the Air Force here has a lot of demands on it. I guess maybe there was some other division on the front that was attacked by two or three Panzer divisions and the Air Force had to help them first"—which everyone present knew was not the case. He even took a pop at another Army unit, Orlando Ward's 1st Armored Division, which held an adjacent sector. "I guess they had motor trouble," he sneered.

Gen. Allen's finest day of the war came on July 11, 1943, the day after the Americans landed in Sicily. It was the largest amphibious landing in history—and it was in trouble. The Americans had stormed ashore in south-central Sicily, with paratroopers and British forces to the east, but high winds and heavy seas had impeded the landings. German forces were counterattacking fiercely, rolling down the island ridgelines toward the Americans splashing ashore. Panzer tanks pushed to within two thousand yards of the water's edge. Allen's infantrymen had burrowed down as the Panzers passed and then attacked the following German foot soldiers. Most of his artillery had not yet come ashore, so Allen called for naval gunfire. Cruisers and destroyers just beyond the breakers, nearly running aground, began to engage the Panzers. That night, when elements of the division were fighting hard just to hold their positions, Allen surprised them with an aggressive order: "THE DIVISION ATTACKS AT MIDNIGHT." It was a brilliant move. Allen could issue the order with some confidence because, atypically for the Army, he long had emphasized training in night fighting, reasoning that some soldiers would be lost in the confusion, but ultimately far fewer than would be killed in a prolonged daylight assault. His sense of combat timing was impeccable: The division's attack surprised German reinforcements, who were marshaling in assembly areas for their own attack, planned for dawn.

Even Allen's nemesis, Lt. Gen. Omar Bradley, was impressed by this surprising rout of the Germans, writing later with evident mixed feelings,

> I question whether any other U.S. division could have repelled that charge in time to save the beach from tank penetration. Only the perverse Big Red One with its no less perverse commander was both hard and experienced enough to take that assault in stride. A greener division might easily have panicked and seriously embarrassed the landing.

Bradley only indirectly praised Allen's leadership. He respected what Allen's division had done, but never went out of his way to praise the way Allen had led it.

After the beachhead was secure, Allen led the 1st Infantry Division into Sicily's hot, mountainous interior, ultimately waging a weeklong battle in the island's center, near Troina, the highest town in Sicily and the anchor point of the German defensive line. It was a difficult encounter with an adversary that launched no fewer than twenty-four counterattacks against Allen's division. Westmoreland, whose artillery battalion was attached to Allen's division, was thrown into the air and nearly killed when his jeep ran over a German Teller mine. Allen and the division won the fight, which in Patton's estimation was "the hardest battle" of the Sicily campaign and, in the opinion of John Lucas, the toughest of the war to that point. Allen later wrote that German prisoners reported "they had been ordered to hold Troina, at all costs." The week that Troina fell, Allen appeared on the cover of *Time* magazine.

Then came an astonishing move. As the battle was ending, Bradley removed Allen as commander of the 1st Infantry Division. Allen was replaced by Maj. Gen. Clarence Huebner, a

Marshall favorite who was available, having been fired the previous month as deputy chief of staff to Gen. Harold Alexander, apparently as a result of Huebner's unwillingness to mutely accept the British commander's persistent disparagement of American troops. Bradley emphasized the point by also relieving Allen's assistant division commander, Brig. Gen. Theodore Roosevelt Jr. Adding to the injury, very little explanation was offered to Allen, who was crushed. The division artillery commander recalled that after the relief "it was painful to see Terry break down. Many wondered if he would ever recover." He had been "shanghaied," Allen would later bitterly tell an aide. It is heartbreaking to read the puzzled notes Allen wrote in pencil to his wife in the wake of his relief as he tried to figure out what had happened and why. He went to see Patton, who unhelpfully told him that perhaps he was being moved out in preparation for promoting him to corps command.

Why was Terry Allen fired? This is a question that bears some examination. His relief cannot be attributed to battlefield failure, for he was among the most successful field commanders the Army had in the European theater in 1942–43.

Official accounts of why Bradley relieved Allen are unclear, and the reasoning given in Bradley's two autobiographies are "inconsistent and confusing," observed Maj. Richard Johnson in a 2009 review of the historical record. In various accounts, it has been explained that Allen was tired (Eisenhower's version), that his troops were undisciplined (one of Bradley's versions), or that he was too aggressive against the Germans (another, less credible Bradley version). But the real reason seems to be simply that Bradley and Eisenhower did not like his type. Bradley thought of Allen as the sort of general who should not be tolerated, writing that "Allen had become too much of an individualist to submerge himself without friction in the group undertakings of war."

But the new men had not read their own boss well. Marshall, as it happened, had visited the 1st Division just before it headed to Sicily and had come away impressed, noting in a letter that it had "won the respect and admiration of all who have seen it in action." When a despondent Allen arrived in the United States, Marshall effectively overruled Bradley's decision. By the end of September, Marshall was looking for a division for Allen to command. Ultimately he gave Allen the 104th Infantry Division, then training in the United States. Unlike many other training generals, Allen would be allowed to deploy overseas with the division and take it into combat. This move was not popular with the generals of the new school. "Terry was nothing but a tramp," said Gen. Wade Haislip, a longtime friend of Eisenhower's who served as chief of Army personnel early in the war. "He was a classmate of mine, but he was just a tramp. . . . Old Terry Allen got relieved for cause and he [Marshall] brought him back home and gave him another division."

A year later, Allen led the 104th Division into Normandy and across France into Germany. Joe Collins, his corps commander, considered Allen a "problem child" but came to judge Allen's new unit, the 104th, as "just as good" as his old one, the 1st Division. True to form, Allen was especially impressive in launching a series of night attacks, breaking through German defenses and demonstrating the sharp training he had given his soldiers. An aide to Gen. Courtney Hodges noted in a headquarters diary, "The whole artillery section functions beautifully according to the book and what the General [Hodges] particularly likes thus far of what he has seen of the 104th is their ability to button up tight and hold the place tight once they have taken it. There is no record yet of the 104th giving ground."

In the short term, Marshall would prevail, with Allen being back in a combat leadership role. But in the long run, in shaping the future of the U.S. Army, Eisenhower and, even more, Bradley would win this argument. There would be few if any Terry Allen types rising to the top in the Army after World War II. Eisenhower and Bradley wanted cooperative team players, not go-it-alone mavericks. Ike believed that the sprawling nature of modern warfare made such nonconformism dangerous. "Misfits defeat the purpose of the command organization essential to the supply and control of the vast land, air, sea, and logistical forces that must be brought to bear against the enemy," he later wrote.

CHAPTER 6
Eisenhower manages Montgomery

Eisenhower also would have bigger problems to handle, most notably that of Bernard Law Montgomery. Nothing illustrates Eisenhower's unusual ability to handle his job like his relationship with the senior British commander in France and Germany during the culminating phase of the war—between D-Day, on June 6, 1944, and V-E Day, some 335 days later.

Among Montgomery's notable traits was the peculiar capacity to spread discontent, beginning with himself. "Certainly I can say that my own childhood was unhappy," he wrote in the third sentence of his memoirs. As an adult, Montgomery remained an odd duck, socially inept and perhaps unable to read others. "I know well that I am regarded by many people as being a tiresome person," he said in a meeting to plan the Allied invasion of Sicily. "I think this is very probably true. I try hard not to be tiresome; but I have seen so many mistakes made in this war, and so many disasters happen, that I am desperately anxious to try and see that we have no more; and this often means being very tiresome."

Montgomery certainly did not go out of his way to put Eisenhower at ease. At their first meeting, early in the war, Montgomery instructed Eisenhower to put out his cigarette, as he did "not permit smoking in his office." The chain-smoking Eisenhower, sensing the insult, stubbed out his cigarette. Even after leaving the meeting, his face was red and the veins in his forehead were throbbing, his driver and close friend Kay Summersby later recalled.

Chester Wilmot, a journalist who covered Montgomery's headquarters during the war and interviewed him after it, appears to reflect Montgomery's view of the U.S. military in his history of the war, *The Struggle for Europe.* In it, he explains with extraordinary condescension that "in their dealings with people, Americans are often unsure of themselves and betray their feeling of inferiority by their behaviour, which Europeans tend to regard as juvenile and even gauche."

Even the more flexible, autonomous command style of the American military in World War II, in which subordinate leaders were told what to do but not how to do it, was interpreted by Wilmot as an unfortunate psychological by-product of American history: "The characteristic American resentment of authority, dating from the birth of the United States, has undoubtedly influenced command policy in their armed forces and has led to a considerable measure of independence and delegated responsibility at every level." This difference may be one reason American generals came to see Montgomery as effective at set-piece battles but poor at improvisation and pursuit. As Wilmot put it, Montgomery's deliberate approach "demanded a degree of patience and restraint the Americans did not possess. Montgomery's approach was scientific; theirs was emotional." Reading such analysis, which almost certainly was inspired by Montgomery's views, one can only marvel at Eisenhower's self-control in dealing with Montgomery and other British officers, especially after Montgomery lost as many as four hundred tanks—one-third of the British total in France at the time—in advancing just six miles beyond Caen in Operation Goodwood, in July 1944.

Throughout the late summer of 1944, Eisenhower and Montgomery sparred over the strategy for the final attack on Germany and also over the command structure that would be used for that campaign, with Montgomery advocating that some senior general—quite obviously himself—be designated the overall "Land Forces Commander." His argument was more or less that any fool could see that Eisenhower was incompetent. For political reasons, Marshall ordered Eisenhower to transfer his headquarters from England to France, even though the communications gear he needed was not yet in place on the Continent. On September 1, Eisenhower formally became the Allied ground operations commander, replacing Montgomery, and moved his headquarters to France, where his staff had taken over a small villa near the monastery island of Mont-Saint-Michel. On the same day, the British parried by promoting Montgomery to field marshal.

The late summer of 1944 brought an awkward and significant shift in this special relationship. The Americans had come late to the war. They had sat out the years during which the British saw the fall of France, the evacuation of more than 300,000 troops from Dunkirk, stinging defeats in Norway and Crete, and then the Battle of Britain and the Blitz. After finally entering the war, the Americans had been considered and treated as a junior partner by the British. The June 1944 landing in Normandy was more bittersweet for the British than the Americans tended to realize. The Americans were *entering* France, while the British were *returning* to it, having been evicted four years earlier. And, of course, Britain had lost a generation of young men in the battlefields of France thirty years earlier. In mid-1944, the balance of power between the two allies was changing, and the newcomers were trying on their primacy. "The British, who had uninterruptedly fought the Germans the longest, and part of the time all alone, were being well and truly elbowed from center stage," commented British historian Norman Gelb.

. . .

On September 2, Eisenhower set out from the villa just established as his headquarters in France for an unhappy round of meetings with Bradley and Patton in Chartres about how, with their forces outrunning their plans, fuel shortages were forcing the curtailment of pending offensives. Patton wanted 400,000 gallons of gas a day, but on August 30 he had received just 32,000. (Patton did not disclose to his old friend Eisenhower that one of his units had just captured more than 100,000 gallons of German aviation fuel.) It was an unfortunate irony that the Americans, who had so quickly risen to dominance in the war because of their capability to churn out goods and manpower, were suddenly coming up short in resources. Patton, always far more vigilant of his own feelings than he was of others', found Eisenhower stuffy at the meeting. "Ike was very pontifical and quoted Clausewitz to us," he wrote. "Ike did not thank or congratulate any of us for what we have done."

Eisenhower's bad day was far from over. On the return flight from the meetings, his B-25's right engine suffered a muffler malfunction and caught fire. The crew returned to Chartres, where Ike got into his L-5 observer aircraft, a two-seater akin to a Piper Cub, driven by a weak 185-horsepower engine. Back over Normandy, the tiny plane ran into a squall that made it impossible to land at the strip that was its destination. The pilot, Lt. Richard Underwood, running short on fuel, diverted and put it down on a flat ocean beach. The powerful Mont-Saint-Michel tide was flooding in, so to preserve the aircraft from the rising seawater, the general and the lieutenant pushed the plane across the wet sand to higher ground—at which point they realized that they did not know whether the beach had been de-mined. In moving the aircraft, Eisenhower badly wrenched his knee—not the left joint, which he had damaged years earlier, but the right, which until then he had considered the good one. Eisenhower's body already was strained by supreme command, which had led him to smoke four packs of cigarettes a day, accompanied by as many as fifteen cups of coffee. (Patton, not always a reliable recorder of facts, also had noted in his diary that spring, "Ike is drinking too much.") Eisenhower hobbled a mile with Underwood along a lightly trafficked back road, "a miserable walk through a driving rain," until by chance an Army jeep came along. They flagged it down. The sergeant at the wheel was astounded to encounter his top general in Europe sodden and limping along a dirt road. Eisenhower's aides were equally surprised when the jeep arrived and two GIs lifted Ike out of it and carried him upstairs.

In the following week, Ike had to sit with his leg straight out, the knee first plastered and then clamped in rubber, making him extremely uncomfortable. It was not the best frame of mind in which to deal with Montgomery, very near the British equivalent of MacArthur: a good general undermined by his own egotism yet untouchable for political reasons. Weigley depicts Montgomery as an "arrogant, hawk-like loner." Montgomery hadn't been Eisenhower's first choice for commander of British forces in the D-Day landings. Ike had asked for Gen. Harold Alexander, whom he liked as a man, admired as a soldier, and respected as a strategic thinker. Eisenhower found Churchill's preference for Montgomery "acceptable," as he had to. It was the most minimal endorsement possible.

Ike wanted to meet with Montgomery, who responded that he was too busy "just at present" to travel to see him. But, Monty added, Ike was welcome to come see him so that Montgomery could convey his views about the way forward against Germany: "If so delighted to see you at lunch tomorrow." Ike declined that invitation. When they discussed possibly holding such a meeting five days later, Montgomery set conditions for the encounter, saying that he did not want others to be present, or that at least they be required to remain silent. Such demands were extraordinary, but Eisenhower was bending over backwards in his dealings with Montgomery and other allies in 1944. Indeed, he was mocked by some American officers as "the best general the British have"—a taunt that reached his ears through an Associated Press reporter returning from a tour with Patton's Third Army. The sarcastic officers could not know it, but this was the highest praise Eisenhower could hear, because it meant that he was rigorously fulfilling Marshall's mandate to maintain the coalition, and was doing it even during the year in which the Anglo-American relationship was fundamentally changing, with the Americans moving up to dominant status even though they were still largely regarded by the more seasoned British as heavily armed amateurs.

The meeting finally occurred on the sunny but cool afternoon of Sunday, September 10, 1944. It was held aboard Eisenhower's aircraft on the tarmac in Brussels. Ike had traveled to Montgomery's headquarters city, but he still managed to hold the encounter on his own turf. Montgomery climbed aboard and began by asking that Eisenhower's administrative officer leave the meeting while his own remained. "I explained my situation fully," he wrote in his memoirs. "It was essential for him to know my views." Montgomery had a difficult time concealing his contempt for Eisenhower, whom he hardly considered a military equal, let alone a superior, the Supreme Allied Commander in Europe. A few weeks earlier he had written a letter to another British general in which he complained that Eisenhower's "ignorance as to how to run a war is absolute and complete." That was basically the same message he had for Ike that day in Brussels.

Montgomery opened the discussion on the tarmac by pulling from his pocket a sheaf of recent memorandums signed by Eisenhower. Holding them aloft, he asked if Ike really had written them. Yes, Eisenhower responded, he had. "Well, they're balls, sheer balls, rubbish," Montgomery informed him. Eisenhower sat in silence, taking it in and perhaps knowing that Montgomery, as socially inept as Ike was smooth, eventually would overstep. When the British officer paused in his condescending tirade, Eisenhower reached out, patted him on the knee, and said, softly but clearly, "Steady, Monty! You can't speak to me like that. I'm your boss." Montgomery, chastened for once, responded, "I'm sorry, Ike."

Ike flew away from Brussels willing to test Montgomery's belief that a narrow, one-front thrust was the way to invade Germany. The trial run would come a week later across southeastern Holland to the German border, beginning with massive paratroop drops and glider landings seventy-five miles behind the front lines. (In addition, Marshall had been pressing Ike to think about more innovative use of airborne forces.) This attack, dubbed Operation Market Garden, would be remembered as "a bridge too far"—one of the worst gambles of the war.

Eisenhower probably was not being so Machiavellian as to give Montgomery enough rope to hang himself operationally, but rather was willing to put the one-front thrust to the battlefield test. "I not only approved Market Garden, I insisted upon it," he would claim years later. That battle would lay bare many of Montgomery's weaknesses, most notably his caution in commanding a highly mobile force. As historian John Ellis wrote,

> Almost every feature of Operation Market Garden . . . simply reaffirmed what had already become evident in North Africa, that Montgomery was generally incapable of conducting anything but stolid defenses or attacks with generous lead times, massive material superiority and no urgent deadline during the battle itself. One might even go so far as to say that Market Garden showed Montgomery and the army he had created in the

worst possible light, revealing serious lapses in planning as well as severe shortcomings in operational and tactical command.

It was indeed a powerful demonstration that Montgomery could not conduct a narrow strike across the Netherlands and into Germany. Eisenhower, still rankled nearly two decades later, having finished with the presidency and retired to his Gettysburg farm, would summarize the outcome of the battle by saying that Montgomery "got driven back and he was still talking, by God, of a thrust. Now, how are you going to make a thrust if you can't get over the river? I think some damn historian ought to just smack him down on such a thing." Montgomery, for his part, muttered about how his attack had been undercut by poor logistical support.

Even if Montgomery recognized how "tiresome" he could be, he rarely seemed to fathom the consequences of such behavior. His view was that Eisenhower, Bradley, and their subordinates simply did not grasp either the military situation or the larger political issues—especially the need of the British, short on manpower and with a struggling economy, to end the war as quickly as possible. "The American generals did not understand," he would write in his memoirs. "The war had never been brought to their home country." Montgomery, not apprehending how the partnership had changed, would continue to treat Eisenhower as his junior. Ike believed that Montgomery had put him on notice that if his "exact recommendations" were not followed, the Allied effort would fail. Again, during the height of the crisis of the Battle of the Bulge, at the end of 1944, the sole major German counter-offensive of the northern European campaign, Eisenhower showed both courage and command ability in transferring control of fielded forces from Bradley to Montgomery, a move Bradley bitterly opposed. Yet Montgomery did not see the skill in the decision and instead decided that Ike had been confused and panicky. Even after that battle, Montgomery continued to harass Eisenhower about strategy.

Montgomery, like many British officers, did not seem to understand that the British and American militaries, though superficially seeming to become more similar as they worked together in Africa and southern Europe in 1943 and in northern Europe in 1944, in fact were growing apart. There were two major reasons for this separation. First was the rapid increase in American mobility and firepower. "The speed of our movements is amazing, even to me," Patton would write in his diary at the height of the Battle of the Bulge. At almost the same moment, J. Lawton Collins, the fast-rising young American general, was arguing with his temporary commander, Montgomery, about a plan to provision a corps, or multidivision formation. "Joe, you can't supply a corps over a single road," the British field marshal said, chiding his American subordinate. Exasperated, and a bit disrespectfully, Collins responded with a hard truth: "Well, Monty, maybe you British can't, but we can."

The second big difference was that the American Army had learned much in the preceding years in Africa and Italy about how to use its advantages. It was, in fact, outstripping the British not just in numbers and mobility but also in military capability and effectiveness. It was more willing to take risks, which meant losing men.

Bernard Lewis, the influential historian of the Middle East, would remember that he took away from his time as an intelligence officer in the British army two dominant impressions of the Americans:

One was that they were unteachable. When America entered the war, we in Britain had been at war for more than two years. We had made many mistakes, and had learned something from them. We tried to pass these lessons on to our new allies and save them from paying again the price that we had paid in blood and toil. But they wouldn't listen—their ways were not our ways, and they would do things their way, not ours. And so they went ahead and made mistakes—some repeating ours, some new and original. What was really new and original—and this is my second lasting impression—was the speed with which they recognized these mistakes, and devised and applied the means to correct them. *This was beyond anything in our experience.*

George Marshall would come to a similar conclusion—as did the German enemy. When British Gen. Harold Alexander made a crack late in the war to Marshall about American troops being "basically trained," Marshall sharply responded, "Yes, American troops start out and make every possible mistake. But after the first time, they do not repeat these mistakes. The British troops start out in the same way and continue making the same mistakes over and over, for a year." Churchill, monitoring this exchange, stepped in and quickly changed the subject. Perhaps even more significantly, German commanders came to similar conclusions about American adaptability. "What was astonishing was the speed with which the Americans adapted themselves to modern warfare," the most famous German general of the war, Field Marshal Erwin Rommel, commented. "The Americans, it is fair to say, profited far more than the British from their experience in Africa, thus confirming the axiom that education is easier than re-education." Another German officer, Maj. Gen. Friedrich von Mellenthin, wrote, even more explicitly, "I don't think the British ever solved the problem of mobile warfare in open desert. In general the British method of making war is slow, rigid and methodical." The disparity between the allies intensified as the mobility of American forces became more evident during the summer and fall of 1944. In a series of battlefield studies that year, the German High Command recognized the quickness with which American forces adapted tactically. In a recent analysis, Meir Finkel, a modern Israeli armored brigade commander turned historian, concluded that the British army suffered in World War II from "low levels of cognitive command and organizational flexibility." In sum, American generals were becoming increasingly different from their British counterparts.

Finally, in late December 1944, Eisenhower threatened to ask for the relief of his nettlesome British subordinate. Montgomery's genial chief of staff, Maj. Gen. Sir Francis de Guingand, sensing trouble, flew to Paris to see Eisenhower, whom he found looking "really tired and worried." Eisenhower told de Guingand that he was weary of the friction with Montgomery and had concluded that he was going to ask the Combined Chiefs of Staff, the military overlords of the war, to choose between the two. Early in 1944, Churchill had pledged to Eisenhower that the British government would not object to any request Ike made for the removal of a British officer. Now Ike was contemplating playing that card. He showed de Guingand the draft of a cable he had prepared to send to Marshall, laying out the situation. The message, Ike said decades later, was "He is going to do what I order or, by God, . . . the Joint Chiefs of Staff are going to throw one of us out and, by God, I don't think it will be me." De Guingand agreed with that assessment: "Since the Americans were the stronger ally, it really meant that Monty would be the one to go." Ike suggested in the cable that Alexander, whom he knew and admired from their days in North Africa, could replace Montgomery. De Guingand pleaded with Ike to hold off on sending the cable for twenty-four hours, during which he would return to Montgomery's headquarters in Belgium and make him understand how much his relationship with the Americans had deteriorated.

De Guingand flew through a snowstorm back to Montgomery's headquarters. "It's on the cards that you might have to go," he informed his commander, who was flabbergasted, "genuinely and completely taken by surprise." Eventually coming to comprehend his tenuous situation, Montgomery agreed to sign and send a careful note of apology that de Guingand had drafted for him while in flight.

Yet those words were not Montgomery's, and he did not seem to take the lesson to heart. Like Patton, he was set in his ways and repeated his mistakes. Barely a week later, Montgomery would again step on Eisenhower's toes, seeming to take credit at a press conference for the Allied victory in the Battle of the Bulge. It had been an American fight—indeed the biggest battle ever fought by American forces—leaving about nineteen thousand American dead and sixty thousand other casualties, compared with British dead of just two hundred, plus twelve hundred other wounded, missing, or taken prisoner. But Montgomery seemed to be taking credit for getting his allies out of a jam. When the Germans attacked, he preened, "I was thinking ahead." Then, he explained, as

> the situation began to deteriorate . . . I employed the whole available power of the British Group of Armies. . . . Finally it was put in with a bang, and today British divisions are fighting hard on the right flank of the First U.S. Army. You have thus a picture of British troops fighting on both sides of American forces who have suffered a hard blow. This is a fine Allied picture.

His comments caused a political storm with the Americans, which, of course, surprised Montgomery. In his obtuse way, he really did seem to think he had been putting the best face on a bad situation. In his memoirs, he concluded that the Americans should have been grateful that he had not revealed what he really thought—that the battle was unnecessary and had been caused by Eisenhower's bumbling. "What I did not say was that, in the Battle of the Ardennes, the Allies got a real 'bloody nose,' the Americans had nearly 80,000 casualties, and that it would never have happened if we had fought the campaign properly after the great victory in Normandy, or had even ensured proper tactical balance in the dispositions of the land forces as the winter campaign developed."

Not all American commanders were as critical of Montgomery. Bruce Clarke, one of the heroes of the Ardennes fighting, later stated, "I think probably the great generalship I saw in the Battle of the Bulge, was the generalship of Marshal Montgomery. He took command of the north half of the Bulge, as you know, and I was under his command in the Battle of St. Vith. The thing that I was impressed about Montgomery was that he was calm and collected. He was not emotional." Likewise, Matthew Ridgway, another aggressive commander, reported that his time under Montgomery's command was "most satisfying." Ridgway explained, "He gave me [the] general outline of what he wanted and let me completely free." However, Lt. Gen. William Simpson, who served under Montgomery for part of the war, told Forrest Pogue, one of Marshall's biographers, that he thought Montgomery could have cut off the German salient, or "bulge," and that Eisenhower made an error by not directing Montgomery to do so.

Eisenhower understood Montgomery perhaps better than the British officer understood himself. "The incident caused me more distress and worry than did any similar one of the war," Ike later wrote. "It was a pity that such an incident had to mar the universal satisfaction in final success." Even Simpson, after Eisenhower probably the most determinedly cooperative of senior American commanders, would come to protest the treatment he received from Montgomery, feeling that his troops were being shunted aside as the fight moved into Germany. Montgomery eventually relented and gave Simpson's Ninth Army a share in the planned crossings of the Rhine.

Marshall believed that Monty was driven by "overwhelming egotism" but withheld his fire until the war was nearly over. Finally, in January 1945, at a stormy meeting in Malta with the British chiefs, he asked for a closed session at which he ripped into Montgomery, venting what Field Marshal Alan Brooke, Churchill's principal military adviser, termed "his full dislike and antipathy." No records were kept of the closed session, but Marshall's biographer, who interviewed him about it, said that Marshall's primary charge was that Montgomery was "unwilling to be a member of the team." That attitude was, of course, in Marshall's eyes ample justification for relief.

Misunderstanding between Eisenhower and Montgomery would only deepen after the war, as each published his own account of what had happened. "Ike is now one of my dearest friends," Montgomery claimed in his 1958 memoir. If that was true, it was a sad indicator of how isolated Montgomery really was. Eisenhower, stung by Montgomery's portrayal of him in that very book, did not agree, telling a historian that in fact he had cut off contact with Montgomery: "I was just not interested in keeping up communications with a man that just can't tell the truth."

For all that, one point upon which Montgomery and his American antagonists did agree was on the need for swift relief. As Montgomery wrote in his memoirs, "Commanders and staff officers at any level who couldn't stand the strain, or who got tired, were to be weeded out and replaced—ruthlessly. . . . There was an urgent need to get rid of the 'dead wood' which was hampering the initiative of keen and efficient young officers." One brutal example he offered was being told that a corpulent colonel might be killed by completing a seven-mile run Montgomery had ordered for all: "I said that if he was thinking of dying it would be better to do it now, as he could be replaced easily and smoothly." His rule of relief was that "if, having received the help he might normally expect, a man fails—then he must go."

With the passage of time, Montgomery's relationship with Eisenhower increasingly appears to resemble George McClellan's with President Lincoln during the Civil War—that is, a small-minded contempt that never comprehends that the less sophisticated superior actually has a stronger and larger sense of strategy. Their eventful meeting in Brussels would stick in Ike's mind, causing him many years later, on September 10, 1959, to pause as president and remember in his diary that "today, fifteen years ago, I met Monty at Brussels airfield. . . . He made his preposterous proposal to go to Berlin."

Ike's handling of Montgomery, and of the British in general, may in fact have been his greatest contribution of the war. He made it look so natural that the lesson of his impressive performance might have been lost. In subsequent wars, American generals often did not treat their coalition partners as thoughtfully. In Vietnam especially, had the Americans worked more closely and less contemptuously with their South Vietnamese allies, not elbowing them aside but instead supporting them whenever possible as the leading edge of the fight, the conduct of that war might have been somewhat different.

CHAPTER 7

Douglas MacArthur

The general as presidential aspirant

D ouglas MacArthur was the great anomaly of World War II, the end of the old order. He does not fit the Marshall template of the low-key, steady-going team player, which might be one reason he was managed at important points as much by President Roosevelt as by Gen. Marshall. Like Montgomery, MacArthur illustrates that when a general believes he cannot be removed, the quality of strategic discourse with his superiors—both military and civilian—tends to suffer, and with it the effectiveness of their collective decision-making process. Historically, he might be most significant for the negative influence he had on civil-military discourse, lingering well into the Vietnam War.

The son of a Civil War general, MacArthur rose to prominence in World War I, when he was chief of staff of the 42nd (Rainbow) Division and later a brigadier general. After the war, he was superintendent of West Point and then, starting in 1930, the Army chief of staff for five years. In the 1940s, when he was the U.S. commander against the Japanese in the Southwest Pacific theater, MacArthur was notably out of step with the Army's emerging style of leadership. Marshall, Eisenhower, and Bradley favored the quiet, determined, cooperative officer. MacArthur had none of those traits. "MacArthur's sense of duty was to himself," concluded the historian Robert Berlin. "His style of leadership was abrupt, emotional and highly personal."

At one point in the early 1930s, when he was chief of staff of the Army, MacArthur may have tried to stymie Marshall's career. "General MacArthur kept General Marshall down until the time he [Marshall] became chief of staff," Omar Bradley once alleged. A lesser man than Marshall likely would have come to resent MacArthur bitterly. "Marshall is the exact antithesis of MacArthur's character," Matthew Ridgway, who served with both men repeatedly over the course of several decades, said near the end of his life. "Marshall was always keeping himself in the background, giving full credit to every subordinate. MacArthur was just the opposite. He wanted to take all the credit for himself."

Ultimately, MacArthur and the political problem he represented may even have been responsible for Marshall's not being given command of the D-Day landings in France, perhaps the greatest invasion in history. FDR famously remarked that he thought Marshall deserved to command the landings but that he could not send the general to do so because, FDR confessed, he wouldn't be able to sleep without him in Washington.

There is no question that FDR needed Marshall as Army chief of staff to help him puzzle through the complex questions of the war. But there also is evidence that Marshall's presence was required in Washington because he was the sole Army officer capable of reining in MacArthur—and even then, just barely. In August 1942, Marshall felt the need to get MacArthur back in line on American strategy, writing to him that a *Washington Post* article sent from his headquarters had created "the impression that you are objecting to our strategy by indirection. I assume this to be an erroneous impression." (Of course, it was not an erroneous impression, but Marshall knew to give MacArthur an avenue of retreat.) In February 1943, Marshall again wrote to MacArthur, this time to get him to cooperate with the U.S. Navy. MacArthur had declined to meet with the secretary of the Navy and the commander in chief for the Pacific, Adm. Chester Nimitz. Marshall noted that he had been told that "a message was received from you pointing out that no useful purpose might be served by such a conference."

In 1944, Henry Stimson, the secretary of war, noted in his diary that Marshall was playing a unique role, "as a matter of fact keeping his hand on the control of the whole thing." Part of that "whole thing" was treading carefully around MacArthur while containing him. The same year, Stimson went out of his way to announce that MacArthur would not be retired from the military at the statutory age of sixty-four. If Marshall were dispatched to lead the D-Day force, then he would have to be replaced as chief of staff in Washington by Eisenhower—who then would face, on top of everything else in a world war, the near-impossible task of managing his former boss, MacArthur, whom he held in some contempt. As Gen. Albert Wedemeyer once put it about Ike and MacArthur, "I heard both of them talk terribly about each other."

Simply removing MacArthur appears to have been out of the question. Whatever his military abilities, he seems to have been kept in command in the Pacific in part because his political standing made it easier to have him inside the Army rather than outside it, criticizing the president. In his monumental study of FDR's relationships with his top military officers, the historian Eric Larrabee went a step further in his analysis. Larrabee argued that the president kept MacArthur on in part because the old general was less politically dangerous while in uniform, but also because of a Machiavellian calculation that MacArthur was exactly the sort of useful idiot FDR needed to maintain a bipartisan coalition in support of the war. It is easy to forget now that there still existed a potentially powerful brew of anti–New Dealers, Republican isolationists, and Midwestern pacifists. "After our entry into the war," Larrabee observed,

> the domestic forces that had passionately opposed it were still in being, momentarily stunned into joining the consensus for victory but still vocal and alert, still amply represented in the Congress. To keep them in the consensus there should ideally be a conservative, neo-isolationist military hero, preferably a figure who was large enough to rally around but naive enough to be no real threat, who was possessed of *bona fide* anti–New Deal credentials yet was located at a safe distance in the Far East. . . . This goes a long way, I think, to explain the President's otherwise enigmatic handling of Douglas MacArthur, who fitted these conditions to perfection and was therefore—up to a delicately chosen point—nurtured and indulged.

Supporting Larrabee's interpretation is the fact that after MacArthur was ordered to leave the Philippines, Marshall pushed to give him the Medal of Honor, in part to obscure the fact that the general, willingly or not, had left behind his besieged troops. The documentation for the award itself was composed by Marshall and polished by Eisenhower—who, even as he edited, argued against bestowing the medal. The awarding of the nation's highest honor to MacArthur may have been one of Marshall's most calculated acts, and it came close to sheer cynicism. "I wanted to do anything I could to prevent them from saying anything about his leaving Corregidor with his troops all out there in this perilous position," he revealed years later. "I thought a Medal of Honor would be helpful. . . . I drafted the citation." MacArthur himself understood well the political uses of medals, in June 1942 giving the Silver Star to Lyndon Johnson, then a visiting congressman, for riding in a malfunctioning aircraft that had come under Japanese attack. "No other crew member, not even the pilot who landed the crippled plane, received a decoration," noted historian and Army officer H. R. McMaster.

But MacArthur's Medal of Honor stuck in the craw of some others. Lt. Gen. Robert Eichelberger remembered being told by Eisenhower, after the war, that his friend Ike had refused a Medal of Honor for the North Africa campaign, "because he knew of a man who had received one for sitting in a hole in the ground—meaning MacArthur." MacArthur's receipt of the medal became especially galling because during the war he had thwarted efforts to bestow the Medal of Honor on Eichelberger and another subordinate, Maj. Gen. Jonathan Wainwright, who, after the surrender of U.S. forces in the Philippines, had become the highest-ranking American prisoner of the war. (After the war, Gen. Marshall would revive the nomination for Wainwright, and this time it would be successful.) MacArthur also turned down a request from Marshall to allow Eichelberger to be transferred to a command in Europe. It is no accident that MacArthur's senior subordinate commanders—Eichelberger, Walter Krueger, Oscar Griswold, and Alexander Patch—are unknown today. "Eisenhower raised his officers' profiles among contemporaries and historians by giving them credit and press for their accomplishments," noted historian Stephen Taaffe, while MacArthur "deliberately denied his subordinates much public recognition."

FDR hardly was naive about MacArthur. He had been keeping a wary eye on the general for years. When MacArthur was Army chief of staff and FDR a presidential candidate, the politician had privately cracked that the general was "one of the two most dangerous men in the country." The other, he explained to friends and aides, was Huey Long—a useful context, because it indicates that Roosevelt saw both men as threats to a troubled American system, the soldier from the right and the senator from the left. The point about Long and MacArthur, Roosevelt continued, thinking ahead to his presidency, was that "we must tame these fellows and make them useful to us."

Not long after becoming president, FDR was confronted by MacArthur, then the Army chief of staff, who was irate over the meagerness of the Army's budget. "I spoke recklessly" at a meeting at the White House, MacArthur wrote in his memoirs, "and said something to the general effect that when we lost the next war, and an American boy, lying in the mud with an enemy bayonet through his belly and an enemy foot on his dying throat, spat out his last curse, I wanted the name not to be MacArthur, but Roosevelt."

Roosevelt roared back: "You must not talk that way to the president!" MacArthur wrote that he promptly apologized, then went outside and vomited on the White House steps.

So if MacArthur was going to be kept in place to play the role of unwitting supporter of the political consensus supporting the war, he would need to be watched closely. And that meant Marshall could not go to Europe.

MacArthur the presidential candidate

MacArthur had a very different conception of the role of a general than did Marshall and other top American military officers of his time. As such, he is the exception who proves the rule in a way that the examples of Patton, Clark, and Allen do not. They were challenges to the Marshall system but operated within it. MacArthur stood outside of it. "Most of the senior officers I had known always drew a clean-cut line between the military and the political," Eisenhower wrote near the end of his life. "But if

General MacArthur ever recognized the existence of that line, he usually chose to ignore it."

The irony of this is that MacArthur actually was not particularly adept at understanding American politics, in part because he had not visited the United States for over a decade—from before the beginning of World War II until he was fired as commander of the Korean War, in 1951. Eisenhower, who was on MacArthur's staff in Washington from 1933 to 1935 and then worked for him in the Philippines in the years before World War II, once fell into a heated argument with MacArthur about who would win the 1936 presidential election back in the United States. MacArthur was so certain that Alf Landon would be the victor that he made plans around it. "The general has been following the *Literary Digest* poll and has convinced himself that Landon is to be elected, probably by a landslide," Ike wrote in one of the few personal entries in his diaries, which generally were more intermittent journals he used to occasionally work out his thinking on issues. "I showed him letters [from a friend in Ike's and Landon's home state] . . . which predict that Landon cannot even carry Kansas, but he got perfectly furious." MacArthur dressed down Ike and an officer who took Ike's side, saying that they were "fearful and small-minded people who are afraid to express judgments that are obvious from the evidence at hand."

MacArthur also had different ethical standards from those of Ike and many other officers. In 1942, he accepted a $500,000 gift from the government of the Philippines. Eisenhower turned down a similar gift, recognizing that accepting such a payment from a foreign government was contrary to both Army custom and regulation. Eisenhower also noted that MacArthur pushed the government of the Philippines to give him the title of field marshal, which Ike found "pompous and rather ridiculous," because the Philippine army was "virtually nonexisting." Ike additionally remembered MacArthur's ire at learning that Marshall, rather than Hugh Drum, his preference, would be nominated to be Army chief of staff: "What he had to say was something out of this world."

It is not clear when MacArthur began considering himself presidential material, but the prospect was certainly on his mind midway through World War II. In 1943 and early 1944, he discussed running for president with his subordinates. "My Chief talked of the Republican nomination for next year," Gen. Eichelberger, then a corps commander, wrote to his wife on June 2, 1943. "I can see that he expects to get it and I sort of think so too." During the war, MacArthur dispatched his chief of staff and his chief intelligence officer back across the Pacific to Washington and New York to explore the notion with Republican luminaries such as Sen. Arthur Vandenberg of Michigan and former president Herbert Hoover. Vandenberg, an influential Republican, calculated that the general's only chance of securing the nomination would be if the nominating convention deadlocked between Thomas Dewey and Wendell Willkie, but by April 1944 Willkie had withdrawn, after being soundly defeated in the Wisconsin primary, leaving Dewey the presumptive nominee. Even so, in the same month, MacArthur scored 550,000 votes in a preferential, nonbinding Illinois primary. Just after that vote, Rep. Albert Miller of Nebraska released two exchanges of letters he had with the general. "I am certain that unless this New Deal can be stopped this time our American way of life is forever doomed," the freshman congressman had written the previous September. "You owe it to civilization and the children yet unborn to accept the nomination. . . . You will be our next president." Miller added that he was certain that MacArthur would carry all forty-eight states. MacArthur had responded in October that he didn't agree with the "flattering predictions," but did "unreservedly agree with the complete wisdom and statesmanship of your comments." There were similar sentiments in a follow-up set of letters early in

1944. By releasing them, Miller had been seeking to reenergize the MacArthur candidacy, but his efforts failed. At the Republican National Convention, Dewey received 1,056 votes, and MacArthur just 1, the unanimity broken by a Wisconsin delegate protesting a fast move by party leaders to keep the general's name from being placed in nomination.

Later in 1944, MacArthur revealed the extent of his political naïveté when he took the astonishing step of lecturing FDR, a political grandmaster, on the possible domestic political implications of any decision to bypass the Philippines in the offensive against Japan. At a meeting in Hawaii, he told the president, according to a MacArthur aide and hagiographer, "I dare to say that the American people would be so aroused that they would register the most complete resentment against you at the polls this fall." Such ill-considered talk must have reassured FDR that he had MacArthur exactly where he wanted him.

MacArthur's presidential campaign that year fizzled, but he didn't learn his lesson. When Ike dined with MacArthur in Tokyo in 1946, the two felt each other out about presidential ambitions. Eisenhower said he did not wish to become involved in politics and invoked the principles of Gen. Marshall, according to an account he gave to Joseph Alsop, a prominent journalist of the time. Alsop continued: "General Eisenhower broke off his recital to me, turned the color of a boiled beet from sheer remembered rage, and said: 'Joe, do you know what that man said to me then?' . . . He leaned over, patted me on the knee, and he had the nerve to say, 'That's all right, Ike. You go on like that and you'll get it sure.'" MacArthur ultimately issued a statement that he would not campaign for the office, but as a good citizen would not shrink from "accepting any public duty to which I might be called by the American people." That call did not come in 1948. MacArthur kept his hopes alive for 1952.

Handling MacArthur as he did may have been the right move for FDR in World War II, but by doing so, Roosevelt planted a political minefield for his successor. Eventually MacArthur would have to be dealt with, but that would be left to Harry Truman, a less artful man than FDR. In 1951, MacArthur's persistent dabbling in politics and his refusal to follow orders would lead to the most dramatic relief of a general in the history of the U.S. military. MacArthur's legacy would be limited in the military realm—he was an influence on William Westmoreland and had little impact after that—but it would be poisonous in American politics, warping President Johnson's discourse with his generals about the conduct of the Vietnam War.

In the Army, MacArthur eventually would become a negative example, an illustration of what future Army leaders would seek to avoid. If today's Army remains wary of the daring, dramatic, outsize personality, the record of MacArthur (and, to a lesser degree, of Patton) is a big part of the cause. The new model for American generalship would be a quite different, and blander, figure. He was quietly helping the Allies win the European war.

CHAPTER 8
William Simpson
The Marshall system and the new model American general

If MacArthur (and, among the Allies, Montgomery) presented to Marshall and Eisenhower the antithesis of the sort of generalship they desired, the Battle of the Bulge, during the snowy final two weeks of 1944, gave them the very model of what they wanted. Ironically, the general who personified that model is forgotten today, even inside the Army. But the values he embodied would be those of the U.S. Army for decades.

The Bulge, the major German counteroffensive in response to the Allied invasion of northwestern Europe in mid-1944, was one of the most important battles of Western Europe in World War II. Eisenhower wrote in very Marshallian tones that

> in battles of this kind it is more than ever necessary that responsible commanders exhibit the firmness, the calmness, the optimism that can pierce through the web of conflicting reports, doubts and uncertainty and by taking advantage of every enemy weakness win through to victory.

Eisenhower did not say so, but the senior commander who best fit that description was not the blustery Patton or the panicky

Hodges but William Hood Simpson, a lanky six-foot-four, egg-bald Texan. The son of a Confederate cavalryman, Simpson was a man of quiet, competent, determined optimism, the very model of the modern Army general. Early in the Battle of the Bulge, he was shown a captured plan for the German offensive. He studied it for a bit, then drily commented, "Well, I think from what we have here I don't feel too much alarmed. We're going to have to do some hard fighting, but I think eventually we'll stop this thing." During this battle, on his own initiative and with little fanfare, he offered and sent five full divisions to the assistance of Hodges in just six days. During the Bulge, notes historian J. D. Morelock, "Simpson actually got more Ninth Army units into combat than did the Third Army [of Patton]—and faster as well."

Like Patton, Simpson was smart, adaptive, and aggressive. But unlike his better-known peer, Simpson was a team player, plain-spoken and self-effacing. He knew how to lay low, having spent fourteen years as a major between the wars. He also knew how to fight, having battled the Moros in the Philippines, Pancho Villa's band in Mexico, and the Germans in World Wars I and II.

He handled his staff well. His corps commanders enjoyed working for him. Simpson was "pleasant, very personal, under-standing, and cooperative," recalled Alvan Gillem, one of his generals and the grandson of a Civil War general of the same name—who, though born in Tennessee, had fought for the Union. Maj. Gen. Ernest Harmon recalled being pleased to have his 2nd Armored Division assigned to Simpson's Ninth Army: "Simpson, though little known outside military circles, was one of the truly great leaders of the European theater, a real general's general. . . . He was a pleasure to fight under." Simpson liked to have his subordinate commanders publicly accept the surrenders of German generals, giving them the credit and the appearances in newspaper photographs. "Even-tempered and composed, he refrained from interrupting and allowed the briefer to complete his presentation before questions were asked," wrote Army Lt. Col. Thomas Stone. The smoothness of Simpson's operation was felt many echelons below that level. Bernard Leu, who had served as a sergeant in the 75th Infantry Division, recalled that once his division joined Simpson's army, it received orders early enough to allow it to plan, which had not happened when the division was part of two other armies.

But what is most striking about Simpson may be that, in a doctoral dissertation and a book largely about him and the Ninth Army, there was almost nothing to relate about him—no stormy meetings, few revealing anecdotes, almost no memorable phrases. There is just an efficient, low-key headquarters operating under an undemonstrative, steady leader. "Simpson could think ahead of time, and he didn't talk too much, either; that's what I liked about him," recalled Gen. Jacob Devers.

Midway through the Battle of the Bulge, Simpson dispatched a note to Eisenhower reporting that his Ninth Army was working smoothly and cheerfully with Montgomery. "Our chins are up," he stated. Privately, Simpson found Montgomery "a very pompous guy" who was overly cautious and could have done great damage to the Germans had he committed three available British divisions to pinching off the northeastern corner of the Bulge. But during the war he kept that to himself. Simpson was exactly what Marshall and Eisenhower had been looking for: an optimistic team player with a small ego and a great ability to work with others. In that sense, the forgotten Simpson personified the ideal of generalship that Army leaders would pursue in the postwar years, and indeed for decades to follow. It was not a bad model, but it contained some hidden dangers.

Eisenhower recognized Simpson's strength and was warmer in summing up this general than perhaps any other individual officer he discussed in his memoirs:

If Simpson ever made a mistake as an army commander, it never came to my attention. After the war I learned that he had for some years suffered from a serious stomach disorder, but this I never would have suspected during hostilities. Alert, intelligent and professionally capable, he was the type of leader that American soldiers deserve. In view of his brilliant service, it was unfortunate that shortly after the war ill-health forced his retirement before he was promoted to four-star grade, which he had so clearly earned.

Bradley also liked Simpson's style, praising his command as "uncommonly normal"—a Bradley-esque phrase if there ever was one. Yet for all that praise, notes historian John English, Simpson has since become "the most forgotten American field army commander of the Western Front" in World War II. Marshall might take that as a compliment, and Simpson probably would, too.

In hands less skilled than Marshall's, the system that produced generals such as Simpson also could result in bland, uninspired, risk-averse leaders. This would be especially true when such leaders were no longer spurred by the prospect of being fired for failure or inaction.

The effectiveness of the Marshall system

After the war, Gen. James Gavin, among others, was critical of the wave of reliefs carried out in the Army in 1944–45, arguing that so many division commanders had been fired that the U.S. Army began to lack plausible candidates for those jobs. Eisenhower, he said, "had to get results. He had to be tough. And he ran out of good commanders, finally, in my opinion." Gavin was not entirely against firing commanders. For example, on June 7, 1944, when he ordered a battalion to attack along a causeway across the Merderet River, the commander told him "that he did not feel well."

So, continues Gavin without skipping a beat, "he was relieved of command and another officer put in charge of the battalion." Yet Gavin was especially critical of firing commanders who were leading green units into combat. "Summarily relieving those who do not appear to measure up in the first shock of battle is not only a luxury we cannot afford—it is very damaging to the Army as a whole."

Gavin made a good point, especially about the removal of new commanders leading untested units. Nor was he alone: Martin Blumenson, one of the Army's best official historians, concluded in 1971 that most World War II reliefs were "unwarranted if not altogether unjustified." He believed that commanders were handled more professionally in the wars in Korea and Vietnam. Blumenson does not pause to address a key difference: The Army was victorious in World War II, but the first of the wars he cites with such approval was a stalemate and the second was a loss—though, of course, those two outcomes hardly can be laid at the feet of the military alone, or even primarily.

What Gavin and Blumenson especially did not seem to weigh in their criticisms was the opportunity cost of not ousting failing officers. In the short run, as Eisenhower noted, a relief sometimes will improve morale. And in the longer run, the removals permitted a new generation of officers—Gavin among the most prominent of them—to emerge in World War II. There clearly was unfairness in some of the removals, notably that of Terry Allen, but it did not seem to damage the effectiveness of the concerned division, the 1st Infantry. In other cases, such as the replacement of the 3rd Armored Division's Leroy Watson by Maj. Gen. Maurice Rose or of the VI Corps's Lucas by Truscott, there clearly was an improvement in the quality of command. It was only in later wars, when generals were *not* removed, that the many costs of not relieving would become more evident.

A better question was whether Marshall, Bradley, and Eisenhower, consciously or not, were intolerant of nonconformists, especially among those from branches other than the infantry. Cavalrymen and their descendants in armored units certainly seemed to think so. Ernest Harmon, who commanded the 1st, 2nd, and (briefly) 3rd Armored Divisions during the war, criticized Hodges's First Army as "a typical infantryman's operation: slow, cautious and without much zip." American command was dominated by the infantry branch, home of Marshall, Eisenhower, and Bradley. Some 59 percent of the Army's four-star generals during World War II came out of the infantry and not the other combat arms—artillery, cavalry, armor, and engineering.

The enemy noticed the sluggish tendencies of its British and American opponents, with one German general commenting that "in contrast to the Eastern theater of operations, in the West it was possible to still straighten out seemingly impossible situations because the opposing armies there . . . despite their enormous material superiority, were limited by slow and methodical modes of combat." At some invisible point, an insistence on teamwork can combine with cautiousness to produce a plodding force—especially if it lacks among its leaders some people with the passion of a Patton or the drive of a Terry Allen.

The manner in which Eisenhower chose to announce the end of the war is strikingly consistent with Marshall's expectations of a general. After the German surrender, Eisenhower's headquarters staff began to compose a wordy message of victory. Eisenhower rejected their lofty prose and instead issued a message simply stating, "The mission of this Allied Force was fulfilled at 0241 local time, May 7, 1945." It was so plain as to be eloquent—or, to use an Army term of the time, it was "'nuff said."

The war's ending also stripped Patton of his shield of combat effectiveness. The next time Patton shot his mouth off, Eisenhower no longer needed him to pursue Germans, and whatever their friendship had meant, Eisenhower removed him from command of the Third Army in October 1945.

The politics of the Marshall system

During World War II, the relief of commanders was also intentionally a political act, making a statement to both insiders and outsiders about the nature and responsibilities of the U.S. military. It was, as FDR once remarked, "a New Deal war." To Marshall's eye, being willing to remove an officer signaled to the American people that the Army's leaders cared more about the hordes of enlisted soldiers than about the relatively small officer corps. Despite his aristocratic demeanor, this was a democratic point he would make to members of Congress who inquired about the fates of generals they liked but whom Marshall had found wanting. In 1943, when queried by Sen. Carter Glass of Virginia about why Col. Robert E. M. Goolrick, commander of Keesler Field in Biloxi, Mississippi, had not been given a shot at generalship, Marshall responded with an explanation of his approach to picking men for top slots. "The only basis upon which we can proceed is that of efficiency without regard to the personalities involved," he wrote.

> We have to be continually on guard against too much emphasis being placed on the honor attached to the rank of general and too little to the choice of leaders who enjoy the confidence of the men in the ranks and who have the skill and physical endurance to bring this war to a successful conclusion without needless sacrifice of American lives. Every contact with the enemy has emphasized anew the importance of dominant and skillful leadership. All other considerations are of minor importance.

Looking out for the common soldier was not an insignificant consideration in a war being fought for democracy, a point

Marshall made repeatedly in his biennial reports on the state of the military. In his 1941 report, discussing his prewar housecleaning of aging officers, Marshall explained, "In all these matters the interests of the soldier and the nation, rather than that of the individual officer, have governed." In the next report, he justified selecting enlisted men to become officers as consistent with "democratic theory." And indeed, that became practice. Two-thirds of the Army's combat officers in World War II were promoted from the ranks. Marshall, in his final wartime report, composed between V-E and V-J days, would begin by stating that "never was the strength of American democracy so evident."

Likewise, when the draft was being designed, Marshall told its planners that it had to be constructed in such a way that it would be supported by the American people. "Those of us who had spent our lives on Wall Street were mainly concerned with solving problems," recalled Paul Nitze, who had been brought to Washington to work on the Selective Service Act of 1940.

> We rarely found it necessary to give much thought to how our actions might impinge on our democratic system. Marshall educated us. Draft selections and deferments were a case in point of how problem-solving had to deal with much more than mere numbers and mechanics. Marshall's point was that men should be selected or granted deferments on a basis that was not only fair and equitable in fact, but that was seen to be so as well.

Once those men were drafted, Marshall insisted that the need to fight the war be explained to them. Disappointed with the pamphlets that were designed for this purpose, Marshall asked Frank Capra, a leading Hollywood director of the time, to make a series of films to educate Army recruits, titled *Why We Fight*.

Marshall did all this not just to have an effective fighting force but also to protect the future of the U.S. Army. He believed that the antimilitarism he had seen in American society in the 1920s and '30s was spurred in part by the harshness with which officers had treated American soldiers during World War I. "They were embittered in a way that they never forgot," he said. So he was determined that, as much as possible, the Army would give decent, rational treatment to these temporary soldiers, or, as he called them, "future citizens." As a lieutenant colonel in China after World War I, Marshall had instructed an officer who was berating a soldier that "you must remember that man is an American citizen just the same as you are." During World War II, this consciousness was reflected in a variety of ways, but it was perhaps captured best in the cartoons of Bill Mauldin, which often mocked the pretensions of officers. ("Beautiful view," one says to another as they gaze at an Alpine sunset. "Is there one for the enlisted men?") Mauldin's work was first carried in the newspaper of the 45th Division, commanded by Maj. Gen. Troy Middleton, who defended the free-spirited cartoonist because he believed it boosted morale and also attracted readers to the division newspaper, which he used to kill unhelpful rumors. When Middleton's commander, George Patton, told Middleton to "get rid of Mauldin and his cartoons," Middleton parried by asking for that order in writing. Patton dropped the subject, Middleton recalled.

It is worth considering whether Marshall's insistence on grooming a certain type of general might have had a less direct political effect: that of encouraging the decline in American life of the *caudillo,* the "man on a white horse" tendency of military leaders to move from the armed forces into political life. There was a strong tradition of elevating a general to the presidency in eighteenth- and nineteenth-century America, beginning with George Washington. All told, thirteen Americans with notable military records have become president: Washington, Eisenhower, Grant, Andrew Jackson, William Harrison, Zachary Taylor, Rutherford B. Hayes,

James Garfield, Benjamin Harrison, Theodore Roosevelt, Harry Truman, John F. Kennedy, and the first President Bush. The first nine in that list actually held a general's rank. In addition, another four generals were losing candidates for president. But since Benjamin Harrison, who for a few months at the end of the Civil War was a brigadier in the Army of the Cumberland and who won the White House in 1888, only one general has been elected to the presidency, and that last general to become president was the least coup-prone of officers: Eisenhower, Marshall's protégé.

The Marshall template, with its studied distance from politics, may have put a stake through the heart of the general as politician. Since Eisenhower, generals who have toyed with running for president have been humiliated in the primaries, emerging from the experience somehow diminished in the public eye. This has been true in both major American political parties, as evidenced by the fizzled presidential campaigns of Gen. Alexander Haig Jr. as a Republican in 1988 and of Gen. Wesley Clark as a Democrat in 2004. In 1968, retired Air Force Gen. Curtis LeMay also ran for national office but had no chance of winning as the running mate on the independent ticket of Alabama's former segregationist governor, George Wallace. At the state level, generals also have fared poorly. In 1962, Maj. Gen. Edwin Walker, having resigned from the Army after getting in trouble for indoctrinating his troops in the 24th Infantry Division with literature drawn from the John Birch Society, ran for governor of Texas but came in sixth and last in the Republican primary. (Early in 1963, he was slightly wounded in a sniper shooting by Lee Harvey Oswald, who according to the Warren Commission used the same rifle he would use later that year to kill President Kennedy.) In 1974, Gen. William Westmoreland lost in South Carolina's Republican gubernatorial primary. In 2011, Lt. Gen. Ricardo Sanchez entered the campaign for the Democratic nomination for senator from Texas but, after raising few funds, dropped out before the primary vote.

The legacy of the Marshall system

George Marshall set the template, and Dwight Eisenhower implemented it, but it may be Omar Bradley's personality that emerged dominant in the postwar Army. Not long after the war ended, the first two men moved on, with Bradley succeeding Eisenhower as chief of staff of the Army in 1948 and then becoming chairman of the Joint Chiefs of Staff a year later. This was a mixed blessing. Even if he was never quite the beloved "GI's general" presented by wartime journalist Ernie Pyle, Bradley was an even-tempered man with a reputation for decency in his personal interactions. Yet during the war he had run an unhappy headquarters, one that during 1944–45 had developed a reputation for "irritable suspiciousness," as the military historian Russell Weigley put it.

Looking back from a perspective of several decades, Weigley judged Bradley to have been "merely competent." In 1944–45, Bradley presided over a force enjoying extreme advantages. He had more men than his foe, and his force was largely a model of tactical efficiency, with trained and disciplined teamwork between the combat arms. The West Wall, or Siegfried Line, was breached by skilled attacks in which, Weigley noted, "forward observers would bring down artillery on a pillbox to clear the enemy from subsidiary positions; tanks would then blast entrances and apertures with armor-piercing ammunition; infantry would close in, at which point the Germans frequently surrendered." Bradley enjoyed a twenty-to-one advantage in tanks. He had even more overwhelming air superiority, with some 13,000 Allied fighters and bombers flying against just 573 serviceable Luftwaffe aircraft.

Despite his advantages, Bradley took months to force his surrounded, outnumbered foe to capitulate. Lt. Gen. Daniel Bolger, who has commanded the NATO transition forces in Afghanistan since 2011, wrote that the Army under Bradley had scored many successes, but also recorded

> a disturbing number of botched battles and, especially, missed chances. The hellish butchery in the Normandy *bocage*, the incomplete Falaise encirclement, the costly confusion before the West Wall in the autumn, the bloody fumbling about in the Huertgen Forest, the shocking initial surprise in the Ardennes and the eventual unwillingness to pinch off the forces in that German salient, the backing and filling in the face of the Remagen bridgehead opportunity—together form a distressing litany that spans the entire length of the campaign.

For Eisenhower, the lesson of the war was that cooperation was more important than anything else. He emphasized this in the introduction to *The True Glory,* a joint British-American documentary about how the European war had been waged, of which he was essentially the producer. "Teamwork wins wars," stated a visibly tired Ike, the skin under his eyes lined and sagging, with no sign of his customary grin. "I mean teamwork among nations, services, and men, all the way down the line, from the GI, and the Tommies, to us brass hats." It was not merely a historical observation, because he made that statement after V-E Day but before the end of the Pacific War, which some military planners thought might continue for several more years.

In the afterglow of victory, the potential pitfalls of this capable, somewhat corporate model of generalship were less noticed. The flaws, when they emerged, largely would be of the kind that George Patton saw in Bradley. "I wish he had a little daring,"

Patton wrote in October 1944. The nature of American military leadership in 1944 and 1945, Weigley agreed, amounted to "unimaginative caution. American generalship by and large was competent but addicted to playing it safe." As Martin Blumenson, a World War II veteran who became a specialist in the history of the European theater in that conflict, would put it, the record of American leadership in Europe "is essentially bland and plodding. The commanders were generally workmanlike rather than bold, prudent rather than daring." James Gavin concluded that the war could have been ended months earlier, "at considerably less cost in blood and resources, if they were willing to take more chances."

It was a mixed legacy. Under the sort of leadership favored by Bradley, Bolger concluded, "one avoids losing, but one can also avoid winning by playing it safe." That is an ominous sentence, given the risk-averse approach often taken by American generals in Korea, Vietnam, and Iraq in subsequent decades and the record of stalemates and worse that they tended to produce.

Perhaps those who rose highest in World War II were organization men. But for the most part they were members of a *successful* organization, with the failures among them weeded out instead of coddled and covered up. That would not be the case in our subsequent wars, in which it would be more difficult to know what victory looked like or even whether it was achievable.

PART II
THE KOREAN WAR

By 1948 the Army was not even a skeleton of the force that so recently had played a major role in winning World War II. It had 555,000 soldiers and, worse, from those it could wring only two and one-third divisions deemed ready for combat. About half of its soldiers were engaged in occupying Germany and Japan as well as Austria, southern Korea, and Trieste, Italy. In Korea in 1950, the Army that had helped defeat the Nazis and the Empire of Japan would be swatted aside by the Korean People's Army, which threatened to drive it into the sea.

CHAPTER 9
William Dean and Douglas MacArthur
Two generals self-destruct

The Korean War began, in June 1950, with the destruction of two American generals—one on the battlefield, the other in top command. Now called by some the "forgotten war," Korea also would bring two of history's finest episodes of American military leadership, the first involving Marine Maj. Gen. O. P. Smith and the second, Army Lt. Gen. Matthew Ridgway.

Few remember how disastrous that first phase of the Korean War was—more humiliating than the first rough months of World War II and in some ways even worse than the dismaying ending of the Vietnam War. Not once but twice, American forces were hurled southward down the peninsula, both times by Asian "peasant" armies (first North Korean and, six months later, Chinese) that often lacked heavy artillery pieces and modern tanks, let alone naval gunfire and logistical support. To a surprising degree, American troops were outmatched in that most basic and essential military element: combat leadership. What's more, these setbacks came just five years after the global triumph of World War II.

One of the first lessons of the Korean War was seeing just how much the American military had deteriorated in the interim. As a result of postwar changes in personnel policy as well as Truman Administration policies that shortchanged the U.S. military, the Army entered the Korean War "not prepared mentally, physically, or otherwise for war," Clay Blair wrote, in one of the best histories of the conflict, with leadership that "at the army, corps, division, regiment and battalion levels was overaged, inexperienced, often incompetent, and not physically capable of coping with the rigorous climate of Korea."

By the time the war ended, in 1953, the Marshall approach to generalship had severely eroded. This was in part because removing senior officers in a small, unpopular war proved politically difficult. A wave of high-level reliefs early in the war provoked fear at the top of the Army that more such actions would lead Congress to ask uncomfortable questions. One must wonder about a system that seemingly was willing to accept the disastrous consequences of leaving unfit generals in command of American troops in order to avoid difficult inquiries from members of Congress.

The destruction of General Dean

The harrowing tale of Maj. Gen. William Dean, commander of the first division to be committed to combat in Korea, illustrates by extreme example the plight of American military leaders at the outset of the war. Korea had been a Japanese colony until the end of World War II, when Soviet forces occupied its north and American forces its south. In 1948, the country was divided into competing regimes. Two years later, when the Communist North invaded the South, Dean was leading the 24th Infantry Division, based in Japan. The first American in Japan to actually learn of the invasion was not Gen. Dean but a young lieutenant named Alexander Haig Jr., the future general and secretary of state, who happened to be the officer on duty at MacArthur's headquarters, in Tokyo, on the quiet Sunday morning of June 25, 1950.

Dean arrived in Korea on July 3 and was thrust into an impossible situation. North Korean forces were driving into the South, South Korean soldiers were fleeing across the front, and the roads were clogged with refugees. American forces hurried to the front, only to find that they were not just undertrained but actually overmatched in firepower. On the afternoon of July 7, Dean dismissed the colonel leading the 34th Infantry Regiment and handed the command over to his longtime friend Col. Robert Martin, "one man who could read my thoughts even before I said them out loud." The next day, a North Korean tank rounded a corner and fired its 85-millimeter gun from twenty-five feet away, cutting Martin in half. American forces began pulling back quickly.

Dean was a decent man, but in the following days he failed as a general. Instead of trying to bring some order to the retreat, as was his responsibility, he essentially demoted himself to a freelance squad leader, leading bazooka teams out to go after individual targets. At one point he became so frustrated that he banged away at a passing North Korean tank with his .45 pistol. He wound up lost and wandering in the hills for thirty-five days, begging food off peasants who stumbled across his hiding places, until finally he was captured, tired and demoralized. "You have to remember that all American generals are not as dumb as I am," he told one of his North Korean interrogators. "You just happened to catch the dumbest." Forbidden to stand or lie down by his captors for much of the time, he would sit with his back against a mud wall and replay in his mind again and again his short combat campaign. In his defense, he at least had been in the thick of things. Lt. Col. Harold Johnson, who later became Army chief of staff, wrote to his mother that during his first week of fighting in Korea, "I didn't see any generals unless I went to the rear a couple of miles." Johnson's regimental commander visited his command post only once in the two months before Johnson was transferred to another position.

Released in September 1953, Dean learned that he had been awarded the Medal of Honor. Unlike MacArthur in World War II, he had the integrity to express embarrassment over it. "There were heroes in Korea, but I was not one of them," he wrote with painful honesty. "There were brilliant commanders, but I was a general captured because he took a wrong road." As for the medal, he continued, "I come close to shame when I think about the men who did better jobs—some who died doing them—and did not get recognition. I wouldn't have awarded myself a wooden star for what I did as a commander."

He was all but destroyed by the experience. Henry Emerson, a young officer who had hunted with Gen. Dean before the war, was shocked when, a few years after the war, he saw the man speak at the Infantry School at Fort Benning:

> I didn't recognize him. He looked 50 years older, gaunt, and he started to talk, and it was immediately evident that he was crazy. I mean, it was just incoherent what he was saying. He read us a poem of what was about 20 verses that he had written, and it was called—you never forget something like this—*Just a Little Sugar in the Mush.* . . . It went on and on and on, and actually some of the guys next to me in the Advanced Class got to giggling. . . . So after it was over, they said General Dean would be glad to shake hands with anyone that served with him. Six or seven guys went up there, and I deliberately got last in the line and I got up to him and I saluted and shook his hand and said, "General Dean, I'm Hank Emerson, Commander from Kangnung and Outpost 24. We goose hunted together." He looked at me like it didn't register at all. He wasn't drooling out of the mouth, but was right next to that. He didn't know me from the man in the moon. I wanted to cry. I wanted to give him a hug. I didn't know what to do.

Not long after Dean was captured, his competent but cantankerous boss, Lt. Gen. Walton Walker, came close to relief. Truman had sent Ridgway and Averell Harriman, then a presidential assistant, to meet with MacArthur. None of the three was satisfied with Walker's performance as the overall ground commander in Korea, but no one wanted to bring it up. "Unknown to either Harriman or Ridgway, at this time MacArthur's confidence in Walker, steadily undermined by Ned Almond, had eroded almost completely," wrote Clay Blair, referring to Maj. Gen. Edward Almond, MacArthur's favorite commander in Korea. MacArthur brought up the subject of removing Walker again in September, when he was riding high, not long after the Inchon landings on the west coast led to the recapture of the South Korean capital of Seoul. MacArthur wondered aloud to subordinate commanders whether a more forceful ground commander was needed.

There were of course poor commanders in World War II, but it is hard to imagine them remaining in command as long as some did in Korea. Consider the case of Lt. Col. Melvin Blair, who, when his battalion of the 24th Infantry Regiment was hit hard, fled and watched from afar as his unit was cut up. He later accused his soldiers of running away. Blair was eventually relieved. He retired from the Army in 1954 but would make headlines in 1957 when he attempted an armed robbery of more than $40,000 from the Bing Crosby National Pro-Am Golf Championship. A year later, he pleaded guilty and was sentenced to five to twenty years but was paroled after serving fourteen months.

MacArthur's downfall

The first year of the Korean War was also the last of Douglas MacArthur's astonishing forty-four years as a senior military commander. Vain and mendacious, MacArthur was always an erratic general, but he was often at his worst at the beginnings of wars, when he tended to be slow to grasp the situation. In December 1941, even after being informed of the Japanese surprise attack on Pearl Harbor, he failed to disperse American aircraft on the ground in the Philippines, where he was in command, resulting in the loss of almost all his advanced warplanes, which were P-40 fighters and B-17 bombers. Similarly, in June 1950, he badly underestimated North Korean capabilities. He compounded misunderstanding with imprudence in his handling of forces and arrogance in his dealings with his superiors in Washington. His defenders maintain that he had successfully overseen the occupation of Japan (although it is not clear that another general could not have done just as well) and then been almost alone in wanting to land troops at Inchon, on Korea's west coast (though such a landing might have been less chancy and equally successful had it been carried out farther south on the coast, where it could have had the same effect of carrying the fight into the rear areas of overextended North Korean forces).

By 1950 MacArthur was seventy years old, well past his prime. But if his physical powers were waning, his sense of self-importance was as robust as ever. During World War II, he could be overbearing even with Marshall and President Roosevelt. Marshall would recount in Washington an exchange he'd had with MacArthur one day during World War II in which MacArthur referred to his staff, and Marshall responded, "General, you don't have a staff, you have a court." In the new war, MacArthur reported to men he hardly seemed to consider peers. The mystery of MacArthur in the Korean War is not that he was removed, but that it took so long to do so. Truman was not the first American president whose orders and policies MacArthur had crossed; he was the third, the first being Hoover, whose orders (according to Eisenhower) he had disregarded during the Bonus March, and the second being

Roosevelt, whom he had attempted to intimidate soon after FDR took office.

Also unlike in the earlier war, MacArthur held all the cards, militarily. The Americans enjoyed control of the air and the sea and possessed an array of land weapons the adversary lacked. The Americans had the ability to move armies quickly by land, sea, and air, while the North Korean army lacked almost all modern forms of support, as did the Chinese army, which would enter the war late in 1950. The Chinese force, for example, had few trucks, and about one doctor for every thirty-three thousand soldiers.

Yet MacArthur imposed on the war a divided command structure that made his operations more difficult, then concocted a series of unnecessarily complex amphibious and airborne assaults that further damaged operations. He split his forces, putting part on the west side of Korea and the remainder on the eastern shore, with a mountain range between them so that they were not able to support one another. MacArthur also stayed in Tokyo, visiting Korea only occasionally, to the point that J. Lawton Collins, by then the Army chief of staff, came to believe that, despite being based in Washington, he had a "far better feel" for the Korean battlefield than MacArthur did.

Perhaps most damaging of all, MacArthur, hardly a subscriber to the Marshall approach, assigned cronies—picked not for their competence but for their personal loyalty—to combat commands, despite their glaring lack of experience. He encouraged sycophantism among his subordinates, accepting from one of them the Distinguished Flying Cross, for flying over enemy-held territory in his passenger aircraft on his way home to Tokyo, despite having seen no enemy aircraft or even enemy troops on the ground during the flight.

MacArthur also was increasingly at odds with Truman. In July, he visited Taiwan at a time when American policy about whether to protect the island against a Chinese attack was undecided. He took sides, in August sending to the Veterans of Foreign Wars a statement that, among other things, seemed to indicate that he supported militarily defending Taiwan against China. When questioned by the White House, he protested, disingenuously, that he had only been expressing a personal opinion—as if the U.S. commander for East Asia could separate himself from American military policy in that region. A month later, in mid-September 1950, Truman fired his defense secretary, Louis Johnson, in part because he seemed to be siding with the general against the White House. Johnson, who had been the chief fund-raiser for Truman's presidential election campaign, was seen by many as an incompetent hack, so the dismissal had the side effect of boosting troop morale. One artillery officer, James Dill, recalled being aboard a ship heading for Korea when the news came out: "The result was a reaction among the troops such as I never saw among American troops at any other time. Cheers broke out all over the ship. Soldiers slapped each other on the back and clapped."

Most memorably, in mid-October Truman flew to see MacArthur on Wake Island, in the mid-Pacific. It was the only time the two men ever met, mainly because MacArthur had not journeyed back to his native land since before World War II—and actually would not go there until he was fired the following year. Before the outbreak of the Korean War, he had rebuffed requests from the Truman Administration to come back to Washington for meetings. At Wake, MacArthur, riding high on the successful landing at Inchon, seemed to see the meeting not as one between equals, but as a case of a great commander being used by a weak president as a political prop. When MacArthur greeted Truman, he shook his hand but did not salute him—an astonishing departure from American military tradition. On the contrary, MacArthur seemed to believe some sort of deference was due him.

It was not forthcoming from Harry Truman. The president

and the general sat together in the rear seat of a 1937 Chevrolet, the only automobile on the small, barren islet. Frank Boring, the Secret Service agent who was driving the car, eavesdropped on their conversation. Truman said, he recalled, "Listen, you know I'm president, and you're the general. You're working for me. . . . You don't make any political decisions; I make the political decisions. You don't make any kind of a decision at all. Otherwise, I'm going to call you back, and get you out of there. If you make one more move, I'm going to get you out of there." It was a good, blunt formulation of the way civil-military discourse is supposed to occur in the American system. But MacArthur was well beyond the point of heeding such an admonition, especially from a president he held in contempt.

After this private conversation, the two men moved to a small one-story building belonging to the Civil Aeronautics Board for a formal meeting that included their aides. MacArthur began the session by assuring the president and his retinue, "I believe that formal resistance will end throughout North and South Korea by Thanksgiving," according to notes compiled by Omar Bradley, then the chairman of the Joint Chiefs of Staff. He also hoped to have the Eighth Army heading back "to Japan by Christmas."

"What are the chances for Chinese or Soviet interference?" asked President Truman.

MacArthur had good news on that front. The Chinese had not yet come in and probably wouldn't, he assured those present at the meeting. But if they did, the general explained, "now that we have bases for our Air Force in Korea, if the Chinese tried to get down to Pyongyang there would be the greatest slaughter." (To be fair, the CIA had just issued an analysis that largely came to the same conclusion.) MacArthur later would bitterly deny, in one of two interviews given on his seventy-fourth birthday and released only after his death, that he had said these things. But MacArthur was not a reliable witness, given his habit of saying whatever he thought was best for his reputation at a particular moment. Most incredibly, in a 1961 interview with Forrest Pogue, one of Marshall's biographers, he claimed that he never had been interested in running for or being president.

At Wake Island, after nearly three hours of talking—during which other Asian issues, such as the problems of France in Vietnam, were discussed—the president concluded the meeting and suggested that they break for lunch while a communiqué was prepared. MacArthur declined the president's invitation, saying he was anxious to get back to Tokyo. This was another violation of military tradition, which holds that an invitation from the president to an officer has the effect of an order.

MacArthur later wrote of the meeting that his private assessment of Truman was that he "seemed to take great pride in his historical knowledge" but that "it was of a superficial character." In particular, he said, "of the Far East he knew little"—MacArthur's standard rebuttal to anyone who disagreed with him on Asian policy. His general conclusion from the Wake meeting was that "a curious, and sinister, change was taking place in Washington," with Truman and those around him losing their nerve. With a different general, the Wake Island meeting might have provided the opportunity to repair a fraying civil-military discourse. But with MacArthur, it was too late, and it was evident from the meeting that the dialogue between the president and his top general in the war was breaking down.

A few days later, MacArthur assured reporters in Tokyo that "the war is very definitely coming to an end shortly." We now know that by this point, Peng Dehuai, who would be the top Chinese commander in the war, already had moved into Korea. In the following week, even as MacArthur was announcing that he would win the war by Christmas, some 180,000 of Peng's troops would pour into Korea. On November 24, MacArthur announced that a new American offensive was being launched that day and that it should, "if successful, . . . for all practical purposes end the war, restore peace and unity to Korea, enable the prompt withdrawal of [the American-led] United Nations military forces, and permit the complete assumption by the Korean people and nation of full sovereignty and international equality." That was a tall order, one that MacArthur would fail to achieve in every one of its particulars. MacArthur and his acolytes later would argue that the American offensive launched in November really had been just a sizable "reconnaissance in force," but that claim is incompatible with the assertion about ending the war that MacArthur had issued on the day the attack began. In addition, MacArthur's orders appeared to violate the Joint Chiefs of Staff directive, issued to him on September 27, not to send American forces to the Manchurian border area.

This string of miscalculations and false assurances alone would have been enough to cause a president to lose confidence in MacArthur and so sack him. But, as in World War II, Douglas MacArthur was not just a general—he was a major political problem. Truman's handling of him in the following months would resemble the new American policy of containing the Soviet Union until it collapsed on its own. MacArthur's end would come after the general issued a series of bombastic statements that undercut his support in the military and finally alienated even his subordinate commander in Korea.

MacArthur's rhetoric, rarely measured, veered toward the hysterical in the late fall of 1950. His statements lacked any sense that competing views might hold merit. He cast minor policy differences in the most absolute and extreme terms. Just nine days after declaring the war all but over, he was talking about facing "the final destruction" of his forces unless he was given the leeway he demanded. When he was ordered to shelve plans to bomb China, he told an aide, "For the first time in military history, a commander has been denied the use of his military power to safeguard the lives of his soldiers and safety of his army." A few days later, informing the Joint Chiefs of Staff of his plan to take all of North Korea, he warned that "any program short of this would completely destroy the morale of my forces and the psychological consequences would be inestimable." Furthermore, he stated, leaving any part of Korea in the hands of the Communists would be an "immoral . . . proposition" that "would be the greatest defeat of the free world in recent times."

On December 6, the president issued an executive order to all theater commanders to clear their public statements with their superiors. This order was clearly aimed at MacArthur.

During this time, MacArthur's favorite, Maj. Gen. Edward Almond, the commander of X Corps, was needlessly antagonizing O. P. Smith, commander of the 1st Marine Division, which had been placed under him, along with two Army divisions, the 7th and the 3rd. Smith was almost exactly the same age as Almond, but Almond condescendingly addressed him as "son." In September 1950, the two had made the Inchon landing together, outflanking North Korean troops, but despite that success, they soon came to loathe each other. Theirs, wrote historian Shelby Stanton, was "the worst working relationship between American generals of the Korean war."

The Chinese intervention proved to be a catastrophe for American troops scattered across northwest Korea, with the 2nd Division alone suffering more than three thousand casualties, many of them incurred as retreating troops passed through a six-mile-long valley remembered as "the Gauntlet," in which Chinese troops on either side of the road saturated their column with machine-gun fire and mortar shells. MacArthur, never one to admit to mistakes, later would insist that "the disposition of those troops, in my opinion, could not have been improved upon, had I known the Chinese were going to attack." Lt. Gen. Matthew Ridgway privately considered that statement an "absolute falsehood. . . . It couldn't have been a worse disposition of troops, as a matter of fact." The Army's official history of the campaign, written decades later, would agree with Ridgway, stating that "the Eighth Army, when hit by the Chinese, was deployed on a broad front with its right flank open and was supported by few reserves."

In the wake of that disaster, the division commander, Laurence Keiser, was removed from his command, but in a fashion markedly more discreet than had been used by the Army in the two world wars. He received a message from Walker's headquarters informing him that he was suffering from pneumonia and that he needed to report to a military hospital in Tokyo. Insulted by the subterfuge, he confronted Walker's chief of staff, Maj. Gen. Leven Allen. "I don't have pneumonia, so cut the bunk," he said. Keiser knew the score, having been chief of staff for John Lucas when Lucas was fired as a corps commander by Mark Clark, at Anzio in February 1944.

Well, Allen responded, the pneumonia message was an order. Would he comply with it? Yes, Keiser said, but only because it was an order. Allen reassured him that Walker would take care of him with some kind of headquarters job. "You tell General Walker to shove his job up his ass," Keiser responded. He would be replaced at the 2nd Division by Robert McClure, who had fought in World War I with the 26th ("Yankee") Division, whose commander had famously been relieved by Pershing. Keiser had suffered the reputation of being an officer who commanded from his headquarters, but McClure was not much better. He privately admitted to S. L. A. Marshall, the Army historian then embedded with the division, that he was over the hill and was drinking too much in order to tranquillize himself. "I can only brace myself by hitting the bottle," McClure said, according to Marshall. One of his first orders was to direct everyone in the division to grow a beard, which he cast as a contest. The ostensible military reason was to make it easier to identify friendly soldiers in the dark. He would be fired within a month of taking command.

The disaster on the western side of Korea would be better remembered were it not for the even more shocking situation to the east, in the frozen mountains around the Changjin Reservoir, which the American military, using maps based on those of the former Japanese occupiers of Korea, knew as Chosin.

CHAPTER 10
Army generals fail at Chosin

The battles around Chosin Reservoir in late November and early December of 1950 would essentially provide a laboratory test for two different American approaches to warfighting and especially to leadership.

The Marines were on the west side of the reservoir, the Army units on the east. Both reported to the same senior leadership and suffered the same winter weather, so cold that rounds for the 3.5-inch rocket launcher froze and cracked open. The Marine division chief of staff at Chosin, Col. Gregon Williams, took a four-minute radio telephone call without a glove on his hand, only to have his fingers turn blue with frostbite later that night. Discussing Chosin years later, Marine corporal Alan Herrington said, "I can still see the icicles of blood." Indeed, one peculiarity of Chosin was that wounds remained pink and red rather than turning reddish brown, because blood froze before it could coagulate. The cold was a lethal curse but also an unexpected medical ally, because wounds froze shut; it also kept corpses from becoming a sanitation problem.

For both the Army and the Marines, Chosin would be one of

the fiercest fights in their history. "I was in the Bulge [in World War II], and it was nothing like this at Chosin Reservoir," one survivor, Army Sgt. First Class Carrol Price, said later. "I lost all my friends."

As vastly larger Chinese forces attacked, both the Army and Marine units retreated almost thirteen miles. The Marine retreat would continue in a second phase, another two dozen miles, after it collected the survivors of the Army units. Though both the Army and the Marines faced the same enemy, the Army unit was wiped out, in one of the greatest disasters in American military history, while the Marine division marched out with its vehicles, weapons, and some of the Army's survivors.

The battle began about three months after the Inchon landings. MacArthur and his followers were riding high. He and his favorite general, Ned Almond, recklessly pressed their subordinates to attack north toward the Yalu River, the border between Korea and China. They did this despite numerous signs that the Chinese government had inserted thousands—perhaps hundreds of thousands—of troops into northern Korea, not far from the Americans. A collision became inevitable.

When Lt. Col. Don Faith Jr.'s 1st Battalion of the 32nd Infantry Regiment arrived on the eastern shore of the reservoir, it was the first Army element to replace the 5th Marines. That Marine unit was being moved to the west side of the reservoir to join the other Marine regiment there, because Maj. Gen. O. P. Smith, the Marine division commander, being worried by Chinese moves and by his open left flank, wanted to consolidate his forces. Lt. Col. Raymond Murray, the seasoned commanding officer of the 5th Marines, had been studying the terrain on the eastern shore. As he turned over the area to Faith, he recommended that the

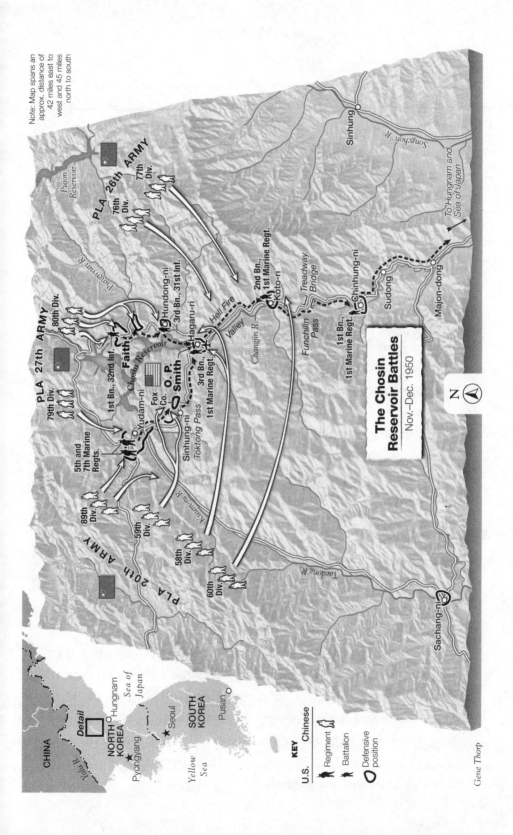

Note: Map spans an approx. distance of 42 miles east to west and 45 miles north to south

PLA 26th ARMY

77th Div.

76th Div.

Pujon Reservoir

Pungnyun R.

PLA 27th ARMY

80th Div.

Hudong-ni

3rd Bn., 31st Inf.

79th Div.

Faith

1st Bn., 32nd Inf.

Hagaru-ri

Hell Fire Valley

2nd Bn. 1st Marine Regt.

Koto-ri

Treadway Bridge

Sinhung

Songchon R.

To Hungnam and Sea of Japan

Chosin Reservoir

O.P. Smith

Yudam-ni

Fox Co.

3rd Bn. 1st Marine Regt.

Sinhung-ni

Toktong Pass

Changjin R.

Funchilin Pass

Chinhung-ni

Sudong

5th and 7th Marine Regts.

1st Bn. 1st Marine Regt.

89th Div.

Kwanu R.

PLA 20th ARMY

59th Div.

58th Div.

60th Div.

Majon-dong

Taedong R.

The Chosin Reservoir Battles

Nov.–Dec. 1950

N

Sachang-ni

Detail

CHINA

Yalu R.

NORTH KOREA

Pyongyang ★

Hungnam

Sea of Japan

SOUTH KOREA

Seoul ★

Pusan

Yellow Sea

KEY

U.S.   Chinese

Regiment

Battalion

Defensive position

Gene Thorp

arriving Army unit dig in and not try to push any farther north. Gen. Smith also passed the word: "Now, look, don't go out on a limb, take it easy up there." The assistant commander of the 7th Division, Brig. Gen. "Hammerin' Hank" Hodes, a veteran of the World War II fighting at Omaha Beach on D-Day, earlier had denied Faith's request to move north. Nonetheless, with the arrival of Col. Allan MacLean, the regimental commander to which he was attached, Faith pressed again for permission to attack north, up the east side of the reservoir. This time he got approval. In his persistence, he had set the stage for a defeat in which more than three times as many soldiers would be lost as at Lt. Col. George Custer's Battle of the Little Bighorn.

The Army units on the eastern side of the water were two battalions from the 7th Infantry Division—one from the 31st Infantry Regiment and one from its sister regiment, the 32nd. The 31st was commanded by Col. MacLean, who had spent World War II as a staff officer planning troop movements and who that fall had been given command of the regiment after his predecessor was relieved for a poor performance after the landing at Inchon. The 1st Battalion of the 32nd was commanded by Faith, who not only had never led a unit in sustained combat before but, incredibly, until the Korean War, actually had never *been assigned* to a front-line combat unit before—not at the squad, platoon, company, or battalion level—having spent all of World War II as an aide to Ridgway. Neither Faith's battalion nor the 31st Regiment had much combat experience in Korea up to that time. Neither had fought on the defensive, and neither had faced enemy forces larger than a battalion. "The sum total of the 1/32 IN [Infantry] battle experience was the unopposed river crossing at the Han River into Seoul and a few days of combat against the scattered resistance from some of the remnants of the North Korean army in the city," noted Maj. Paul Berquist in a study done later at the Army's Command and General Staff College.

Hubris rode north with Col. Faith. The first ominous sign came on the afternoon of November 27, when MacLean sent the 31st Infantry's Intelligence and Reconnaissance Platoon to establish an outpost on the northeastern side of the reservoir near an inlet. The platoon, mounted on jeeps with machine guns, headed north and vanished, reporting back by neither radio nor runner. It was never heard from again. Faith's intelligence officer also was picking up word from Korean civilians that Chinese troops were telling them they "were going to take back the Chosin Reservoir but everyone more or less pooh-poohed the idea," recalled Capt. Ed Stamford, a Marine forward air controller who was attached to Faith's Army battalion so he could coordinate support from Marine aircraft. "They couldn't take it from us."

On the same day, Gen. Almond was being briefed on the operations of the 7th Marines. "I already know all this," he interrupted. "Where's your intelligence officer?"

Capt. Donald France stepped forward. Almond asked him, "What's your latest information?"

"General, there's a shitload of Chinamen in those mountains," France bluntly told him.

Almond later would insist that the Marines' chief of intelligence had not seen a threat, stating that he'd been briefed on November 26 that "the G-2 of 1st Marine Division did not give the enemy an offensive capability in the Chosin Reservoir area." This is shameless quibbling on the part of Almond, because the record is clear that the Marines were reporting substantial columns of Chinese forces moving through the countryside. Almond here is hiding behind the point that the Chinese appeared to be moving north and so were not attacking. Rather, as Gen. Smith correctly feared, they were maneuvering to draw the Marines northward into a trap.

Nor was Maj. Gen. Charles Willoughby, MacArthur's intelligence chief, crediting any talk of a looming clash with Chinese forces. When the Marines started moving north, they ran into a Chinese force and captured fifty of them. "Those aren't Chinese soldiers," Willoughby said. "They are volunteers." *No,* Almond responded, siding with the Marines. *They have been interviewed, and they say they are regular troops.* He invited Willoughby to come look at them. "That's a Marine lie," Willoughby responded.

Willoughby was an unusual character. Born in Germany, probably under the name Adolph Weidenbach, he changed his name after coming to the United States before World War I. By 1951, Willoughby had served MacArthur continuously for ten years, the only senior subordinate to do so. Like MacArthur, he enthusiastically dabbled in politics while in uniform, lobbying Congress in the late 1940s, for example, to extend the hand of friendship to Spain's Fascist leader, Generalissimo Francisco Franco. He persisted in this even after Omar Bradley, then Army chief of staff, told him in writing to desist. (The same year, Robert McCormick, the right-wing publisher of the *Chicago Tribune,* wrote to Willoughby that he had confirmed with the American ambassador to France that "it is the Jews who are keeping us from recognizing Spain." McCormick added, "I was told Mrs. Harriman is a Jewess but doubt this. I met her some time ago and saw no indication of it.")

Not long before the Chinese attack, Willoughby, despite his role as the chief intelligence officer for the American military in the Far East, was busying himself lobbying Congress. He took time to write to Sen. Owen Brewster of Maine "to congratulate you and the able GOP management in obtaining a magnificent and highly suggestive victory in the recent elections. I hope this trend will continue in the future." He lauded the work of Brewster's political ally, Sen. Joe McCarthy, and applauded the Republican victory in the midterm elections as "a repudiation of the Administration's Far Eastern policy." In January he sent a fan note to McCarthy himself, saluting the Wisconsin Red hunter as "a lone voice in the pinco [*sic*] wilderness." A few months later, at a dinner in Tokyo, Willoughby would propose a toast "to the second greatest military genius in the world—Francisco Franco." MacArthur chuckled at such talk, referring to Willoughby as "my pet fascist."

While Willoughby was working the Congress on behalf of Franco, the Chinese, more focused on the task at hand, were concentrating around the Chosin Reservoir. On the night of November 27–28, Chinese soldiers attacked Faith's outpost and quickly worked around the ends of his incomplete, horseshoe-shaped perimeter. "One minute we were planning an attack," recalled Capt. Erwin Bigger, one of Faith's company commanders. "The next, we were fighting for our lives in a situation where we knew little of what had hit us."

In the middle of the night, Capt. Stamford, the Marine air controller attached to Faith's Army force, heard gunfire and then some nearby "chattering." The poncho serving as a door to his bunker was pulled aside to reveal the fur-rimmed face of an enemy soldier, who tossed a small hand grenade his way. He survived the blast, but many other soldiers did not make it through the night. The two Army encampments along the east side of the reservoir took heavy casualties that night and were cut off by roadblocks not only from each other but from the Marines to the south. The isolated U.S. Army unit was being hit by the 80th Division of the People's Liberation Army.

Despite the Chinese assault, the next afternoon, Almond landed at the forward headquarters of Faith and MacLean, and ordered them to get on the ball. "We're still attacking, and we're going all the way to the Yalu," about seventy-five miles to the north, he told them, according to an official Army history. "Don't let a bunch of Chinese laundrymen stop you." Never was such racist advice so ill-advised. When Faith reported that his battalion had been attacked by parts of two Chinese divisions, Almond exploded, telling him that "there weren't two Chinese divisions in all of Korea." The only opposition Faith was facing, the general reassured him, was from Chinese stragglers fleeing north. Almond also told Faith that it had been a command failure not to have occupied the high ground. "Faith agreed," he recalled. Almond pinned the Silver Star, a high decoration, on three soldiers, including Faith. "After the helicopter carrying General Almond left the area, I saw Colonel Faith rip the medal off his uniform and throw it on the ground," recalled Staff Sgt. Chester Bair.

The regiment was about to be smashed head-on by a full Chinese division. Both of the commanders Almond had been exhorting would be dead within three days. By the next afternoon, on both sides of the reservoir, a total of four U.S. Army and Marine regiments were isolated and besieged. Alarmed by what it was hearing, the Joint Chiefs of Staff sent an inquiry to MacArthur, asking whether his units were overly exposed. MacArthur coolly reassured Washington that he had ordered Almond not to let units become isolated. At any rate, MacArthur soothed, "While geographically his elements may seem to be well extended, the actual conditions of terrain make it extremely difficult to take any material advantage thereof."

Col. MacLean, the regimental commander, was killed early in the fighting as he approached a group of soldiers he thought were his but who were actually Chinese. The two other battalion commanders present were seriously wounded, so command of the cut-off Army units on the east side of the reservoir devolved upon Faith. An Army tank unit located a few miles to his south made several attempts to break through to him, but all failed. Unfortunately, and quite negligently, this crucial fact was not communicated to him at the time.

This was the moment when good generalship could have made

a lifesaving difference. Faith needed a senior officer to step in and guide him, to coordinate his movements with supporting aircraft, to establish better communications, to find out what help could be given in other ways, and generally to help him organize his withdrawal and also use rank to summon the formidable assets of the U.S. military. None of this happened. Faith was not well served by his superiors. His division commander, Maj. Gen. David Barr, helicoptered in to visit him on the morning of November 30. "The situation was much more serious than he realized," Barr recounted three months later in a lecture at the Army War College. That appears to have been all the advice that Barr brought. It is amazing, Maj. Berquist later wrote, to consider "that MG Barr did not coordinate a breakout attempt with LTC Faith right at that moment. MG Barr knew the true extent of the situation and only he, not LTC Faith, was in a position to coordinate anything." Like Faith, Barr had been a staff officer in World War II, not leading troops in combat. What Faith needed at this point was not a pat on the back and some demoralizing assessments but concrete support from Barr and Almond in the form of coordinating his retreat with an attack from Army tanks to the south. Barr's assistant division commander, Gen. Hodes, a seasoned combat veteran, was nearby and easily could have been put in charge of the effort—but wasn't.

The situation continued to deteriorate. "Nothing was working out," recalled PFC James Ransone Jr. "We were being shot up bad. We were just in a terrible situation. We were being annihilated."

That evening brought the most determined Chinese attack so far. At three in the morning, Chinese soldiers overran part of the Army perimeter, giving them devastating control of a small hill overlooking the entire Army encampment. Faith's position had never been good, but now it was untenable. The following morning, after three days of intensifying Chinese attacks, running low on ammunition, and with wounded dying from lack of medical care, Faith and the regiment set out to try to make it four miles south, to where they believed—incorrectly—that friendly lines began. "They had been fighting for over eighty hours in below zero weather," observes Berquist. "Few had had much sleep or much to eat," because what food they did have was frozen. "Dead and wounded soldiers were everywhere and wounded soldiers who could not move froze to death." The dead performed a final posthumous service, becoming the supply depot for the living, who stripped the corpses of their comrades for clothing, weapons, and ammunition.

What could go wrong did. Faith did not know it, but the temporary Army outpost he was aiming for had pulled out, so safety was not four miles away, as he thought, but seven miles away, at Smith's Marine base at the southern end of the reservoir—and it had fewer troops than Faith had. As the column of about thirty trucks formed, each carrying fifteen or twenty wounded, a barrage of Chinese mortar shells wounded several key leaders. Marine aircraft appeared overhead to provide air support. The column began to creep southward, only to come under Chinese rifle fire almost immediately. Lt. James Mortrude, who was in the lead vehicle, recalled, "We had proceeded only a short way beyond the perimeter when a furious burst of enemy automatic weapons fire drove me and the gunner down behind the shield of our open turret." A call went out for air support, only to result in the lead Marine aircraft dropping napalm on the vanguard of the Army column. Mortrude was able to crouch down in the turret and let the wave of flame pass over him, but others were not so fortunate. Maj. Hugh Robbins, lying wounded in the bed of a truck, ducked as the bomb hit, then peered through the slats of the truck to glimpse about fifteen soldiers enveloped in fire. "Looking back up I could see the terrible sight of men ablaze from head to foot, staggering back or rolling on the ground screaming," he recalled.

"It was terrible," recalled Pvt. Ransone. "Where the napalm had burned the skin to a crisp, it would be peeled back from the face, arms, legs. It looked as though the skin was curled like fried potato chips. Men begged to be shot." One officer, epidermis burnt black, asked a soldier for a cigarette and then walked into the frozen distance, never to be seen again.

The column moved on at less than walking speed as the trucks were raked endlessly with fire from Chinese rifles and machine guns. Some of the wounded were hit two or three more times while lying in the back of a truck. Drivers, sitting in the left sides of their vehicles, were particularly vulnerable, as the column was heading south and was overlooked by a parallel ridge to the east—that is, on the drivers' side of the convoy.

Two hours into its crucifixion, the convoy encountered a nasty surprise: The bridge leading across a stream had been blown. No one had thought to ask the Marine pilots flying overhead to report to them on the state of the road. At this point, the M19 vehicle in the lead, carrying a set of powerful .50-caliber machine guns that could scythe down attackers, ran out of ammunition. But it still made itself useful by winching the trucks through the streambed adjacent to the destroyed bridge. This was a one-by-one process that consumed two hours of daylight. The M19 then ran out of fuel. Both these outages might have been prevented by better communication, coordination, and support between Faith and his superiors. While the American convoy was tugged across the stream, the Chinese enemy used the time to move south and take up positions along the hillside the Americans would next have to ascend. When the convoy resumed moving, some of the soldiers who could walk began running away, mainly heading downhill, out to the ice of the reservoir, where they had a chance to walk south to the Marine outpost at the southern end of the reservoir. Among the first to run, survivors reported, were those assigned to defend the rear of the column.

At the top of the hill, the convoy hit a Chinese roadblock. Soon the winter evening began to fall, which meant the Americans would lose their air support, the only major weapon remaining to them. Discipline was eroding rapidly. Soldiers and officers sent up a hill to flank the roadblock declined to assault the Chinese and instead continued down its other side, eventually angling out to the ice of the reservoir. One exception was Capt. Earle Jordan, who assembled a group of ten soldiers who fought their way toward the roadblock, only to run out of ammunition when they got to it, so they continued their assault "by yelling, shouting and making as much noise as possible," according to historian Roy Appleman.

About one-third of the sixteen thousand men in the U.S. Army's 7th Division were Koreans who had been pulled in from the streets, hastily trained, and put into American units to round them out. This was an ill-conceived plan that impeded the units when they were under pressure. Faith found two of his Korean soldiers under a truck, apparently trying to hide by tying themselves to its undercarriage. He pulled them out and executed them with his .45. "It was a sad and outrageous moment," historian Martin Russ comments. "Faith did not shoot any of the American soldiers who were equally demoralized—and who had received far better training than the hapless ROKs."

Whatever Faith's shortcomings, he was still trying to provide leadership. A few minutes later, when he was struck in the chest by grenade fragments, all semblance of organization went with him. "After Colonel Faith was killed, it was everyone for himself," recalled Sgt. Bair. "The chain of command disappeared." The column moved on about another quarter-mile, only to run into another roadblock. Those who survived the massacre were primarily those who now cut to the west and walked or even crawled south on the ice toward Marine lines. When three trucks loaded with wounded were abandoned by their drivers, a fourth truck tried to push them aside and wound up overturning them down the hillside. "Wounded men inside were spilled and crushed," an official Army history relates. "The frantic screams of these men seemed to Lieutenant [James] Campbell like the world gone mad."

That was the end of the convoy, which now was stalled and defenseless. Hundreds of wounded were left behind, lying stacked in trucks. Chinese soldiers trotted along the column tossing white phosphorus grenades into the vehicles, burning to death many of those who had not already been killed by the cold. Still, some survived: A Marine pilot who flew low over the column the next day reported that he saw some wounded trying to wave.

Out on the frozen reservoir, Gen. Smith recalled, "some of these men were dragging themselves on the ice, some of them had gone crazy and were walking in circles." Many of the soldiers were rescued by Marine Lt. Col. Olin Beall, the crusty commander of the 1st Motor Transport Battalion, who, on his own initiative, over three days, repeatedly took five Marines and a Navy corpsman in jeeps out onto the ice, where they collected 319 Army survivors, almost all of them wounded, frostbitten, and disoriented. The grizzled Beall had enlisted in the Marines at the outset of World War I but left the Corps in 1922 to try his hand at minor league baseball. After a season in which he posted an unimpressive 0–1 record as a pitcher for the Class D Blue Ridge League's Martinsburg, West Virginia, Blue Sox, he reenlisted and eventually became an officer. (His Blue Sox teammate Hack Wilson did better, with a 1922 batting average of .366 and thirty home runs in eighty-four games. Wilson eventually went on to the New York Giants and then into the Baseball Hall of Fame.)

Operating under the eyes of Chinese riflemen who were some-times just one hundred feet away but generally did not fire at them, Beall and his men attached sleds to their vehicles to pull stacks of the wounded. After two days of rescue work, Beall finally arrived at the charred remains of the Army convoy and inspected its hulks, looking for more survivors. He counted about three hundred dead but found no one still breathing. Ultimately, the 31st Regimental Combat Team, which included Faith's battalion, lost all its artillery pieces and vehicles and left behind many of its wounded soldiers and all of its dead. Overall, the casualty rate for the 3,288 men of the 31st Infantry Regiment was an astonishing 90 percent.

The Marines fed the survivors hot soup and evacuated the seri-ously wounded by air; then they took the 358 men deemed capa-ble of fighting and put them into a provisional battalion, plugging them into their perimeter. The Army officer put in charge of them later suffered a mental breakdown, according to Gen. Smith. At this point, the generals, so sluggish a few days earlier, sprang to action. All the far-reaching, powerful tools of the U.S. military establishment, seemingly so unable to help these men when they were besieged, now came to their aid. Within twenty-four hours of being shot up in the hellish convoy, some of the sol-diers were sleeping in the clean sheets of Army hospital beds in Japan.

Less noticed in the debacle, and not much mentioned by the Marines subsequently, was the fact that, by getting in the way of the Chinese attack, the Army regiment may have bought a day or two of precious time for the 1st Marine Division. Without Faith's last stand, the Marines might not have been able to hold the key junction of Hagaru-ri, at the southern end of the reservoir, where they built an airstrip and which they held with a small contingent while the two Marine regiments on the far northwest side of the reservoir fought their way back down to them. But this does not excuse the utter failure of the Army generals in the chain of command: Hodes, the seasoned assistant division commander, who might have stepped in; Barr, the division commander, who should have; Almond, the corps commander, whose arrogance made matters worse; Willoughby, the intelligence chief general who refused to recognize the reality of a Chinese intervention in the war; and, most of all, MacArthur, the top commander, who had insisted on the harebrained drive to the Yalu through the Korean winter. In World War II, several of these men would have been removed for their poor leadership at Chosin. In Korea, only Barr was. MacArthur's firing, when it came a few months later, would be for a different reason.

CHAPTER 11
O. P. Smith succeeds at Chosin

One of the little-known aspects of the Chosin Reservoir Campaign was that Maj. Gen. O. P. Smith, the commander of the Marines there, was far more of a Marshall man than were the Army generals to whom he reported. Ned Almond, the Army general over Smith, "was a MacArthur man, and anything MacArthur said, nothing could change it. . . . MacArthur was God," recalled Smith.

Smith, rail-thin and white-haired, seemed to have been cut from the Marshall cloth. When he was seven years old, Smith lost his father, a Texas lawyer. His widowed mother took him to California and raised him in penury. As a young man, Smith arrived at the University of California, Berkeley, with just five dollars in his pocket and worked his way through school, often as a gardener. He joined the Marines at the outset of World War I but spent the war in Guam, a setback to his career that would help keep him at the rank of captain for almost two decades during the interwar period.

In the early 1930s, though it was unusual for a Marine officer, Smith attended the Army's Infantry School, then run by Lt. Col.

George Marshall. There, he and his classmates Bedell Smith and Terry Allen were instructed in the use of machine guns by Omar Bradley, and in tactics by Joseph Stilwell. "Colonel Marshall was pretty definite in his ideas," O. P. Smith remembered admiringly. "He was a pretty tough hombre."

Like Marshall, Smith disliked military sentimentalism or romanticism, even about his own Marine Corps. During the 1930s, he wrote a paper that debunked the bayonet as a weapon. For his evidence, he researched the use of the bayonet by Marines against German soldiers in Belleau Wood in World War I. "But when you run down the history," the bayonet lacked the shock value often attributed to it, he found. "Where I got the dope was from the medical officers, how many bayonet wounds they treated, and there weren't many."

As a general, the quiet, pipe-smoking Christian Scientist hardly fit the gung-ho popular image of a Marine, which may be one reason his name is hardly known today. On the eve of landing for the Battle of Peleliu, in World War II, for example, he passed the time by reading, among other things, a biography of Oliver Wendell Holmes. Peleliu proved to be a bloodbath for the American landing force, which according to Adm. Chester Nimitz suffered the highest casualty rate—nearly 40 percent—of any amphibious assault ever by American forces. This experience surely helped steel Smith for the carnage he would see during the hardest days of the Chosin fight.

It is said that the essence of generalship is what one does before the outbreak of fighting. That is certainly the case with O. P. Smith at Chosin. The three most important decisions of the campaign may be those Smith made before it even began. First, he insisted on consolidating his regiments so they could support one another. This meant bringing the 5th Marines in from the east side of the reservoir and turning that area over to the Army.

Second, he made it a top priority to have his engineers scrape out two airstrips in the frozen ground, enabling the Marines in the following days to fly in supplies and reinforcements and move out their wounded, unburdening their units and enabling them to move faster through the frozen roads and mountains. A total of 4,312 wounded or frostbitten Marine and Army personnel were flown out in the mere five days that the northernmost airstrip, at Hagaru-ri, was operational, from the afternoon of December 1 to the evening of December 6, 1950, when the retreating Marines abandoned that base. Third, he put himself at what he believed would be the key point of the battle. The American forces around Chosin Reservoir were essentially in a giant formation resembling the letter *Y*, with the Marines on the left arm, to the west of the reservoir, and the Army on the right, to the east. Smith understood that if the Marines held their position west of the reservoir but lost the outpost to the south of it, where the forks met, they would be doomed. So on the morning of November 28, he left his rear headquarters and flew to that junction, where the two branches came together and the single road out of the mountains, south to the sea, began. This spot, he had determined, would be the decisive point geographically in the coming battle. "Hagaru-ri had to be held at all costs," he later explained. "Here was the transport plane airstrip. . . . Here was accumulated the wherewithal to support the subsequent breakout from Hagaru-ri. Here was a defended perimeter where the 5th and 7th Marines [who were isolated to the northwest] could reorganize, resupply, reequip, and evacuate their casualties preparatory to the breakout therefrom."

In the American system, every general has a boss. A seldom-discussed aspect of generalship is understanding the person to whom one reports, whether that is a president, a prime minister, or another general. What are that superior's concerns, his skills, his shortcomings? Gen. MacArthur, for example, was poor at this, whether in grasping FDR's mastery of politics or sensing the threshold of Truman's temper. A significant aspect of the Chosin campaign, by contrast, was that Smith soberly assessed the combat skills and judgment of Lt. Gen. Almond, the Army general to whom he was reporting.

Almond's record might give any colleague pause. A 1915 graduate of the Virginia Military Institute, he rose quickly during World War I, commanding a machine-gun battalion in the fighting late in the war. His record was less distinguished during the next big war. One of George Marshall's biggest mistakes during World War II stemmed from a certain misperception about race. Marshall believed that white Southerners best understood how to work with black soldiers, so he officered the Army's segregated units with white Southerners. One of the most prominent of his picks was Almond, a proud Virginian steeped in the traditions of the Confederacy, who was given command of the 92nd Division and led it in Italy during World War II—with notably poor results. Marshall was to write to Eisenhower that the 92nd's "Infantry literally dissolved each night abandoning equipment and even clothing in some cases." When the Army concluded that the 92nd Division's performance had been "unsatisfactory," Almond blamed his black soldiers, who, he said, were unwilling to die for patriotic reasons. He claimed his background gave him special insight into the race issue: "People think that being from the South we don't like Negroes. Not at all. But we understand his capabilities. And we don't want to sit at the table with them." Almond's unhappy troops developed reciprocal feelings, at one point booing their commander. One anonymous member of the division denounced it as "a slave unit for white masters." Despite the 92nd Division's weak combat record in World War II, Almond manned his corps headquarters in Korea with six veterans of its staff. Ridgway, who would take over command of the war from MacArthur, had a very different view of the black soldier, commenting later that "there was nothing wrong with him if he had the right surroundings, the right officers, the right training and the right leadership."

It was said of Gen. Almond that "when it pays to be aggressive, Ned's aggressive, and when it pays to be cautious, Ned's aggressive." Chosin Reservoir was developing as one of the latter cases. When Almond visited Smith's headquarters, he told the general and his Marine division staff, "We've got to go barreling up that road." Smith bit his tongue until Almond left and then said to his staff, "We're not going anywhere until I get this division together and the airfield built." Before the battle, Smith also wrote a personal letter to the commandant of the Marine Corps, putting his unease on the record. "Our left flank is wide open," he noted. "I have little confidence in the tactical judgment of X Corps or in the realism of their planning. There is a continual splitting up of units and assignment of missions which puts them out on a limb. Time and time again I have tried to tell the Corps Commander that in a Marine Division he has a powerful instrument, and that it cannot help but lose its effectiveness when dispersed." At one point in mid-November 1950, Almond had spread his five divisions (three American and two South Korean) across a five-hundred-mile front. Smith's Marine division had a gap of eighty miles on its left and 120 miles on its right. "We went cautiously," he said later. "We never sent our patrols out of the range of artillery. . . . That meant they could get out to six or seven miles."

Smith so distrusted Almond's judgment that, expecting that his forces eventually would be compelled to retreat, he established along the road back to the sea three fortified base camps, about one day's march apart, loaded with supplies and well protected by infantry units. "In effect, 1st Mar Div stood in column on a line of strong points within enemy country," wrote Army historian S. L. A. Marshall in a 1951 report that was classified as secret and published only three decades later. When the Chinese force attacked, he continued, it "proceeded to impale itself upon this line of strong points." Gen. Smith would tell the historian that he felt he had "the upper hand" throughout the campaign.

The tactical layout of the strongpoints and other outposts also was distinctive, reflecting Smith's calculations about the fight he was facing. As long as his perimeters held, he figured, he could keep his artillery and mortars in operation, which meant the Marines could keep fighting even while heavily outnumbered. This led to the conclusion that it was preferable to have guaranteed close-in kills than just good chances far out. He wanted to prevent as much as possible having handfuls of Chinese soldiers slip inside his lines to suicidally attack machine gunners and artillery and mortar crews. So Smith drew his units together, sacrificing some tactically significant positions atop hills in order to establish extremely tight perimeters. "Instead of going to positions which might improve the prospect for an effective kill at long range, 1st Mar Div built its defenses so as to be certain of stopping CCF [Chinese Communist Forces] at short range," S. L. A. Marshall explained.

As for Almond, his account of what happened at Chosin frequently rings false. The evidence indicates that Almond lied in his official oral history and elsewhere, repeatedly claiming that he had all but forced Smith to build the landing strips that would prove so vital. "The airstrip was 'ordered prepared' by the X Corps and repeated supervision was necessary to insure the speed with which it was constructed," he insisted in his oral history. "The Marine division commander either was not especially in favor of it or thought little of its advantages." Almond held to this account for decades, asserting in writing to the official Army historian, Roy Appleman, in 1975, "Yes, I did order the construction of this airstrip." But Almond's assertions run contrary to both logic and the documentary record. He was urging the Marines to charge a hundred miles northward, so why would he want them to pause to establish an airfield just a short way from the sea? As Matthew Ridgway later wrote, "Almond seems to have remained optimistic, but Smith and the 1st Marine Division anticipated trouble and began to prepare for it with measures which later proved to be the salvation of a good part of his command." Also, as it happens, Smith, in a letter to his wife weeks earlier, had mentioned that among his concerns, he considered building airstrips absolutely necessary for supporting any combat operations around the Chosin area. Also, when Smith asked for the help of Army engineers to build the airstrips, X Corps staff refused his request. As Smith put it in an interview decades later, "The [X] corps at the time [early November] wasn't interested in any field up there. I told Almond that we ought to have a field that would take transport planes to bring in supplies and take out casualties. He said, 'What casualties?' That's the kind of thing you were up against. He wouldn't admit there ever would be any casualties. We took 4,500 casualties out of that field."

Smith also had problems with his own superiors in the Marine Corps. By putting his foot down and insisting on consolidating his troops and moving north carefully, he was bucking his Marine chain of command. At the beginning of November, he had met with Lt. Gen. Lemuel Shepherd, chief of Marines in the Pacific, and had expressed his concerns about Almond. Shepherd told Smith to get with the program. "I talked to him and said, 'O. P., play the game; don't get so mad with Almond, he's trying to do the right thing,'" Shepherd said later in his official Marine Corps oral history. "I kept urging Smith to push forward more rapidly, as he had the North Koreans on the run. . . . Smith, as you know, wanted everything done right by the book. And in battle you can't always do things by the book. You've got to take the initiative in combat—take chances when the opportunity to gain a victory appears probable." Shepherd believed at this time—correctly, it would turn out—that he would be the next commandant of the Marine Corps, so he might not have wanted to rock the boat and make it appear as though he could not get along with the Army. He also was friendly with Almond: "Having been a schoolmate of mine at VMI, [he] always made me welcome at his headquarters, and he treated me with the greatest courtesy." Almond's chief of staff, Maj. Gen. Clark Ruffner, also was a Virginia Military Institute (VMI) man.

But Smith saw mounting reasons to be careful. Even as Almond urged him to charge north to the Yalu, Smith and his Marines began to notice ominous signs around them. Korean children, normally eager to beg for candy, were nowhere to be seen. Deer were moving down from the ridges, as though displaced by something. When Smith learned that the Chinese had left a bridge intact over a chasm, he was alarmed, believing that it was part of an enemy plan to lure the Marines northward. History has revealed that Smith's suspicions were correct: Marshal Peng Dehuai, the top Chinese commander in the war, had told his subordinates at a campaign planning meeting on November 13, "We will employ a strategy of luring the enemy forces into our internal line and wiping them out one by one." The Chinese gambit of entrapment was exactly the right move to make against Almond, who was being overaggressive while underestimating his enemy.

Chinese commanders in North Korea had explicitly been given the mission to "encircle and exterminate the U.S. Marines around the Changin [Chosin] Reservoir." Sensing this, Smith's plan "was to slow down the advance and stall until I could pull up the 1st Marines behind us and get our outfit together. I was unable to complete that until the 27th of November."

That Marine consolidation came just in time. The same night, November 27–28, the two Marine regiments isolated at the northwestern end of the Marine line were attacked by two Chinese divisions. A third division swept in behind them to try to cut off their line of retreat to the southern end of the reservoir. A typical comment from this time in the campaign came from PFC Peter Holgrun: "We spent the night shooting gooks as they approached, one bugle-blowing wave after the next. It was pure battle. You had no idea of who was winning and who was losing." Lt. Col. Ray Davis, commanding a battalion of the 7th Marines, was surprised by the eerie sound a bugler would make when shot. "Their buglers sounding some kind of battle call would get hit right in the middle of a note, and it'd just die off," he said.

The confidence of the Marines' response to these relentless attacks was striking—and infectious. They knew they had lavish and accurate close air support available. Army soldiers and Marines at Chosin alike would recall looking down from hillsides and waving at Corsair pilots flying in the valleys below them. At night, when those planes could not operate, the Marines had artillery batteries standing by, ready to fire at prearranged coordinates in the draws and gullies in which Chinese attackers were most likely to creep toward American lines. When Smith asked Col. Lewis "Chesty" Puller how he was doing, Puller responded, with no irony, "Fine! We have enemy contact on all sides." Capt. William Hopkins reported that by the next morning five Marines had happily repeated Puller's comment to him.

Gen. Smith found out later that when the Chinese attack began, Gen. Omar Bradley, then the chairman of the Joint Chiefs, concluded that the Marines would suffer the same terrible fate as the Army units on the east side of the reservoir. "The Army figured we were finished up there and we wouldn't get out," Smith recalled. "I found later that General Bradley, in talking to General McGee, who was at that time on the Joint Staff, told him that the 1st Division was lost."

But there was a key difference in leadership. Unlike Faith and those around him on the eastern shore of the reservoir, the two Marine regiments fighting on the western shore and the third regiment, trying to hold open the road to the south, were led by commanders who knew how to use communications, logistics, maneuver, and fire support. Because of that, they would bring out all their wounded and most of their vehicles and artillery pieces, as well as many of the wandering Army soldiers they encountered. When their infantry attacked, it generally could count on swift and effective supporting fire from mortars, artillery, and aircraft. Both the enlisted men and their officers had stored up hundreds of small combat ruses and ploys in World War II: When the enemy makes a noisy probing attack, he probably is trying to locate your machine guns, so respond only with grenades and rifle fire if possible. When withdrawing, buy a few precious moments by building a fire and throwing in some bullets as you depart, which as they cook off could make the enemy believe the abandoned position is still being contested. In icy weather, have soldiers and medics tuck morphine syrettes inside their mouths so the painkiller will not be frozen when it's urgently needed.

There was a hardness in the Marines. The 7th Marines' Fox Company had been left atop a hill in a key pass to try to keep the road back to the southern end of the reservoir open. Resupplied by air, Fox Company fought for five days, finally operating from behind improvised barricades that included stacks of frozen Chinese corpses. "Word had been passed to kill all enemy wounded," recalled Fox's PFC Ernest Gonzalez. It was so icy in the cutting

wind of the pass, recalled another member of the company, PFC
Robert Ezell, that one morning, when warm milk was poured over
his cereal, by the time he sat down on a stump to eat, the milk
had frozen. Another Marine, Cpl. Robert Kelly, was so cold that
he did not notice he'd been hit by rifle fire in the right foot, a fact
he discovered only after the battle, when a medic noticed his limp
and sat him down to examine his foot. The medic looked up at
him and began laughing, saying, "You dumb asshole, you're shot."

The key to getting the two Marine regiments from their outposts on the west side of the reservoir down to the junction at
Hagaru, where Smith and supplies were waiting, was to break
through the Chinese roadblocks and get the road open. Two
attempts were made to clear the road directly; both failed. The
regimental commanders, Lt. Col. Raymond Murray of the 5th
Marines and Col. Homer Litzenberg of the 7th Marines, recognized that a radically different approach was needed.

In what might have been the crucial tactical moment of the
entire campaign, Murray and Litzenberg sent Lt. Col. Ray Davis
to lead his 1st Battalion of the 7th Marines overland through
enemy-held territory. The temperature was twenty-four degrees
below zero, according to reports from artillery units in the valley.
Few movements are as physically draining as going up and down
hills covered with snow, but Davis's battalion marched eight miles
through waist-high drifts and over three frozen ridges. In steeper
sections, Davis said, "we had to climb on our hands and knees,
hold on to roots and twigs to keep from sliding back down." At
times the Marines were so near Chinese troops that "we could
smell the garlic and hear them talking," recalled Sgt. Charles
McKellar.

The weather was a physical threat but also a tactical ally. The
snapping wind covered the sounds of hundreds of heavily laden
men moving and climbing in the snow, and encouraged enemy

soldiers to keep their ears well covered. It was too cold, and the men were too fatigued, to allow any stops, so the column moved almost continuously for twenty-four hours, then collided with the rear of the enemy along the road, ambushing the would-be Chinese ambushers and relieving the beleaguered Fox Company. When Lt. Col. Davis's battalion arrived, it saw some 450 Chinese corpses splayed out around the company's perimeter. Over the course of six days, Fox had suffered 26 killed, 89 wounded, and 3 missing, out of about 220 Marines in the reinforced company. The dead were stacked outside Fox Company's aid station, recalled McKellar, "probably twenty feet high," topped by the pilot of a helicopter downed that morning, still in his leather flight jacket. "That sight is burned into my brain," he said. All of Fox's survivors had suffered either frostbite or dysentery. Davis and Fox's commander, Capt. William Barber, would both receive the Medal of Honor. (A total of fourteen Marines in the Chosin campaign would receive that highest of American military honors.) Davis's battalion then moved down and held open the pass until the Marine column could move southward through it.

Over four days and three nights, this epic march and attack enabled the 5th and 7th Marines to push the fourteen miles back down the left arm of the *Y* to Hagaru, fighting Chinese attackers most of the time and the cold always. There were seven Chinese roadblocks along the way that needed to be attacked and cleared. Moving slowly and carefully, the two regiments brought with them all fifteen hundred of their wounded—six hundred of them in stretcher cases—as well as their dead. "The dead were stacked in trucks like so many cords of wood," recalled PFC Doug Michaud of the 5th Marines. "When they ran out of truck-bed space, they laid the dead on fenders, across hoods, tied on the barrels of artillery pieces. God, there were a lot of them." Patrick Roe, an intelligence officer for the rearguard battalion, wrote later, "No one ever doubted the troops from Yudam-ni would make it, but there was always a question of how many would."

Smith and his chief of operations, Col. Alpha Bowser, were in a tent at Hagaru one night, working on the issue of how to replace a blown bridge on their line of retreat, when they heard an unfamiliar noise, one of human voices gradually growing louder. Bowser went outside to look and found hundreds of Marines marching into camp from the northwestern side of the reservoir, "singing in the midst of this falling snow," he said. "The place was a fairyland to look at if you could just detach yourself for a split second and look at the scenery. It was like a fairyland. . . . Beautiful, really beautiful to look at." The voices were those of the lead element of the two regiments coming into camp, singing the Marine Corps Hymn and other familiar tunes. Bowser looked at Gen. Smith and said, "Our troubles are over. We've got it made." The mood was less cheerful inside the medical tents, where arriving casualties were packed. "We had so many patients lying, sitting, and standing that we could hardly see the floor," recalled Charles Holloway Jr., a Navy surgeon attached to the 1st Marine Division. "I stacked patients in like sardines in the commandeered pyramidal tents, 25 casualties in a circle around the center stove. Their own body heat and warmth from the heater kept them from freezing until we could load them on planes."

Hagaru itself was under assault by yet another Chinese division. Smith took two days to allow the two arriving regiments to recuperate and refit, and also to fly out all the wounded and then some of the dead. (The aerial supply and evacuation effort was overseen by Air Force Maj. Gen. William Tunner, who just two years earlier had been in charge of the Berlin Airlift.) With the additional infantrymen, plus ammunition brought in by air, Smith calculated that he now had sufficient combat power to hold Hagaru indefinitely, despite being greatly outnumbered by

Chinese attackers. "I considered that the critical part of the operation had been completed," he wrote not long after the battle. "Even with two depleted RCTs [regimental combat teams] I felt confident we could fight our way to Koto-ri where we would gain additional strength." But the newly arrived regiments were hardly put on a regime of rest for their two days at Hagaru. PFC Fred Allen of the 5th Marines remembered being put into the Hagaru line upon arrival and told to "dig in and be prepared." At midnight, an illumination flare launched high overhead revealed a memorable sight: "It looked like half of China was coming down that valley."

Elements of six Chinese divisions stood along the sole road leading from the junction of the *Y* south to the sea. On December 6, Smith began the march of his ten thousand Marines to the coast. It was planned even more carefully than an attack, with Marines moving along the flanking ridgelines to protect the column. There were a thousand trucks, tanks, and other vehicles in the column, but by Smith's order, only drivers, radiomen, medics, and the wounded were allowed to ride. Everyone else would walk, the better to stay warm and to ward off enemy attacks. "This was a very powerful force," Smith later wrote. "It was well-supplied with ammunition, fuel, and rations; was powerfully supported by Marine and carrier-based air; possessed organically artillery, tanks and the whole gamut of infantry weapons; and had dedicated officers and men to carry the fight to the enemy." Even so, it took thirty-nine hours and cost six hundred more casualties to fight southward eleven miles through nine more roadblocks to the next of Smith's prepared strongpoints, at Koto-ri. Gen. Almond flew over the convoy and was outraged to see it stopped at points, so he had his aircraft land at Koto-ri, where he lectured Gen. Smith on the need to move rapidly.

When the Marines marched into Koto-ri, the last of Smith's

strongpoints, PFC Paul Martin, a member of the 1st Marine Division's reconnaissance company, went looking among them for friends in the 5th and 7th Marines. "Found most of them had been killed," he said.

On the final leg, south from Koto-ri down to the coastal plain, one of Lt. Col. Davis's officers, Joseph Owen, encountered combat in a whiteout blizzard. "The tracers were weird streaks of orange that flew at us out of blinding snow clouds," he wrote. Chinese soldiers, ill-clad and at the far end of their supply lines, were found frozen to death in their foxholes. Chinese mortars were zeroed in on a point in the road where it was crossed by railroad tracks. The Navy Reserve surgeon Charles Holloway, who had been pulled from civilian life just months earlier, was frightened out of his wits but still conscious enough to observe that the fragments of exploding mortar rounds hit the icy canyon walls with a sound "like gravel being thrown against glass."

The final obstacle, where the road ran along the top of a fifteen-hundred-foot cliff face, was a deep notch in the cliff whose bridge had been almost completely destroyed by the Chinese. Without it, troops could walk out, but Smith's fourteen hundred vehicles (he had picked up four hundred more at Koto-ri) were stuck—and on them lay the truck-bound wounded. "To leave them was unthinkable," said Lt. William Davis of the 7th Marines. The division engineer, Lt. Col. John Partridge, came up with a novel way to address the problem: Drop bridge sections by air.

Partridge is one of the unacknowledged heroes of Chosin, having already overseen the emergency construction of the northern airstrip that permitted the evacuation of more than four thousand casualties. The end of that runway was only three hundred yards from the base perimeter, and the engineers occasionally had to put down their construction tools and pick up weapons to help repel attackers. But Smith was skeptical of the unprecedented plan for the bridge and questioned Partridge closely about it. "He was kind of a grouchy guy," Smith recalled of his engineer. "He admitted that the Air Force had never dropped Treadway bridge sections." Smith pressed him, asking how he knew it would work, whether test drops had been conducted, what would happen if some sections were damaged while being parachuted in, and whether there was a backup plan. Finally Partridge tired of the questions and exclaimed, "I got you across the Han River. I got you the airfield. And I'll get you a bridge." Smith laughed and told him to proceed. The bridge project worked, and the Marines were able to move out of the mountains. Surprisingly, despite his heroic efforts and Smith's support, Partridge would not be promoted beyond lieutenant colonel.

Evenness under extreme strain is a vital leadership skill, one that both George Marshall and O. P. Smith appreciated, and that Lt. Col. Ray Davis demonstrated for weeks during the Chosin campaign. An officer in his 1st Battalion of the 7th Marines recalled Davis raising his voice just once during the campaign, when he was informed that one of his companies had been pushed off a hill. Near the end of the retreat, Cpl. Ray Pearl heard a voice in the frozen darkness. It was Davis. "Is that you, Pearl?" he asked.

"How you been, Colonel?" Pearl responded.

"No complaints. How's things with you?" said Davis.

"Fine, sir. Just fine."

"That's good. . . . Take care, Pearl."

It was the most ordinary of exchanges, made memorable because it occurred in the most stressful of circumstances. When Davis reached the sea at the conclusion of the retreat, he was surprised at how hungry he was, eating first "five or six of these great large Tootsie Rolls" and then "something like 17 or 18 pancakes in two hours." One of Davis's Marines, Charles McKellar, reported that when he landed at Inchon he had weighed 170 pounds, but when he left Chosin he was down to 120.

Gen. Smith, vastly outnumbered, had mauled the Chinese divisions—at least nine of them, and perhaps even twelve—arrayed against his one division. Afterward, he wrote to the commandant of the Marines that his men "came down off the mountain bearded, footsore, and physically exhausted, but their spirits were high. They were still a fighting division."

Smith's pride was justified. According to Russell Spurr's groundbreaking history of Chinese involvement in the war, *Enter the Dragon*, after the Chosin battles, the Chinese commander in Korea, Marshal Peng Dehuai, a coal miner turned guerrilla from Hunan Province and a veteran of the Long March of 1934–35, flew to Beijing. There he confronted Chairman Mao Zedong, telling him bluntly that the forces given him were unequipped, untrained, and undersupplied. As a result, he said, the attack on the Marines had been a disaster. (Twenty-three years later, during the last phases of Mao's Cultural Revolution, Peng would be repeatedly beaten by Red Guards in a series of more than 130 interrogations and also paraded with a humiliating placard hung around his neck, before he succumbed to cancer.) The Chinese divisions that attacked the Marines at Chosin suffered twenty-five thousand dead, twelve thousand more wounded, and tens of thousands of frostbite cases. These divisions were withdrawn from fighting until March of the following year.

Nonetheless, the campaign was a strategic victory for the Chinese. They had taken on the Americans, the world's leading military power, and, fielding an illiterate, unmechanized peasant army, had pushed them out of northern Korea. And they had done it against one of America's most prominent generals, Douglas MacArthur, the conqueror of Japan. "Communist China—until then considered to be a rogue regime of doubtful legitimacy—

had become a power with which to be reckoned," concluded Patrick Roe, a Marine intelligence officer at Chosin.

Gen. Ridgway admired O. P. Smith's performance at Chosin. "If it wasn't for his tremendous leadership, we would have lost the bulk of that division up north. His leadership was the principal reason it came out the way it did. He was a great division commander." When Smith retired, S. L. A. Marshall, the Army historian, went even further, calling his Chosin performance "perhaps the most brilliant divisional feat of arms in the national history." It is difficult to overstate what he achieved. Had he simply followed orders and charged toward the Yalu, he might well have lost more than ten thousand Marines, which would have been perhaps the greatest military disaster in the nation's history. If the 1st Marine Division had been wiped out, it would have been a triumph for Communism, with consequences for the Korean War and the larger Cold War that are incalculable. The United States might have withdrawn from the peninsula and into isolationism, or it might have escalated and used nuclear weapons in Korea. Neither prospect is appealing.

Surprisingly, Smith is not much remembered or honored in today's Corps. Ask a Marine who commanded at Chosin, and he is likely to say Chesty Puller or perhaps, even more mistakenly, Gen. H. M. Smith, the "Howlin' Mad" officer of World War II fame. A major reason for the relative obscurity of Gen. O. P. Smith likely is the friction between him and Gen. Shepherd, his immediate superior in the Marine Corps during the Chosin campaign, which probably is why he was never invited to the Marine base at Quantico, Virginia, to teach fellow officers about the campaign. "Regimental commanders spoke, company commanders spoke—everyone spoke but O. P. Smith," wrote his granddaughter, with evident bitterness.

This neglect continues even now. The exhibit on the Chosin

campaign at the big new Marine Corps museum near the Quantico base is magnificent. Especially chilling is the room-size re-creation of Fox Company's hilltop stand, with its depiction of tracer fire arcing across the night as mortarmen run low on shells and the dead are covered by snow. "Chosin remains a touchstone of Marine Corps history," a nearby sign states. Yet the exhibit treats O. P. Smith as an afterthought, sharing a small display case in a corner with Chesty Puller. The only Marine general from the Korean War honored with a prominent yellow-on-red biographical plaque, oddly enough, is Gerald Thomas, who succeeded O. P. Smith as commander of the 1st Marine Division in Korea.

Upon retiring, Smith and his wife, having never owned a house, at first found it difficult to obtain a mortgage, but eventually they were able to buy a small rambler not far from Stanford University, in Los Altos, California. There he gardened in the combat boots he had worn at Chosin. He died on Christmas Day of 1977.

Why the difference in leadership?

Years later, Faris Kirkland, an Army veteran of Korea turned academic historian, wrote a careful analysis of the Chosin campaign that is heartbreaking in its conclusions. Sifting the historical records and mulling the different outcomes of the Marine and Army units, he found little difference between the 13,500 Marines and the 4,500 Army troops in the performance of their enlisted men and junior officers. But in their more senior officers— majors, lieutenant colonels, colonels, and generals—he detected crucial distinctions. "Marine commanders at Chosin demonstrated knowledge of tasks, obstacles and the means to overcome them," Kirkland wrote. "Army commanders showed dash, bravery and hope; but little understanding of such matters as communications, reconnaissance, fire support and logistics."

The key factor, he concluded, was the combat experience of

those in command. As Kirkland noted, the officer officially designated as the Army's hero of the battle, Lt. Col. Faith, who took
over after the regimental commander was killed, had no combat
experience, nor even much formal schooling in his profession.
Rather, Faith, the son of an Army general, had been plucked
directly from Officer Candidate School during World War II to
become an aide to Matthew Ridgway. He never attended the
Infantry Advanced Course for officers or the Command and General Staff College. Eight years after OCS, leading a beleaguered
regimental combat team in Korea, he knew how to look like a
commander. "On the battlefield, Faith was a clone of Ridgway:
intense, fearless, relentlessly aggressive, and unforgiving of error
or caution," wrote the historian Clay Blair. Yet for all that, Kirkland noted, Faith did not really know how to command:

> [He] had not mastered the fundamentals of military operations
> in the field. He ordered all the mortars and howitzers destroyed.
> He made no arrangements for communications within or between
> the infantry forces or the truck column. He did not ask Marine
> aviators, who had provided close support throughout the period
> 27 November–1 December, for information about the condition
> of the route he was to traverse or the dispositions of the enemy;
> neither did he send out patrols. He assigned no intermediate
> objectives and made no plan for spending one or more nights on
> the road. At least one company of 3-31 Infantry did not know
> there was going to be a breakout until leaders saw a line of trucks
> driving out of the perimeter. The commander of the artillery
> battalion asserted that he never had oral, telephonic or radio
> contact with Faith from the time he assumed command until the
> 31st RCT was annihilated.

The list goes on. "There is no evidence that any effort was
made by Faith . . . to establish communications when the means

were at hand to do so through the daily radio contact of the TACP [tactical air control party] with pilots overhead," noted Roy Appleman, formerly an official Army historian. "It apparently never dawned on Faith or his principal staff officers that this means of establishing communications with the 1st Marine Division at Hagaru-ri, and through it with the 7th Infantry Division and X Corps, was available."

Faith, posthumously awarded the Medal of Honor, was "both the beneficiary and the victim of officer personnel policies," concluded Kirkland. The histories of the Chosin fight tend to take their cue from the official accounts compiled by Army historians. As Kirkland noted, the lead Army historian, Appleman, chose not to write anything critical of Faith. "About Faith, I have not placed in the [manuscript for the book *East of Chosin*] any unfavorable views that may have been uttered to me by others—only the favorable," Appleman wrote in a letter. "I owe his memory and personal valor that much. I do not know if *anyone* could have done better in the exact circumstances. I do believe he overlooked some possibilities open to him while he was at the inlet. This is the extent of my criticism. I place far greater blame on higher command for the result."

Sadly, Kirkland noted, Faith's lack of combat experience would not have made him stand out in the Army units sent to Korea that year: "Of the six generals initially assigned to command divisions in Korea, four had not held a combat command at any level during the Second World War." Had the commanders above him been more seasoned in combat, they might have been better prepared to assist Faith, especially with communications and support. "The communications breakdown . . . bordered on command criminal negligence," concluded historian Shelby Stanton. Maj. Gen. David Barr, Faith's commander in the 7th Division, had been a chief of staff for Gen. Jacob Devers in the earlier war.

Likewise, Kirkland observed, of the eighteen colonels commanding infantry regiments in the initial phase of the Korean War, fifteen had never before led units in combat.

In reading histories of the Korean War, when new regimental and division commanders are discussed, it is striking how often they are introduced with phrases such as "had not previously led troops in combat." Instead they had spent World War II in the Pentagon war-planning division, or had trained troops, or had been a staff planner in the Mediterranean Theater, or had been a corps chief of staff. This extended even to the chief of staff for Gen. Almond, Clark Ruffner, who had spent World War II as the chief of staff for his father-in-law, Gen. Robert "Nelly" Richardson, who oversaw Army troop training in the Pacific. In Korea, the Marines still had a bad taste in their mouth from Richardson, who had played a major role in the Army's querulous response to the firing of Army Gen. Ralph Smith by Marine Gen. H. M. Smith during the Battle of Saipan, in 1944.

Trying to be fair to officers can be lethal to the soldiers they lead on the battlefield. The Army was using the Korean War to give the staff officers of the earlier war "their chance" to command in combat—with disastrous results. Well before Chosin, the Army had recognized that it had a problem with inexperienced combat leadership in the war. In August 1950, the Army sent a team of expert colonels and lieutenant colonels to Korea. They produced a thick report that, among other things, warned that the Army's approach to filling command slots with inexperienced officers "has often resulted in poor leadership, especially at the regimental and lower levels. The career program has been detrimental to combat efficiency." Some commanders were found to lack "the ability to command under adverse conditions, resulting in a defeatist attitude." Gen. Mark Clark, then commander of Army Field Forces, sent the report to Gen. J. Lawton Collins, the

Army chief of staff, along with a "Dear Joe" cover letter explaining that "the detrimental effect of the [officers'] career program on combat efficiency is an inescapable corollary of the program as a whole which seeks, by variations in assignment, to produce well-rounded and versatile officers." In response to complaints about the quality of officership, the Army tried to change its approach. In February 1952, it instituted a new program to send better officers, especially colonels, to Korea. The focus of the program was to find and deploy "officers considered by their seniors to be potential high-level commanders, but who had not had a combat command during World War II."

This supposed "solution," which actually intensified the leadership problem, is inexplicable until one remembers that the Army of this era was focused on the Soviet threat. If World War III came, the Army's plan was to field eighty or more divisions, so it was desirable to have on hand as many seasoned officers as possible to lead regiments and divisions in combat. The United States had to keep its eye on the Red Army in Central Europe, and it feared that Korea, a secondary theater, might be a Communist diversion intended to weaken it in Europe. Even so, the approach the Army took meant that for the rest of the Korean War, complaints about the character and competence of Army officers would be rampant.

The Marine Corps, by contrast, was dealing with the more immediate threat of doubts in Washington about whether the Corps should even continue to exist, so it had an incentive to send its best commanders to Korea. After the initial emergency of the war, when it sent anyone it could find, the Marines tried to stick to their practice of requiring anyone commanding a unit to have led the next-lower level of unit in combat. Thus, a colonel leading a regiment had to have overseen a battalion that fought, and a battalion commander needed to have done so with a company. O. P. Smith had been an assistant division commander on Peleliu.

The officers leading his regiments were some of the best the Corps has ever had. Col. Homer Litzenberg, who had a reputation for crankiness with both superiors and subordinates, had not only commanded in the Pacific War—he had been relieved there. Despite that, Smith said later, "I gave him the 7th Regiment. He was difficult to handle but he did a good job with the 7th. I had no complaint. I gave him good fitness reports, and he made brigadier general. And he made major general, but he could not get along. They tried him out at Lejeune and pulled him out, tried him out at Parris Island, and pulled him out—he was just too tough on his subordinates."

Lt. Col. Raymond Murray, commanding officer of the 5th Marines, had fought at Guadalcanal. He then received command of a battalion after Col. Lewis "Chesty" Puller, the regimental commander, not only relieved his predecessor but busted that officer from lieutenant colonel to lieutenant. At Guadalcanal, Ray Davis sometimes had the mission of extinguishing grass fires touched off by Japanese strafing before the flames ignited bombs stored there. "I spent many a moment standing atop a 500-pound bomb beating out a fire around it," he would recall. "It's a good thing they weren't fused, but still it was a hairy way to spend an afternoon." At the age of twenty-eight, Davis led a battalion at Tarawa and then at Saipan, which he considered the toughest fight he had ever faced; he was seriously wounded there and received a Navy Cross to join his two Silver Stars. Chesty Puller, "perhaps the most famous Marine of all time," who had received an extraordinary four Navy Crosses even before the Korean War, was alongside Davis at Chosin, still commanding a regiment. As a battalion commander at Guadalcanal, Puller had held off the Japanese at Henderson Field, despite being shot twice and being hit by three pieces of shrapnel. Smith's operations chief, Col. Alpha Bowser, had commanded an artillery battalion on Iwo Jima. His chief engineer, Lt. Col. John Partridge, was a veteran of Saipan, Tinian, and Iwo Jima. Capt. William Barber, who received the Medal of Honor for his leadership of the encircled Fox Company, had led a platoon at Iwo Jima.

One would expect that it must have given the Army pause to receive such a devastating analysis, one that clearly argued that its officer management policies had led to disaster in the Korean War. But Kirkland said that the Army, even decades after the event, chose to ignore him. He said he offered his article to *Parameters,* the journal of the Army War College, for which he had written before, but was turned down. Instead he published it in *Armed Forces & Society,* an obscure academic journal specializing in military sociology.

MacArthur's reaction to the disasters of the Gauntlet and Chosin Reservoir, which resulted directly from his impulse to drive the Communists from Korea and from his misapprehension of Chinese intent and capabilities, was typical of his behavior, though it was still surprising. He had just taken an amazing gamble. In October 1950, the United States had a total of twelve divisions globally. Seven of those were under MacArthur's control in Korea, and he sent them, as one historian put it, "in an uncoordinated rush toward the border of a hostile nation that possessed an army of more than 5,000,000 in 253 divisions. . . . All this was done in the face of explicit Chinese warnings not to do so and in defiance of orders from the Joint Chiefs of Staff." MacArthur responded to his military setback by launching a series of blistering public attacks on the Truman Administration. Most notably, he told *U.S. News & World Report* that he had been handicapped by Washington's limits on him, "without precedent in military history," and accused Western leaders of being "somewhat selfish" and "short-sighted."

Lt. Gen. Matthew Ridgway, the Army's G-3, or deputy chief for operations, and others were puzzled about why MacArthur was being allowed to talk like that. After a meeting of the Joint Chiefs of Staff during the Chosin battles, Ridgway approached the Air Force chief, Hoyt Vandenberg. He asked why the Joint Chiefs did not just issue direct orders to MacArthur telling him what to do. "What good would that do?" Gen. Vandenberg responded, shaking his head. "He wouldn't obey orders. What can we do?"

Ridgway was exasperated by such talk. He knew what he would do. "You can relieve any commander who won't obey orders, can't you?" Vandenberg's astonished reaction to this suggestion, he remembered, was such that "his lips parted and he looked at me with an expression both puzzled and amazed."

Privately, Ridgway blamed MacArthur for the debacle at Chosin. "I regard General MacArthur's insistence on retaining control from Tokyo, 700 miles from the battle areas, as unwarranted and unsound," he wrote years later. "In my opinion, this was largely responsible for the heavy casualties and the near disaster which followed." He also said that Army schools "could well choose this operation as a perfect example of how not to plan and conduct a campaign."

This was the general to whom Ridgway would report just a few weeks later.

CHAPTER 12
Ridgway turns the war around

Not long after the end of the Chosin retreat, on the morning of December 23, 1951, in Korea, Lt. Gen. Walton Walker, the overall ground commander in Korea, notorious for ordering his driver to speed, had his jeep doing forty miles per hour on a road glazed with ice as they headed north from Seoul toward the nearby town of Uijeongbu. His driver was trying to pass a convoy cautiously moving at ten miles an hour when the jeep slammed into the back of a South Korean weapons truck, throwing Walker from the jeep and killing him. On the same day, Ridgway was ordered to replace him. There long have been rumors that one reason the succession could occur so quickly was that MacArthur had been on the verge of firing Walker and already had lined up a replacement. No hard evidence of this has ever surfaced, but there was enough talk of it that Korea veteran T. R. Fehrenbach, in his history of the ground war there, remembered that "for days a whisper had run through command channels of the Eighth Army that Walker was through."

In Washington, on the other side of the world, it was still the evening of December 22. Ridgway was sipping a highball at a pre-Christmas cocktail party when he got word that he was to take command in the war. He flew out of Washington the next night. The approach he would take in his first hours, days, and weeks in command was perhaps as fine a performance as any by an American general in the twentieth century. Had it occurred in World War II, the Ridgway takeover likely would be immortalized in film. But it happened in the small, divisive, unpopular Korean War and so, unfortunately, has largely been forgotten.

Ridgway had enjoyed maybe the most satisfying career of his generation of Army officers. He had worked under MacArthur at West Point, where he stood out for his organizational skills and in fact turned down a job offer from the New York Giants, who in the early 1920s stood atop the baseball world, just as the Yankees would later. But he was closer to Marshall, whom he first met in 1919, than he ever was to MacArthur. Ridgway and Marshall served together several times—in the 15th Infantry Regiment in China in 1925–26, at Fort Benning's Infantry School in 1929–30, and in Chicago in 1933–36. At the Infantry School, Ridgway remembered, Marshall had been a strong and constant presence:

> There was hardly a tactical exercise, during the time that I attended that course, that he did not personally attend. . . . He put great emphasis on simplifying our very complicated field orders at that time. They had grown up in the staff procedures during World War I, so that it took you hours to really digest an attack order, or something. He put great insistence on stripping that thing down to essentials. He put great emphasis on an officer being able to stand up and dictate an order orally, and somebody just take down notes.

Marshall was staying at Maj. Ridgway's house at the Presidio, in San Francisco, in 1939 at about the time he was notified that he had been selected to be the next chief of staff of the Army, back when that job was far more significant than it is today. That same year, Marshall and Ridgway carried out their special mission in South America to secure military transit rights through Brazil. Years later, after commanding in the Korean War and then being Army chief of staff, Ridgway would dedicate his book *The Korean War* to Marshall.

In World War II, Ridgway enjoyed a meteoric rise. He began the war as a colonel who prepared and delivered Marshall's morning briefing, summarizing developments in the war over the previous twenty-four hours. Copies of the briefing also were delivered to Secretary of War Stimson and President Roosevelt. From there he went on to be assistant commander of the 82nd Airborne Division, then to command that division in Sicily and Normandy, and finally he commanded the airborne corps at the Battle of the Bulge and in Germany.

In the crucible of Normandy, Ridgway's division, with just twelve battalions, lost fourteen battalion commanders in four weeks. He found combat in the Bulge later that year to be even tougher. "No one knew where anyone else was," he said. "Just sheer luck that I wasn't picked up by the Germans."

One of the hard lessons he took away from that war was that

> the best of troops will fail if the strain is big enough. . . . I have commanded in World War II the finest troops the U.S. had. . . . I have seen individuals break in battle, and I have seen units perform miserably. The latter was always because of poor leadership. But sometimes, failure of the individual was not due to leadership. It just gets to the point where a man can't take it anymore—that's all. . . . I saw men in Normandy in a few cases where the strain was too damn much for them. Casualties were

very, very heavy, men were falling all around them, and they just walked off crying. Always be easy on a man like that. Help him get back to the rear. Nine times out of 10 he will come out of it all right. Sometimes he can be ruined for life, though.

This was a sharp contrast to the attitude Patton had shown in World War II. Ridgway was indeed different from Patton and MacArthur—a younger man, with a more modern approach to leadership and a strong democratic streak. Once, explaining why he did not like to speak to soldiers from stages or platforms, he said, "I always disliked standing above people. I'm no better than they are. In rank, yes; in experience, yes; but not as a man. . . . When reviewing troops I would never permit them to raise a reviewing stand. I always stood there on the field, six to eight feet from the right flank of the unit going by. Then I could look into the eyes of the men going by. Looking into their eyes tells you something—and it tells them something, too." Knowing how to read the mood of soldiers is also part of being a general, and Ridgway would give a memorable display of that skill during his first days in Korea that winter of 1950–51.

Ridgway's actions in the weeks after his arrival were a model of how to revitalize the spirit and reverse the fortunes of a sagging military force. He left Washington determined to switch the Americans in Korea to the offensive. He stopped in Tokyo to see MacArthur, his first problem to defuse. He did not trust the aging commander, nor did he think that MacArthur had handled the war well. He also knew that MacArthur had considered relieving Walker. "Everybody in life has their fallibilities and MacArthur had them to an extraordinary extent, which apparently he concealed from the public," Ridgway said later. "I was well aware when I reported to General MacArthur on the day after Christmas of 1950 that I was on dangerous ground. I'd have to be very careful. I knew his temperament. I knew there would be no hesitancy in relieving me if I did something he disliked. But he couldn't have been more generous."

Ridgway would have to be especially careful not to get caught in the crossfire between Gen. MacArthur and President Truman. Ridgway thought MacArthur had failed in his duty to Truman, writing later that "beginning in 1950, the presidential authority was treated with disrespect, insidiously at first, then with increasing boldness, and finally with flagrant, if not with deliberate disobedience of orders." Unlike MacArthur, Ridgway believed Truman was pursuing an understandable and explainable strategy in the war:

> I thought the president had made it unmistakably clear that his primary concern was not to be responsible for initiating World War III. . . . His instructions to MacArthur were categoric, and disregarded in most cases, that he did not want to start World War III. MacArthur had been pressing to attack China, to bring [Nationalist] Chinese troops onto the Korean Peninsula, and to impose a blockade of the Chinese coast.

After meeting with MacArthur in Tokyo, Ridgway flew to Korea. That afternoon, he released a letter to his troops. "You will have my utmost," he vowed. "I shall expect yours."

The next morning, he set out to study the rugged terrain on which he would fight. He climbed into a B-17 bomber, crawled along its catwalk across the bomb bay and into the bombardier's compartment, and ordered the pilot to fly the old four-engined warplane over the hills and rivers of central Korea at an altitude of just three thousand feet. Ridgway sat in the Plexiglas-enclosed nose with a map unfolded across his lap and looked down. "The granite peaks rose to six thousand feet, the ridges were knife-edged, the slopes steep, and the narrow valleys twisted and turned like snakes," he recalled. "The roads were trails, and the lower hills were covered with shrub oaks and stunted pines, fine cover for a single soldier who knew how to conceal himself. It was guerrilla country."

After he landed, Ridgway took care of politics, visiting South Korean president Syngman Rhee for thirteen minutes and assuring him that the Americans would not abandon him. "I intend to stay," he told Rhee. At that point, he said, the Korean leader's "impassive face broke into a broad smile. He took my hand in both of his."

Next, and most important, he headed out to spend three days visiting his battlefield commanders and assessing their states of mind, asking himself each time, "Is he confident, does he know what he is doing, does he know the terrain in his area?" These sessions proved even more worrisome to him than did the rugged landscape. He was taken aback to find out that some generals were not moving around the front lines of their assigned sectors. "These division commanders did not know the terrain," he concluded. Seeing some prominent mountains, he asked one of the commanders their names. "He did not know them. He didn't even know the name of the river that ran through his sector. I asked what about that ground over there—is that feasible for armor? Well, he did not know that either." It was a worrisome finding for Ridgway. Lower echelons were equally dismaying. He found battalion commanders "roadbound," neglecting the surrounding ridges and also failing to cooperate with adjacent units. "Your infantry predecessors would roll over in their graves the way you have been conducting operations here," Ridgway told one officer. His next step was to see as many enlisted soldiers as possible. This also was a surprise to him. "The troops were confused—they had been badly handled tactically, logistically. . . . They didn't know just what was going on."

When Ridgway visited the front lines, the lack of confidence was palpable throughout the ranks. "I could sense it the moment I came into a command post. I could read it in their eyes, in their walk. I could read it in the faces of their leaders, from sergeants right up to the top. They were unresponsive, reluctant to talk. I had to drag information out of them. There was a complete absence of that alertness, that aggressiveness, that you find in troops whose spirit is high." His overall conclusion: "The consensus from private to general was, 'Let's get the hell out.' That was the prevalent spirit through the Eighth Army. . . . The only way to go was up. It couldn't get worse." Lt. Col. Walter Winton, his aide, later succinctly summarized the war situation as "Weather terrible, Chinese ferocious, morale stinko."

Ridgway also was troubled to find that the Eighth Army's headquarters was located in a warm, comfortable, well-lit building some 180 miles south of the front lines. It was Fredendall in North Africa all over again. He found the Eighth Army's staff "very mediocre." He ordered the headquarters moved northward, far closer to the front, and there made his office out of two eight-by-twelve tents, where he would sit for hours to study a giant relief map of the Korean Peninsula. At his first meeting with Marine Gen. O. P. Smith, the Chosin commander, Smith informed him that the Marines did not want to serve under Almond anymore. "I told him frankly that we had been put out on a limb and we'd gotten ourselves off that limb, that we'd lost some confidence in higher command," Smith recalled. It was a damning comment—Smith was effectively firing his superiors. A sympathetic Ridgway promised that he would do his best to see that the Marine division would not again be placed under Almond's command.

Ridgway dropped down several echelons of command to both encourage and assess commanders below the level of general officers. He told them to begin patrolling vigorously, at first in small groups and then in company and battalion size. This was designed to boost both their confidence and their knowledge of the terrain. "Ridgway was such a breath of fresh air," recalled one of the best regimental commanders, Col. John Michaelis. "Spit and fire. I'll never forget. He came to my CP in a jeep, grenades hung on his shoulder harness, brisk-walking, beetle-eyed, looking right at you." Ridgway told Michaelis that if his regiment could attack and hold the ground, he would be reinforced by a division in twenty hours, and by a full corps a day after that. All Ridgway was saying was that success would be recognized and strongly supported, but it was not the message that Michaelis had been hearing from his previous commanders.

The forty-eight-hour tour of the battlefield led Ridgway to two conclusions. First, despite his aggressive intentions, it was just not the time to launch a major attack. "What was perfectly, clearly apparent was that this army was in no condition for a major offensive action," he recalled. Second, he would need some new commanders. "The leadership I found in many instances sadly lacking, and I said so out loud. The unwillingness of the army to forgo certain creature comforts, its timidity about getting off the scanty roads, its reluctance to move without radio and telephone contact, and its lack of imagination in dealing with a foe whom they soon outmatched in firepower and dominated in the air and surrounding seas—these were not the fault of the GI but of the policymakers at the top." But, he thought, "you can't relieve them right away. . . . You'd tear the whole thing apart." Instead, "little by little, we ease them out."

The lively correspondence that followed between Ridgway and Army chief of staff Gen. J. Lawton Collins is fascinating to read even now, six decades later. "Everything is going fine," Ridgway wrote in one of his first messages, on January 3, 1951. "We shall be in for some difficult days but I am completely confident of the ability of the Eighth Army to accomplish every mission assigned."

Not just the substance but the style of his language was a world away from MacArthur's pompous, Latinate, and overwrought messages.

Five days later, Ridgway dropped the other shoe in a long letter to Collins warning that both he and Collins would need to "be ruthless with our general officers if they fail to measure up." He explained, in an underlined sentence, that he was concerned by "a lack of aggressiveness among some Corps and Division commanders." In a separate message sent the same day, he also asked Collins to send him three "young, vigorous, mentally flexible Brigadiers already marked for high command by reason of demonstrated leadership." Ridgway already was contemplating replacing some division commanders. In fact, that was item six on his agenda for a meeting with his senior commanders the same day. In a meeting a few days later, he stated flatly to MacArthur's new chief of staff, Maj. Gen. Doyle Hickey: "Can't execute my future plans with present leaders." He repeated that phrase in a follow-up memorandum to Collins.

Ridgway's reliefs

Ridgway's first sacking in Korea became notorious, probably intentionally so. Ridgway was being briefed by Col. John Jeter, the operations chief (or G-3) of I Corps. He grew uneasy when Jeter dwelled on a series of defensive positions the corps planned to take as it fell back. "What are your attack plans?" the general asked.

There were none. "Sir, we are withdrawing," Jeter said.

"You are relieved," Ridgway snapped, or so went the story that rocketed around the Army in Korea. In fact, Ridgway did not say exactly that—he acted more formally, going through channels— but the effect was the same: Jeter was ousted, and word got out, probably as Ridgway intended. (This was at least the second snap relief of Jeter's career: Late in World War II, he had been fired as a regimental commander by Maj. Gen. Donald Stroh, then commander of the 8th Infantry Division, but was given command of another regiment in another division.) Jeter was replaced by Col. Harold K. Johnson, who thirteen years later would become chief of staff of the Army—and who would react differently to a wave of firings by one division commander in Vietnam.

Ridgway was sending a message. He was preparing for a sweep of most of the Army's leadership in Korea. He was doing what Pershing had done in World War I and Marshall in World War II: conducting a housecleaning of generals. Over the following three months, he relieved one of his corps commanders (John Coulter, who was shuffled into a liaison job and retired a year later), five of his six division commanders, and fourteen of his nineteen regimental commanders.

But in Korea there was a key difference that would make Ridgway's reliefs far more difficult to carry out: He was commanding not in a world war, but rather in a small, limited, controversial "police action." The Marshall model did not work as well in such circumstances. In response to pressure from the Pentagon, he would take pains to disguise the moves as normal rotations. He did that so successfully that even today some historians insist that Ridgway did not relieve generals but simply rotated out the tired—a contention that is disproved by a review of Ridgway's correspondence at the time.

Ridgway's first relief of a general set off alarms in Washington. On January 14, Maj. Gen. Robert McClure was fired by Ridgway and Almond after just thirty-nine days in command of the 2nd Division, where he had replaced Maj. Gen. Laurence Keiser, who himself had been sacked. Two days later, Ridgway received a classified message of concern from Lt. Gen. Edward Brooks, the

Army's chief of personnel: "Press here has played up relief of McClure. With return of Barr and Church already scheduled plus possibility of Gay and Kean, Gen. [Wade Hampton "Ham"] Haislip fears if not handled most skillfully, what has appearance of wholesale relief of senior commanders, may well result in congressional investigation."

Ridgway apparently did not take the admonition to heart. In mid-February, he got a rocket from the Army vice chief of staff himself, Gen. Haislip, who warned him that the reliefs might raise too many questions in Washington's political circles. "We are still very much concerned about the proposed rapid release of officers in Korea as it may result in a Congressional investigation and a loss of all the new confidence the people are now showing," wrote Haislip, who is remembered now, if at all, for having introduced Dwight Eisenhower to Mamie Doud in 1915. "I suggest very strongly that you go slowly and think of the possible effect on us that each proposed change may cause." Collins, the Army chief, who had been an advocate of swift relief during World War II, had shifted his position and now worried about the way it would look to the public. Haislip added that Collins, in his public remarks, was being less than candid about the reliefs that had occurred so far, of the 7th Division's Barr and the 24th Division's John Church: "Thus far Joe has justified Barr's and Church's return by stating that we will take advantage of their experience in training but the more who come home the more unconvincing such an answer will be."

Ridgway was a protégé of Marshall's, but the system of generalship Marshall employed in World War II was being strained by the politics of this very different war. "Dear Ham," Ridgway wrote back apologetically. "I am disturbed lest I may have acted in deviation from your wishes in the matter of this home coming [sic] general officers."

Ultimately, Ridgway would be permitted to go forward with his planned series of reliefs—as long as he did them slowly and did not discuss them much in public. While this might have soothed Congress, the low-key approach might have made the reliefs more alarming internally than they would have been. Normally, command of a division in combat is a stepping-stone to the top jobs in the Army, but in this case, as often happened with reliefs in World War II, the removed commanders moved to training posts in the United States and thence to obscure retirements. (Of the ousted generals, Barr was sent to the Armor School at Fort Knox, Kentucky; Church to the Infantry School at Fort Benning, Georgia; and the 2nd Division's Keiser to the Infantry Replacement Center at Indiantown Gap, Pennsylvania. The 25th Division's William Kean was given command of III Corps at Camp Roberts, California, while Hobart "Hap" Gay, who had led the 1st Cavalry Division, was tucked away as the deputy commander of the Fourth Army at Fort Sam Houston, on the outskirts of San Antonio, Texas.) Despite his efforts to play down the reliefs, Ridgway was unambiguous in describing his approach to the novelist James Michener: "Try to find good men to fill the key spots. Give them full authority for individual action, but check them relentlessly to see they speed the main job. And if they don't produce, fire them." He had captured the Marshall system in a nutshell, but subsequent events would prove his comment to be more an epitaph than a prescription for it.

"Dear Matt," Collins, the Army chief of staff, wrote on May 24, 1951, in a long letter that approved the relief of John Coulter. "I expect he will elect to retire, which I hope he will do with no trace of bitterness." But he told Ridgway that if he insisted on getting rid of another corps commander, Frank "Shrimp" Milburn, Ridgway would need to find a place to park him, because there was nowhere for him in the Army back in the continental United States. "It would be very helpful if you feel Shrimp has lost some of his steam as a Corps commander, if you could use him as a Deputy Commander to Van Fleet." Ridgway also requested the removal of several South Korean commanders, including one corps commander.

Interestingly, one commander Ridgway did not seek to relieve was Almond. Almost certainly, he did not want to pick a fight with MacArthur, who had been Almond's protector. But he also liked the Army officer's aggressive streak and knew that all he needed to do was occasionally restrain the crusty Virginian: "Almond was a very able officer. Almond is one of the few commanders I've had that, instead of ever having to push at all, I would have to keep an eye on unless he, maybe in his boldness, would have jeopardized his command or executed a risky operation." Still, Ridgway said he saw how others were rubbed the wrong way by Almond, who, he once observed, "was apt to be pretty rough on other people's sensibilities, and he could be cutting and intolerant."

Ridgway's wave of reliefs in Korea in early 1951 would prove to be a fulcrum point for the U.S. Army in its history of how it handles its leaders. Ridgway was firing an entire group of generals, yet at the same time he had been told by the Pentagon to veil his moves. The Army was in an odd position, fighting what Mark Clark, always politically sensitive, would call "the most unpopular war in United States history." Truth be told, the war was not even much welcomed inside the Army. "He [Ridgway] told me he had a hell of a time getting generals to want to come to Korea," remembered Roger Cirillo, a historian of the modern U.S. Army. Also, the optics of relief are more difficult in a war that is going badly than in one in which victory is increasingly apparent, as was the case with most World War II reliefs after mid-1943. It is human nature that it is more difficult to admit to a failure when one is failing broadly.

These firings by Ridgway also came during the one-year period in which George Marshall stepped in as defense secretary. Ridgway almost certainly knew that his old mentor would approve of the reliefs. Painfully aware that his mental powers were declining, Marshall decided to step down after just one year as secretary of defense. When Dean Acheson, who knew Marshall from the State Department, argued with Marshall against his leaving, he was surprised to see a flash of irritation from the old general. Marshall then confessed to Acheson that "he had increasing difficulty in recalling proper names even when he knew the persons well. He was much humiliated by the weakness." Marshall's memory deteriorated rapidly in the ensuing years. He would die in October 1959.

In just a few short months of dynamic action, Ridgway turned the Korean War around. At the end of January 1951, the Americans for the first time not only stopped a full divisional assault by the Chinese but "virtually annihilated" the attackers. A few weeks later, the Eighth Army drove the Chinese back, taking a key airfield near Seoul. With the same number of troops that MacArthur had overseen in defeat in the fall of 1950, Ridgway turned back a Chinese offensive in the spring, with half of the fourteen Chinese divisions in Korea badly mauled and generally withdrawing north of the 38th parallel.

Strong, determined, considered leadership went a long way. When Ridgway arrived, "it was a disintegrating army," said Harold K. Johnson, a staff officer and then regimental commander in Korea who later became Army chief of staff. "It was something that was bordering on disgrace. In a matter of about six weeks Gen. Ridgway had turned a defeated army around." To be sure, not everyone was impressed with Ridgway. Allan Millett, the preeminent American historian of the Korean War, called him "as mean-spirited an American officer as ever wore stars." Ridgway, wrote Millett, "had a short temper and made snap judgments of people and operations that could not be challenged. Ridgway could be jealous, moody, hyper-competitive and harsh in public comments about his peers. He had a tendency to cut corners yet expect perfection of subordinates, and he held a Copernican view of the Army that put Matthew B. Ridgway in the center of that universe."

One thing Ridgway did not see in Korea was the Sun King of the Army, Gen. MacArthur, who remained in Japan for many weeks. "He didn't come to visit me until I got the Eighth Army turned around and started forward," Ridgway remembered.

Ridgway's performance on the battlefield also had a surprising side effect on American civil-military relations. His success suddenly deflated the standing of MacArthur, making the old general seem far less an indispensable man and much more just a troublesome blowhard. As Ridgway arrived in Korea, the Joint Chiefs of Staff were engaged in a frenetic debate with MacArthur about whether to abandon Korea in a Dunkirk-like amphibious evacuation or to start a major war with China, which appeared to be the only two alternatives under discussion. The Joint Chiefs favored the former option, instructing MacArthur at the end of 1950 to determine when to evacuate Korea. "It appears from all estimates available that the Chinese Communists possess the ability of forcing United Nations Forces out of Korea if they chose to exercise it," the Chiefs wrote. "We believe that Korea is not the place to fight a major war. . . . Since developments may force our withdrawal from Korea, it is important, particularly in view of the continued threat to Japan, to determine, in advance, our last reasonable opportunity for an orderly evacuation."

MacArthur thought it would be better to go to war against Communist China. He responded the next day with a recommendation to the Joint Chiefs that he be allowed to carry out operations to "blockade the coast of China, . . . destroy through Naval gunfire and Air bombardment China's industrial capacity to wage war," and encourage the Chinese Nationalists on Taiwan to attack the mainland. When the Chiefs rejected starting a regional war, MacArthur reverted to discussing bugging out. Gen. Collins, the Army chief of staff, would recall that as 1950 ended, MacArthur's cables were "pretty frantic." Early in the new year, MacArthur informed Maj. Gen. Maxwell Taylor, the Army's deputy chief for operations, that "it can be accepted as basic fact that, unless authority is given to strike enemy bases in Manchuria, our ground forces as presently constituted cannot with safety attempt major operations in North Korea."

Yet even as MacArthur was writing that letter, Ridgway was proving its assertion wrong. That basic fact, combined with MacArthur's increasing belligerence in his policy recommendations to Washington, was altering the political balance of power between MacArthur and Truman.

CHAPTER 13
MacArthur's last stand

By January 1951, Gen. MacArthur had become, as Secretary of State Dean Acheson succinctly put it in his memoirs, "incurably recalcitrant and basically disloyal to the purposes of his Commander in Chief." MacArthur dug into an all-or-nothing position against his superiors in Washington, refusing to permit any middle ground. Whatever their question, his answer was: *Either we go to war with China or American forces in Korea will be destroyed.* Anyone disagreeing was deemed an appeaser, a defeatist, or worse. Ridgway, by contrast, less flamboyantly but demonstrating more military effectiveness, decided to advance to the Han River, in central Korea, and then dig in and use his advantage in firepower to destroy Chinese forces as they attacked him.

During this period, with Ridgway taking the reins in Korea, MacArthur increasingly became a figurehead, bypassed and ignored as much as possible by Washington. In early 1951, he repeatedly violated Truman's executive order of the previous December to stop issuing independent policy statements. No one but MacArthur knew why he acted in this manner. One theory is that he became publicly insubordinate in order to extricate himself from the war, using "every means at his disposal to provoke President Harry Truman to relieve him so that he, MacArthur, would not have to face the indignity of the inevitable stalemate in Korea," wrote one historian. Another, equally plausible theory is that MacArthur genuinely believed he could take on Truman and perhaps succeed him as president. A third is that MacArthur did not believe, despite the warning reportedly given him at Wake Island, that Truman would call him on it—that a failed haberdasher and accidental president could take on a general who had been a major figure in American life for decades.

Whatever was going on inside MacArthur's head, he was becoming a major problem in the conduct of the war. When the Joint Chiefs of Staff sent a memorandum to MacArthur making suggestions about how to improve the command structure in the war, MacArthur "wrote back a very insulting telegram," recalled Bradley, then the chairman of the Joint Chiefs. "I say insulting. If you read between the lines, he just thought we were a bunch of kids and didn't know what we were talking about. And we were kids to him. We were only fifty-eight and sixty years old." By mid-February of 1951, MacArthur was spinning in circles, finding himself at odds not only with the president and the Joint Chiefs but even with Ridgway, his subordinate commander in Korea. In a Tokyo press conference, he all but denounced Ridgway's approach: "The concept advanced by some that we should establish a line across Korea and enter into positional warfare is wholly unrealistic and illusionary." But that was just what Ridgway was doing— and operating far more successfully than MacArthur had the previous fall.

An often overlooked aspect of Ridgway's generalship was his shrewd handling of MacArthur in this difficult period. It is always a delicate task to manage relations with a shaky superior. In order to minimize the impact of MacArthur's bombast, especially during his flying visits to Korea, Ridgway took time early in 1951 to brief reporters on an impending American offensive. He used the occasion to praise the "freedom of action" MacArthur had given him, and so tacitly underscore it. He also made careful records of his private conversations with MacArthur, with exact quotations noting the time and place of the old general's words to him. He was, possibly, establishing a paper record to protect himself in case his erratic commander turned on him.

Yet MacArthur still found a way to undercut Ridgway, arriving in the midst of the successful offensive to announce that, because of the restraints placed on him by Washington, the war was becoming deadlocked. "Assuming no diminution of the enemy's flow of ground forces and material to the Korean battle area, a continuation of the existing limitation upon our freedom of counteroffensive action, and no major additions to our organizational strength, the battle lines cannot fail in time to reach a point of theoretical military stalemate," he announced to reporters, reading from a penciled manuscript, according to historian Robert Leckie. He highlighted the "abnormal military inhibitions" imposed on him by his civilian overseers. This soon became known to skeptical American soldiers as MacArthur's "die for a tie" proclamation. One can imagine Ridgway's frustration at that phrase, coming after his months of work to improve American troop morale.

Ridgway responded five days later, distancing himself from MacArthur's formulation. "We didn't set out to conquer China," he responded at his own press conference. "We set out to stop Communism. We have demonstrated the superiority on the battlefield of our men. If China fails to throw us into the sea, that is a defeat for her of incalculable proportions. If China fails to drive us from Korea, she will have failed monumentally." In Ridgway's view, charging to the Chinese border at the Yalu River, as MacArthur advocated, was no solution, he explained later:

> The seizure of the land [in northern Korea] . . . simply would
> have meant the seizure of more real estate. It would have greatly

shortened the enemy's supply lines by pushing him right up against his main supply bases in Manchuria. It would have greatly lengthened our own supply routes, and widened our battlefield from 100 miles to 420. Would the American people have been willing to support the great army that would have been required to hold that line? Would they have approved our attacking on into Manchuria? On into the heart of the great mainland of Asia, a bottomless pit into which all the armies of the whole free world could be drawn and be ground to bits and destroyed? I doubt it.

MacArthur, by contrast, believed it was the right time for a war with China. In late March 1951, he issued a statement that seemed to threaten the new Communist Chinese government with destruction, saying that it should be "painfully aware" that "expansion of our military operations to his coastal areas and interior bases would doom Red China to the risk of imminent military collapse." MacArthur had recovered from his despair of December 1950 and swung back to the bellicose optimism of November. Marine Gen. Smith, who saw MacArthur and some of his aides in March, said later, "I got the impression talking to his staff officers that they had an absolute contempt for the Truman Administration. Their idea was that the only man in the world who knew anything about the situation in the Far East was General MacArthur."

MacArthur spoke up again in response to a speech by Rep. Joe Martin, the House Republican leader, who had concluded, "If we are not in Korea to win, then this Truman Administration should be indicted for the murder of thousands of American boys." When Martin sent a copy of the speech to MacArthur, the general wrote back to express his agreement with this denunciation of his commander in chief. He added, "There is no substitute for victory," effectively challenging the administration's more limited goals for the war. Martin released the general's letter to the public.

Those two final violations of the presidential order to cease making policy statements lit the fuse for MacArthur's firing. The dismissal finally came on April 11, 1951. Through a series of mis-communications, word leaked out early, forcing the White House press secretary to hold a dramatic press conference at 1 A.M. Truman's statement opened with a concise one-statement summary of the issue: "With deep regret I have concluded that General of the Army Douglas MacArthur is unable to give his wholehearted support to the policies of the United States government and of the United Nations in matters pertaining to his official duties." This explanation had the benefit of being true.

MacArthur, who had treated Truman with such contempt, was surprised to be so disrespected himself. "No office boy, no char-woman, no servant of any sort would have been dismissed with such callous disregard for the ordinary decencies," he railed in his memoir, still indignant thirteen years after the event. It was, wrote his intelligence chief, Gen. Willoughby, an "infamous purge." The gap between the president and the general was so wide that each concluded that the other must be mentally unhinged. MacArthur privately told Ridgway that Truman was an unhealthy, confused man, suffering from "mental illness." Tru-man, for his part, later said that there were times when MacAr-thur was "out of his head and didn't know what he was doing."

MacArthur returned home to the welcome of a conquering hero. He was given one parade in Honolulu, two each in San Francisco and Washington, and a final triumph in New York City, bigger than that given for Charles Lindbergh. He addressed a joint session of Congress and used it to accuse the Truman Administration of appeasement of Communism and "defeatism." It was time to take on China, he said, though he pulled his punches a bit and did not call for bombing of its air bases, as he had recommended internally. If the United States did not prevent a Communist takeover of Taiwan, he added, then it might well start think about defending itself "on the coast of California, Oregon, and Washington."

But after the initial hoopla, seeing MacArthur up close seemed not to build his support among Americans but to erode it. At congressional hearings on his firing, beginning on May 3, 1951, he used three days of testimony to try to cast the debate over the conduct of the Korean War as one of military professionals being frustrated by inept civilians. That gambit failed when it became clear from other testimony that he also had been deeply at odds with the Joint Chiefs of Staff.

In fact, Truman's ouster of MacArthur did not provoke outrage among senior military officers. The men running the American armed forces in the early 1950s had been the successful younger generals and admirals of World War II, and they knew how MacArthur had abused his subordinates, always insisting on glory for himself and denying it to underlings. During the war, they knew, he had killed a recommendation of Lt. Gen. Robert Eichelberger for a Medal of Honor, and after that action had found other ways to humble the man. One afternoon in 1947, one of Eichelberger's aides was called into that general's office, only to find him looking out the window with tears coursing down his cheeks. Eichelberger explained that he had been summoned to MacArthur's office for a 10 A.M. appointment, only to be kept waiting in an anteroom as others came to see MacArthur and left. Finally, at 2 P.M., Eichelberger was told that MacArthur simply was too busy to see him. "I have never been so humiliated in my life," Eichelberger confessed to the aide. He retired the following year.

The most memorable line from the congressional hearings on MacArthur's dismissal came not from the old bull but from a younger Army general, the far less eloquent and flamboyant Omar Bradley, the Joint Chiefs chairman who had rejected

MacArthur's advocacy of taking on China by bombing its military bases and blockading its ports. "Frankly," he stated, "in the opinion of the Joint Chiefs of Staff, this strategy would involve us in the wrong war, at the wrong place, at the wrong time, and with the wrong enemy."

For his part, MacArthur's most striking statement during the hearings might have been his laughable insistence that "no more subordinate soldier has ever worn the American uniform." His credibility was further undermined by the deliberate leak of the Wake Island meeting minutes, given to a reporter from the *New York Times* on the "direct order" of Truman, according to the White House staff member who did it. The record of the meeting showed the public that MacArthur had badly miscalculated the likelihood and impact of a Chinese intervention in the war, damaging his credibility and even making him look a bit foolish. At first, mail to the White House ran overwhelmingly in favor of MacArthur, but eight weeks later, by the end of the hearings on his dismissal, on June 27, polls ran against him.

Despite being officially still on active duty, MacArthur spent the following twelve months barnstorming the country, wearing his Army uniform while giving speeches in which he denounced Truman and those around him. His travels were bankrolled by, among others, a trio of wealthy Texas ultraconservative oilmen—H. L. Hunt, Roy Cullen, and Clint Murchison. Meanwhile, a less ideological, more business-oriented group of Texas oil billionaires led by Sid Richardson were intent on enticing MacArthur's old assistant, Dwight Eisenhower, into the presidential race.

In 1952, according to longtime MacArthur aide Charles Willoughby, the general entered into a private agreement to join Robert Taft on the Republican ticket if Taft won the nomination. MacArthur would be more than a mere vice president—under a written agreement Willoughby reported drafting with Taft, he also would be named "deputy commander-in-chief of the Armed Forces." By the time the Republican National Convention got under way in Chicago in July 1952, the MacArthur-for-president boomlet was waning, but he had one last chance: He was to deliver the keynote address at the convention. It would be his first time speaking in civilian clothes, which may have affected his delivery. "A tremendous demonstration preceded his arrival on the dais, and there was enormous excitement during the first 15 minutes of his address," C. L. Sulzberger, a *New York Times* correspondent, wrote in his diary that night. But as MacArthur droned on, he continued, "One could feel the electricity gradually running out of the room. I think he cooked his own goose." By the time MacArthur finished, witnesses agreed, it was difficult to hear him over the chatter of the delegates. In his presidential memoirs, Eisenhower offhandedly mentions that MacArthur was the Republican convention's keynote speaker but coldly says nothing else about the speech or his former commander's appearance in Chicago. In a sign of the times, MacArthur's speech was followed by an appearance by Joseph McCarthy, the Communist-hunting senator from Wisconsin.

The convention would in fact go on to nominate a famous Army general as its presidential nominee, but it would not be MacArthur. Instead, in one of history's more remarkable rebukes, the party turned to the man he had demoted fourteen years earlier: the quiet, steady, and discreet Eisenhower, who had departed MacArthur's headquarters in Manila to become, a few years later, George C. Marshall's most prominent protégé. Ike, when he left, had not been happy with MacArthur. In January 1942, barely six weeks after Pearl Harbor, he commented in his diary that MacArthur was "in many ways . . . as big a baby as ever." Ike probably had heard by 1948 that MacArthur had referred to him in his headquarters as "that traitor Eisenhower." He certainly knew that

MacArthur, meeting with journalists near the end of the war, had been openly critical of Ike's handling of Europe.

Eisenhower certainly was more of an internationalist than the Republican Old Guard was. By 1952 he was concerned about the future of Europe and the new North Atlantic Treaty Organization, and that may have encouraged him to run for president. But he also may have been motivated by his loathing of MacArthur and a concern that if he did not run, MacArthur might become president. According to his longtime friend Mark Clark, Ike years earlier had seriously considered eventually running for president, telling Clark one night just after World War II ended, while they were on a trip to hunt Alpine chamois in Austria, that "I'll have to see when I get home just what the situation is." But in 1948, Ike was so persuasive in telling his wartime aide and confidant Harry Butcher that he would not run for president that Butcher stated in a radio broadcast that it would not happen. A year later, when his old friend Gen. Charles "Cowboy Pete" Corlett implored him to consider running, Ike flatly responded that he would not. "Dear Pete," he wrote, "I simply hate the thought of my direct connection with partisan politics—I cannot think of any more difficult chore for me than to touch that field ever, even indirectly."

Yet a problem remains here, in what Eisenhower's decision to run for president might say about the Marshall system. Even if Ike became president in order to stop MacArthur from doing so, it still is difficult to reconcile Marshall's studied distance from politics with the fact that his chief protégé moved into politics and in fact into the White House. Marshall hardly was responsible for Eisenhower's actions. The two were very different men. Indeed, Ike managed in the presidential campaign to mistreat his old mentor. Traveling and appearing in Wisconsin with that state's Senator McCarthy, who had denounced Marshall, Eisenhower—in a moment of weakness—allowed advisers to delete a defense of Marshall from the draft of a speech he was to deliver in Milwaukee. This act of cowardice "haunted Eisenhower for the rest of his life," according to one of Marshall's best biographers, Mark Stoler. Ike would argue, rather weakly, that he allowed the portion of the speech supporting Marshall to be removed because he already had defended Marshall in a speech in Denver.

As for MacArthur, he went to his grave believing that he could have won the Korean War if only he had been allowed to start a nuclear war with China. In January 1954, he boasted in an interview with Bob Considine of Hearst Newspapers, a sympathetic journalist who twelve years earlier had written a biography titled *MacArthur the Magnificent,* that he could have won the Korean War in just ten days. All he would have needed, the general insisted, was thirty to fifty atomic bombs, two Marine divisions, and a half-million of Chiang Kai-shek's troops. This was delusional thinking. There was discussion at the top of the Truman Administration about whether to use nuclear weapons, but it was extremely unlikely that the United States would attack China. Also, there was no evidence that the Nationalist Chinese, newly evicted from the mainland and escaped to Taiwan, would be able to provide anywhere near that number of troops, especially as it would leave their island base vulnerable to the new Communist regime.

In the end, for those watching closely, the Korean War stripped MacArthur of much of the image he had cultivated for decades, revealing him to be, as Eric Larrabee concluded, "a shell of tarnished magnificence, a false giant attended by real pygmies." This was understood in the Army, where MacArthur left little legacy. Unlike Marshall's, none of his protégés would rise to major positions in the service or elsewhere in government. Today MacArthur seems forgotten in American society. This was a remarkable outcome, considering that he was an Army chief of staff, a recipient of the Medal of Honor, and a senior American commander in two wars.

Inside the Army, MacArthur is remembered, if at all, as a bit of an embarrassment, except perhaps at West Point. "MacArthur was guilty of contumacy, which a general must never allow himself to be," concluded Gen. Bruce Clarke, a hero of the Battle of the Bulge who was later the U.S. Army commander in Europe. A minor exception to MacArthur's modern obscurity was provided by Caspar Weinberger, secretary of defense for most of the Reagan years, who displayed in his Pentagon office a bust of the general. This was in part to remind visitors that, unlike several of his predecessors, Weinberger had served in the military during wartime—as an intelligence officer on MacArthur's staff during World War II. Yet MacArthur would have a profound effect on America's next war, in Vietnam.

MacArthur would be very much on President Johnson's mind in December 1964 as he discussed whether to bomb North Vietnam. Maxwell Taylor, then the American ambassador to Vietnam but brought home for the meeting, expressed doubt that Hanoi would retaliate. Johnson snapped back at him, "Didn't MacArthur say the same just before the Chinese poured into Korea?" When Johnson met with Gen. Westmoreland in Hawaii in February 1966 and Westmoreland was pushing him for a sharp escalation in troop levels, it again would be the malign example of MacArthur that Johnson invoked. "I have a lot riding on you," the president told the general, who the previous month had been named *Time* magazine's Man of the Year, succeeding the 1965 selection for the same honor, Johnson himself. "I hope you don't pull a MacArthur on me," the president said to the general.

CHAPTER 14
The organization man's Army

In the mid-1950s, under the direction of Defense Secretary Charles Wilson, the former CEO of the General Motors Corporation, the Army was fast becoming a collection of "organization men," to use the term of William Whyte, author of *The Organization Man,* one of the biggest-selling nonfiction books of that decade. Underscoring this was the unhappy departure of three prominent individualists—Ridgway, Taylor, and Gavin—who left the Army to file public dissents in the form of books.

As Whyte wrote, the organization's managers did not welcome such rebellious types. This is how he summarized the emerging culture of corporate America in the 1950s:

"The rough-and-tumble days are over."

"Unorthodoxy is dangerous to The Organization."

"Ideas come from the group, not from the individual."

"Creative leadership is a staff function." That is, when the organization needs new thinking, the leader "hires staff people to think up the ideas."

These characteristics were remarkably similar to those of the Army in the 1950s. In such organizations, where competition was submerged and a great emphasis was placed on cooperation, Whyte perceived a new, unsettling social atmosphere. People tended to have a friendly mien, but it was "a rather automatic, and icy, bonhomie" that in fact masked a certain distance. Corporate rotation policies that moved executives every few years deepened this impersonal conformism, with a tendency to avoid developing "a personal identity that depends upon a particular place," noted William Henry, an academic who specialized in the psychological makeup of corporate executives.

In the military, similar rotation policies would mean, among other things, being less wedded to the regiment or a similar unit and being more of a person known for getting along in all situations. It would be an Army with little place for the Terry Allens of the world but with rich opportunity for ambitious micromanagers such as William Westmoreland.

Looking at Col. Westmoreland when he led an airborne regiment in Korea in 1952, one can glimpse the looming future of the Army. "To his paratroopers, the most impressive thing about their new commander was his care for details," wrote one of his biographers. "He wanted to check every turn in a patrol route, often suggesting alterations. . . . One of his battalion commanders characterized Westmoreland's command: 'He makes you feel like he's looking over your shoulder all the time.'" Westmoreland struck Maj. Frederick Kroesen, a future four-star general, as a fine commander, if somewhat misguided by his careerism. "I remember . . . someone saying he'd court-martial his wife if he thought it would get him another star," Kroesen recalled.

The military's trend toward a corporatist approach was reinforced by developments in strategic thinking. During the 1950s, Thomas Schelling, an influential economist turned nuclear strategist, began to argue that, in intellectual terms, fighting a war was little different from operating in a market. "There is more than a semantic connection between price war and real war," he wrote, with more wit than wisdom. "There is at least a touch of similarity between, say, a threat to retaliate with nuclear weapons and a threat to retaliate by calling a strike." Schelling, who decades later would win a Nobel Prize, perceived in this similarity the opportunity to rethink military strategy:

> Today's strategy is less concerned with how to conduct a war that has already begun than with using potential military force in the conduct of foreign affairs. "Deterrence" is a strategic concept, but not a purely military one. Certain military capabilities are necessary to deter aggression; but essentially deterrence is concerned with manipulating or working on or influencing a potential enemy's preferences, intentions, and understandings. Deterrence depends not only on what one can do in a purely military sense but on how one can display what he can do.

Nor, he continued, was this applicable only to considering how to deal with the Soviet Union. He also proposed it as a way to think about smaller engagements:

> Limited war is essentially a bargaining process in which violence and the threat of violence is used, in which one tries to coerce or to deter an enemy and cause him not to pursue all of the actions of which he is currently militarily capable.

That sentence essentially captures the strategy of "gradual escalation" that President Lyndon Johnson would employ half a decade later in the Vietnam War as he sought to use increasingly heavy bombing to try to bring the North Vietnamese to the negotiating table.

The logic seemed compelling. In 1957, Robert Osgood argued

in his influential work *Limited War: The Challenge to American Strategy* that the United States, with all its vast wealth, would prevail in any war of attrition, even against the millions of people of China. Indeed, he assured his readers, that "would be precisely the kind of war in which our superior production and economic base would give us the greatest advantage. As one writer has observed, a war of attrition is the one war China could not win." Both these theories would be put to the test a few years later—not against the Chinese but against Vietnam's Communists, presumably a smaller and easier case. As Osgood would write much later, "If the early 1960s saw the height of enthusiasm for limited war, the late 1960s witnessed in Vietnam the greatest blow to that enthusiasm." Ironically, spirit and enthusiasm—what George Marshall had called "determination"—were exactly the elements that Schelling's rationalist approach lacked.

The post–Korean War Army's search for a mission

The post–Korean War Army was a surprisingly troubled institution. By the mid-1950s, noted William DePuy, the tough little veteran of slaughter in Normandy who was on his way to becoming a general, "the Army was feeling sorry for itself." Coming home from a frustrating war in Korea, the Army faced difficult and unexpected problems. On Capitol Hill, the Army's leadership was under attack by Sen. Joseph McCarthy, a boorish Wisconsin Republican who accused it of harboring Communists.

More significantly for the Army, as one service historian put it, the 1950s was "the decade of doctrinal chaos." The service came to doubt its future. The first major issue was the question of the Army's role in an era of nuclear weapons, which were proving revolutionary for the other armed services. The Air Force was rapidly expanding, opening scores of new bases in the United States and overseas and, in 1955, fielding its first genuinely intercontinental bomber, the B-52. It also was moving smartly into space, launching reconnaissance satellites. The Navy introduced its first nuclear-powered submarine, the USS *Nautilus,* in 1955, and later in the decade developed an intermediate-range nuclear-tipped missile, the Polaris A-1 SLBM. For the first time in the nation's history, land power was no longer seen as the paramount form of military force. Rather, as one Army historian put it, ground combat had begun to seem almost quaint. Just a decade after playing a central role in the biggest war in history, the U.S. Army's size was reduced from twenty to fourteen divisions.

The irony of the Army's losing its way in the 1950s is that it occurred on the watch of our last general turned president, Dwight D. Eisenhower—"a man," as historian Adrian Lewis put it, "whose very being was so deeply associated with the U.S. Army, whose character was shaped by the institution." Even the president's son, John Eisenhower, himself an Army officer, told his father about the Army's malaise, saying that as an institution, its lack of a clear mission "has left them somewhat unsatisfied and even bewildered," according to Ike's military aide Col. Andrew Goodpaster. "Their role is rather hazy to many of them."

The feeling of being adrift extended to the field. Reporting to Fort Dix in 1956, Maj. John Collins found the New Jersey base had a ghost-town feel to it, with decrepit barracks and antique plumbing. His first battalion commander committed suicide. The second one was an alcoholic who sowed salt into the roots of shade trees in order to eliminate leaf raking in the fall. When Norman Schwarzkopf moved from West Point to Fort Campbell, Kentucky, in 1957, he was surprised to find many of its officers and sergeants wallowing in alcohol. "The ones who were still in the junior ranks were too often the dregs—guys who were just marking time, who had no sense of duty or honor, and who saw the world through an alcoholic haze." One of Schwarzkopf's routine tasks was to collect his company commander at the base's "rod and gun club" around six every evening, when the commander, who left the office early, passed out from drinking. "If you didn't show up for happy hour at the officers' club on Friday afternoon, you were regarded as a weak sister," Schwarzkopf recalled. "Drinks cost a quarter, and the object was to put away as many as possible before seven o'clock." The Army of that time, he wrote decades later, was "in many ways . . . ethically and morally bankrupt."

"When I came back to Washington" in June 1955 to be Army chief of staff, Gen. Maxwell Taylor said later that year in a talk at Fort Benning, "some people told me that the Army was 'in the dog-house,' that it was consistently in a minority position in the important decisions taken by the Joint Chiefs of Staff, that it was a forgotten service." He insisted that he did not share that feeling. His lack of candor in that talk is somewhat forgivable, because he was trying to rally the Army troops at Benning. What is unforgivable is Taylor's proclivity for not telling the truth, which would haunt the country a decade later. In fact, a few years later Taylor would bitterly describe the mid-1950s as the Army's "period of Babylonian captivity." As one of Taylor's aides at the time, John Cushman, would remember, "The Army [was] . . . fighting for its existence."

As Army chief of staff, Taylor led his beleaguered service's attempt to respond to the ascendancy of the Air Force and the Navy. In 1956, he unveiled a muddled response, the "Pentomic Army," in which Army divisions were re-formed into five independent "battle groups" that would operate in a more dispersed, semi-independent fashion. The Army hoped the change would make soldiers more likely to survive on "the atomic battlefield." The characteristic weapon of the time would be the new "Davy Crockett" tripod-mounted recoilless rifle, which fired a fifty-one-pound, ten-kiloton warhead just over a mile. Soldiers, calculating that the portable nuclear weapon's range was smaller than the area of its lethal radioactivity, joked that it was a new Darwinian form of an intelligence test. Nevertheless, by 1957 half the instruction at the Army's Command and General Staff College was about how to operate during nuclear warfare. In 1959, Taylor lamented, the Army's allocation of the Pentagon budget was 23 percent, precisely half the Air Force's 46 percent share.

At the same time, another answer to the question of the Army's future was emerging. If the Air Force and the Navy were focusing on atomic war, at the high end of the spectrum of conflict, the Army could show its flexibility and move to the lower end, into the area historically occupied by the Marine Corps: small wars. Taylor lit this particular spark not long after he became Army chief of staff, in 1955. In a letter to the Army's retired generals, he stated, "We must be able to deter or win any kind of war. It is particularly important to prevent or to put out the brush fire war before it can spread into a general conflagration." In 1957, eight Army officers wrote an article for *Military Review* titled "Readiness for the Little War—Optimum Integrated Strategy," which argued against the Eisenhower Administration's doctrine of "massive retaliation." "Small aggressions do not warrant big bombs," they stated. At the same time, the Command and General Staff College began putting a new emphasis on counterinsurgency. Also in 1957, Taylor established the new "Special Warfare School" at Fort Bragg, North Carolina. Taylor's Pentomic Division would be discarded soon after he stepped down as Army chief, in 1959, but his emphasis on being able to respond to "brush fire wars" lived on, especially when a new administration came into power, led by a president attracted to Taylor's notion of flexible response—and deeply influenced by Taylor's views. It is not overstating the case to say that the Army's doomed voyage to Vietnam grew in part out of its search for a mission in the mid-1950s.

Also contributing to the Army's melancholy were problems

with its structure and culture. By the mid-1950s, only about seven years after the personnel-law changes of 1947 were instituted and only four years after combat rotation was introduced in the Korean War, a spate of articles appeared complaining about over-supervision, or what is now called micromanagement. These critiques identified different causes but agreed that the Army was becoming increasingly bureaucratized, to the point that, as military journalist George Fielding Eliot put it, the service was at risk of losing its soul. "From corporals to colonels," he wrote,

> the men whose main job it is to train fighting soldiers and forge them into fighting units find themselves instead mere cogs in the vast machinery of the "system"; martyrs to the American devotion to the idea that the American businessman is the most efficient individual in the world and therefore all American institutions should be "run on business lines."

A major part of the problem, Eliot added, was the constant rotation of soldiers and officers: "The noncoms who receive [new soldiers] are rotated out before they've gotten acquainted; their officers are being constantly changed." Also, this was the first time in its history that the Army had been manned by a draft during peacetime, so it was dealing uncomfortably with many soldiers and officers who wore the Army uniform for just two years.

Rotation and micromanagement proved to be mutually re-inforcing flaws. The more soldiers and officers moved, the less familiar they were with one another and, therefore, the more leaders tended to oversupervise, because they could not be sure of who was competent and who was not. Rotation also tended to reward abusive leadership that aimed for short-term results at the long-term expense of those who produced them. In this sense, a star performer might not necessarily be a good leader. In some units, an officer would enjoy personal advancement but, as he moved to his next position, would leave a demoralized and exhausted unit behind him. "The leader is often rewarded as a top performer in spite of being responsible for serious organizational problems," Col. Steven Jones pointed out decades later, as the problem persisted.

Others sensed a larger and growing depersonalization in the Army. Capt. Roger Little lamented in 1955 that

> like the mass society in which we live, military units have become more like crowds than neighborhoods or regiments. Membership is constantly changing, with persons moving in and out, up and down, and to widely different stations. . . . They don't really "know" one another. The regiments are like crowds, anonymous collections of people, constantly changing before their members develop common standards, and sharing few if any memories of the battle or the bivouac.

By 1957 the Army was sufficiently concerned that it surveyed students at its Command and General Staff College, at Fort Leavenworth. A full 81 percent said they believed that commanders oversupervised junior officers. Among the causes they cited were an unrelenting demand for perfection, the use of excessively detailed orders, and overall lack of confidence in younger officers. Maj. Gen. Lionel McGarr, the commandant at Leavenworth, in a follow-up letter to the Army's personnel chief, reported a consensus among students and faculty that the way the Army was managing its officers tended "to reward caution and conformity and to penalize progressive initiative."

The Army tried to address the problem but had little success. In September 1957, Army chief Taylor sent a letter to his senior generals expressing a concern about this tendency of junior officers to perceive that they were being micromanaged. The following year, the Army's manual FM 22-100, on military leadership, warned, "Over-supervision stifles initiative and creates resent-ment." Senior Army commanders also were sent a letter summa-rizing the issue. But not much was done besides this discussion. Most significantly, there was no indication that anyone saw the problem as a structural one arising from the way the Army man-aged and promoted its officers.

One reason for inaction might have been that those who rose to the top in an era of micromanagement saw nothing worrisome about the close supervision of subordinates. It was, after all, what had helped them climb the ladder. "Why do so many generals pay so much attention to details?" wrote Maj. Gen. Aubrey Newman. "That they paid attention to important small matters is one rea-son they were made generals." It was a maddening, but accurate, formulation: Micromanagement was becoming part of the Army's culture—or, as George Fielding Eliot would have put it, its soul. As Gen. Newman's comment indicates, general officers as a class were extremely resistant to outside criticism. After all, they could always say, they were the generation that had won World War II. After defeating the Nazis, everything else was deemed less of a challenge.

By 1961, there was growing evidence that the Army was losing hold of the concept of command. Lt. Col. David Ramsey Jr. took to the pages of *Military Review* to argue that, despite what many of his comrades seemed to believe, "command and management are not the same thing."

From the outside, the Army looked terrific, in part because so much effort had been put into looking good. "It can be said with-out exaggeration that the Army . . . has never entered a war situa-tion as well led as it is today," *Fortune* magazine would report as the Vietnam War intensified. Part of its evidence was that "all but a fraction of the serving general officers and colonels have seen action or done staff duty in one or another of the great campaigns of World War II or Korea." But there were signs of rot inside the service. Henry Gole, who had left the Army after the Korean War and returned in 1961, was shocked by the change he saw. "Officers were doing the tasks NCOs had done in 1953," he recalled. "There was a lot of show . . . white rocks, short hair, shiny boots, the appearance of efficiency, over-centralization, fear of risk."

In the early 1960s, Peter Dawkins was a celebrity within the Army, a captain better known than most generals. As a youth he had overcome polio. At West Point he became the first person ever to be captain of the Corps of Cadets, student body president, in the top 5 percent academically, and captain of the football team. It was almost anticlimactic that he also won the Heisman Trophy in 1958, as the nation's outstanding collegiate football player, and then became a Rhodes scholar. But by 1965 he had grown unimpressed with the Army's sense of leadership. "The ideal almost seems to be the man who has done so little—who has exerted such a paltry amount of initiative and imagination—that he never has done anything wrong," he charged in an article for *Infantry* magazine. "There was a time when an individual wasn't considered a very attractive candidate for promotion unless he had one or two scars on his record. . . . If [a man] is to pursue a bold and vigorous path rather then one of conformity and acquiescence, he will sometimes err."

By this time, both elements of the Marshall system had begun to crumble: Generals were not selected for the qualities Marshall described, and were not relieved at the rate his model expected. Thus misapplied, the Marshall template of generalship tended to promote organization men who were far less inclined to judge the performance of their peers. They were acting less like stewards of their profession, answerable to the public, and more like keepers of a closed guild, answerable mainly to each other. Becoming a general was now akin to winning a tenured professorship, liable to be removed not for professional failure but only for embarrassing one's institution with moral lapses.

Without realizing it, by ceasing to police its own generals for competence, the Army had spurred the rise of a new practice: the relief of top generals by civilians, as occurred in Korea with MacArthur and would continue in Vietnam and subsequent wars. One of the few predictors of how well a war will go is the quality of discourse between civilian and military leaders. Unfortunately, in America's next war, it was not the benign spirit of Marshall but the malign spirit of MacArthur that would hover over presidents' discussions with their generals.

This was the Army that would go into Vietnam—and that already was advising the Vietnamese military to take what now appears to have been entirely the wrong direction.

PART III
THE VIETNAM WAR

For the Army, the 1950s had been a brush with institutional extinction, as many wondered aloud whether there would even be a role for ground forces in the new era of nuclear weapons. Gen. Maxwell Taylor, chief of staff of the Army from 1955 to 1959, would refer to the era as the Army's "Babylonian captivity." The Navy had been developing nuclear-powered submarines and nuclear-tipped missiles, while the Air Force, with its strategic bombers, became the star of the military establishment, for a spell enjoying a budget double the size of the Army's. The Army rebounded somewhat under a new president, John Kennedy, who authorized an increase in its conventional forces from eleven to sixteen divisions and also encouraged the rapid growth of Special Forces. The Army eyed Indochina as the place to demonstrate its continuing relevance. But it also had to keep an eye on the Soviet Union and so was never permitted to deploy more than one-third of its soldiers to Vietnam.

CHAPTER 15

Maxwell Taylor
Architect of defeat

The same men we have lionized as part of "the Greatest Generation" were the generals we have demonized, rightly, for their part in the Vietnam War. The generals of Vietnam, William DePuy once noted, were the frontline combat commanders of World War II. "All the way from Westmoreland down through the division commanders, most of us were battalion and regimental commanders in World War II," he observed.

These men were not just survivors; they were winners on a global scale. Born around the time of World War I, they had gone through the Depression as adolescents and had scrambled to get college educations. "We never had very much," Gen. Walter "Dutch" Kerwin recalled decades later. "We never had radios and we never had a car. Along came the Depression and my father lost his job and, well, for about four years or so, we were in dire straits. So it was always impressed on me as a young kid that if I wanted to go anywhere I was going to have to fight for it." During World War II, they not only survived but thrived. They rose quickly in rank as they took on and crushed the greatest external threat that ever faced the United States. These were men who in an Army of millions had been star performers. Kerwin, for example, as a major on the besieged beach in Anzio, Italy, in early 1944, effectively had been given the power of a general to sort out and make artillery fires effective against the German counterattackers. He was severely wounded in France later that year and, after recuperating for months, ended the war in Ridgway's old post as the morning briefer to Gen. Marshall. Waiting his turn outside Marshall's office, he would see "brigadier generals and major generals coming out of there with the shakes. He was very understanding, but a very disciplined man, and hard as nails." In 1967, Kerwin would become Westmoreland's chief of staff in Vietnam.

It is difficult to put aside the miserable end of the Vietnam War and recall that, as the United States entered it, an overwhelming optimism pervaded the Army's generals. Their outlook, verging on arrogance, was shared by their civilian overseers at the Pentagon and the White House. These men stood astride the world. Even now, it is startling to consider the awesome capacity of a nation that could simultaneously wage and lose a war on the far side of the planet, undergo a social revolution at home, and also launch a space program that placed human beings on the moon.

But in a hot, wet, strategically insignificant corner of Southeast Asia, this world-beating generation of Army generals would become bogged down in frustration, so much so that the support of the American people, which they had learned to take as a matter of fact, began to erode. "It was the strangest thing that we have ever gotten mixed up with," Gen. Bruce Palmer Jr., who at age thirty-one had been the chief of staff of the 6th Infantry Division in World War II, said not long after the end of the Vietnam War, in which he was a corps-level commander. "We didn't understand the Vietnamese or the situation, or what kind of war it was. By the time we found out, it was too late."

This generation was led into Vietnam by Maxwell Taylor, who, slightly older, had commanded the 101st Airborne Division during World War II, though he missed its most celebrated engagement, at Bastogne in the Battle of the Bulge. In 1960, a year after stepping down as Army chief of staff, he published a bitter critique of Eisenhower's defense policies titled *The Uncertain Trumpet*. (The first draft of the book was written largely by Taylor's staff aides, among them William DePuy and John Cushman, about whom more will be said later.) During the presidential campaign of 1960, Taylor and his book became favorites of the Democratic nominee, John F. Kennedy. "We had been affected tremendously by his book," said the president's brother and closest adviser, Robert Kennedy, who named a son after Taylor. Taylor's book "may have influenced the United States involvement in Vietnam more than any other," concluded Lt. Gen. Dave Richard Palmer.

In the early 1960s, Taylor would become almost the opposite of George Marshall. Despite having worked for Marshall as a young officer in 1941–42, Taylor became a highly politicized officer who, rather than keep the White House at arm's length, made his personal relationship with the president his base of power. Though out of uniform when John Kennedy became president, he would have more influence on the American entry into the Vietnam War than any general on active duty, playing Pangloss to Kennedy's Candide.

As Army chief, Taylor had felt unappreciated by President Eisenhower. But under Ike's successor, the Army would reclaim the spotlight as Kennedy focused on the non-nuclear uses of the military. In 1961, even as Taylor's misbegotten Pentomic concept was being hastily dropped by the Army, his influence was growing at the White House. Early in Kennedy's term, in mid-April 1961, Taylor was given an opening by the Bay of Pigs debacle. The CIA-led attempt to send Cuban exiles into Cuba to depose Fidel

Castro had caused the president to distrust the Joint Chiefs of Staff; he felt they had distanced themselves and failed to warn him of problems they foresaw. "Those sons of bitches with all the fruit salad just sat there nodding, saying it would work," he reportedly complained.

Taylor first came to the White House to lead an investigation into the Bay of Pigs fiasco for the president. He stayed on to become the president's personal military adviser, a new position in which he effectively supplanted the chairman of the Joint Chiefs, Gen. Lyman Lemnitzer, enjoying far more access to the Oval Office than did anyone in the military. "I would often see him several times a day on many different subjects," Taylor recalled of the president. He was seen not just as a general but as an important White House official with an open portfolio. "General Taylor had an influence with President Kennedy that extended far beyond military matters; rightly he regarded him as a man of broad knowledge, quick intelligence, and sound judgment," said Gen. Earle "Bus" Wheeler, who became Army chief of staff in 1962. Wheeler recalled that the first issue Taylor took up, once he was officially a member of the White House staff, was what to do about Vietnam.

In 1962, Kennedy made the de facto situation de jure by naming Taylor to succeed Lemnitzer as chairman of the Joint Chiefs, a position Taylor held until 1964. He was regarded warily by the other members of the Chiefs as the White House's man, according to his not unsympathetic biographer, retired Army Brig. Gen. Douglas Kinnard. Discourse between the Chiefs and their commander in chief was strained under Kennedy, and would remain so under his successor. After two years as chairman of the Joint Chiefs, Taylor again retired from the military, this time to become the American ambassador to South Vietnam, where he officially held the powers of a proconsul, overseeing both the civilian and military sides of the American effort. After leaving Vietnam,

Taylor served as a consultant on the war to President Johnson for three years. He also was instrumental in putting in place two of the three top American commanders in the Vietnam War—first one of his former aides, Paul Harkins, and then another, William Westmoreland.

American memory scapegoats William Westmoreland as the general who lost the Vietnam War, but Taylor should bear much of the blame for getting the country into it. As the strategic expert Bernard Brodie once put it, Taylor "bears as much responsibility as any other military man for the sad story of our commitment to Vietnam," having been the man who peddled the idea of an intervention and who then shaped the American military's approach to the conflict. Gen. Nathan Twining, a member of the Joint Chiefs for most of the 1950s, first as Air Force chief and then as chairman of the Joint Chiefs, said in 1967:

> He is largely responsible for our position in Vietnam right now. He's the one that wanted to do that, against all our advice. We argued this day after day, many times. . . . Taylor believed, at least he said so, that we could fight a war over there. Oh, we've argued this in the JCS time and again. He was the only advocate of it. All the Navy and the Marines and the rest of us were against it, but his statement was that we could fight a war over there by not shooting, not a shooting war, but have our forces there in not too big numbers, but we would supply the equipment, the training and all that for these people and let them do the fighting for us. . . . He was as much responsible for this as anybody.

Twining here is overstating the extent and nature of JCS opposition to involvement in Vietnam during the 1950s—and especially misstating his own role—but the essence of his point is nonetheless correct: Taylor led the way.

Taylor tugged the Joint Chiefs of Staff into supporting American involvement in a ground war in Vietnam. Before Taylor was involved, the Joint Chiefs had concluded that Vietnam was at the periphery of American interests. In the spring of 1954, Matthew Ridgway, who succeeded J. Lawton Collins as Army chief of staff, spearheaded a vigorous internal campaign to keep the American military out of a direct combat role in Indochina. Early in April 1954, Adm. Arthur Radford, then chairman of the Joint Chiefs, polled the Chiefs on whether they would support limited American military support for the beleaguered French forces at Dien Bien Phu. Radford was for it, and the representatives of the Navy and the Air Force were inclined to go along with him. "My answer is a qualified 'yes,'" responded Twining, who thought "about three A-bombs" would take care of the Indochina problem.

If it came to a vote, it looked as though the Joint Chiefs would favor air strikes. Two American aircraft carriers, the *Boxer* and the *Philippine Sea*, steamed in the South China Sea with small nuclear bombs in their weapons lockers. But what Ridgway lacked in votes he made up for in energy. "My answer is an emphatic and immediate 'NO,'" he wrote in his own memo. "Such use of United States armed forces . . . would constitute a dangerous strategic diversion of limited United States military capabilities, and would commit our armed forces in a non-decisive theatre to the attainment of non-decisive local objectives," he told his fellow members of the Joint Chiefs on April 6, 1954. Nor, he stated in another document, would the use of atomic weapons reduce the number of ground forces required to fight in Vietnam, which he estimated would be seven to twelve divisions (that is, at least 300,000 men, including support troops), depending on whether the French withdrew and the Chinese intervened. Over Radford's objections, the Army's dissent was briefed to the president. Ridgway was joined in his objection by the commandant of the Marine Corps. He likely also gained strength from knowing that his commander in chief agreed with him. In 1951, not long before becoming president, Ike had written in his diary about Vietnam, "I'm convinced that no military victory is possible in that kind of theater." In a 1954 meeting, according to Douglas MacArthur II, the State Department official who was a nephew of Gen. MacArthur, Eisenhower vowed, "As long as I'm president we will not go in with ground troops to Vietnam." In a meeting with Radford and Taylor on the morning of May 24, 1956, Eisenhower expanded on that view, emphasizing that "we would not . . . deploy and tie down our forces around the Soviet periphery in small wars." Finally, Ridgway had history on his side: Everyone involved knew that just four years earlier, MacArthur had assured President Truman that any Chinese intervention in Korea would be halted by air strikes, which, painfully, had proven not to be the case. Ultimately—at least as far as 1954 was concerned—the minority view of the chief of staff of the Army and the commandant of the Marine Corps prevailed: America would not go to war in support of the French.

Yet Ridgway and his allies were not able to keep the United States out altogether. There is a subterranean aspect to the first ten years of American involvement in Vietnam, from 1955 to 1965. In the wake of Dien Bien Phu, the Americans stepped in to take over the military burden from the French—not in fighting but in advising and training South Vietnamese forces. Patterns and tendencies that became obvious later were set then, most notably an American inclination to push the Vietnamese toward building a conventional military designed to repel a North Vietnamese invasion, rather than a force tailored to conduct a domestic counterinsurgency campaign. As Gen. Westmoreland would observe years later, "American advisers in the 1950s saw the main threat to South Vietnam not from within but from the North Vietnamese army. In organizing and training the South Vietnamese forces, the Americans thus created conventional forces much in their own image." Unfortunately, invasion from the North was not the threat South Vietnam would face, at least until much later in the war.

The senior American adviser in Saigon from late 1955 to late 1960 was "Hanging Sam" Williams, recovered from his battlefield firing in Normandy in 1944. Despite their facing a guerrilla insurgency, which generally calls for paramilitary forces performing police functions while living among the people, ideally among their longtime neighbors, Williams and his comrades tried to create versions of the U.S. Army divisions of World War II—that is, regular forces designed for regular, state-on-state war.

Lt. Gen. Williams "was convinced that that was the way the war was going to go . . . and that was the way he trained and organized the Vietnamese forces," said Army Col. James Muir. "I don't recall anybody ever trying to talk him out of it because that was one of those things you just didn't do with General Williams." Nor did Williams restrict his tongue lashings just to Americans. Describing his plans for the Vietnamese military, he was interrupted by a French officer who said that the Vietnamese were not capable of fighting. "Hell," Williams responded, in a manner reminiscent of John Wayne's film persona, "they just whipped your ass at Dien Bien Phu." Elbridge Durbrow, the U.S. ambassador, in an official report on Williams, questioned his "tact, judgment on other than military matters, and his ability to cooperate with other members of the Country Team."

The paradox of Williams is that he was advising South Vietnamese president Ngo Dinh Diem to engage in pacification programs. "The real danger lies in the local Viet Minh cadre," Williams told Diem, according to a memorandum of a conversation between the two in December 1955. Diem apparently agreed; the memo noted, "The President stated that to be successful against the Viet Minh [the nationalist and Communist opposition] you must use the same tactics they employ."

Yet Williams did not follow through on that thought. Instead, in 1958, at his encouragement, the South Vietnamese government disbanded its six light infantry divisions, which Williams had criticized as being unable to hold their own against North Vietnamese divisions. When the Communists attacked in the late 1950s, they concentrated on heavily populated rich rural farmlands, which Gen. Cao Van Vien, chief of South Vietnam's general staff from 1965 to 1975, noted were "precisely the areas which had not received adequate attention in the RVN [Republic of Vietnam] defense system." The disbanded light divisions would have proven useful when small Viet Cong guerrilla units, conducting hit-and-run operations, "gradually gained control in rural areas," recalled Lt. Gen. Ngo Quang Truong, generally regarded as one of the most combat capable and tactically sharp of the South Vietnamese officers. He continued:

> When fighting finally broke out, it did not take the form of a conventional, Korean-style invasion. It rather began as a brushfire war fought with subversive activities and guerrilla tactics away from the urban centers. Day and night, this small war gradually gained in tempo, nipping away at the secure fabric of rural areas. In the face of a growing insurgency, ARVN [Army of the Republic of Vietnam] units found themselves ill-fitted to fit this type of war, for which they had not been trained.

In February 1960, the government of South Vietnam began a new program designed to improve counterinsurgency operations in the countryside—which, in retrospect, was exactly the right thing to do, and which the Americans would support vigorously nine years later. But at the time, their American advisers were appalled. Williams denounced the move as "hasty, ill-conceived and destructive to overall instruments of power." Williams departed Vietnam in September of that year. His legacy, said Gen. Truong, was that of "a long and valuable time . . . irretrievably lost," during which security could have been built up in the villages of Vietnam. (Lest this be dismissed as sour grapes, a March 1966 study by the U.S. Army staff would arrive at the same conclusion: "From 1954–61, our predominantly military advice nurtured a conventional GVN [Government of Vietnam] military force structure to repel overt armed invasion. Events have proved this formulation to be grossly in error.")

Williams was replaced late in 1960 by Lt. Gen. Lionel McGarr, who was a bit of an eccentric. He made a habit in Saigon of staying in his house for days at a time, its steel shutters closed tight, while tape-recording instructions that he had delivered to his subordinates. He was even less congenial than his predecessor. "General McGarr was not an adept change agent," wrote John Cushman, who worked with McGarr on "the Atomic Field Army" and would go on to become a lieutenant general. "McGarr came across as blunt, rough, humorless and suspicious—not easy to like." Even the Army's official history concludes that during his Vietnam tour, "Splithead" McGarr "made himself thoroughly unpopular in Saigon and Washington."

In 1961, when the British proposed a classic counterinsurgency plan for Vietnam that was aimed more at winning control over the population than at killing insurgents, McGarr objected to it, worrying that, among other things, it would take too long to implement and also would undercut the "offensive spirit" he thought needed to be inculcated in the South Vietnamese army. Throughout the 1960s, recalled Brig. Gen. Tran Dinh Tho, chief of operations of the Vietnamese general staff for seven years, the Americans would show only "lukewarm interest" in counterinsurgency and pacification operations, which they did not regard as their mission. Meanwhile, American focus on the conventional South Vietnamese military would intensify, with such intense "mirror imaging" of American forces that by the mid-1960s, recalled one American general, every South Vietnamese division had its own marching band, just like American units. Gordon Sullivan, who went on to become Army chief of staff in the 1990s but was then a young adviser in Vietnam, recalled, "I never got the feeling that the U.S. advisory effort was coherent and 'Okay, guys, here is what we are trying to do.'"

Part of the incoherence was due to a difference between what was needed and what was done. One of the jobs of generals is to ensure that the military bureaucracy responds to instructions. This was a problem in Vietnam. Robert Komer, the CIA officer who took over the pacification program in 1967, wrote years later that there was a striking "discontinuity between the mixed counterinsurgency strategy which U.S. and GVN police called for at the outset, and the overwhelmingly conventional and militarized nature of our actual response." He concluded that the military bureaucracy had done not what it was told to do but rather what it knew how to do.

The attitude of the Joint Chiefs toward Indochina shifted somewhat after Gen. Taylor became a power at the Kennedy White House, with the Chiefs beginning to support direct military involvement. "Kennedy's preferred battleground appeared to be Southeast Asia, an area that the Army had not wanted to enter in 1954," wrote Army Major Jay Parker. "That reluctance was not gone, but gradually the Army became willing to accept military involvement as both a national security imperative and as a means of validating its role." Taylor also appears to have been the first American official to discuss bombing North Vietnam, in a memorandum to the president in November 1961. "The risks of backing into a major Asian war . . . are present but are not impressive," he assured Kennedy, in large part because, he assumed, "NVN [North Vietnam] is extremely vulnerable to conventional bombing." When the nature of such a campaign was being discussed in 1964, he and Gen. Westmoreland would jointly argue for a graduated response, which they termed "a carefully orchestrated bombing attack."

Yet the Chiefs still had their own ideas, which neither Taylor nor the other Kennedy men much liked. In April 1961, Gen. George Decker, then Army chief of staff, told Kennedy, "we cannot win a conventional war in Southeast Asia; if we go in, we should go in to win, and that means bombing Hanoi, China, and maybe even using nuclear weapons." Decker would serve as Army chief for just two years, half the normal tenure, as would Lemnitzer as chairman of the Joint Chiefs. Taylor advised the president to replace Decker with Earle Wheeler, a pliable officer, while Taylor himself became the Joint Chiefs chairman.

Taylor in the early 1960s became almost the opposite of George Marshall. He was intensely politicized. He did not seek to allay distrust between generals but instead played on it. He made a habit of saying not what he knew to be true but instead what he thought should be said. In a study written decades later, Maj. Gen. H. R. McMaster concluded that Taylor's character flaws had played a central role in deepening American involvement in Vietnam:

> When he found it expedient to do so, he misled the JCS, the press, and the NSC. He deliberately relegated his fellow military officers to a position of little influence and assisted [Defense Secretary Robert] McNamara in suppressing JCS objections to the concept of graduated pressure. . . . To keep the Chiefs from

expressing dissenting views, he helped to craft a relationship based on distrust and deceit in which the president obscured the finality of decisions and made false promises that the JCS conception of the war might one day be realized.

To extend his influence even further, Taylor suggested another key change: a new top officer for the American presence in Vietnam. He had in mind Paul Harkins, who had been on Patton's staff during World War II, helping draft the plan for the invasion of Sicily. Harkins said that, after Patton's death, "Taylor . . . had sort of adopted me." Under Taylor's influence, Harkins was dispatched to Vietnam to take over the American advisory effort.

Harkins almost certainly was not a good fit. "I think General Harkins was an unmitigated disaster," said John Dunn, later an Army general but at this point a lieutenant colonel working as an aide to Harkins's bureaucratic foe, Ambassador Henry Cabot Lodge. "He was totally insensitive to all the political considerations and simply gave his blind loyalty to whoever was running things at the time" in the government of South Vietnam. "He was not a clever man." Early in 1964, about six weeks after Lyndon Johnson succeeded the assassinated Kennedy, national security adviser McGeorge Bundy informed the new president, in a memo labeled "TOP SECRET—EYES ONLY," that his top general in Vietnam was a loser. "I do not know anyone except perhaps Max Taylor, in the top circles of your government who believes that General Harkins is the right man for the war in Vietnam now," he began.

> Harkins has been unimpressive in his reporting and analyzing, and has shown a lack of grip on the realities of the situation. . . . Harkins and Co. have been dead wrong about the military situation for months. . . . McNamara himself thinks Harkins should be replaced.

Defense Secretary McNamara certainly was underwhelmed by Harkins, telling the presidential historian Henry Graff that the old tank officer "wasn't worth a damn so he was removed." The problem, McNamara added, was a basic one: "You need intelligent people." Gen. Donn Starry, who considered Harkins "a good friend," agreed with McNamara about the nature of the general's ouster. "When they relieved General Harkins and brought him out of there, it was in large part because things were not going well in the countryside." The U.S. Army's official histories of its wars usually are extremely discreet about personnel moves, to the point of not even mentioning them, but the volume that covered the Harkins era stated that in May 1964 the general "abruptly" was told by the president to travel back to Washington and then told not to return to Vietnam, an order that a "dismayed and embittered Harkins" viewed "as a thinly disguised dismissal."

The way had been cleared for Westmoreland.

CHAPTER 16
William Westmoreland
The organization man in command

The selection of William Westmoreland to replace Harkins came during an unsettled time, not long after Kennedy's death, and was approved by a new president neither familiar nor comfortable with his generals. The result was that, even though his choice of Harkins had not worked out, Maxwell Taylor likely enjoyed a disproportionate influence in picking Harkins's successor. "I think that General Westmoreland sort of was a pick of General Taylor's," recalled Gen. Harold K. Johnson, who at the time was the Army's deputy chief of staff for operations.

Indeed, Westmoreland was, more than anything else, another Taylor man. The two had first met in Sicily in the summer of 1943, when Westmoreland, looking for action, had wandered over to Taylor's headquarters to volunteer his artillery battalion to support Taylor's paratroopers. The offer was eagerly accepted, in part because the artillery unit possessed trucks that the light infantrymen lacked. Twelve years later, when Taylor became the head of the Army, he selected Westmoreland to be the secretary of his general staff—essentially the chief of staff to the Army's chief of staff.

In 1960, Westmoreland had become superintendent of West

Point, where he was perhaps best remembered for rejecting a plan to hire Vince Lombardi to coach the academy's football team. "Lombardi was too tough, too obsessed with winning, and he had slapped around a cadet while he had been Red Blaik's assistant," Westmoreland told his friend and subordinate Gen. Phillip Davidson. "This was not the kind of man I wanted around cadets." Westmoreland's habit of wanting to look good, even when he was not, apparently extended to his tennis game. His best biographer, Lewis Sorley, tells about his aide calling a captain on the faculty who was a frequent opponent of Westy on the courts and suggesting that he let the general win more often. The speaker at the 1963 commencement, Westmoreland's last as superintendent, was Gen. Taylor.

Westmoreland's shortcomings were well known in the Army. Gen. Johnson was not pleased with the choice of Westmoreland, an artillerist by training before becoming an airborne infantry officer. "I felt at the time that he went out to Vietnam he was not the best qualified to put out there. My reason for that opinion was that I felt it was an infantry war, really a squad leader's and a platoon leader's war, to be fought in a way that would not alienate large segments of the population." Johnson added, "I don't happen to be a fan of General Westmoreland. I don't think I ever was, and I certainly didn't become one as a result of the Vietnam War or later during his tenure as chief of staff of the Army." When Westmoreland's name emerged as the likely choice to command in Vietnam, Brig. Gen. Amos Jordan intervened with the secretary of the Army, Cyrus Vance, to warn against it. "He is spit and polish, two up and one back," said Jordan, who was on the faculty at West Point when Westmoreland was superintendent. "This is a counterinsurgency war, and he would have no idea of how to deal with it." Vance responded that the decision already had been made.

William Westmoreland himself was a new thing in the Army,

an organization man more educated in corporate management than in military affairs. He was an odd combination of traits: energetic and ambitious, yet strikingly incurious, and prone to fabrication even as he considered himself a Boy Scout in his ethics, according to Sorley. He did well in World War II as a battalion commander, especially at a crucial moment early in the war, at Kasserine Pass. Yet in his subsequent career, he would embody the empty approach of looking good rather than being good— the opposite of the old Terry Allen type, but dismayingly common in the uncertain Army of the 1950s. For example, in his memoirs he depicted himself as a student of military history, someone who always kept a few classics at his bedside. This was untrue. "He simply doesn't have any interests," Charles MacDonald, the military historian who helped Westy write his memoirs, told Sorley. "I would venture to guess that the man has not read a book from cover to cover in a hell of a long time." Another officer, Lt. Gen. Charles Simmons, said that "General Westmoreland was intellectually very shallow and made no effort to study, read or learn. He would just not read anything." Westmoreland told people he had no idea that he had been invited to address a joint session of Congress while in Washington in April 1967, yet in fact he had been notified of this before leaving Saigon and had prepared for it for weeks.

Such minor instances of mendacity probably were harmless, but the habit carried over into his conduct of the war and his defense of it for decades afterward. He provided false evidence in 1967 that his attrition strategy was working, telling the president during his April trip that "the crossover point" had been reached and claiming on *Meet the Press* that November that North Vietnamese "manpower cannot be replaced." As Sorley notes, this was "in no way accurate." As Army chief of staff, he oversaw the preparation of a history of the Vietnam War that was laden with omissions and evasions, yet he would assert to the editor of *Reader's Digest* that "the fact remains that this is the only authentic publication on the war." Westmoreland would persist in making such statements late into his life, sometimes flatly denying facts that historians knew from documents to be demonstrably true. For example, he would deny to historians working for the Marine Corps that he had developed a low opinion of Marine tactical abilities, a statement that, wrote Sorley, was "not only false, but reckless, given the existing paper trail." Ultimately, the habit of saying whatever sounded good at the moment would catch up with him when he sued CBS News for libel, only to have the network's defense lawyer read to him passages from his memoirs that undercut his testimony.

Was Westmoreland stupid? He certainly often struck people as being not very engaged intellectually, and perhaps even worse than that. Walter Ulmer, who served in Westmoreland's Saigon headquarters and went on to become a three-star general, recalled that "General Westmoreland's capacity for handling cognitive complexity was severely limited." Brig. Gen. Edwin Simmons recalled Westy announcing to a roomful of commanders in Vietnam that he would read to them the principles of war that he had carried on a card in his wallet since World War II. It turned out to be rules about getting the troops hot meals and their mail and checking their feet, which, as Simmons said, were "platitudes of squad leading." This is yet another example of a commander under pressure regressing to his previous level of competence, a tendency American generals repeatedly showed in Vietnam as they became squad leaders in the sky.

As Army chief, Westmoreland often did not impress others at the Pentagon. "He seemed rather stupid," said Air Force Lt. Gen. Robert Beckel, who was an aide to the chairman of the Joint Chiefs. "He didn't seem to grasp things or follow the proceedings very well." Russell Weigley, one of the foremost historians of the U.S. Army, concluded that Westmoreland's dullness reflected poorly on President Johnson, because, he wrote, "no capable war president would have allowed an officer of such limited capacities as General William C. Westmoreland to head Military Assistance Command Vietnam for so long." But Brig. Gen. Douglas Kinnard, himself an intellectual who went on to earn a doctorate at Princeton after retiring from the Army, and who knew Westy well, having worked for him at the Pentagon in the 1950s and in Saigon a decade later, said Westmoreland was not stupid but rather that "he was not interested in theory. He was not analytical. He was pragmatic."

Most notably, the man who took command of the U.S. ground war in Vietnam in 1964 and would run the Army into the ground in the following three years had attended only two Army schools— the Airborne School at Fort Benning and an Army Cooks and Bakers School in Hawaii. "He was uniquely unschooled by the Army's formal educational system," wrote Lt. Gen. Phillip Davidson, who served as Westmoreland's intelligence officer in Vietnam. "Westmoreland told me he considered his lack of formal military education to be an advantage in Vietnam." He attended neither the Army War College nor its Command and General Staff College but—in keeping with the Army's new emphasis on corporate management—became the first Army officer to attend the Harvard Business School while on active duty, taking a thirteen-week course in advanced management in the fall of 1954. "Westy was a corporation executive in uniform, a diligent, disciplined organization man who would obey orders," Stanley Karnow wrote in his history of the Vietnam War. "Like Taylor, he saw the war as essentially an exercise in management."

In Vietnam, Westmoreland would become the most prominent example of the Army's shift from leadership to management. As

Lt. Col. Andrew O'Meara Jr., who was decorated for valor as an intelligence officer with the 11th Armored Cavalry Regiment in Vietnam in 1969, put it,

> The U.S. involvement in the Vietnam war some day may be considered one of the most magnificently managed major campaigns in the records of military history. Directed against enemy strongholds thousands of miles from home territory, the U.S. military employed a combat force of half a million men in sustained combat over many years; they had less disease, better medical treatment, better maintenance, better food and better equipment than any other military force of its size in history.

Yet, O'Meara continued, it was all for naught. Army generals failed in their fundamental task of understanding the war in which they were engaged and finding an effective way to respond. "We were beautifully managed and inadequately led," O'Meara wrote. "We were Mr. McNamara's Army, materially the richest and spiritually one of the poorest armies that ever took to the field."

Westmoreland was an acolyte of Taylor's, but the star by which he seemed to steer was MacArthur's. The old general looms over Westmoreland's memoirs, which open with an anecdote about an encounter with him, quote him approvingly three pages later, and invoke him repeatedly throughout the text. The book's penultimate chapter is titled "No Substitute for Victory," a conscious echoing of MacArthur's battle cry against the Truman Administration.

As with MacArthur, Westmoreland's greatest failing might have been a matter not of misunderstanding his war, but of misunderstanding how he should deal with his civilian overseers. He had inherited the MacArthur mind-set that held that political leaders should state their long-term goals and then get out of the way of the military professionals. In a major conflict such as World War II, this attitude was merely troublesome, and both President Roosevelt and Prime Minister Churchill were strong and confident enough to sweep it aside. In smaller wars, such as Korea and Vietnam, this view would prove to be disastrous, because the essence of these conflicts was not military but political—most notably in how they ended. Neither war was a fight to the finish, as was World War II. In fact, in the Vietnam War, the politicians were not meddling in Westmoreland's affairs; rather, he was dabbling, incompetently, in theirs. Yet he seemed to believe that civilians were ignorant and venal and simply interfered with his work, harassing him with questions and suggestions. "The Chairman of the Joint Chiefs has a difficult job living with his civilian bosses, the Secretary of Defense and the President, striving to convince them in terms they can understand of matters that he views as military necessity," Westmoreland wrote in terms that MacArthur almost certainly would endorse.

Moreover, Westmoreland's command of the war in Vietnam would suffer from a lack of strategic direction that could only compel his superiors to get involved in what he considered his province. His explanation of how American ground troops were introduced into the war, perhaps one of the two or three most important decision points of the conflict, is worth noting for the backward way in which it came about. When President Johnson decided to bomb the North in order to encourage it to enter negotiations, Westmoreland said, "I realized that the airfields— and we had three jet-capable airfields—were extremely vulnerable. If that strategy was to be a viable one, we had to protect those airfields. I feared the Vietnamese did not have the capability of protecting the American aircraft on those airfields, and therefore, my first requests for troops were associated with the essentiality of protecting the airfields." Like his idol, Westmoreland also tended to view events back in Washington in conspiratorial terms. "The cut-and-run people had apparently gotten to McNamara," he stated, in trying to explain why he no longer enjoyed the full-throated support of the secretary of defense. In a meeting in Hawaii in 1966, Johnson had explicitly warned Westmoreland against trying to "pull a MacArthur on me." The admonition might have been lost on the general. "Since I had no intention of crossing him in any way, I chose to make no response," Westmoreland later wrote. One wonders whether President Johnson was reassured by that silence.

Westy took to South Vietnam the most conventional of approaches. "It is always the basic objective of military operations to seek and destroy the enemy and his military resources," he believed. This axiomatic approach certainly falls in the mainstream of American military thinking, but destroying the enemy is hardly the only possible objective, and so cannot "always" be the goal of military operations. For example, weaker foes frequently will seek to run away from the enemy rather than confront him, which can stretch an adversary's supply lines, making him more vulnerable not just to military operations but to pilfering and poor weather—one of the major lessons of the British loss in the American Revolution. Or a military force can try to make its enemy irrelevant, or try to make him turn on the population and so lose popular support—another lesson of that earlier war. Or, as in Vietnam, a foe might just want to hunker down and outlast the Americans.

Westmoreland and William DePuy, his chief of operations in Vietnam, tended to regard the Vietnamese people more as an impediment than as the prize. They were hardly alone. One of the most striking moments in Norman Schwarzkopf's autobiography is his recollection that in 1965, when he was an adviser in Vietnam, he had tried to take his Vietnamese counterpart to an

American officers' club, only to be told by the club manager, "We don't serve Vietnamese." That was a symbolic error, but the approach also carried significant tactical costs. When Westmoreland chased the enemy away into the hill country, the Viet Cong would move into the areas left uncovered, the people there now unprotected from Communist retaliation.

Frederick Weyand commanded the 25th Infantry Division from 1964 to 1967, leading it into Vietnam. He eventually would become the last American commander in Vietnam and then in 1974 would become the chief of staff of the Army. Looking back, he charged that the Westmoreland approach was essentially futile:

> I, of course, was not at all happy when my division would be ordered by General Westmoreland to move north to deal with an enemy base area. Sometimes the main force units were in there. More often than not, they weren't. Whenever I had to go off on these missions of search and destroy, looking for main force units, I had to leave some or all of Hau Nghia province uncovered. My experience was not a happy one because when we returned I would find that once again the VC had moved in, intimidated the local officials, assassinated school teachers, and intimidated the people who were raising crops. . . . In general [it] set back a lot of progress we'd made. I was continually objecting . . . about this business of going off to fight the big war.

Westmoreland came to embody a certain facelessness on the part of American leadership. Few people relate anecdotes about Westy as a war leader, and when they do, the stories often are unflattering. It is no accident that one of the most illuminating studies on American generals in Vietnam, by retired Brig. Gen. Douglas Kinnard, is titled *The War Managers*. Historian John Gates observed that "Vietnam seemed to be a war fought by committee."

The two most remembered officers of the war, he added, probably are Gen. Westmoreland and Lt. William Calley, of My Lai notoriety. Maxwell Taylor, the general who might be most responsible for getting us into the war and for some of its basic missteps, is hardly remembered in connection with it, or at all, except by military historians.

CHAPTER 17

William DePuy

World War II–style generalship in Vietnam

Unlike Westmoreland, William DePuy was a brilliant general, thoughtful and dedicated to constantly improving his understanding of his profession and of the conflict at hand. Unfortunately, in Vietnam, his understanding of both would be proved lacking.

As a young officer in Normandy in 1944, DePuy had seen ineptitude among American commanders lead to two months of slaughter of the soldiers of the hard-luck 90th Division. "We went to war with incompetents in charge," he said about Normandy. "That incompetence trickled down and caused the tactical failures . . . and the incredible casualties. All this was indelibly stamped on my mind and attitude ever after for both good and bad." That summer, he saw two of his division commanders fired. In Vietnam, in March 1966, DePuy finally became a division commander himself, moving from Westmoreland's staff to take over the 1st Infantry Division, of which Marshall had been a member during World War I, and which Terry Allen had commanded in World War II. In an astonishing irony, DePuy would himself come close to being fired.

In leading the 1st Division, DePuy, a charismatic "banty rooster" of a man, at five foot seven and 145 pounds, applied two lessons he had learned in World War II. First, he focused on applying a tremendous amount of firepower—mainly artillery and air strikes—on enemy positions. Second, he removed anyone he deemed ineffective. Sadly, neither lesson really worked. The lavish use of firepower was inappropriate in the conditions of Vietnam, a limited war fought among the people.

The second lesson, the swift relief of failing officers, was unwelcome in the U.S. Army of the 1960s. "I wanted people who were flexibly minded, didn't need a lot of instructions, would get cracking, and would get out and do something useful on their own once they were given a general direction," he later explained. In his one year of leading the 1st Infantry Division, DePuy would fire eleven of his top officers, including seven battalion commanders, plus many majors, captains, and sergeants major, for a grand total of fifty-six reliefs in one year, according to Gen. Donn Starry, who had his office review Army personnel records to arrive at that number. Starry did not disagree with this approach and in later years would argue that the problem in Vietnam was that other division commanders had not followed DePuy's unforgiving example.

DePuy's ax-swinging approach to officer management caught the unhappy attention of Gen. Harold K. Johnson, by then the Army chief of staff. "If every division commander relieved people like DePuy, I'd soon be out of lieutenant colonels and majors," Johnson complained to subordinates. "He just eats them up like peanuts." Johnson wrote to DePuy instructing him to slow down on reliefs, to give people second chances, and to stop being so capricious. Part of the division commander's job, Johnson noted, was to train people. It was a striking line to take, in particular because Johnson, as a colonel in the Korean War fifteen years earlier, had witnessed the turnaround in morale and battlefield success brought about by Gen. Ridgway, in part through a series of dismissals of division and regimental commanders.

The written message did not take, so on Christmas Day of 1966, Gen. Johnson, on a trip to Vietnam, repeated it in person to DePuy. Only a bit more than two decades had passed since Dwight Eisenhower and Omar Bradley led American forces in Europe with the philosophy that a division commander must relieve failing subordinates, and if he will not, he must be relieved himself. As Bradley wrote in his memoirs, "Many a division commander has failed not because he lacked the capacity for command but only because he declined to be hard enough on his subordinate commanders." But times had changed, and now the Army chief of staff came with a far different message: Instead of pushing a division commander to relieve subordinates, he would all but order him to stop.

Gen. Johnson's Christmas visit began with a briefing by DePuy to the visiting chief of staff and his entourage. DePuy began discussing personnel issues, complaining that "he was not getting his share of the qualified people." Gen. Johnson said nothing, but after the briefing, as they were walking to the mess hall, DePuy brought up the subject again. The Army chief finally said to him, "Bill, to me the mark of a great leader is a man who can make do with the resources he has."

DePuy was nothing if not tenacious. Later that day, DePuy and his assistant division commander, Brig. Gen. James Hollingsworth, met with the Army chief of staff in DePuy's "hootch," his personal living quarters. Gen. Johnson turned to Hollingsworth, who was as much a natural-born brawler as DePuy. "You are relieving too many battalion commanders," Johnson said to Hollingsworth. "You are supposed to train them."

"I'll answer that," DePuy intervened.

"No, sir, he asked me," Hollingsworth said. Then Hollingsworth looked at the Army chief and said, "General, I had the idea that you were going to train them and we were to fight them over here and save soldiers' lives." It was a remark verging on impudence.

DePuy backed Hollingsworth. "I'm not here to run a training ground," he shouted. "They get people killed!" In DePuy's view, command was a privilege to be earned, not a right. He thought it unfair to soldiers to saddle them with battalion commanders who had never been prepared by serving time as battalion executive officers or operations officers.

DePuy explained to Johnson his formative World War II experience. "I fought in Normandy with three battalion commanders who should have been relieved in peacetime," he once told an interviewer, and he likely said something similar to Johnson. "One was a coward, one was a small-time gangster from Chicago . . . and the other was a drunk." Harking back to World War II was not the most politic of approaches, given that Johnson had been captured at Bataan early in that war and spent the rest of it in a Japanese prison camp. DePuy told the Army chief of staff how, back in 1944, "we suffered inexcusable and enormous casualties" because of the failure to remove clearly incompetent commanders. "In the six weeks in Normandy prior to the breakout, the 90th Division lost 100 percent of its soldiers and 150 percent of its officers. . . . That's indelibly marked on my mind."

DePuy dug in deeper. As a matter of personal integrity, he told the Army chief, he couldn't change. It was quite a challenge. "I either would have to be removed," DePuy later recalled, "or I would continue to remove officers who I thought didn't show much sign of learning their trade and, at the same time, were getting a lot of people killed. You can't get a soldier back once he's killed."

Gen. Johnson held to his sharply different view. "I can't have you be the filter for all the best officers we have in the Army to see if they meet your approval," he replied.

DePuy emerged from the half-hour confrontation dejected. "The chief of staff just left, and I'm probably going to be relieved," he confided to Sidney Berry, commander of his 1st Brigade. He followed up by writing a letter of self-defense to Johnson, listing the relieved officers and the reasons for their ousters:

a. LTC Simpson, William J.—G2—[intelligence chief] . . . Col. Simpson was a fat, disheveled officer without any soldierly characteristics whatsoever who made a bad impression on all those people whom he briefed as a representative of the 1st Division.

b. LTC Dundon, James—Provost Marshal—LTC Dundon is completely without talent of any kind whatsoever. He had no initiative, no imagination and repeatedly performed his duties in a sluggish, unintelligent manner.

And so on. Lt. Col. John Hunt was "Valueless." Lt. Col. James Koenig, an artillery battalion commander, "did not have the character to stand up and be counted" and to admit responsibility for "gross errors" in the firing of guns that had led to civilian and friendly military casualties. Another artillery battalion commander, Lt. Col. Elmer Birdseye, "was simply a weak officer." Maj. Ronald Theiss, an infantry battalion commander, "led a verbal existence. He had all the right answers to all the questions" but did not really know what was happening in his unit. "He is a third rate officer who should not be entrusted with command of soldiers in combat." DePuy also continued to tell subordinates, "I can tell if a commander is competent. He is going to take care of his people or get them killed. I don't waste any time with that. I replaced them because no person's career is worth the sacrifice of soldiers."

Some of DePuy's subordinates marveled at his combat skills.

"When it came to the tactics of small units, DePuy was a genius," said Alexander Haig, who served under the general as the division operations officer and then as a battalion commander. Paul Gorman, who also went on to become a general and who succeeded Haig as DePuy's operations officer, concluded that DePuy "was an ideal commander. Above all, I learned to respect his instincts for finding the enemy and anticipating his next moves. He knew the larger aspects of the war and its finest details, right down to the rifleman's level. I consider him an authentic military genius."

But others found DePuy too quick to pull the trigger against subordinates, firing them when he should have been counseling them. Frederic Brown served several tours of duty under DePuy, both in Vietnam and at the Pentagon. The general mentored him closely, and the two men's families dined together on occasion, despite the notable difference in their ranks. Yet Brown, who would retire as a three-star general, came away from his experience in the 1st Infantry Division profoundly ambivalent about DePuy's handling of subordinates. "There was no question of brilliance of tactical command or of the presence of an exceptional professional standard," he recalled. "The sun simply did not go down without platoons dug in, fires registered, et cetera." At the same time, he said, there was "no [time allowed for] learning— immediate exceptional performance expected." So, he concluded, "I believe the overall effect approached dysfunctional," especially given that other units were harmed as the Army scrambled to send only its best officers to DePuy. Brown added, "Once he was away from combat he was a superb teacher, trainer, mentor to those who worked for him."

Frederick Weyand, whose 25th Infantry Division operated just across the Saigon River from DePuy's 1st Infantry, also disapproved of his colleague's handling of personnel. "Bill would not accept officers that didn't meet his standards from the onset. . . . Bill, I think, injured a lot of good officers who had the potential to be good leaders without giving them a chance to show it."

Oddly, just as Terry Allen had appeared on the cover of *Time* magazine at around the time of his firing as commander of the 1st Infantry Division, DePuy was featured on the cover of *Newsweek* as the commander of the 1st ID a few weeks before his confrontation with the Army chief of staff. The parallel is meaningful, because DePuy effectively was the "Terrible Terry" of his time, an anachronism who brought old attitudes to a new war—and ran into trouble with his superiors because of it. The differences in the careers of the two men as commanders of the 1st Infantry underscore just how much the Army changed in the twenty-two years between Allen's firing and DePuy's meeting with Gen. Johnson. In World War II, a general so at odds with the system almost certainly would have been relieved, as Allen had been.

Ironically, because of the institution's growing rejection of relief as a tool for managing generals, DePuy was more secure in his position than he realized. Gen. Johnson would not oust him. Instead, Johnson's revenge would be to deny him command of the Army's Infantry School, which DePuy had hoped to attain, nor would he allow him a position on the Army staff at the Pentagon. Rather, Johnson would send him into the Army's version of exile at the time, expelling him into the uncertain, colder world of joint assignments—where, ironically, given DePuy's emphasis on "search and destroy" firepower, he became the special assistant to the chairman of the Joint Chiefs for counterinsurgency, a capacity in which he essentially advised the chairman on Vietnam.

After Gen. Johnson retired, DePuy would be welcomed back into the institutional Army, where his career revived. He would be promoted twice again, to full general, as he went on to lead the post-Vietnam rebuilding of the Army. His focus on tactics, discipline, and firepower likely was exactly what the Army needed in the 1970s and '80s, and it would pay off in 1991 in the one hundred hours of fighting that forced Iraqi forces out of Kuwait.

In retrospect, relieving DePuy probably would have been the right thing for Gen. Johnson to do, in terms of fighting the Vietnam War. It is far from clear that DePuy's enemy-focused, firepower-heavy approach was the correct course to take in Vietnam. He had the right answer—but to the wrong question. In World War II, the issue had been how to bring firepower to bear on the enemy, and DePuy had worked hard to become a master of that. "We are going to stomp them to death," DePuy told a reporter in 1965. He added, revealingly, "I don't know any other way." But in Vietnam, killing the enemy was not the right way, or at least not the most important one. CIA veteran Robert Komer—like Westmoreland and McNamara a former Harvard Business School student—had been no shrinking violet in his own prosecution of the war, overseeing the Phoenix Program, which targeted Viet Cong cadres in South Vietnamese villages. But as Komer, whose nickname was "Blowtorch Bob," put it, "firepower alone was not the answer to Vietnam's travail."

Unfortunately, firepower was the only answer the Army knew. As one Army historian wrote, "firepower became the dominant characteristic of American operations in the war." Army Specialist 5 Donald Graham, who decades later would become chairman of the Washington Post Company, once noted that when one Vietnamese sniper pinned down four American soldiers, the Army used three air strikes, several helicopter rocket runs, and more than one thousand rounds of artillery to extricate them. Carlton Sherwood, a Marine, also saw a battalion commander call in air strikes against a solitary sniper. On one day alone, November 8, 1966, artillerymen in one operation fired more than fourteen thousand rounds.

Not noticed sufficiently in this storm of firepower was the civilian population, which was the real prize in the war but which the American military tended to treat as the playing field. Stuart Herrington, a young Army intelligence officer advising a Vietnamese unit, recalled working for months to pacify a rural area, including building a school and digging wells for an irrigation system. Then a two-man Viet Cong cell began sneaking into the village at night and sniping at a conventional Army unit that was temporarily in the area. The American commander wanted to respond by shelling the village. "With one salvo from his unit's formidable array of howitzers and other weapons, that American unit could have undone all of the progress we had made," Herrington said. "It took a lot of convincing and intervention with his chain of command to 'persuade' him that he could not do this, that the people living in that hamlet could not be wasted because of something they could not control."

Such recklessness with weaponry was hardly confined to this instance. When William Fulton took over a brigade in the Mekong Delta in mid-1967, he regarded his predecessor as derelict for not responding to mortar fire, for fear of hitting villagers. On his first night in command, he recalled, his ground radar system picked up "over 675 sightings, and I shot artillery at every one of them. Whether it was a water buffalo or a farmer clinking around in the bush, I leveled it. After that I never had another mortar round land in Dong Tam." Fulton did not comment on the effect of the strikes on the loyalties of the villagers, which indicates that he either did not know or did not care. As Army Col. Gregory Daddis wrote decades later, "That the Army never could determine if it was winning or losing goes far in explaining the final outcome of the war in Vietnam."

DePuy was the foremost proponent of this ham-fisted approach, magnificent in bringing firepower to bear on the battlefield but never seeming to pause to consider whether this might be counterproductive or even irrelevant. In that role, he personified the Army's approach to Vietnam. It was only years later, after much reflection, that he confessed to some second thoughts. "You only see the things you've been doing well, not the big mistakes you've made," he said in 1989. "When I was commanding the 1st Division, I was totally preoccupied with trying to find the 9th VC Division and the other main-force elements in my area." While he had been tactically sound, he concluded, "I was deficient at the next level up—the operational level. I wasn't thinking that way in Vietnam also and we paid the price for that." Had DePuy as a general officer focused less on delivering firepower and more on its larger effects, he would have been a more effective officer, better serving his soldiers, his superiors, his cause, and his country. As his nemesis Harold Johnson would later say, "We got into a firepower war out there, where firepower was not really effective." Expending enormous numbers of shells and other explosives meant little to an enemy who often was not there. Years later, DePuy's protégé Donn Starry would come to agree: "The time gap between when the infantry contacted the enemy and engaged him with fire [through calls for artillery or air strikes] was sufficient for the enemy to get away," he said. "So, in every case, we dumped this enormous load of firepower on an enemy that didn't exist [at that spot], because he had had time to react."

In February 1967, not long after his confrontation with Gen. Johnson, DePuy turned over command of the 1st Infantry Division and headed home. A month later, he wrote a letter of thanks to Maj. Gen. Terry Allen, long retired but still eager to help his old division learn to fight more effectively. "I have looked over your training guides and find them both interesting and useful," DePuy wrote. "I have always hoped to meet you at some time." Just six months later, Allen's son and namesake, Lt. Col. Terry Allen Jr., would be killed in an ambush soon after taking command of a battalion in the 1st Infantry Division.

With DePuy's departure from the 1st ID, the World War II approach to relief ended. Ironically, just as the Army was abandoning the practice of relief, Peter Drucker, the great expert on American management, cited the Army in his book *The Effective Executive*, first published in 1966 and influential in American business life for several decades:

> It is the duty of the executive to remove ruthlessly anyone—and especially any manager—who consistently fails to perform with high distinction. To let such a man stay on corrupts the others. It is grossly unfair to the whole organization. It is grossly unfair to his subordinates who are deprived by their superior's inadequacy of opportunities for achievement and recognition. Above all, it is senseless cruelty to the man himself. He knows that he is inadequate whether he admits it to himself or not.

The first example Drucker cited in support of his argument came not from the world of business but from the Army of the 1940s: "General Marshall during World War II insisted that a general officer be immediately relieved if found less than outstanding." But the Army of the 1960s was a long way from the model Drucker highlighted in his book.

CHAPTER 18

The collapse of generalship in the 1960s

a. At the top

Under Lyndon Johnson, the discourse between civilian leaders and top generals that is essential to the conduct of war in the American system of government, already strained under Kennedy, began to break down altogether. President Johnson's distrust of his generals extended well beyond the possibility of being challenged or misled by Westmoreland. "That's why I am suspicious of the military," Johnson told the most intimate of his biographers, Doris Kearns Goodwin. "They're always so narrow in their appraisal of everything. They see everything in military terms. Oh, I could see it coming. And I didn't like the smell of it. I didn't like anything about it, but I think the situation in South Vietnam bothered me most. They never seemed able to get themselves together down there. Always fighting with one another. Bad. Bad."

Policy is best formulated by using straightforward, candid dialogue to uncover and explore differences. But LBJ was afraid of those differences ("Always fighting with one another. Bad. Bad.") and used the process designed to formulate policy instead to obscure and minimize differences. A popular myth, persisting even in today's military, is that senior civilians were too involved in the handling of the war. In fact, the problem was not that civilians participated too much in decision making but that the senior military leaders participated too little. President Johnson, Maxwell Taylor, and Robert McNamara treated the Joint Chiefs of Staff not as military advisers but as a political impediment, a hurdle to be overcome, through deception if necessary. They wanted to keep the Chiefs on board with policy without keeping them involved in making it or even necessarily informed about it.

Under President Johnson, the U.S. government pursued a policy of graduated pressure, summarized thusly by Gen. Westmoreland:

> The campaign of escalating pressure through bombing continued in the hope that ground and air action together would prompt Hanoi to negotiate. Appropriate pauses were to be made in the air war to signal American intent and to allow time for a North Vietnamese response.

Had the policy formulation system been working, the wisdom of that approach would have been explored. Instead the White House excluded the senior generals, and the senior generals did not appear to listen to other generals. The Westmoreland-DePuy approach hardly enjoyed universal support among military leaders. "It just seemed ridiculous on the face of it," said Gen. Weyand, who especially disliked the emphasis on measuring progress by counting the number of enemy dead. "I don't know what the body count of the 25th Division was, and I didn't care a hell of a lot." Attrition, body count, and "search and destroy" were the holy trinity of the Westmoreland approach to the war, Weyand said, and "I didn't like any of them."

Weyand was hardly alone. When retired Army Brig. Gen. Douglas Kinnard surveyed Army generals who had served in Vietnam about the conduct of the war, they were fairly evenly divided into three camps about the efficacy of the search-and-destroy concept. Thirty-eight percent said it was "sound," 26 percent said it was sound at first but "not later," and 32 percent called it "not sound." DePuy himself would concede decades later that the strategy of attrition rested on an unexamined premise: "We . . . didn't know about the redoubtable nature of the North Vietnamese regime. We didn't know what steadfast, stubborn, dedicated people they were. Their willingness to absorb losses compared with ours wasn't even in the same ballpark." Another general, Bruce Palmer, came to a similar conclusion: "We were searching and destroying, and fighting a battle of attrition, and trying to break the will of Hanoi simply by chewing up people. But we underestimated those people. They don't quit that way." He added, correctly, that the other crucial factor the generals misunderstood was "how long our people back home would stand for it." Had the policy formulation system not broken down, President Johnson and those around him might have better understood the military concerns about the conduct of the war, and his top generals might have grasped the domestic political limitations that approach would encounter.

Gen. Taylor, the chairman of the Joint Chiefs of Staff from October 1962 through June 1964, further eroded the quality of civil-military discourse by playing down to McNamara the misgivings the other members of the Joint Chiefs had about the policy of attrition. McNamara, in turn, further reduced those concerns when conveying them to the president. The Chiefs, for their part, allowed themselves to be kept in the dark, cut off from the president. Defense Secretary Robert McNamara (another graduate of Harvard Business School) and Gen. Taylor actually worked to reduce communication between civilian and military officials, cutting off back channels between the military and the White House. Such alternate lines of communication are important to help fix the policymaking process when it fails to examine key assumptions or bring to the surface lingering differences in views.

No one had asked the American people whether they wanted to engage in a lengthy war of attrition on the other side of the planet, and in fact all the historical evidence at the time suggests that they would not. Nonetheless, Westmoreland would blame them for interfering with his strategy: "One reason they [Hanoi] could not read our signal was that the message was garbled by the loud and emotional voices of dissent on the domestic scene and sensational news reporting by the mass media." It could be argued that, if anything, the gradualist signals sent were interpreted in Hanoi to mean that the Americans would not launch a full-scale attack.

The Joint Chiefs did not fail utterly in their duty. Irked by the gradualist approach, they came close to rebelling against Taylor near the end of his time as chairman, in June 1964. On May 30 of that year, they met without him present and produced a statement for the defense secretary that expressed their concern over the "lack of definition, even a confusion in respect to objectives and courses of action related to each objective." They also expressed doubt about the entire approach of using military force to send signals and messages. The Chiefs intended their message to be read by McNamara before he joined Taylor, Secretary of State Dean Rusk, and other high officials for a meeting in Honolulu about the war. But on June 1, Taylor directed the memo to be withdrawn from McNamara's office, on the grounds that he was unsure that its wording accurately reflected the views of the Chiefs. Incensed, the Chiefs met again, revised some of the language, and sent the new version to Hawaii with an explicit request that Taylor give it to McNamara. The Marine commandant also used his own

Marine Corps back channels to verify that Taylor had represented the memo accurately. Such suspicions were well founded. "Despite the Chiefs' urging, Taylor refused to submit their paper to the conferees, and after suppressing the memo, directly opposed the JCS position at the conference," wrote Maj. Gen. H. R. McMaster.

Once obfuscation became accepted as the approach, it was hard to drop it. When Sen. Wayne Morse of Oregon asked Taylor skeptical questions about the Gulf of Tonkin incident of August 1964, "Taylor gave misleading answers," McMaster noted.

Later in 1964, the Chiefs again made a run at expressing dissent. Taylor had been sent to Vietnam as U.S. ambassador and had suggested that Earle Wheeler succeed him as chairman of the Joint Chiefs. Wheeler, growing frustrated in the post, eventually told McNamara that the Chiefs were prepared to state to the president that unless the war was taken vigorously to North Vietnam, they wanted to withdraw American forces from South Vietnam. McNamara met with the Chiefs and kept them from bolting by promising that he was willing to entertain the possibility of a series of major escalatory actions, from heavily bombing the North to confronting China in a land war—none of which he really wanted to take. When the Chiefs submitted a memo to the president stating their views, McNamara omitted a key phrase from it. The result of such evasion, concluded McMaster, was that "the assumptions that underlay the president's policy went unchallenged by the one formal body charged by law and tradition with advising the president of the United States about strategy and warfare."

Johnson was certainly a poor wartime commander in chief, but he remained a canny manipulator of men. In mid-1965, he cajoled the Joint Chiefs, "You're my team; you're all Johnson men." At this point, duty should have overcome courtesy and impelled the Chiefs to correct their president, as Marshall almost certainly would have: They were *not* his men, they should have said—they were the nation's men. Yet the president had measured them well, for, in fact, they would behave as his minions when they met with members of Congress and failed in their duty to be truthful.

Finally, in November 1965, Wheeler and the other members of the Joint Chiefs of Staff got up the nerve to go to the White House and present President Johnson with a united front. They called for an end to his policy of gradual escalation and lobbied to replace it with a major military offensive against North Vietnam. They wanted to pound North Vietnam hard from the air, with both Air Force and Navy jets, and also to mine and blockade its harbors. Furthermore, they wanted this application of "overwhelming naval and air power" to be done quickly. Johnson made it clear that this was not a welcome meeting. He did not offer them seats, though he listened attentively as they stood in a semicircle to present their recommendations.

When the Chiefs finished, the president turned his back on them for about a minute, leaving them standing while seeming to weigh their counsel. Then he whirled on them in a fury. "He screamed obscenities, he cursed them personally, he ridiculed them," recalled Charles Cooper, then a Marine major, who had been brought to the meeting to hold maps. Among the names the president spewed, recalled Cooper, who later rose to the rank of lieutenant general, were "shitheads, dumbshits, pompous assholes." After the Army chief of staff and the Marine commandant confirmed their support for a sharp, swift escalation of the war, Johnson again yelled at them. "You goddam fucking assholes. You're trying to get me to start World War III with your idiotic bullshit—your 'military wisdom.'" Then he ordered them to "get the hell out of here right now."

In his car afterward, Adm. David McDonald, the chief of naval operations, said, "Never in my life did I ever expect to be put through something as horrible as you just watched from the president of the United States to his five senior military advisers." Johnson had counterattacked powerfully. Henry Kissinger, meeting Gen. Wheeler three years later, saw him as a beaten dog, resembling "a wary beagle, his soft dark eyes watchful for the origin of the next blow." Gen. Harold K. Johnson, the Army chief of staff, told students at the Army War College years later that at one point he had decided to resign as chief of staff of the Army. "And then on the way to the White House, I thought better of it and thought I could do more working within the system than I could by getting out," he recalled. "And now I will go to my death with that lapse in moral courage." He also seemed to retreat in place emotionally and professionally. "I acquired the feeling, the sense, that I was an observer, I was not a participant—particularly in my role as a member of the Joint Chiefs of Staff."

Johnson's tantrum was a modern low point in discourse between generals and presidents. Among other things, President Johnson's explosion recalls George Marshall's wisdom in trying to maintain a social and emotional distance from the president. Had FDR spoken to him in the degrading fashion Johnson spoke to the Joint Chiefs, Marshall almost certainly would have replied that he clearly had lost the confidence of the commander in chief and so was obliged to submit his resignation as chief of the Army. It was a sign of the decline in the quality of the nation's military leadership that none of those present in that November 1965 meeting did so. As Gen. McMaster put it in *Dereliction of Duty*, his scholarly study of the professional and moral failures of the Joint Chiefs in dealing with the war, that lapse invited tolerance of greater sins. "The president was lying, and he expected the Chiefs to lie as well or, at least, to withhold the whole truth. Although the president should not have placed the Chiefs in that position, the flag officers should not have tolerated it when he had." It was equally a sign of how Lyndon Johnson had failed to live up to the example of Franklin Roosevelt, whom Goodwin called "his patron, exemplar, and finally the yardstick by which he would measure his achievement." Unlike FDR, Johnson never really explained his war to the nation. "At no time that I was aware," wrote Joseph Alsop, who became almost the last "hawk" among prominent journalists, "did President Johnson or his advisers seek to prepare the American people for the grim consequences of a protracted military battle, nor did they adequately explain to the public the reasons for the fight." Neither the president nor the Joint Chiefs of Staff did their duty during the Vietnam War.

b. In the field

Here is the history of the American involvement in combat in Vietnam in a nutshell: In 1964, the situation in Vietnam was eroding quickly. Then came 1965, the year of emergency, when the South Vietnamese government looked as if it might collapse if not reinforced by American forces. In 1966, the Army and the Marines fought to establish themselves and secure bases in Vietnam. In 1967, the Americans began to take the fight to the enemy, going after his bases and lines of communication. They were surprisingly successful in doing so. In Chau Thanh, just south of the Plain of Reeds, senior Communist cadres criticized local fighters for retreating. The fighters protested, "We met with very strong enemy units that were ten times stronger than we. Therefore, we dared not resist their operations. If we stood against them, we would have been completely eliminated. The enemy . . . has mechanized equipment and modern weapons." Military setbacks carried political consequences for the Viet Cong, or National Liberation Front, explained a village secretary from an area just to the northwest: "The Tam Hiep villagers' confidence has been shaken, and they want to cut all ties with the Front. Most of them still pay taxes, but it is simply to have the Front leave them alone."

The two sides were heading toward a major clash that would come early in 1968 and prove to be the determinative campaign of the war. Until then, it was possible for both sides to develop a genuine sense of progress—a situation surprisingly common in war. If the Americans were pushing back the Viet Cong and their Northern backers in 1967, the Communists could conclude at the same time that they had met the world's most powerful military on the battlefield and, despite lacking its tanks, bombers, and helicopters, had survived and even learned something about how to handle the newcomers. Vo Nguyen Giap, the North Vietnamese defense minister, would write in September of that year that "the situation has never been as favorable as it is now. The armed forces and the people have stood up to fight the enemy." By then the Communists were planning the major offensive they would launch five months later.

In fact, by late 1967, there were signs that the Vietnam War was beginning to sour for the U.S. Army. It was an unwanted war for which the Army had not prepared. "The officer corps of the 1960s was trained to fight Russians," Charles Krohn, an Army intelligence officer in Vietnam in 1967–68, wrote decades later. "They envisioned massive tank and mechanized infantry battles. Force versus force. In Vietnam every American officer dreamed of the day when the little beggars would come out and fight, but they never did"—at least not during his time there. As it fought in Vietnam, the Army was not much interested in the theories or tasks of counterinsurgency that lay outside "its standard operational repertoire," Army analyst Andrew Krepinevich noted. This included tactics such as "long-term patrolling of a small area, the pervasive use of night operations, [and] emphasis on intelligence pertaining to the insurgent's infrastructure rather than his guerrilla forces."

The U.S. Army in Vietnam displayed a willful ignorance. It did not see a need to send senior officers to the British Jungle

Warfare School, in Malaysia. Nor did it choose to study the French experience in Vietnam a decade earlier, even though the French arguably had fought harder, with higher casualty rates. Pentagon analyst Thomas Thayer recalled being told by the French defense attaché in Saigon—a veteran of fighting in Vietnam who was chosen for the diplomatic post because of his excellent English—that during the first eighteen months of his assignment, only one American had visited him to inquire about the lessons the French might have to share. Even more strikingly, when Army Special Forces troops under a CIA program began training villagers to defend themselves, the program worked, with armed locals posting "a record of almost unbroken success" against the Viet Cong. Areas around villages in the training program recorded a noticeable improvement in their security. Maxwell Taylor, by then the American ambassador, directed the CIA to turn the program over to the U.S. military, resulting in a major drop in the effectiveness of the mission. "Our direction was you organized these villages for their own defense, and that expanding defense then excludes the enemy," remembered William Colby, who was the CIA station chief in Saigon from 1959 to 1962 and then chief of the agency's Far East Division until 1968. "When the military took over, it was 'You take these forces and use them on offensive missions.' They sent them up on the Cambodian border and they chased around in the woods and it never had a damn thing to do with the overall strategy." In other words, they were misused just as Weyand's 25th Infantry Division had been misused, with the same poor result. Under military control, over the following year the village defense program collapsed.

Nor did Army leaders pay much attention to the fact that during the early part of the war, the Viet Cong's primary form of support was local: It drew almost all of its recruits from the surrounding population and its weaponry from government forces, through either capture or purchase. For example, Truong Nhu Tang, then a Viet Cong official, recalled that his subordinates had been able to buy cigarettes and radios—and even weapons such as hand grenades and antipersonnel mines—from South Vietnamese officers. "The rationale that ceaseless U.S. operations in the hills could keep the enemy from the people was an operational denial of the fact that in large measure the war was a revolution which started in the hamlets and that therefore the Viet Cong were already among the people when we went to the hills," Francis "Bing" West wrote in a 1969 study. Nor, he noted, were local South Vietnamese particularly worried by large Viet Cong units, because they knew the Americans could and would track and confront those units. Rather, West wrote, what concerned those officials far more was "the local VC forces with their cunning, their killing of selected targets, and their dedicated commitment."

The Army's leaders in Vietnam chose to ignore even the knowledge of its own best-informed members: When advisers in the field, close to the action, disputed the optimistic reports coming out of the American military headquarters in Saigon, their views were generally ignored. Early in his tenure as commander in Vietnam, Westmoreland ordered the advisers to put aside their frustrations and to "accentuate the positive" in their reports. One of the most outspoken advisers, Lt. Col. John Paul Vann, effectively demanded a hearing, traveling to Washington and using Army connections to line up an opportunity to brief the Joint Chiefs of Staff on his notably pessimistic views. Taylor, then still the chairman of the Joint Chiefs, learned about the planned briefing a few hours before it was to begin and, in collaboration with his protégé Gen. Earle Wheeler, the Army chief of staff, canceled it at the last minute. A similarly skeptical State Department report titled "Statistics on the War Effort in South Vietnam Show Unfavorable Trends" was swatted aside with a note from Defense

Secretary Robert McNamara to Secretary of State Rusk: "Dean: If you promise me that the Department of State will not issue any more military appraisals without getting the approval of the Joint Chiefs, we will let this matter die. Bob."

The Army in Vietnam even managed to disregard formal internal reports that "noted the absence of an overall counterinsurgency plan and the excessive use of firepower, particularly in pacification operations," wrote Krepinevich. In March 1966, a lengthy report commissioned by Gen. Johnson concluded that "the war has to be won from the ground up." The Army chief of staff went on to make a series of somewhat muddled recommendations on how to bring about that reorientation. On the one hand, the report, which reflected the views of young officers who had served as advisers in Vietnam, stated that the American approach to the war had been "inappropriate" and "marginally effective." The report found that "present U.S. military actions are inconsistent with that fundamental of counterinsurgency doctrine which establishes winning popular allegiance as the ultimate goal. While conceptually recognizing the total problem in our literature, Americans appear to draw back from its complexity in practice and gravitate toward a faulty premise for its resolution—military destruction of the VC." It also stated that the Viet Cong were "relatively self-sustaining," winning support locally. Yet it denounced the enclave approach with which the Marines had been experimenting in coastal population centers, seeing it as too static and passive. Rather, it said, the "bulk" of American forces should continue to be used to confront "main force" Communist units and attack their lines of supply. But after making that case, it continued on into a massive contradiction: "At no time should U.S. . . . . combat operations shift the American focus of support from the true point of decision in Vietnam—the villages." In other words, the central task of the war, the decisive fight, somehow was not a mission for the Americans—it was some-one else's job. If that were the case, the center of gravity of the American effort should have been supporting South Vietnamese forces. But it did not do so. Instead, as Vietnam veteran and histo-rian James Willbanks observed, "the South Vietnamese were vir-tually shunted aside and relegated to a supporting role."

Westmoreland loathed the PROVN report, as it was known in the Army. Gen. Davidson, his intelligence officer, while sympa-thetic to Westmoreland, faulted his handling of the report:

> The study deserved more mature consideration. Its executioner was General Westmoreland, and while he does not even mention PROVN in his memoirs or in his Official Report on the War, his reasons for throttling it are obvious. PROVN forthrightly attacked his search and destroy concept, which, correctly or incorrectly, Westmoreland sincerely held to be the right strat-egy. . . . He could not embrace the study's concept (that search and destroy operations were unproductive) without admitting that he and his strategy were wrong.

So rather than shift to what it needed to do, the Army would continue doing what it knew how to do, which is how bureaucra-cies act when they lack strong leadership. "We went and fought the Vietnam War as if we were fighting the Russians in the plains of central Europe for a very simple and straightforward reason—that was what we were trained, equipped, and configured to do," said Komer, who revitalized the pacification effort in Vietnam in 1967. "We over-funded and over-invested in a military war we couldn't win the way we fought it, and we really didn't do enough for what was, even from the outset, proving to be at least a limited success, and that was the pacification effort." The Army believed, institutionally, that winning wars meant killing enemy soldiers and disrupting enemy operations by cutting supply routes, and that was what it intended to do, even if it meant fighting a grinding war of attrition that was perhaps irrelevant. In the Army view, Krepinevich wrote, "all that was needed was efficient application of firepower." Indeed, when Westmoreland was asked at a press conference about the best way to respond to an insurgency, he replied with one word: "Firepower." In light of all this, it can be argued that the United States really never launched a genuine counterinsurgency campaign in Vietnam. In fact, by one measure, financial expenditures, the war was foremost an air effort (with $9.3 billion spent in fiscal year 1969) and secondarily an attritional ground campaign (with spending of $4.6 billion in the same period). The total tonnage dropped by American aircraft during the war averages out to seventy tons of bombs for every square mile of Vietnam, noted the Pentagon's Thayer. "Pacification was a very poor third," he concluded.

"They [the Americans] didn't want to pacify," concluded Tran Van Don, one of the South Vietnamese generals who led the plot against President Diem in 1963. "They wanted to make war."

The enemy learned how to deal with the American approach. Two years later, the Communists purposely would encourage it as they neared the launch of their city-centric Tet Offensive, taking actions that would lure American forces into the countryside and borderlands. As Truong Nhu Tang, the former Viet Cong official, put it, the result of the Americans' concept of the war was that they never really participated significantly in the most important fight in Vietnam: "The military battlefield upon which the Americans lavished their attention and resources was only one part of the whole board of confrontation. And it was not on this front that the primary struggle was being played out."

But the Army, like a football team that had shown up at the wrong stadium and played its game there anyway, would continue to insist that it was not responsible for the outcome of the war. In a poll of 976 teachers and students at the Army's Command and General Staff College conducted in February 1972, 40 percent of those asked blamed "the politicians," and 21 percent blamed "the general lack of commitment" among American youth. Only 5 percent thought the Army was at fault for conducting the war poorly. (The rest provided a variety of other answers.) Retired Army Col. Anthony Wermuth was even more emphatic, insisting in 1977 that "the American Army fought magnificently in Vietnam." Gen. Alexander Haig agreed, arguing, "The war was not lost on the battlefield in any sense of the word." So did the man probably as responsible for the war as anybody, Gen. Maxwell Taylor, whose view was that "our American leadership, I think, has been superb. I don't know of any improvement that anyone could make to the general tactics and the strategy, under the ground rules which have been decided for the armed forces."

As such comments indicate, during the Vietnam War there was a lack of willingness among general officers to examine their own performance, as well as a lack of curiosity about it. "By the second decade after World War II, the dominant characteristics of the senior leadership of the American armed forces had become professional arrogance, lack of imagination, and moral and intellectual insensitivity," causing otherwise intelligent men to act stupidly, wrote Neil Sheehan in one of the best books about the Vietnam War, *A Bright Shining Lie.*

One result of such attitudes was the end of the relief of generals. If in Korea the Army had begun to find it difficult to relieve generals, during Vietnam it found it all but impossible. Firing senior officers would have been seen as a confession of failure. Furthermore, in a hazy war with a muddled strategy, what constituted success was less clear, so rewarding it and punishing failure became even more difficult. The result was that by the arrival of the Vietnam War, firing a general officer amounted to an act of dissent, a public questioning of the way the Army worked, because it involved someone who had risen through a demanding process over two decades. To say that he was not fit for a position was tantamount to a rejection of the process that had produced him. So where relief was once a sign that the system was working as expected—rewarding success and punishing failure—it had become seen inside the Army as a hostile critique of the system. As Gen. Westmoreland put it, "If an officer progresses through the United States Army's demanding promotion system to reach the rank of general, he is, except under the most unusual circumstances, clearly competent, even if he may not be the best man for every assignment."

The Marine road not taken

Despite Maxwell Taylor's claims, there were alternatives available. In 1964, John Cushman, then a lieutenant colonel, twice briefed Gen. Westmoreland on classic counterinsurgency techniques he was employing in a province in Vietnam's Mekong Delta. Both times, Westmoreland conveyed utter boredom. "No reaction, no questions, no exploration, no curiosity," recalled Cushman, who later became a lieutenant general and an important figure in the Army's post-Vietnam recovery.

Tucked away at the northern end of South Vietnam, the Marine Corps was less under Westmoreland's control and was able to take the counterinsurgency idea further. The Marines developed a different concept of the war, arguing that the way to win was not to pursue the enemy through the unpopulated jungle but instead to move small units into villages to try to protect the people and cut them off from the enemy, separating the foe from his base of supply of recruits, food, and other necessities of war.

"The Vietnamese people are the prize," Marine Lt. Gen. Victor Krulak wrote in a 1966 memorandum, while attrition, he said, is "the route to defeat." Neil Sheehan reports that President Johnson read a copy of Krulak's memo that summer and met with Krulak, but essentially blew him off. Later that year, Krulak commented to a fellow Marine general regarding the overall war effort, "I am deeply concerned that the enemy has played the tune, and induced us to dance to it." But by focusing on villages instead of territory, the Marines could not display to visiting officials on their maps that they controlled large swaths of land. This inability would antagonize Army leaders.

The Marines established a three-layered approach. First, they would use operations of battalion size and larger to go after main forces and reduce their ability to move freely. Second, smaller counter-guerrilla patrols would aggressively seek to constrain Viet Cong movements in population centers; recognizing that the VC lived by requisitioning rice from farmers in the rich lands along the coast, the Marines launched operations to cut off those supplies. Third, and most memorably, they would put small numbers of infantrymen into the villages themselves. The notion was to separate the people from the enemy and to protect and arm the people so that they would feel able to talk and cooperate with the Americans or their Vietnamese allies. Under this program, called Combined Action Platoons (CAPs), the Marine Corps, starting in August 1965, put teams of soldiers—the goal was thirteen Marines, a Navy corpsman (that is, a medic), and around thirty-five Vietnamese militiamen—into nearly eighty villages. The teams actually had only about thirty people on average, in part because Army leaders did not like the program and directed the Marines to man it by taking people from units already in Vietnam.

The key to the Marines' CAP effort was their sustained presence in these villages. They developed a familiarity with the local people and their living conditions and thereby understood what "normal" looked like, so they were able to detect aberrations from everyday patterns. "In the process of operating within the same area over a prolonged period, an intelligence network was eventually established," wrote historian Michael Hennessy. One CAP that was almost entirely surrounded by enemy forces survived in part because the local woodcutters would see the enemy move in and warn the Marines. It was hardly a hand-holding program. Marines in the program accounted for just 1.5 percent of all Marines in Vietnam but suffered 3.2 percent of casualties—and inflicted 8 percent of enemy casualties. In other words, they were hit disproportionately, but they were effective militarily. These efforts would become the road not taken in Vietnam: the harder but better alternative to firepower-oriented search-and-destroy operations.

The Army's leaders in Vietnam, being focused on big battles as the way to win the war, objected vigorously to the Marine programs. Maj. Gen. Harry Kinnard, who commanded the first full Army division sent into Vietnam, reported later that he was "absolutely disgusted" with the Marine Corps. "I did everything I could to drag them out and get them to fight. . . . They just wouldn't play. They just would not play. They didn't know how to fight on land, particularly against guerrillas." DePuy felt similarly, telling the historian Krepinevich that "the Marines came in and just sat down and didn't do anything. They were involved in counterinsurgency of the deliberate, mild sort." Westmoreland felt that the Marine Corps leadership back in Washington was meddling in his war; he wrote in his diary in 1965 that "I detect a tendency for the Marine chain of command to try to unduly influence the tactical conduct of III MAF [Marine Amphibious Force] which is under my operational control."

DePuy, then chief of operations for Westmoreland, reportedly urged him to order the Marines to launch large-scale operations.

Westmoreland dismissed the Marine programs as too troop-intensive, too consuming to implement across Vietnam—a view that ignores the fact that the Marine program was intended to spread like an oil spot, with Marines expanding areas of security and Vietnamese forces filling in behind them. Westmoreland's senior intelligence officer in 1967–68 was Lt. Gen. Phillip Davidson, who had served under Patton in World War II and then, during the Korean War, had served as chief of plans and estimates under Maj. Gen. Willoughby, MacArthur's intelligence chief. In Vietnam, Davidson said, "Westmoreland's interest always lay in the big-unit war. Pacification bored him." The Army remained focused on killing the enemy rather than protecting the population. It would not explore the Marine alternative, despite the fact that it was a more cost-effective option. As Thomas Thayer pointed out, it was far cheaper to pay the enemy to quit fighting than to kill him. The cost of bringing in a Communist defector under the amnesty program called Chieu Hoi ("Open Arms") averaged out to less than $350, with a total of 176,000 such turncoats during the war. The cost of killing an enemy combatant with firepower, by contrast, averaged out to $60,000. Of course, we do not know how many stayed turned, while the dead stayed that way.

As Gen. DePuy put it to Daniel Ellsberg, then a trusted counterinsurgency specialist, over lunch in his 1st Infantry Division headquarters, "The solution in Vietnam is more bombs, more shells, more napalm . . . till the other side cracks and gives up." His view would prevail, as the Army, by late 1966, had 95 percent of its combat battalions in Vietnam carrying out search-and-destroy operations—a term coined by none other than DePuy, who drily noted, "It turned out to be infelicitous." In one two-month operation in 1967, code-named Junction City, American forces killed fewer than two thousand Viet Cong while firing 366,000 artillery rounds and dropping more than 3,000 tons of bombs.

By 1967, the new Marine commander in Vietnam, Lt. Gen. Robert Cushman, was ready to give up the struggle with the Army. "I soon figured out how Westy liked to operate and tried to operate the same way, and get on with the war and not cause a lot of friction for no good reason," he said years later. In February 1968, Westmoreland, not quite mollified, established a forward headquarters near the Marines to keep an eye on them. The move was taken as a sign of distrust. "I thought it was the most unpardonable thing that [the U.S. military headquarters in] Saigon ever did," said Maj. Gen. Rathvon Tompkins, commander of the 3rd Marine Division. Marines continued to believe that a counterinsurgency campaign built around protecting the Vietnamese people and separating them from the Viet Cong would have worked. "Westmoreland never understood it thoroughly," Gen. Krulak said at Annapolis in 1969. "He doesn't yet."

DePuy's search-and-destroy approach was a constant in Army operations, from Korea to Vietnam and then into the first years of the Iraq war, in 2003–4. In each war, Army officers often maintained, the Americans could have prevailed if only they had been allowed to unleash all their firepower. The problem with this hawkish view is that it has never been proven, while the lavish application of firepower that did occur over several years in Vietnam tends to argue against it. Those who say that more bombing would have led to success offer no explanation for why the bombardment of Laos did not succeed. The campaign there, not subject to political constraints, was extremely heavy, with some 8,500 sorties by B-52s in 1970 alone—more than twice as many sorties as there were in South Vietnam that year—yet it did not succeed in cutting the flow of supplies on the Ho Chi Minh Trail. "The allies had enormous firepower, combat support and the ability to move forces quickly," noted the Pentagon's Thayer. "But the communists won."

Another view, heard more often outside the military, was that neither the Marine approach nor a more intensive use of firepower would have worked, because both represented doomed attempts by an outside force to counter the fundamental facts of culture and politics in a far-off part of the world quite foreign to the Americans. The most comprehensive and balanced study of American pacification efforts in Vietnam concluded that it probably would not have led to eventual success, for much the same reason that the attrition strategy did not work: The price, in blood, money, and time, was more than the American people would be willing to pay. "Given the iron determination of the communists to unite Vietnam, their patience and resilience, their strategic and tactical flexibility, on the one hand, and the systemic problems of the Saigon government, on the other, the answer is no," wrote Richard Hunt. "The advocates of pacification hoped it would cause a fundamental transformation of South Vietnam. But even if that transformation had occurred, it would most likely have taken too long and would in any case have exhausted the patience of the American people, inevitably eroding support in the United States." Ironically, this entire argument about whether to work with the people would be repeated almost word for word four decades later in Iraq and Afghanistan—the major difference being that a small group of Army officers who rallied around the new American commander in Iraq in 2007, Gen. David Petraeus, would become the main proponents of the new counterinsurgency school, following the path not taken in Vietnam.

Less heard in this debate were the voices of the South Vietnamese military, which favored the local security approach long before the Americans became attuned to it. Its commanders have argued that a strategy based on providing security in villages could have worked—especially if the Americans had been better focused on enabling the South Vietnamese people to carry more of the load. "Tactics employed by the CAPs were founded on three basic principles: tactical mobility, economy of force, and credible permanence," recalled Lt. Gen. Truong. "The basic

Gen. George C. Marshall was the father of the modern U.S. armed forces, the military of the American superpower. He is shown at left in October 1941, just weeks before the United States entered World War II. Despite his position atop the biggest armed force in history, he was foremost a soldier. Below, he washes his face in Normandy, France, in June 1944, not long after the D-Day landings.

Pictured here in World War I are two officers who would play key roles in World War II. Above, Marshall's reserve is evident in his expression. Right, Douglas MacArthur's imperiousness was already well developed.

Four unusual lunch partners in Casablanca, Morocco, in January 1943. From left: White House adviser Harry Hopkins (an unlikely ally of Marshall's throughout the war), Lt. Gen. Mark Clark, President Franklin Roosevelt, and, back to camera, Maj. Gen. George Patton. Roosevelt's relations with his senior generals were a model of civil-military relations.

Maj. Gen. Terry de la Mesa Allen (left), commander of the 1st Infantry Division, and Lt. Gen. Omar Bradley examine a map in Sicily in July 1943. The following month Bradley would fire Allen, one of his most successful commanders—only to see Gen. Marshall send Allen back to Europe in command of another division.

Two of the major players in the Battle of Chosin Reservoir, one of the most memorable engagements in American military history. Gen. Douglas MacArthur (center) ordered Maj. Gen. O. P. Smith (right), commander of the 1st Marine Division, to charge northward to the Chinese border. Smith resisted that directive and so probably avoided a major military catastrophe that could have wiped out thousands of Marines.

Before and after Chosin: Above, members of the 7th Marine Regiment, part of Gen. Smith's 1st Marine Division, march toward the reservoir in November 1950. Left, the following month, Smith stands at a Marine's grave after the battle.

TOP SECRET

DECLASSIFIED
E.O. 11652, Sec. 3(E) and 5(D)
White House Press Release 4/10/51
By NLT-65c., NARS Date 3-7-75

PROPOSED ORDER TO GENERAL MacARTHUR TO BE SIGNED BY THE PRESIDENT

I deeply regret that it becomes my duty as President and Commander in Chief of the United States military forces to replace you as Supreme Commander, Allied Powers; Commander in Chief, United Nations Command; Commander in Chief, Far East; and Commanding General, U. S. Army, Far East.

You will turn over your commands, effective at once, to Lt. Gen. Matthew B. Ridgway. You are authorized to have issued such orders as are necessary to complete desired travel to such place as you select.

My reasons for your replacement, ~~which~~ will be made public concurrently with the delivery to you of the foregoing order, ~~will be communicated to you by Secretary Pace.~~ and are contained in the next following message.

Harry Truman

MacArthur fired: Above, President Truman's order removing him in April 1951. Below, the ousted general speaking at Soldier Field in Chicago two weeks later, at the height of his popularity. At this point he still may have thought he would be elected president the following year.

Two more doomed Army generals: Lt. Gen. Walton Walker (far left) talks with Maj. Gen. William Dean early in the Korean War. By the end of the year, Walker would be dead and Dean captured by the North Koreans. Dean was the highest-ranking American to be taken prisoner during the war.

Lt. Gen. Matthew Ridgway (left) would succeed Walker and, early in 1951, turn the war around, in the process undercutting MacArthur's political standing.

Maxwell Taylor arguably was the most destructive general in American history. As Army chief of staff in the 1950s, he steered the U.S. military toward engaging in "brushfire wars." As White House military adviser during the early 1960s, he encouraged President John F. Kennedy to deepen American involvement in Vietnam. As chairman of the Joint Chiefs, he poisoned relations between the military and the civilian leadership. He was also key in picking Gen. William Westmoreland to command the war there. Here Taylor (center) meets with Defense Secretary Robert McNamara and President Kennedy.

President Lyndon Johnson tries to clean up the mess he inherited in Vietnam. His relations with senior military leaders were even worse than Kennedy's. Here he meets with advisers on his Texas ranch in December 1964. Counterclockwise from Johnson (third from left): Air Force Gen. Curtis LeMay, Army Gen. Earle Wheeler, Deputy Defense Secretary Cyrus Vance, Gen. Harold Johnson, Adm. David McDonald, Gen. Wallace Greene, Maj. Gen. Chester Clifton, and Defense Secretary McNamara. Johnson would eventually treat the Joint Chiefs in a manner that Marshall would not have tolerated.

Gen. Creighton Abrams (far right) would succeed Westmoreland as the American commander on the ground in Vietnam and by many accounts did a much better job. Here he speaks with Maj. Gen. George Forsythe, then the commander of the 1st Cavalry Division.

The life of Gen. William DePuy (left) is in many ways the story of the modern U.S. Army. He fought in a hard-luck unit in Normandy in the summer of 1944. He commanded a division in Vietnam, where he was credited with inventing the term "search and destroy." And he played a central role in the post-Vietnam rebuilding of the U.S. military. Here he instructs a soldier in tactics, his favorite subject.

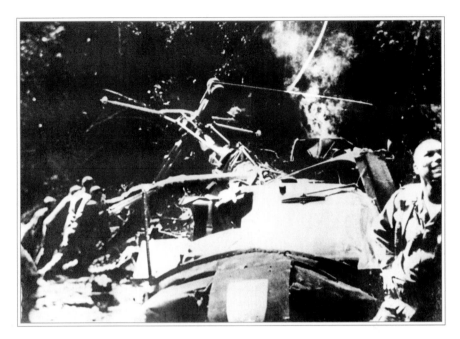

Two future generals deeply influenced by their time in Vietnam: Colin Powell (above right) stares upward after being injured in the crash of the helicopter behind him. Norman Schwarzkopf (below left) helps carry a wounded South Vietnamese soldier.

Powell and Schwarzkopf (above) during their month of triumph, February 1991, when the forces under their command made short work of the Iraqi military. Defense Secretary Dick Cheney sits next to Powell. But Schwarzkopf and many other generals missed the message of the Battle of Khafji (below), resulting in a war plan that instead of destroying the Iraqi military pushed its most important units back into Iraq.

Schwarzkopf's odd handling of his generals was best illustrated by his miscommunications with Gen. Frederick Franks (above). Franks suffered from Schwarzkopf's overestimation of the effectiveness of the Iraqi foe. Schwarzkopf would describe Franks in his memoirs as jittery and overcautious.

Schwarzkopf (left) arranges a ceasefire with Iraqi generals at Safwan, Iraq, in March 1991. He and his superiors thought they were ending the war. Iraqi leader Saddam Hussein could not understand why he was being given the gift of a ceasefire, which he interpreted as a victory for Iraq. That is, he had been assaulted by the Americans but lived to tell about it. So began two decades of American fighting with Iraq—first, twelve years of patrolling "no-fly zones," followed by eight years of fighting on the ground. But the ragged outcome of the war was more the fault of American civilian leaders than that of generals.

Gen. Tommy R. Franks, who mishandled the wars in Afghanistan and Iraq, is seen by many in the Army as a mistake or aberration, someone promoted well past his level of competence. In fact, he was not an accident but the natural outcome of Gen. DePuy's post-Vietnam rebuilding of the military, with its overemphasis on tactics and its failure to educate generals to think strategically about war. As retired Lt. Gen. John Cushman put it, "His development approached the ideal career pattern of senior officer development at the time."

Gen. David Petraeus cleaned up much of the mess made by Gen. Tommy Franks in Iraq but was less successful when sent to try to conclude the Afghan war. Petraeus is an anomaly among contemporary American generals. He earned a Ph.D. at Princeton, enjoyed talking to reporters, and generally was more successful than many of his peers, who saw him as an outsider.

Lt. Gen. Ricardo Sanchez (left), the most junior three-star general in the Army, was put in charge of a situation in Iraq that he did not understand; a full-blown insurgency emerged on his watch. He was given command in Iraq essentially because he was available. He would retire in bitterness. He was succeeded by Gen. George Casey (below left, walking on an Iraqi tarmac with Defense Secretary Donald Rumsfeld). Casey would do better than Sanchez but ultimately would be ousted by President George W. Bush.

Long after the war in Iraq sputtered to an end, American soldiers fought in combat in Afghanistan. Above, soldiers of the 101st Airborne Division fighting in Kunar Province in 2011.

tactical idea was to lay out a screen of ambushes on the approaches to the hamlet instead of putting up a static defense wall around it. . . . By virtue of this quality of elusive mobility, the CAP seemed to be everywhere but never predictably anywhere." The effect of this was to deny Viet Cong fighters crucial sources of manpower, food, and taxes, he concluded. "The advantages of the CAP were obvious. It provided continuous protection to the village; it trained and motivated a local self-defense force; and it was a potential source for the type of intelligence that would ultimately break the enemy infrastructure." Lt. Gen. Dong Van Khuyen, a former chief of staff of the South Vietnamese general staff, argued that the village defense approach was effective in part because it was consistent with Vietnamese traditions of local self-government. "Had it been fully developed and implemented, the enemy would have been beaten at his own game," he wrote in 1978. "Since the Communist infrastructure and guerrillas could operate only if supported and sheltered by the people, then only the people could single them out and destroy them."

That approach was flatly rejected by senior American commanders. Instead, as Westmoreland himself put it, the United States engaged in "a protracted war of attrition"—never a good bet to win the support of the American people, especially in a small, hot country on the far side of the world. Nor did it make fundamental sense in operational terms. Search and destroy was a tactically offensive approach, but it was carried out while the American military was in a strategically defensive position, sitting in South Vietnam and waiting for attackers to move in from the North. This meant that even if the United States could pour firepower onto the battlefield, the enemy could moderate the pace of combat at will and, as a result, adjust its casualty rate—which undercut the attritionist approach. Even DePuy, that most aggressive of commanders, was surprised, when leading the 1st Infantry Division, at the difficulty his units had in finding and pursuing the enemy. "It turned out they controlled the tempo of the war better than we would admit," he said decades later. "We beat the devil out of 'em time after time, and they just pulled off and waited and regained their strength until they could afford some more losses. Then they came back again. . . . So we ended up with no operational plan that had the slightest chance of ending the war favorably."

In other words, the enemy was allowed to determine the time, place, and pace of battle and so, to a surprising extent, could regulate his level of casualties. This, in turn, called into question the entire strategy of attrition. And that meant that the American strategy was essentially a recipe for an open-ended war that could not be won. "As long as they could control their losses, there was no way you could bring the war to any kind of a conclusion," DePuy would conclude in 1985. A strategy of attrition might possibly have succeeded *only* if the United States had been willing to fight a much broader and riskier war, sending several divisions to invade North Vietnam and also to cut the Ho Chi Minh Trail in Laos. It was not willing to take that risk, especially given the possibility that such a campaign would have provoked a large-scale Chinese intervention, as had happened in Korea in 1950. So, like a full-blown counterinsurgency approach, this remains a road not taken, an unknowable theoretical alternative.

c. In personnel policy

In Colorado Springs, one evening in March 1976, four military officers were discussing American personnel policies in the Vietnam War. "If you attempted to run a business like that, it would go under," commented an Air Force officer.

"Ours did," an Army infantry major responded.

There is an old military saying that amateurs talk tactics, while

professionals talk logistics. In fact, real insiders talk about personnel policy, which as they know shapes the American military to a
surprising extent. Even had the Vietnam War been better conducted by American generals in the field, the personnel policies
put in place by generals back at the Pentagon still might have
undercut the American effort. During the American foray in Vietnam, the Pentagon used an approach to personnel that verged on
the bizarre, with troops coming and going under a policy of individual one-year rotations and commanders moving on at about
the time they began to understand their tactical situation. "It's
the stupidest damn thing I've ever seen," Gen. Donn Starry said
later.

The Army began a policy of rotating troops midway through
the Korean War, in 1951, on the humane grounds that men should
not be left in combat indefinitely. This tactic also allowed seasoned
soldiers to move into other units where they would be useful
should war break out with the Soviet Union. Yet this policy carried
a surprisingly high price for the people it supposedly was helping:
It likely led to the deaths of many American soldiers, and also
undercut larger military aims. Under the rotation policy, the performance of combat units in Korea began to decline. By late 1952,
most of the younger officers with World War II experience had
gone home, replaced by green men with "little or no acquaintance
with the battlefield," records an official Army history. "Most of the
troops sent over from the United States lacked field training and
had to learn the hard way. By the time the new men became proficient soldiers, they had amassed enough points to qualify them for
rotation and the process had to start all over again." Patrolling by
frontline units, an all-important function for keeping troops on
their toes and commanders aware of enemy moves, especially suffered. If a patrol is ordered to go forward five hundred yards to
see whether an enemy machine gun is in place, but it goes only

three hundred yards and returns to state that it went the entire distance and saw nothing, troops may well die. In a surprising report for someone in a semi-official position, S. L. A. Marshall, the Army historian, noted in a memoir that by late in the Korean War, "patrol leaders had learned to lie with some proficiency."

The effect of rotation on the 65th Regiment late in the Korean War was a case in point. "Stripped of its experienced leadership and spirited volunteers, the 65th sank into a gradual decline that was to result, finally, in a scandalous bugout [soldiers running away from an attack in October 1952], after which the Army court-martialed 92 of its men," noted Clay Blair. Paul Gorman, later a general but then a young lieutenant, was surprised to find soldiers in the 65th smoking marijuana "every night." The regiment's commander blamed its weakness on excessive rotation. In the first nine months of 1952, the 3,500-man unit had a total of more than 9,000 men among its ranks. (That is, 1,334 lost as casualties; 3,963 rotated; and 3,825 replacements.) That is a level of turbulence that destroys cohesion and trust, and so undermines combat effectiveness.

It might not have seemed possible to come up with a worse method of rotation than the Army had used late in the Korean War, but in Vietnam it found a way. In a new wrinkle, under a system devised in 1964 by Gen. Johnson, the Army chief of staff, officers were given a break. Enlisted soldiers would continue to spend a year fighting, as they had in the Korean War, but their officers would spend six months in staff positions followed by six months leading a unit, or vice versa. The Army's leaders argued that commanders were worn out after six months of sustained combat, but evidence indicates that this was a fatuous argument. First, as historian Adrian Lewis, himself a former Army officer, noted, "few units were in sustained combat," and most support units, such as those providing logistics, were not in combat at all. Also, dispositive data, when collected, disproved the assertion: After the war was over, a survey of officers at the Army Command and General Staff College found that only 8 percent reported "burn-out" at the end of their six months of command. Rather, the authors of the survey, Maj. Arnold Daxe Jr. and Capt. Victor Stemberger, found that "the major deterrent to true professionalism was that an officer did not stay in the same job in the same place long enough to become knowledgeable in the specifics of their situation." Another Army personnel expert, Walter Ulmer, agreed, saying later that "the problem with six-month or twelve-month command tours is that you can do some really dumb things and they don't come back to haunt you until after you are gone. . . . It is easy to be a spectacular commander for six months. It is tougher to be a spectacular commander for eighteen months."

Even less considered was how changes in personnel policies—promotion, relief, and rotation—altered the long-term rules governing military careers and so changed combat behavior. Explicit or not, there is always an incentive structure built into such policies. What gets an officer ahead? What does the organization expect, and what does it flatly reject? What is deemed intolerable behavior? For example, there tends to be a connection between rotation and risk aversion. If one is in a war for the duration, and the road home goes through Berlin and Tokyo, as the World War II saying had it, then there is a clear incentive to take some risks. In such a situation, inaction not only postponed the inevitable but also gave the enemy a chance to rest, recover, and build up his defenses. By contrast, if everyone rotates home at a set time regardless of the state of the war, and there is little relationship between one's performance in a tour of duty and subsequent promotions, there is less incentive to take risks and there is every incentive to simply serve the time, protect one's people, and move on. Even if a commander does not succumb to that logic, but his

278 | THE GENERALS

peers do, then his risk taking will be easier for the enemy to counter and so more likely to fail, because the foe is not being challenged by risk taking elsewhere along the front. Rotation thus tends to push commanders toward the average, as the incompetent are tolerated along with the excellent. Whatever their performance, everyone simply rotates, and combat tours become a matter of "ticket punching."

Rotation also reinforced the disinclination of the Army in Vietnam to relieve failing officers and instead encouraged simply micromanaging them. If someone was going to go home in a few months, why go to the trouble of moving him out and finding a replacement? By the time a commander became certain a subordinate was unfit for his position, the time to rotate that officer often was approaching. Thus, it frequently was easier simply to bypass the problem and wait for the rotation. This could be done by pulling the officer's unit back from frontline combat or by relying heavily on the executive officer (the commander's deputy) or, most commonly, by simply monitoring the officer closely, watching his every move—that is, relying on micromanagement. The new policies represented a triumph of management over leadership, making it easier to run the organization but not necessarily making the organization more effective. In other words, the Army would be easier for bureaucrats to manage on a day-to-day basis, but it was not being developed to prevail in combat. Historian Keith Nolan, author of eleven books about the Vietnam War, judged that the rotation policy "cast an amateurish quality over the war effort as a whole and resulted in needless casualties."

Intentionally churning personnel was one way to run an Army, but it was no way to win a war. In Vietnam, as in Korea, the Army seemed more interested in taking care of its own officer corps than in winning. DePuy said as much: "With regard to having six months in command and trying to rotate everybody through, I've always said that was running the war for the benefit of the officer corps."

Sometimes an odd or stressful personnel policy can be justified on the grounds of combat effectiveness, but here the opposite was the case. A 1968 Pentagon study, "Experience in Command and Battle Deaths," found that units operating under experienced commanders had roughly two-thirds the death rate of units with less experienced leaders. Also, American soldiers fighting in Vietnam were more than twice as likely to die in the first halves of their yearlong tours than in the second halves: Some 18,991 Army soldiers were killed during their first six months, while 6,759 were killed in their second six months.

Rotation also left tactical commanders unfamiliar with some basic facts about the country. For example, noted Thayer, the Pentagon analyst, over the years a seasonal pattern emerged in which fighting peaked in May and subsided in the last quarter of the year. This may have contributed to the waves of optimism that occasionally swamped American analyses. "Major offensives or waves of communist activity did not occur during the last three months of the year and this was when the year-end reports of progress were being written." He added that he had never met an American who had fought in Vietnam who was aware of this predictable yearly cycle.

The rotation of Americans also would prove dangerous to the Vietnamese population. One of the root causes of the 1968 My Lai massacre of villagers by American troops, the Army's official investigation would find, was personnel turbulence created by rotation and the policy of six-month command tours for most officers. "This inquiry found that the resulting lack of continuity and the problems created with the personnel replacement process were detrimental to unit effectiveness," Lt. Gen. William Peers wrote.

The policy also strained relations with the Vietnamese military, observed Lt. Gen. Truong: "The relatively rapid turnover of advisers at battalion level had a definite adverse effect on the advisory program." During the course of the war, tactical commanders in the South Vietnamese military typically went through a total of twenty to thirty American advisers, noted a study conducted after the war by former South Vietnamese officers.

The short-tour policy for officers even hurt the very people it was supposed to help by corroding the professionalism of the officer corps. Lt. Col. David Holmes charged in an Army publication that it probably reinforced what he called "the 'ticket-punching' careerist syndrome still visible in today's officer corps."

It also might have encouraged the risk-averse tendencies of the Army's officer corps. By the end of the Vietnam War, retired Army Lt. Col. Wade Markel concluded, the Army had stumbled into a

> culture of insecurity that engendered a general predilection for prudence and caution. That general predilection for prudence found its expression in the adoption of the perimeter defense as battalion and brigade commanders' preferred form of maneuver in Vietnam. . . . Thus an Army whose pre-WWII traditions and wartime practice inclined its members to seek enemy weakness reflexively and to exploit that weakness relentlessly became an Army obsessed with covering its own weakness, an Army that avoided error rather than exploited opportunity.

Combat ineffectiveness

Given all this, it should not be surprising that, while Americans often fought hard in Vietnam, it is not clear that they fought well on the whole. For all its firepower, the American military was less intimidating to its enemy than might be expected. Army commanders actually tended toward "excessive caution" in waging their war, one Army historian noted. This was measurable: Pentagon studies found in 1967 that more than 90 percent of company-size firefights were initiated by the foe. "The great majority of all ground battles were at the enemy's choice of time, place, type and duration," noted historian Guenter Lewy. The enemy also tended to decide when to break contact, and generally was not followed far. "Pursuit became a forgotten art," observed retired Army Lt. Gen. Dave Richard Palmer. "No sizable communist force was ever hounded to its lair and wiped out."

Americans also showed a lack of professionalism in the field, tending, for example, to disclose too much information while talking over their radios, said Air Force Maj. Gen. George Keegan, an intelligence specialist: "Our ground, naval and air forces have paid an enormous price for their near total lack of communications discipline. The enemy always knew where we were, what we intended to do, and when." Overall, conceded Lt. Gen. Davidson, the top American military intelligence officer in Vietnam at that time, U.S. communications security was "atrocious," with even senior officers routinely discussing plans and troop movements over unsecured radios. There were, he added, "all sorts of other things that were dead giveaway indications of American operations," all the way down to when units did their laundry.

Veterans of the Viet Cong and the North Vietnamese Army agreed with that assessment. One reason for their superior intelligence was a focused infiltration program that in part capitalized on the Americans' eagerness to have sex with Vietnamese women. "We placed our own girls in the various hotels and offices to service" the Americans, said Nguyen Thi Dinh, a woman who was the deputy commander of the Viet Cong and later a major general in the regular Communist army. She explained:

> When it became necessary for us to attack the Americans, these women would be the ones to place the bombs and the mines. We even had people in the High Military Command of the

Americans. In fact, we had people in every enemy office and we were able to have a firm grasp of the enemy's situation as a result. And whenever we decided to attack, our targets were always very significant targets. We never hit the ordinary American targets.

As a result, some Communist veterans would recall a confidence about attacking Americans, especially as the U.S. Army began to deteriorate rapidly in 1968–69. "The U.S. soldier is very poor when moving through the terrain," one Communist fighter told his interrogators. This assessment of the Americans might reflect a bit of resentment, given that captured fighters complained in interrogations that every time they got close to American lines, the Americans would pull back and call in artillery fire and air strikes. That same fighter added, "An American unit cannot take or destroy a machine-gun position in a properly prepared bunker except by calling for air or artillery." Huong Van Ba, an NVA artillery colonel, said, "Their idea was to surround us with ground forces, then destroy us with artillery and rockets, rather than by attacking directly with infantry. Usually we could get away from that, even when they used helicopters to try and surround us, because we knew the countryside so well and we could get out fast. That happened at Soi Cut, where they destroyed three villages while they were trying to catch us."

Communist veterans also came to doubt the tenacity and adaptability of American forces, especially later in the war. "They had a lot of bombs and shells, they were very powerful as far as war materials were concerned, but they did not fight very well at all," said Nguyen Van Nghi, a Northerner who fought as a member of the Viet Cong from 1967 to the end of the war. "They were very slow in moving around, they were not really that mobile. In combat you have to be quick physically and mentally. But in combat the Americans were not very quick—they reacted very slowly."

Nguyen Thi Hoa, who as a teenage girl fought with the Viet Cong in the Battle of Hue in 1968, said she thought the Americans' sentimentality made them vulnerable: "When the American soldiers fell down and died, three or four others would jump in to carry the body away, crying. . . . So we took advantage of the situation to kill the rest of the group." A third VC veteran, Dang Xuan Teo, said that many of his comrades actually preferred combating the Americans: "The puppet troops were also Vietnamese and, therefore, they were quite devious in many ways. The Americans in general were quite naive. It was easy to fight them."

In particular, the Communists found the perimeters of American bases to be remarkably porous. A captured North Vietnamese lieutenant who had been badly wounded told his interrogators, "All the U.S. defensive positions are easy to get through. I can say that I have never encountered a tough one in my experience. We just crawl slowly through the wire, cutting the bottom strands."

Perhaps most important, Communist fighters seemed to have a better grasp of the nature of the conflict in which they were engaged. As the lieutenant said in his interrogation, "We know we cannot defeat the Americans, as it is almost impossible to defeat you, but the military operations exist just to back the political aspects. We will win the war politically, not militarily." Though it was coming from a junior officer, this comment indicates a better understanding of the war than Westmoreland and other American generals possessed.

Everyone makes mistakes, especially when operating under the extreme mental and physical stress of combat. Indeed, part of the art of combat is forcing the enemy to commit errors. But victory in war often goes to those who are able first to recognize their mistakes and then to correct them. The American generals did not seem able or even willing to do so in Vietnam. For years, American generals refused to recognize mistakes, to the point of self-deception. As historian John Gates put it, "The stubborn commitment of the high command to error defies belief, but the evidence of it would seem to be overwhelming."

Seemingly unable to do their own jobs, the American generals of the Vietnam War often sought to do the work of their subordinates. One of the enduring images of the Vietnam War is that of commanders hovering over the battlefield in command helicopters. William Rindberg recalled being a platoon leader in a serious fight: "The battalion commander was almost forced off the air, and the brigade commander was on the net controlling one of the platoons, the division commander was talking with the company commander. All this was going on and the company commander was getting pretty frustrated. He couldn't even talk to his own platoons because everybody was on his net."

The relatively new technology of the helicopter might have enabled generals to try to escape their roles. Instead of trying to improve strategy, generals and colonels climbed into aircraft and became what one general called "squad leaders in the sky." They found themselves in a situation where the fundamental task of a general—to understand the nature of the fight and adjust his force to it—may have been all but undoable. When strategy becomes inexplicable, the natural tendency is to retreat into tactics. "Kill more Viet Cong" was at best a tactical imperative, but it became the mantra from the White House and the Pentagon down to the headquarters of the U.S. military in Vietnam.

CHAPTER 19

Tet '68

The end of Westmoreland and the turning point of the war

War is always a gamble, a venture into uncertainty. To paraphrase a famous comment by the historian and Anzio veteran Michael Howard, the victor is not necessarily the side that gets it right at the start but the side that adjusts more quickly. In launching the Tet Offensive of 1968, the Communist leadership was not correct in its understanding of what would happen, but it was less wrong than the Americans were.

In November 1967, Westmoreland had stated, "We have reached an important point when the end begins to come into view." Two months later, such talk would seem at least foolish and perhaps even mendacious. At 3 A.M. on January 31, 1968, some eighty thousand Communist fighters nearly simultaneously attacked across South Vietnam, hitting Saigon, thirty-nine provincial capitals, and seventy-one district capitals. Militarily, this was unwise, because it spread forces terribly thin. But the primary purpose of the offensive was not military but political, aimed at sparking a nationwide uprising of the people of South Vietnam. If that occurred, then military reinforcements would be unnecessary: The people would rise up, finish the war, and oust the Americans.

The planning toward that end was careful and elaborate—and would quickly falter. One Viet Cong battalion was ordered to liberate the five thousand inmates of Saigon's prison, many of them held on political charges. The unit's guides were killed en route, and it became bogged down in battle before reaching the prison. The 101st Viet Cong Regiment, which had been trained to operate South Vietnamese tanks and artillery pieces, was directed to attack the headquarters of South Vietnamese armored forces and fight using gear it confiscated there, but it was unable to do so. Lt. Ngo Minh Khoi, a South Vietnamese paratrooper stationed at Tan Son Nhut air base, outside Saigon, was astonished to see Viet Cong soldiers charge into the minefields surrounding the base. "The majority of them clearly was killed by the mines, and the rest was killed by the firing of the unit that was defending," he said. Assassination squads were sent to kill the South Vietnamese president, the American ambassador, and various chiefs of police and intelligence organizations. All these efforts failed.

Some were almost successful. Another specialized unit was sent to take over the government radio station. The infiltrators arrived at 3 A.M., dressed as South Vietnamese police. A guard asked who they were. Reinforcements, they told him. None had been requested, he replied. They shot him. A platoon of genuine South Vietnamese airborne troops on duty on the station roof was wiped out by Viet Cong machine gunners from an overlooking apartment building. The attackers then escorted a radio technician trained to operate the transmitting gear into the station. They brought with them tapes to play, which would announce that the people had risen and liberated the capital. What they did not know was that the station's director had instructed that, in the event of an attack, the station would be taken off the air, to be replaced by a remote station—which turned out to have on hand only "Viennese waltzes, the Beatles, the Rolling Stones and

Vietnamese martial music." The Communist tapes were never broadcast. At 10 A.M., the surviving Viet Cong fighters blew up the station and themselves.

A Viet Cong platoon wearing South Vietnamese uniforms rocketed the gates of the Independence Palace but were fended off by the palace guard, which had two tanks on hand. The VC unit retreated into a nearby unfinished apartment building, where, over the following two days, thirty-two of its members were killed and two captured. An attack on the headquarters of the Vietnamese navy also failed. The assault on the American military headquarters for the country, located at Tan Son Nhut air base, was more successful, as three Viet Cong battalions hit it simultaneously from the west, north, and east. Unfortunately for them, a full Vietnamese battalion was at the base, waiting to be flown north, and was quickly thrown into the fight.

A team of nineteen Viet Cong used a satchel charge (a small explosive device) to breach the compound wall of the American embassy and fought for several hours to try to get inside the building. They also were wiped out. But as one of the leading historians of Tet, James Willbanks, wrote, "This small squad of VC sappers had proven in dramatic fashion that there was no place in Vietnam that was secure from attack."

There would be additional political fallout from Americans seeing news photographs that showed the true face of the war. The following day, the chief of the national police force, Gen. Nguyen Ngoc Loan, executed a Viet Cong guerrilla in the streets of Saigon. The image was splashed on the front pages of newspapers around the world. After firing his revolver, Nguyen turned to the reporters watching him and said, in English, "They killed many Americans and many of my men. Buddha will understand. Do you?"

One bright spot during Tet '68, now all but forgotten, was the performance of Lt. Gen. Fred Weyand, who by this point had been promoted from division command to overall leader of American forces in the Saigon region. At the time, Westmoreland, his commander, was focused on the besieged mountain outpost of Khe Sanh, which Westy mistakenly believed threatened to become his Dien Bien Phu—the climactic defeat that all but ended the French war for Vietnam in 1954. In addition, on December 15, 1967, the Americans had turned over responsibility for defending Saigon to the South Vietnamese. But Weyand was not so easily distracted. He discussed the movements of the Viet Cong with his friend John Paul Vann, and they concluded, " 'Hey, something is going on here that we don't have a good handle on. It doesn't look like they are going to be where we thought they were going to be if we move north.' " Westmoreland ordered Weyand to move forces to the border, but Weyand argued against that and ultimately got grudging permission to shift fifteen of his battalions from the countryside to positions closer to the capital, nearly doubling American forces there. This move, commented Lt. Gen. Dave Richard Palmer in his history, was perhaps one of the most significant and perceptive tactical decisions of the war. Characteristically, Westmoreland would fudge the facts in his memoir, asserting that Weyand's concerns only reinforced doubts he already held. This claim is at odds with his actions at the time.

Westmoreland would argue that Tet had proven to be a defeat for the enemy. When it was over, between 45,000 and 58,000 North Vietnamese soldiers and members of the Viet Cong lay dead. (By contrast, the total number of U.S. and South Vietnamese soldiers killed in the offensive was about 9,000.) The general went to his grave considering the Tet Offensive to be the Vietnamese equivalent of the Battle of the Bulge, a last-gasp effort by an enemy facing total defeat. "We saw the Germans do this . . . when Von Rundstedt made the attack into the Ardennes, and the Allied troops were tremendously set back, but the Germans were defeated, and it was downhill the rest of the way," he asserted in 1981. There is no doubt that the offensive had failed to achieve its explicit goal of inciting insurrection. The Hanoi government's official history of the war concedes, "Our soldiers' morale had been very high when they set off for battle, but . . . when the battle did not progress favorably for our side and when we suffered casualties, rightist thoughts, pessimism, and hesitancy appeared among our forces." When the people of South Vietnam did not rise up, many Viet Cong cadres became "confused," to use the Communist euphemism. So Westmoreland was correct that it had been a demoralizing tactical defeat for the Communists.

But in strategic terms, Tet '68 was a triumph, and the turning point in the war for the Communists. The people are the prize, holds one of the key tenets of insurgency and counterinsurgency, and the North Vietnamese seemed inadvertently to have hit the American people squarely: The American center of gravity in the war was not Saigon or the Vietnamese people, nor even the American military in Vietnam, but the willingness of the American people to continue supporting an open-ended war of attrition. The American public had been growing unhappy with the war for months, particularly since the previous fall, when President Johnson had proposed a 6 percent war surtax. "The president's tax proposal made a lot of new doves," Secretary of State Dean Rusk had observed to his staff on October 5, 1967.

In the wake of Tet, "the American imperialist will to commit aggression began to waver," noted Hanoi's stilted war history. "We had brought our war of revolution right into the enemy's lair, disrupted his rear areas, and made a deep and profound effect on the puppet army, the puppet government, U.S. troops, and on the American ruling clique." Robert Komer, one member of that "clique," recalled, "Washington panicked. LBJ panicked. Bus

Wheeler, chairman of the Joint Chiefs, panicked. . . . The Chiefs have decided, because they too panicked, that we're losing." Richard Holbrooke, then a young foreign service officer, said that when he went to see senior officials in Saigon, "they were all in a state of shock." DePuy seemed to capture the mood best with his observation that Tet had ruined internal American discourse: "Nobody believed anything that anybody said for a while after Tet." Most skeptical of all were the American people, who were rapidly losing faith in the leadership of American officials in both Saigon and Washington. In November, two months before Tet, 50 percent of Americans interviewed for the Gallup Poll said the United States was making progress in the war, while 41 percent thought it was losing or standing still. By February those numbers had essentially reversed, with just 33 percent still believing that progress was being made, while 61 percent thought it was losing or standing still.

Like his predecessor, Westmoreland was now seen as a failure by his civilian overseers. As the offensive was being extinguished, Johnson, on a visit to California, helicoptered to visit Dwight Eisenhower in Palm Springs. "He told me some stories about General Marshall," Johnson related to Secretaries Rusk and McNamara, among others, the following day over lunch. "He said that Marshall was an impersonal man." That was not the whole of it, according to the well-connected British journalist Henry Brandon, who had socialized with the Kennedys for years and would go on to enjoy unusual access to President Johnson, holding private conversations with him. Brandon spoke with Johnson a few days later and learned that Johnson had gone to inquire of Eisenhower how to know when to relieve a general. Ike, following what Marshall had taught him, said that it was necessary to do so when one lost confidence in that general.

Just five days later, Johnson sent a telegram telling Westmoreland that he was taking him out of Vietnam. Westmoreland's biographer's grim conclusion was that

> in virtually ignoring pacification and the upgrading of South Vietnam's armed forces, Westmoreland failed to advance the security of the populace or the capacity for self-defense of South Vietnam's armed forces. He likewise failed to diminish the enemy's combat forces, despite his near-exclusive focus on that task, as the casualties inflicted were simply replaced. What he had done was squander four years of his troops' bravery and support by the public, the Congress and even most of the news media for the war in Vietnam.

Westmoreland's departure, following that of Harkins and indeed that of MacArthur seventeen years earlier, continued the new pattern in America's wars: The only general removed was the topmost one, reassigned for political reasons by the defense secretary or the president. This was the new form of relief.

Tet '68 also knocked off a president. Two weeks after moving against Westmoreland, President Johnson announced that he would not run for reelection. Vietnam tormented the president even in his dreams. "Every night when I fell asleep I would see myself tied to the ground in the middle of a long, open space," he told Doris Kearns Goodwin. "In the distance, I could hear the voices of thousands of people. They were all shouting at me and running toward me: 'Coward! Traitor! Weakling!' They kept coming closer. They began throwing stones. At exactly that moment I would generally wake up."

The war effectively was lost. When Johnson's successor, Richard Nixon, became president in January 1969, he moved into the White House determined to terminate American involvement in the war. His chief foreign policy aide, Henry Kissinger, later would write, "Even before assuming office, we decided to withdraw American forces as rapidly as possible."

Coda: The Hue massacre

Almost unnoticed at the time were the mass murders conducted by the Communists as they occupied parts of Hue City for twenty-five days. Among the executed were not just government officials but also teachers, students, priests, foreigners, and anyone else thought to possibly oppose Communist rule. At least 2,800 bodies were found in mass graves. "In any area where the grass was green, there was a body underneath it," recalled Nguyen Cong Minh. Some had been buried alive. Many were buried in remote areas far from the city, apparently because prisoners taken along with retreating Communist forces became cumbersome and were killed for fear that they would reveal the routes of withdrawal. In the city, many more corpses were taken away for burial by the families of the dead, who often had been assured by Communist officials not to worry, that the family member simply was being taken to attend a meeting. "You had this horrible smell," recalled Marine Capt. Myron Harrington, who was a company commander at Hue. "It was there when you were eating your rations. It was almost like you were eating death."

CHAPTER 20
My Lai
General Koster's cover-up and
General Peers's investigation

Unlike what happened in Hue City, the My Lai massacre has lived on in American memory—but only as an instance of a rogue platoon led by a dimwitted lieutenant. What has been forgotten is that the Army's subsequent investigations found that the chain of command up to the division commander was involved either in the atrocity or in the cover-up that followed. The triggers were pulled by young men, but several senior officers were deeply at fault as well. In fact, it was the modern low point of Army generalship, and of the Army itself.

When he left command of the 23rd ("Americal") Division in mid-1968, Maj. Gen. Samuel Koster filed an end-of-tour debriefing report with the Army that depicted his outfit doing a difficult job effectively. "The Americal Division strives to maintain rapport with the local government and populace," he reported. "Among the major subordinate areas in which the Americal Division has extended unique services are public health, commodities/resources control, transportation and movement of supplies, refugee assistance, civil employment, claims and indemnities, mobile training teams, and measures to minimize the effects upon the civilian population caused or which would be caused by VC/NVA [North Vietnamese Army] initiated actions." When he signed that report, Gen. Koster was well aware that a few months earlier, one of his units had murdered many Vietnamese civilians in a small village near the coast. He flew over the village in a helicopter on the day of the mass killing and participated in the subsequent cover-up of the incident.

On the morning of Saturday, March 16, 1968, about one hundred members of Charlie Company, 1st Battalion, 20th Infantry Regiment, 11th Light Infantry Brigade, American Division, had slaughtered at least four hundred Vietnamese civilians in a fishing-and-farming village between the coast and Route 1 that the soldiers called "Pinkville" and the locals called Thuan Yen, a part of Son My that the world now remembers as My Lai, after a general area of the map in which Thuan Yen was listed as the sub-hamlet of "My Lai 4." Revelation of the atrocity came the following year, and the ensuing revulsion would provoke a new wave of questioning about why the United States was in Vietnam, as well as about the state of the Army and its officer corps.

The Army in Vietnam suffered "a collective nervous breakdown," wrote Ronald Spector, once an official Army historian of Vietnam. If that is accurate—and it almost certainly is—then My Lai was the place where the collapse became apparent to the world and no longer deniable by the Army's generals. Even half a century later, the incident is painful to study. Charlie Company was not a unit driven around the bend by months of unrelenting loss. It had been in the country for just three months, and in a combat zone for just half that time. It had suffered four deaths and thirty-eight wounded, almost all inflicted by mines. "They had received casualties, but they had received most of their casualties by taking shortcuts," said Hugh Thompson, an Army helicopter pilot who intervened to try to stop the killings. "Our enemy knew us a whole lot better than we knew them. They knew a new unit would take shortcuts, the easy way out."

Charlie was an odd company in a division that itself was something of an orphan, having been cobbled together from three separate infantry brigades and then staffed poorly.

As is often the case with the formation of new units, Americal tended to be used as a dumping ground by other divisions. "The people we received at mid-level and lower, I suspected, were those who had difficulty finding a home," Gen. Koster later said. He thought his staff was solid, but some of its members disagreed. "It was the most unhappy group of staff officers and unhappy headquarters that I ever had any contact with," stated Lt. Col. Jesmond Balmer, the division's assistant operations chief.

Like William DePuy, Koster was one of those officers who had risen swiftly during World War II, graduating from West Point in 1942 and commanding a battalion by age twenty-six. But unlike DePuy, he was not embraced by Westmoreland. Rather, in Vietnam he himself was a bit of a stray, the only Army division commander in the country who had not been personally requested by Westmoreland but rather sent by the Army chief of staff. "He was a protégé of Harold K. Johnson, who wanted to make him superintendent of West Point, and thought it was well for him to get the division command experience before he went to West Point," recalled Gen. William Knowlton, who would replace Koster at West Point years later, when Koster was forced to step down because of revelations about his role in covering up what his soldiers had done at My Lai.

Command arrangements further isolated Koster. Because the division was located in the far north of South Vietnam, where the Marines were in command, Koster reported to a Marine general. Given the history of tension in command relationships between the Army and the Marines in World War II and in Korea, as well as in Vietnam, the Marines probably were inclined to let Koster and his Army division go their own way. "Terribly difficult command and control problem, in perhaps the toughest part of Vietnam to fight in, 'Indian Country' that the Viet Cong had owned for generations, far removed from Army supervision and working under the Marines," commented a regretful Gen. Bruce Palmer Jr. It was a recipe for disaster: an understaffed, poorly manned unit led by an isolated general in a remote corner of the country, with a huge "tactical area of responsibility." In addition, Palmer noted, Koster really did not have much time leading soldiers in combat—a repetition of a mistake the Army had made in the Korean War. "When we really looked at Sam's troop record, it showed very little troop experience. So we gave the toughest job in Vietnam to our most inexperienced commander, who was least qualified to be a division commander."

Even in the ragtag American Division, Charlie Company stood out as notably undisciplined. "When I was assigned to Charlie Company, I knew there was something wrong," said Michael Bernhardt. "You could smell it and feel it. . . . They were just a bunch of street thugs doing whatever they wanted to do. It was a group that was leaderless, directionless, armed to the teeth, and making up their own rules out there." Army investigators later would determine that, even before My Lai, rapes of Vietnamese women and girls were often committed by members of the company.

The crime at My Lai began the night before the massacre, when Charlie Company's commander, Capt. Ernest Medina, briefed the next day's mission. He would later testify that he had said not to kill women and children, and would pass a lie detector test about that issue, but twenty-one soldiers would testify that he had been clear that the plan was to kill all enemies in the village— and that anybody in the village was considered to be an enemy. "When we left the briefing we felt we were going to have a lot of resistance and we knew we were supposed to kill everyone in the village," one Charlie soldier, William Lloyd, told Army investigators. Most significantly, Lt. William Calley, the leader of Charlie's 1st Platoon, believed, according to his subsequent testimony, that the order of the day was, simply, "Waste them." He elaborated, "I was ordered to go in there and destroy the enemy. That was my job on that day. That was the mission I was given. I did not sit down and think in terms of men, women, and children. They were just all classified the same, and that was the classification that we dealt with, just as enemy soldiers." Robert Jay Lifton, a Harvard psychiatrist specializing in how war affects people, probably got it right when he summarized, "There are many versions of what happened at the briefing, but it was kind of a license to kill."

At around eight the following morning, Charlie Company's 1st Platoon began walking into the western end of the village. They were led by Lt. Calley, a short, pudgy 1963 dropout from Palm Beach Junior College who had drifted into the Army while down on his luck in Albuquerque and had somehow been selected to become an officer. The killing began then, according to the Army's official report:

> As the 1st Platoon moved into the hamlet, its soldiers began placing heavy fire on fleeing Vietnamese, throwing hand grenades into houses and bunkers, slaughtering livestock, and destroying foodstuffs. Several witnesses testified to having observed an old Vietnamese man being bayoneted to death by a member of the platoon and to having seen another man thrown alive into a well and subsequently killed with a hand grenade.

The unit encountered fifteen villagers huddled together. "Kill everybody, leave no one standing," Capt. Medina ordered, according to Herbert Carter, who would become the sole American casualty of the day when he shot himself in the foot and was helicoptered out. At around nine o'clock, about sixty villagers who had been rounded up and herded into a ditch were shot by members of the 1st Platoon. "I walked over to the ditch," Dennis Conti later testified. "As I walked up to it, Lieutenant Calley and Sergeant Mitchell were firing into the ditch. I looked into the ditch, and I saw women, children, and a couple of old men, just regular civilians. I saw a woman get up, and Calley shot her in the head."

Meanwhile, in the nearby sub-hamlet of Binh Tay, Charlie's 2nd Platoon, which had stood out in the company for its proclivity for rape, rounded up a group of ten to twenty villagers, made them squat in a circle, and fired several 40-millimeter rounds from an M79 grenade launcher into their midst. The wounded were then finished off with small-arms fire. This platoon also engaged in "at least one gang-rape of a young Vietnamese girl, an act of sodomy, and several other rape/killings."

Charlie's 3rd Platoon also was busy. One of its members, Varnado Simpson, later testified, "I killed about eight people that day." He also watched as five members of his platoon raped a girl. "When they all got done, they all took their weapons, M-60, M-16s, and caliber .45 pistols and fired into the girl until she was dead. Her face was just blown away and her brains were just everywhere."

During much of the bloodbath, Lt. Col. Frank Barker, commander of the provisional battalion of which Charlie Company was part, was circling overhead in one helicopter, and the brigade commander to whom he reported, Col. Oran Henderson, was in another. This was not the action of one or two platoons or even one company gone berserk. "This was an operation, not an aberration," said Ron Ridenhour, a soldier who later would play a key role in disclosing the atrocity. "What happened at My Lai was a plan. . . . We have officers, lieutenant colonels, a task force commander, a brigade commander, and the division commander in the air over those villages for significant periods of time, all morning long."

Larry Colburn, a door gunner on an arriving helicopter, watched in astonishment as Medina kicked a woman, stepped back, and shot her. It was only then that Colburn realized, "It was our guys doing all the killing." Colburn's pilot, Hugh Thompson, landed his aircraft between one remaining group of civilians and the soldiers and ordered Colburn to open fire on the soldiers if they tried to fire into the group—or tried to shoot Thompson for intervening. Asked years later why he had acted to stop the killings when no one else did, Thompson said, "I was brought up in the country. My mother and father probably would be called abu-, sive now by today's standards. . . . But they always taught me to help the underdog. Don't be a bully and live by the golden rule. . . . They taught me right from wrong."

When the soldiers of Charlie Company finished committing mass murder, they sat down at the eastern end of the village and ate lunch. The nearby dead totaled 400 or more. Of them, some 120 were children aged five or less. Of about twenty females raped, the youngest was eleven years old and the oldest about forty-five.

Thompson flew back to his base, landed, and flung his flight helmet to the ground. He angrily reported what he had seen to his company commander, Maj. Frederic Watke. "There's a ditch full of dead women and children over there," Thompson said. "We saw one armed VC all day. We never captured one damn weapon. They're killing women and children!" Watke went to Lt. Col. Barker, the battalion commander, who said he would look into Thompson's allegations. That afternoon Barker encountered

Watke and told him not to worry, that he had determined that Thompson was incorrect. Rather, Barker said, he had found that a small number of civilians had been killed in the village but that their deaths were "a result of justifiable situations." What Thompson and his company commander did not know was that Barker was complicit in the massacre, which was the act not just of one company but of the three companies operating under his command. While Charlie was butchering the people of My Lai, the other two companies in the battalion had sealed off the village, and in the process, one of them, Bravo Company, carried out a smaller slaughter in an adjacent hamlet, probably killing ninety civilians. Even so, Thompson's intervention had had an effect: Shortly after he made the allegation, word went out over the radio telling Bravo and Charlie companies to "stop the killing."

So began the second major crime committed by Army officers in connection with My Lai. The first was the killing itself; the second was how the chain of command in the Americal Division handled the incident. That afternoon, Gen. Koster, the division commander, took the next significant step in the cover-up. He was flying near My Lai and overheard an order from Col. Oran Henderson, the brigade commander, who requested that soldiers return to the village to tally the dead by gender and approximate age. "Negative," Koster countermanded, according to subsequent testimony by Medina and Henderson. Koster would tell investigators that he did not remember the conversation that way, but his testimony would prove to be unreliable. At any rate, he said, there was no specific need to return to the village, because "there was no set requirement for reporting civilian casualties or injuries and this type of thing."

Two days later, Col. Henderson was told to determine what had happened at My Lai, but his actions in fact appeared to have had "as their goal the suppression of the true facts concerning the events of 16 March," the Army subsequently concluded. Henderson gathered a group of Charlie soldiers and asked them all if they had seen a massacre. Most replied in the negative, but one said he had no comment. Henderson did not pursue that interesting response. Rather, he seemed mainly out to discredit Thompson, the helicopter pilot. He reported on March 19 that there was no basis to the allegations. As Koster recalled much later, when he was under investigation, "he felt the pilot had been confused and that he was a young man who had become overly excited and had probably imagined some things that hadn't really taken place."

By this point the cover-up was well under way. On March 28, Lt. Col. Barker submitted a routine "Combat Action Report" that offered his summary of events in My Lai twelve days earlier:

> This operation was well planned, well executed, and successful. Friendly casualties were light and the enemy suffered heavily. On this operation the civilian population supporting the VC in the area numbered approximately 200. This created a problem in population control and medical care of those civilians in fires of the opposing forces. However the infantry unit on the ground and helicopters were able to assist civilians in leaving the area and in caring for and/or evacuating the wounded.

The next month, Vietnamese on both sides of the war began talking about something terrible happening at the village. In response, Col. Henderson wrote a document he titled "Report of Investigation." It began with a lie: "An investigation has been conducted of the allegations." Under questioning, Henderson eventually would concede that this was not the case and that in fact he had not conducted a series of interviews or taken signed statements from participants. His "report" also falsely stated that 128

Viet Cong soldiers had been killed in the My Lai operations, as well as "20 noncombatants caught in the battle area." But, he emphasized, "at no time were any civilians gathered together and killed by U.S. soldiers." He concluded on a note of moral indignation. Such allegations, he wrote, were "obviously a Viet Cong propaganda move."

The cover-up, which also included destruction of documents, was so extensive that it held for about a year. Then Ron Ridenhour sent a letter to his congressman and to various other officials in Washington that alleged that something awful had happened in the Vietnamese village the troops called "Pinkville." With clarity and precision, he related how he had been told that a "Lieutenant Kally (this spelling may be incorrect)" had played a central role in it.

Col. William Wilson, a World War II veteran who had been wounded in Normandy while a member of the 101st Airborne, was given the task of investigating Ridenhour's allegations. He went into it skeptical about the charges. "But if the Pinkville incident was true, it was cold-blooded murder," he continued. "I hoped to God it was false, but if it wasn't, I wanted the bastards exposed for what they'd done." In the late spring and summer of 1969, as Wilson quietly traveled around the country interviewing former members of Charlie Company, "a repugnant picture was forming in my mind."

The clincher came late on the afternoon of July 16, 1969, when Wilson interviewed Paul Meadlo, a former Charlie Company soldier who had lost a foot to a mine the day after the killings and had been working at a gas station since coming home from the Army and Vietnam. Meadlo began the interview, held in a room in a Holiday Inn in Terre Haute, Indiana, by almost immediately confessing to having committed murder at My Lai. "We just moved on in and we just started wiping out the whole village. That is it. We burnt the village and killed all the people and just one mass slaughter, just like you do a bunch of cows, you know, just killed them all." He added a key detail, telling Wilson that he had been one of those who pulled the trigger when about fifty villagers had been rounded up: "Lieutenant Calley opened up on them first and then I joined in."

Wilson interrupted Meadlo's extraordinary confession to advise him of his right to remain silent. When the interview resumed, Meadlo expressed puzzlement: "Can you really get me for anything like that or for killing people when I was just following orders?"

That night, Wilson wrote, "Something in me died. . . . I had prayed to God that this thing was fiction, and I knew now it was fact."

One of the few senior Army officers who looked better because of his handling of My Lai was William Westmoreland, who insisted that the investigation be wide-ranging, looking at not just what had happened but how and why it happened, and what was done about it. "We investigated this thing fully and let the chips fall as the evidence was produced," he recalled, correctly. The Nixon White House seemed intent on politicizing the investigation, which Westmoreland strived to resist. At one point he asked Alexander Haig, then an Army officer detached to work for National Security Adviser Henry Kissinger, to stop by his house for a drink. After some preliminary chatting, Westmoreland delivered a message. "I have been getting pressure not to push the My Lai investigation, and I want you to understand, and I hope the president will understand, that if these pressures don't cease and desist immediately, I am going to exercise my prerogative and I am going straight to the president." Haig seemed upset for a moment, but he got the message, Westmoreland recalled. After that conversation, he said, the pressure ceased.

In November 1969, after news of the massacre and the Army's investigation broke, the Army appointed Lt. Gen. William Peers, who had commanded the 4th Infantry Division in Vietnam, to investigate the larger aspects of the incident—how and why the massacre had happened, and how it was covered up. To his credit—and the Army's—Peers did the right thing, conducting an exhaustive investigation in which more than four hundred witnesses were interviewed, some repeatedly. He was operating under an extreme time limit of less than four months, because on March 16, 1970, the two-year statute of limitations would expire on many crimes short of murder. Like Wilson, Peers initially doubted Ridenhour's allegations, but he concluded that the situation was even worse than the Ridenhour letter had depicted. One day, Peers and his investigators asked the chief of staff of the American Division why he had not pursued what he had heard about the incident. "There was no use in me taking this up with General Koster," the officer replied. "The generals were handling the situation." It was a damning statement.

One of the most striking moments in the entire sprawling investigation came when Gen. Koster, who by this point was the superintendent of the U.S. Military Academy at West Point, was called back for a second round of questioning. The general had repeatedly insisted that he had carried out his duty and ensured in the days after the My Lai incident that a formal investigation had been conducted. In fact, he said, he remembered that a sheaf of written, sworn statements had been attached to that report. This was the essence of his defense. If that internal inquiry had erred, or if Peers's investigators could not locate the report, he implied, that was certainly not his fault. He probably knew that almost every single document relating to My Lai had disappeared, somewhat mysteriously, from the division's files. As one frustrated investigator told Koster, "We have not only searched everything in

Vietnam, but all the file retentions from Okinawa and over here. And there isn't any trace of any papers from the division. . . . There are no logs. These are supposed to be retained for two years, the classified documents. There are no documents. There are no destruction certificates. There is no nothing."

Peers had known Koster for decades, admired him, and considered him a close friend. Yet he found Koster's initial round of testimony "almost unbelievable." In a second round of testimony, in February 1970, Peers challenged Koster's account. Peers and his staff informed Koster that they had traveled to Vietnam and had talked to dozens of people, including the involved company commanders, and found not a single person who had given a sworn statement. In fact, they had concluded, the testimony about the statements was a lie. The statements simply had never been given. "They made no statements, and to further compound the problem, there is no record of such a report ever having arrived at headquarters, Americal Division," one Peers investigator said to Koster. "There is no copy of the report available. There is no information whatsoever [that such a report ever had been done] aside from that which you and Colonel Henderson have indicated."

"Yes, sir," Koster responded. "I can't explain that." But the investigators had developed an explanation: The absence of evidence was so total as to be dispositive. The complete absence of evidence was evidence of a cover-up.

Peers's report made it clear that he was shocked by the behavior not only of the soldiers who pulled the triggers, threw the grenades, thrust the bayonets, and committed the rapes at My Lai but also of the chain of command above them. "Efforts were made at every level of command from company to division to withhold and suppress information," he wrote in March 1970. "Efforts initiated in 1968 to deliberately withhold information continue to this day. Six officers who occupied key positions at the time of the incident exercised their right to remain silent before this Inquiry, others gave false or misleading testimony or withheld information, and key documents relating to this incident have not been found in U.S. files."

Peers listed thirty soldiers, among them two generals and three colonels, who appeared to have committed offenses in the cover-up. This was on top of the criminal charges that would be brought for the massacre itself. Of the accused, the Army for legal reasons chose not to prosecute those who had left the service. William Eckhardt, a career Army lawyer, was tapped to be the lead prosecutor. He flew to Atlanta to begin reading the investigative files. By the end of his first day of work, he recalled, he was nauseated. "I threw the files against the wall and went and ran about five or six miles." His horrified conclusion resembled that of Gen. Peers: "The facts are worse than are reported. There are over five hundred [dead]. They didn't report to you the sexual abuse, the rapes, the sodomy, the looting."

The Army ultimately brought charges against sixteen men, but the charges were dropped against twelve of them after the initial trials went badly. Of the five soldiers who were tried, only one, Lt. William Calley, was convicted. Ernest Medina, the company commander, and Oran Henderson, the brigade commander, were acquitted. (Frank Barker, the battalion commander, had died in combat.) "This prosecutorial record was abysmal," conceded Eckhardt, the prosecutor, who noted that his efforts were subjected to a series of unusual political pressures. Even the punishment of Calley, the lowest-ranking officer in the chain of command, was reduced by President Nixon, who ordered that he be released from jail and allowed to live under house arrest in his Army apartment while his case was appealed. Calley's sentence of life in prison was eventually commuted to ten years, and he was paroled well before that was served, in November 1974.

Despite Peers's efforts, the Army also protected Koster, the division commander. Peers believed that Koster had been derelict in his duty, had given false testimony, and had conspired to cover up what had happened. As the general who presided over the My Lai massacre, Koster had brought more disrepute upon the Army than any general in American history since Benedict Arnold. Westmoreland ordered Koster to step aside as superintendent of West Point and replaced him with William Knowlton, who was surprised to find that Koster would not vacate Quarters 100, the superintendent's official residence. "Poor Sam Koster, once the fact hit him that he was no longer the superintendent, really went into kind of a state of shock and just continued to live in the house for another month or two," Knowlton recalled.

Yet Lt. Gen. Jonathan Seaman, the officer selected to decide the disposition of the case against Koster, chose not to send Koster's case to a court-martial and instead gave him the minimum punishment possible: a demotion to brigadier general and a letter of reprimand. "My opinion was that there was insufficient evidence . . . for obtaining a conviction," Seaman later told an Army historian. "I wrote Koster a strong letter of censure. He had failed to carry out a division commander's duties. Failed to send anyone to the battlefield to investigate." This was an extraordinarily lenient interpretation that ignored Koster's role in the cover-up and his lies to investigators. Koster nevertheless protested that even this lightest of punishments was "unfair and unjust."

Koster was allowed to stay in the Army, wearing the uniform he had disgraced, until January 1, 1973. Peers, disturbed by Seaman's light hand, told Gen. Westmoreland that it was "a travesty of justice and would establish a precedent that it would be difficult for the Army to live down."

Seaman's decision had the ripple effect of poisoning the cases against subordinate officers. If the commanding general was not going to prison, soldiers on court-martial juries were likely to reason, then those he commanded should not, either. Maj. Gen. Kenneth Hodson, the Army's top lawyer and its judge advocate general during this period, said that charges had to be dropped against most of those involved, because military juries simply were not going to hold the soldiers responsible. In his official oral history, recorded just months after he retired in 1972, Hodson seemed remarkably detached from the entire affair, not only unable to remember the number of officers charged ("I think it was in the neighborhood of about 12") but also getting the date of the massacre wrong ("Along about the latter part of February 1968").

One of the soldiers who suffered most after the revelations was Hugh Thompson, the helicopter pilot who had intervened to stop the killings and had repeatedly tried to get his superiors to look into what had happened that day in the village. Some of his comrades called him a traitor. When he appeared before a congressional committee in April 1970, he was treated as a hostile witness. When Thompson hesitated in one response and said "I think," he was blasted by Rep. Edward Hébert, the Louisiana Democrat, who asked, "What has blunted your memory so dramatically between December and April? At that time you were vocal and articulate. . . . This is almost the end of April, and I find a different man on the stand. The man I find on the stand today has a hard time remembering. He is not positive. He halts." Thompson defended himself simply, even humbly. Asked if he had charged that "indiscriminate firing" had occurred, he responded, "No sir, I didn't use those words, because I stay away from big words."

Thompson found little peace. For years he would endure, in his own words, "death threats at three o'clock in the morning, mutilated animals on your doorstep, and I'm sitting here confused as hell."

Peers's core conclusion about the affair was that Army leadership had been wanting. "It appeared to the Inquiry that at all levels, from division down to platoon, leadership or the lack of it was perhaps the principal causative factor in the tragic events before, during, and after the My Lai operation." This was the third great sin of My Lai. The first had been the crime itself, the second was the chain of command's cover-up, and now we come to the last: the failure of Army leaders to react properly to all of it. "Thus," Peers wrote, "the failures of leadership that characterized nearly every aspect of the My Lai incident itself had their counterpart at the highest level during the attempt to prosecute those responsible." In other words, the Army failed in its response to My Lai.

This was the low point of the U.S. Army in the twentieth century. In contrast to the extreme accountability practiced by George Marshall during World War II, the Army of the Vietnam era failed to hold its generals accountable. Instead it went into a defensive crouch, letting the general responsible for the affair off the hook and blaming others for its problems. In sum, the generals who were running the Army acted less like stewards of their profession and more like the keepers of a guild, accountable only to themselves. This posture would have long-lasting pernicious effects on American generalship.

A stunning Army study of Army officers

My Lai held one more surprise for Gen. Westmoreland. When Gen. Peers finished his report on the cover-up, he delivered a separate, confidential memorandum to Westmoreland. My Lai, Peers warned, was not just a matter of a criminal platoon leader or even a rotten battalion. Rather, Peers had come to believe that the Army officer corps had drifted far from its stated values. It had become an organization in which lying and hypocrisy were widespread and tolerated, perhaps encouraged and required. What concerned him most was that "so many people in command positions—perhaps as many as fifty—had information that something most unusual had occurred during the My Lai operation and yet did nothing about it. . . . Had any of these persons made their knowledge known to the proper investigative authorities, the whole blanket of obscurity covering the incident would have been rolled back and the true facts brought to light." Why had so few Army officers done the right thing? Why had a helicopter pilot been the only one to speak up on the day of the killings, and why was an enlisted soldier the one to write the letter that triggered the investigation? Where was the officer corps? Peers recommended that the chief of staff order a review of the state of Army ethics and morals.

One of the most striking paragraphs in Peers's lengthy memo to Westmoreland addressed this failure of leadership:

> Because men's lives are at stake in combat, there can be no acceptance of mediocre leadership nor mediocrity in performance of other duties relating to the support of combat. *Failures in leadership or in the performance of duty in combat are due cause for and should demand the removal or reassignment of the officer concerned to positions of lesser responsibility.*

What was most extraordinary about this statement was that it needed to be said at all. Removing poor combat leaders had been a long-standing Army practice, as seen in the two world wars. But it had been lost in the previous twenty years, and now the chief of staff of the Army had to be told that failures should not be left in positions of command.

Westmoreland did not mention this memo in his memoirs, but it, along with Peers's evidence of lying up and down an entire division chain of command, led to perhaps the most memorable act of Westmoreland's four years as chief of staff. "The memo shook Westy to the core," recalled Maj. Gen. Franklin Davis. Exactly one month later, Westy ordered the commandant of the Army War College to conduct an analysis of the "moral and professional climate" of the Army officer corps. He asked that it be given to him by July 1.

The report was compiled and written in just ten weeks, by Col. LeRoy Strong, Lt. Col. Dandridge Malone, and Lt. Col. Walter Ulmer. When it landed on Westmoreland's desk, it startled him. "He said that we should use it, but we should keep it close hold because the Army had just been beaten over the head and this was just another reason to be beaten over the head," recalled Ulmer. Westmoreland likely was right about how the report might be used. Yet he missed an opportunity, because he cast a shroud over a work that showed three Army officers—Strong, Malone, and Ulmer—at their best, being clear-sighted and doing their utmost to serve the country as they candidly examined the flaws of their institution.

"The traditional standards of the American Army officer may be summarized in three words: Duty—Honor—Country," the report began. But, it continued, "officers of all grades perceive a significant difference between the ideal values and the actual or operative values of the Officer Corps." One of the report's authors, Col. Malone, an Army infantry officer turned social psychologist, later concisely condensed the report into one sentence: "Duty, honor and country" had been replaced by "Me, my ass and my career." This perception held true across the service, with 450 officers surveyed, from the combat arms to support functions and from junior officers to senior ones, the report noted. If that were not enough, it also pointed toward a new model of officer that was emerging. This, it said, was

> an ambitious, transitory commander—marginally skilled in the
> complexity of his duties—engulfed in producing statistical

results, fearful of personal failure, too busy to talk with or listen to his subordinates, and determined to submit acceptably optimistic reports which reflect faultless completion of a variety of tasks at the expense of the sweat and frustration of his subordinates.

Close to half the officers surveyed described a lack of honesty in reporting data, in everything from body counts to the number of soldiers going AWOL. If there were too few of the former or too many of the latter, a commander might well fear for his chances of promotion. "Nobody out there believes the body count," one officer stated. "They couldn't possibility believe it. . . . We had one lad even tell us of an experience where he almost had to get in a fist fight with an ARVN adviser over an arm, to see who would get credit for the body, because they were sorting out pieces." One of the dismaying lessons that soldiers took away from My Lai, reported one officer, was that they should always carry an AK-47 rifle, the Communists' weapon of choice, "so that if they did kill someone they've got a weapon to produce with the body." Another officer reported being ordered by a major general "that there will be no AWOLs." He concluded that "dishonesty is across the board."

The Army as an institution was all too willing "to accept mediocrity," said one colonel, who added that "with few exceptions what I feel to be the most serious problems stem from this prevalent attitude." But that was not the worst of it, the respondents reported. Senior officers, "including generals," showed a "moral laxness," yet this did not stop them from being promoted, added a major. "Ratings are solely on results, no matter how obtained." Maintaining one's integrity had become a career impediment in the Army, said one major: "The honest commander who reports his AWOLS, etc., gets into trouble while the dishonest commander gets promoted." Another major reported that he had been under the command of a colonel who "led by fear, would double-cross anyone to obtain a star, drank too much and lived openly by no moral code. He is now a BG!"—that is, a brigadier general. The Army forced officers into acting immorally, said another officer: "Unless you are willing to compromise your standards . . . you will not survive in the Army system." A captain agreed that "it's necessary today to lie, cheat and steal to meet the impossible demands of higher officers."

The Army's leaders did not see the problem, younger officers believed, because they were "isolated, perhaps willingly, from reality." "Senior officers appear to be deluding themselves and actually talking themselves into believing these false statistics, all the way up the line," said one officer, in an accusation that must have given pause to Westmoreland, in his position at the head of the line. Senior leaders were portrayed by survey respondents as a cause of the problem, offering a "poor example" in both competence and ethics. A third major spoke of a superior who would " 'bleed' his troops dry to make a good impression—and then stab his subordinates in the back when they were no longer useful." A lieutenant told the Army War College study group that he saw a behavioral pattern of "cover your ass." A colonel agreed that "endless CYA exercises create suspicion." Nor did senior officers show much loyalty to subordinates, in part because they rotated through their billets so quickly. "True loyalty among men is not developed overnight," one captain said.

Because the people who thrived in this system naturally did not see a need to change it, it would be difficult to fix the problem, the report warned. That "the leaders of the future are those who survived and excelled within the rules of the present system militates in part against the initiation of any self-starting incremental return toward the practical application of ideal values," it read, in a somewhat cautious, Latinate style that might have reflected the trepidation the authors felt in labeling the Army's general officers as a group of bad apples. All the more worrisome was that the respondents in this study were "winners in the system," as one expert on the modern Army put it, top-half officers who had been selected for the staff and war colleges.

When the report was briefed to Westmoreland in July 1970, "he kept shaking his head," as if to disagree, recalled Col. Malone, who had helped compile it. "But the facts started backing each other up." In the following week, Westmoreland spent more than twenty-five hours with his staff, weighing the conclusions and implications of the report, as well as whether to follow its recommendations. One reaction was almost immediate: Within a few weeks, the six-month command tour, that characteristic personnel policy of the Vietnam War, was eliminated.

Westmoreland eventually decided to handle the report in a contradictory manner. He ordered its findings briefed across the Army but ordered that the document itself be kept "close hold." "I mean close," wrote Malone. "Locked it up. And that's how it was for about two years." As Ulmer put it, "We put a couple of hundred copies in some bathroom up at the War College and locked the door." The unfortunate effect of that decision was that a consequent series of policy changes ordered by Westmoreland appeared unrelated and even confusing, rather than what they were: part of a considered strategic response to a stated problem that was being seriously studied.

CHAPTER 21

The end of a war,
the end of an Army

The history of the Vietnam War is far more complex than what is rendered in popular culture. Even now, almost four decades after it ended, it is probably the least understood of America's wars. No authoritative military history of the Vietnam War exists. There is no narrative that captures the ebb and flow of the war tactically and strategically, showing both battlefield actions and the deliberations of senior officials. Existing histories of the war give a taste of combat and thereafter tend to concentrate on the political and diplomatic discussions among senior American officials in Saigon and Washington.

The Vietnam War certainly was not one long, steady descent into a quagmire, as some books, films, and songs would have us believe. Rather, it was a series of complicated interactions between four major military forces: the South Vietnamese forces, the American military, the Viet Cong, and the North Vietnamese Army. By late 1968 and early 1969, each of those forces had been altered by its experience in the conflict. The Viet Cong had been decimated and demoralized by the Communist offensives in February and May of 1968, which also had brought to the surface the

VC's clandestine network in the South and shown its face to local officials, making it far more vulnerable. In 1965, Communist forces in the South were about three-quarters Viet Cong, while by 1970 they were about three-quarters North Vietnamese Army, according to a comment made by Gen. Creighton Abrams in the latter year. (However, some contemporary historians caution against accepting the notion that the Viet Cong had only a small role in the war after Tet, noting that it has been in the interests of the Hanoi government "to minimize the role of local forces in the conquest of South Vietnam.") "By winter of 1969 the VC were just sort of running around like a bunch of chickens and it really was no contest," said Lt. Gen. Julian Ewell, who commanded the 9th Infantry Division in the Mekong Delta in 1968 and then was promoted to lead a corps-level headquarters.

The conventional North Vietnamese Army moved in large numbers into the South, but the new Northern troops who replaced the Viet Cong were largely inexperienced. "The NVA were tenacious but not very successful against U.S. forces," said Al Santoli, who served with the 25th Infantry Division in Vietnam in 1968–69. "They suffered needless mass casualties attempting frontal assaults on U.S. positions and, in most cases, where they used concealment of terrain for ambush, they were unable to sustain initiative beyond immediate surprise against U.S. infantry." By the spring of 1970, military mail intercepted en route from North Vietnam "was pleading with the units and the party cadre not to get engaged in military ground action at all," recalled Maj. Gen. Elvy Roberts, a veteran of the Battle of the Bulge who commanded the 1st Cavalry Division in 1969–70. "They realized they couldn't sustain it. They were too weak. The letters said, 'We're winning the war at the conference table in Paris, so don't fight the Americans.'"

On the other side, South Vietnamese forces were increasingly seasoned, but they were not much respected by their American allies. The Americans also brought many of their own problems to the battlefield. Despite serving the most powerful nation on earth, U.S. troops at this point in the war often were short on combat experience and led in the field by similarly green sergeants and platoon leaders, largely because of shortsighted and inept personnel policies that had their origin in a fateful decision by President Johnson. In mid-1965, the Army, its eye on Vietnam, had written plans to call up 100,000 reservists for two years of active duty and also extend the enlistments of active-duty personnel. But President Johnson had vetoed that plan and instead, on July 28, 1965—a key date in the history of the war—publicly stated that he had "concluded that it is not essential to order Reserve units into service now." It is difficult to overstate how damaging that decision was. The Army was not designed to go to war without the reserve forces. Their absence was felt in Vietnam, where the Army lacked logisticians, but perhaps even more in the United States, where reservists normally would have performed many of the tasks of training new recruits. The president's refusal to activate the Army Reserve meant that the Army would use up its active-duty sergeants and lieutenants quickly in the following three years, with some killed and others leaving the military after their tours of duty or moving to less hazardous positions in rear-echelon units. Ironically, by not mobilizing the reserves, LBJ forced the Army to rely on involuntary conscripts much more heavily, which ultimately intensified political opposition to the war much more than a reserve call-up would have done.

Often in warfare, it is the first year of fighting that seasons forces, which become more effective as those who survive gain skill, good leaders rise to the top, and units become more cohesive over time. Counterintuitively, as the Vietnam War progressed, the American frontline force weakened. In 1966, remembered Paul Gorman, the battalion he commanded had fourteen senior sergeants who had been in the unit for more than ten years, all of them trained by a legendary sergeant major who had landed at Normandy with the Big Red One. By contrast, he said, five years later, when he was commanding a brigade in the 101st Airborne, good sergeants who could provide the backbone of units, especially by maintaining standards and enforcing discipline, were hard to find. "I didn't have the NCOs [non-commissioned officers]. The NCOs were gone." By 1969, draftees made up 88 percent of the infantry riflemen in Vietnam. Another 10 percent was made up of first-term volunteers, meaning that the fighting force was almost entirely inexperienced and often led by novice first-term NCOs and officers. In one company in 1970, of two hundred men, only three—the captain, one platoon sergeant, and one squad leader—had been in the Army for more than two years. In addition, because of the rotation policy, units not only arrived green but stayed that way. "After only two months in Vietnam, I had more experience than half the men in Vietnam," recalled one sergeant. There were plenty of career soldiers in Vietnam, but they disproportionately served at higher headquarters, not in line units doing the fighting. Small units in the field were "appalling," agreed Donn Starry, who took command of the 11th Armored Cavalry Regiment at the end of that year:

> There would be a lieutenant as the company commander—he might be a captain, but if he was a captain he was a two-year captain, and he didn't have a long tour as a lieutenant. Then you had some very junior sergeants. . . . You had absolutely no experienced leadership, and there they were out there groping with a problem of some enormity. As a regimental commander, you just had to look at the situation and say, "What have we done to ourselves? It's not fair." And it wasn't their fault. It was the Army's fault. We did that to ourselves.

Westmoreland, in his new role as chief of staff of the Army, would compound the problem in 1969 by insisting that the most experienced soldiers be allowed to leave Vietnam first, further stripping the force of much-needed field knowledge. "Individual personnel redeployments destroyed unit integrity, increasing turbulence in units remaining," wrote Starry. "In the end, it caused leaders to go forth to battle daily with men who did not know them and whom they did not know. The result was tragedy."

Abrams takes command

In 1968 and 1969, three personnel changes at the top resulted in a major shift in the American conduct of the war. In mid-1968, Gen. Westmoreland was replaced by Gen. Abrams. Six months later, President Johnson was succeeded by Richard Nixon. Robert McNamara, meanwhile, had left office earlier in the year, replaced at the Pentagon by Clark Clifford, who would then be replaced, under Nixon, by Melvin Laird.

There has been a running battle for decades among American military historians about whether in late 1968 and 1969, with the shift from Westmoreland to Abrams, the conduct of the war really improved. The Army itself probably has overemphasized the change, elevating it to mythic importance. At one low point in the war in Iraq, for example, commanders were recommending that subordinates read Lewis Sorley's *A Better War*, a history of Abrams's time in command in Vietnam, as evidence that things could get better in Iraq. In fact, there were more continuities between Westmoreland and Abrams than not—most units continued to do pretty much the same things in pretty much the same ways. Even so, there were significant changes in what Abrams chose to emphasize about those operations, with less talk of "body counts" and bringing the enemy to battle and more of pacification and protecting the population. More important, the nature of the war began to change, and this led to some changes in American tactics. Walter "Dutch" Kerwin, who had been Westmoreland's chief of staff, perceived a sharp difference between the two U.S. commanders:

> The way Westy ran the organization was just the opposite from the way General Abrams would have run it. . . . [It] was quite evident that almost immediately after General Westmoreland left, we pulled out of Khe Sanh. General Abe did not believe that was the way to run a war. . . . He changed the tactics, techniques and methods of handling the corps commanders.

Abrams put aside Westmoreland's strategy of attrition. "In the whole picture of the war, the battles don't mean much," Abrams told subordinates in a comment that would have been heresy to Westmoreland, DePuy, and other generals earlier in the war. Nor, he said, did he care to be briefed on tallies of enemy killed. "I don't think it makes any difference how many losses he takes."

Instead, in his meetings and briefings, Abrams expressed more interest than Westmoreland ever had in the nuts and bolts of pacification, especially about programs that supported security in the villages. What a commanding general emphasizes will ripple throughout his organization—indeed, on a day-to-day basis, the subjects he chooses to focus on might be the most important thing he can do. Abrams was using more of the approach the Marines had advocated years earlier, which was one reason he got along better with the Marines than Westmoreland had.

It was a good time to change the emphasis, for there was a new opportunity emerging in rural areas. "Hanoi had pushed most of the best Viet Cong cadre into the cities during Tet, and so the Tet Offensive really destroyed the flower of the Vietnam insurgency," said Robert Komer, who was overseeing the rural pacification program. "I argued there was a vacuum in the countryside."

But the biggest change was over Abrams's head and was made by the new president. By early 1969, the American priority was no longer winning the war but getting out of it. This shift was felt down to the front lines. "When Johnson rolled out and Nixon came in, the emphasis was black and white from where I sit," said Lt. Col. Gary Riggs, who was in Vietnam from 1966 to 1970. "The emphasis became, 'Let's get the damn thing over. Let's close it out, with as much dignity as we can, but let's just back off and come home.'" This became known as the "Vietnamization" of the war. And while Westmoreland "was very aggressive, 'We're going to win this mother,'" Riggs said, Abrams "came with a different message, which was, 'Contain, pacify.'"

Oddly, the Americans were starting to leave just as their years of struggle were paying off. It was not really seen by the American public at the time, but there is little doubt now that the Communists were rapidly losing control of large parts of the South Vietnamese countryside in late 1968 and for the following three years. At the end of 1964, only 40 percent of the population had been under government control, Komer said. By the end of 1971, he noted, about 97 percent of the population was considered to be in "relatively secure" areas.

The change in the American stance took the enemy by surprise and led to one of the most difficult phases of the war for the Communists. Hanoi's official history of the war drops its triumphalist tone for several pages as it grimly relates how this period unfolded. "During late 1968 the enemy discovered our vulnerability in the rural areas," the history stated. It continued:

Because we did not fully appreciate the new enemy schemes and the changes the enemy had made in his conduct of the war and because we underestimated the enemy's capabilities and the strength of his counterattack, when the United States and its puppets began to carry out their "clear and hold" strategy our battlefronts were too slow in shifting over to attacking the "pacification" program and we did not concentrate our political and military forces to deal with the enemy's new plots and schemes.

In a startling change of tone, the Communists' history seems almost admiring of the effectiveness of the new approach:

The political and military struggle in the rural areas declined and our liberated areas shrank. . . . The enemy built thousands of new outposts, upgraded puppet forces, drafted new troops, and expanded the puppet army, especially local forces and people's self-defense forces used to oppress the population. They blocked our entry points and attacked our supply routes from the lowlands to our base areas. The enemy also collected and tightly controlled the people's rice crops in order to dry up local sources of supply for our armed forces.

That paragraph is a very good summary, through the eyes of an adversary, of how to carry out an effective counterinsurgency campaign.

The Hanoi history mentioned in a footnote that, in one region, the Communists lost all but three or four of their forty-two rice collection points, a loss that had grim consequences for Communist forces. Some units were reduced to eating less than one hundred grams of rice a day. Hungry and dismayed, Communist soldiers began defecting in greater numbers. "The enemy's horrible, insidious pacification program and his acts of destruction created immeasurable difficulties and complications for our armed forces and civilian population," the history dolefully observed.

This official history conceded that during 1969, North Vietnamese main-force units had retreated from the lowlands, and
American soldiers, working with local South Vietnamese security
units, had begun to push the Viet Cong out of large parts of the
South. By the end of that year, it stated, "the population of our
liberated areas had shrunk to 840,000 people," while "the enemy
established 1,000 new outposts and gained control over an additional one million people." Recruitment began to dwindle, starting a vicious cycle of decline for Communist control of the
countryside. In 1968, some sixteen thousand new Viet Cong had
enlisted in the lowlands of the South. But in the same area in all
of 1969, the Hanoi history related,

> we recruited only 100 new soldiers. . . . Our liberated areas were
> shrinking, our bases were under pressure, and both our local
> and strategic lines of supply were under ferocious enemy attack.
> We had great difficulty supplying our troops. . . . Some of our
> cadre and soldiers became pessimistic and exhibited fear of close
> combat and of remaining in the battle zone. Some deserted their
> units to flee to rear areas, and some even defected to the enemy.

Hanoi's official account is consistent with those given by Viet
Cong veterans. "There's no doubt that 1969 was the worst year we
faced, at least the worst year I faced," recalled Trinh Duc. "There
was no food, no future."

Huong Van Ba, a North Vietnamese artillery officer, also had
harsh memories of that time. "When the Tet campaign was over,
we didn't have enough men left to fight a major battle, only to
make hit-and-run attacks on posts. So many men had been killed
that morale was very low. We spent a great deal of time hiding in
tunnels, trying to avoid being captured. We experienced desertions." In mid-1969, orders from the Central Committee in Hanoi

were conveyed to field commanders as "COSVN Resolution 9," telling them to hunker down in force-preservation mode—that is, hang back, harass the Americans with sappers, and try to outlast them. "The Communists are simply avoiding contact with us," one general said that summer. "The reasons are not clear. But there is no doubt that right now there is a very peculiar situation on the battlefield." From 1965 to 1968, the Communists launched an average of seventy battalion-size assaults annually. In 1969 and 1970, the rate fell to twenty. This led to a virtuous cycle: Smaller and fewer operations by the enemy meant that the Americans could reduce large-scale search-and-destroy sweeps and instead conduct more small-unit patrols in the countryside, reinforcing their control.

In addition, the Phoenix Program, aimed at rooting out the Viet Cong command infrastructure, expanded rapidly in 1968, with devastating effect. "In some locations . . . Phoenix was dangerously effective," remembered Truong Nhu Tang, a Viet Cong official, who saw the VC network "virtually eliminated" in the province near his base area. The success of the program illustrates the point that winning over a defector is more damaging to the enemy than simply killing one of his soldiers. Nguyen Thi Dinh, the deputy commander of the Viet Cong, said in an interview years after the war ended that the Phoenix Program was greatly feared,

> because they were able to infiltrate our infrastructures, using Vietnamese to kill Vietnamese. . . . What they did was to train and organize demoralized and disenchanted people to come back into our areas and to reveal our infrastructures to the Americans. We considered this a most dangerous program for us. We were never afraid of a military operation with a full division of troops, for example. But for them to infiltrate a couple of

guys deeply into our ranks would create tremendous difficulties for us.

In a remarkable tribute to the twin policies of pacification and Vietnamization, the Communists decided to imitate the American and South Vietnamese tactics, dispersing main-force troops into villages to bolster their hold on local security.

But for the Americans and South Vietnamese, the chimera of victory appeared too late. By the time the U.S. Army generals started getting Vietnam right—that is, operating effectively—the U.S. military had been involved in Vietnam for thirteen years and fighting there in large numbers for three. The situation had improved for the Americans tactically, but strategically they were facing an enemy force that knew they were leaving and was thus operating with the goal of simply dodging and outlasting them. "The problem was that it came too late," Gen. DePuy later said, speaking specifically of the success of pacification and of local Vietnamese forces. "We were ready to pull out. And the North Vietnamese just kept coming."

Most important, the American people were tired of a war they had not asked for and never understood. Jeffrey Record, who served as a pacification adviser during the war, concluded, in one of the most balanced appraisals of those years, that "the United States could not have prevented the forcible reunification of Vietnam under communist auspices at a morally, materially, and strategically acceptable price."

Even if the American people had been willing to pay a higher price and support fighting for many more years, the Army itself was probably too weak to carry such a burden. "By '69, it was just a joke" trying to train soldiers in the Army, recalled Herb Mock, who fought with the 25th Division in Vietnam. Charles Cooper, the Marine officer who had listened to President Johnson curse at the Joint Chiefs in 1965, was serving in Vietnam as a battalion commander in 1970. "Things were going to hell in a handbasket," he thought. "They were just flooding us with morons and imbeciles." Even good career officers were avoiding Vietnam, recalled William Richardson, a brigade commander at about this time. "It was very difficult to get outstanding battalion commanders to come to Vietnam. I knew one, in particular, who I tried to recruit to come to Vietnam. An outstanding officer, he didn't want to come to Vietnam and be a battalion commander. I was distressed to see an attitude of, 'I may damage my career.'"

In other words, when victory was a possibility, the Army was too depleted to grasp the chance. Judith Coburn, a reporter, summarized the dilemma eloquently: "When I hear people say we could have won the war, I always think: Where were you going to get the soldiers?" As a result of Westmoreland's and Johnson's squandering of people and resources from 1965 to 1968, the Americans and their South Vietnamese allies were unable to take lasting advantage of the huge opportunities that emerged from 1969 to 1971.

Massacre at Firebase Mary Ann

By late in the Vietnam War, the U.S. Army was a mess. In October 1970, it was losing a soldier a day to death by drug overdose. Desertions and AWOL incidents were going off the charts. Combat refusals and other forms of mutinous insubordination were becoming more common. According to a statement made by Sen. John Stennis in a hearing, there were at least sixty-eight refusals to fight among the seven divisions in Vietnam in 1970. In at least two instances, U.S. military police were used as assault forces against other American troops. On September 25, 1971, fourteen soldiers of the 35th Engineer Group barricaded themselves in a bunker behind machine guns. They surrendered after an explosion in the rear of the bunker. A month later, military police were sent into a signals outpost near Dalat after fragmentation grenades were used against the company commander two nights in a row. The MPs remained to police the outpost for a full week. Newcomers were inducted into "a bogus combat-veteran culture that was in reality no more than an accumulation of bad habits," recalled Norman Schwarzkopf, who took command of a battalion in the Americal Division late in 1969. He saw units in which the notion of maintaining perimeter security had been all but abandoned, with collapsed bunkers, barbed-wire fences with "yawning gaps," and Claymore antipersonnel mines whose detonating wires had rusted and separated, and even some mines that had been turned so they faced in toward the outpost.

Even as the Army was disintegrating, officers were rewarding themselves more. Close to half the generals who served in Vietnam received an award for valor. In 1968, a year in which 14,592 Americans were killed in action in Vietnam, some 416,693 awards were bestowed. In 1970, when only 3,946 men were killed, some 522,905 awards were given. Once again, the Army seemed to be putting the interests of its officer corps first.

The final insult to the Americal Division, and perhaps to the U.S. Army as a whole, came in March 1971. It was a particularly bitter phase of the war for both leaders and those they led. There were 120,000 Army personnel in the country, down from an American personnel peak of 543,000 in April 1969. Everyone knew the Americans were leaving, and the attention of many Americans was moving elsewhere, but small numbers of American soldiers were still engaged in combat. Rear areas were in a shambles, with racial tensions high, discipline becoming optional, and marijuana and heroin widely available at rock-bottom prices. Gayle Smith recalled working as a nurse in a U.S. military surgical hospital, in the Mekong Delta town of Binh Thuy, in which heroin usage was rampant. "These guys would work stoned all the time. My medics would shoot up my patients. . . . I caught them in the bathroom shooting each other up." George Cantero, another medic during this phase of the war, recalled, "In my units, the majority of people were high all the time." A rigorous series of tests and interviews concluded that almost half the Army enlisted men who departed Vietnam in one month in late 1971 had tried heroin or opium. Even more were using marijuana.

Cantero, the medic, also noted that "fragging," or the murder of officers with grenades, was common, but said that "the person that got fragged usually deserved it. . . . You only frag incompetent officers." According to an official Army history, between 1969 and 1971, there were eight hundred attacks involving hand grenades that, in sum, killed forty-five officers and sergeants.

The situation in frontline units was somewhat better but still problematic. Some saw head-spinning turnover in leadership. Keith William Nolan, in his melancholy portrait of the Army in Vietnam in 1971, offhandedly mentions one infantry company that went through five commanders in seven months. Platoon leaders felt especially squeezed between regular Army superiors who were trying to keep fighting the war and enlisted men who were just trying to survive and get home in one piece, and who sometimes were willing to maim or kill leaders they found overly aggressive in going after the enemy. "There were times I was very frightened, not just of what was in front of me, but what was behind me," one former lieutenant, Peter Doyle, told Nolan. "Sandbagging" patrols—going only part of the way, then lolling in the bush instead of seeking signs of the enemy—became more common. Combat refusals also probably were far more frequent than reported. When one platoon refused to move out from the position in which they had "laagered" the night, Nolan wrote, their company commander reminded them that it was battalion policy to hit such sites with an artillery barrage an hour after moving out in order to kill enemy scavengers. "So you got a choice," he informed them. "You can move out or get blown up."

In 1965, the Army's rate of court-martials in Vietnam had been 2.03 per thousand. In 1970, the American Division, a unit of perhaps 15,000 troops, had 5,567 nonjudicial punishments and court-martials. The two figures are not equivalent, but they are indicative. More directly comparable is that in 1965 the Army in Vietnam had 47 "apprehensions" for drug violations, while in 1970 it had more than 11,000.

At 2:40 A.M. on March 28, 1971, the North Vietnamese called in the debts being run up by soldiers in an American Division out-post who routinely got "buzzed" on marijuana before going on guard duty, or fell asleep during it, or did not even bother to get out of their bunks to report for duty. About four dozen members of the Viet Cong's 409th Sapper Battalion slipped through the perimeter defenses of Fire Support Base Mary Ann and roamed through the base, killing soldiers in their sleeping bags and toss-ing explosives and tear gas into the command post and other bunkers. There were extraordinary acts of heroism during the following hours, but at dawn, when the shooting and explosions were over, the fact remained that the base had been poorly defended by soldiers who had grown lax and commanders who had grown tired of pushing them or become wary of doing so for fear of retaliation. The Army as a whole seemed to be coming apart—one soldier recalled being surprised to see the crews of Cobra helicopters dispatched on the rescue mission leisurely walking to their aircraft. "They were just walking, and it made me pretty mad," Spec. 4 James Carmen later told Army investigators. Ultimately, of the 231 American troops at the firebase, 30 were killed and 82 wounded. It was the biggest single loss for American forces in their final phase of the war. The outpost, which had been sited poorly and could be easily observed from a nearby hill, was abandoned a few weeks later.

In the wake of the debacle, Maj. Gen. James Baldwin was relieved of command of the Americal Division by Gen. Abrams, the overall American commander in the ground war. "It was a mistake to make him a division commander," said William Richardson, who commanded a brigade in the Americal and then became its chief of staff. Abrams also wanted to reduce Baldwin in rank but was overruled by the secretary of the Army, who instead issued a formal letter of admonition for permitting defensive laxity under his command. Baldwin was replaced by Maj. Gen. Frederick Kroesen and sent home to retire the following year. This obscure personnel action, barely remembered today, appears to have been the last combat relief of an Army division commander up to the present day.

After My Lai, the jinxed Americal Division was far too notorious, so, in an unusual move, it effectively was fired as well. In December 1971, the Army did away with the division altogether, deactivating it and withdrawing two of its brigades from the war, leaving a third brigade as a stand-alone unit.

The end of an Army

By the end of the Vietnam War, the system of running the Army that had been devised decades earlier by George Marshall, a man of integrity, discipline, and objectivity, had collapsed. The new system of generalship rewarded officers without character and promoted distrust between generals and those they led, as well as the civilians to whom they reported. In the Army of 1972, "the atmosphere was somewhat poisonous, characterized by a vociferous loss of confidence in the Army leadership," William DePuy would recall many years later. In a public opinion poll of the perceived truthfulness of twenty occupations, Army generals ranked fourteenth, behind lawyers (9), television news reporters (11), and plumbers (12) but ahead of TV repairmen (15), politicians (19), and used-car salesmen (last).

While addressing young officers at Fort Benning, Georgia, where Marshall had taught infantry leadership forty years earlier, Gen. Westmoreland was nearly booed off the stage, according to one account. He also received a rowdy reception from officers at Fort Leavenworth. An officer serving then recalled that "the senior officer corps was thoroughly discredited by the Vietnam War. The majors were in revolt. They didn't give a shit about what the senior officers said."

Gen. Kroesen tried to explain how this had happened. He had seen the American Army through three wars. Not only had he replaced Baldwin at the American Division, but he had commanded troops in World War II and Korea. This is how he summarized the effect of the Vietnam War on the force:

We reached a condition in which the chain of command was in a state of dysfunction. I have always maintained that a chain of command must function from the bottom up as well as from the top down—with every squad leader making squad leader decisions and reporting to his platoon leader, "Here's what I found, here's what I did, and here's why I did it." When squad leaders have someone telling them not only what to do but also how to do it, they stop being leaders, and so do platoon leaders and company commanders. Initiative is stymied, and decision making is replaced by waiting to be told. Combat action becomes tentative, and military action bogs down.

In Vietnam many low-level commanders were subject to a hornet's nest of helicopters carrying higher commanders calling for information, offering advice, making unwanted decisions and generally interfering with what squad leaders and platoon leaders and company commanders were trying to do. There is no more effective way to destroy the leadership potential of young officers and noncommissioned officers than to deny them opportunities to make decisions appropriate for their assignments.

The Army continued to decline even after it left Vietnam. It was riven not only by the war but also by drugs and racism. "Those were the dog days of the Army in the post-Vietnam mid-seventies," recalled Gen. Montgomery Meigs. "The Army was more than hollow; parts of it were very rotten." Barry McCaffrey, a future general who was then the executive officer of a battalion based in West Germany, recalled gang rapes in the barracks and officers carrying loaded pistols for fear of assault. "The Army was really on the edge of falling apart," he said.

By the end of World War II, Marshall had built an entirely new Army—huge, mechanized, and powerful. By the end of the Vietnam War, thanks mostly to John F. Kennedy and Lyndon Johnson but also to Maxwell Taylor, Earle Wheeler, Harold K. Johnson, and William Westmoreland, Marshall's Army was close to destruction. "An entire American army was sacrificed on the battlefield of Vietnam," wrote historian and Vietnam veteran Shelby Stanton. "When the war was finally over, the United States military had to build a new volunteer army from the smallest shreds of its tattered remnants."

Col. Richard Sinnreich, who would be involved at Fort Leavenworth in the intellectual rebuilding of the Army, would say later, "As a young officer, I watched the Army come as close to dissolution, I think, as it has since the Revolution. . . . The glue that held us together was very thin." Not only would the Army have to be rebuilt, but so would its relationship with its civilian overseers.

PART IV
INTERWAR

Coming out of Vietnam, the Army was shattered. It was, said one general, "on its ass." As in the 1950s, it faced a basic question. This time the issue was whether it could exist without a draft. Over the following twenty years, it would remake itself. It recruited a force of volunteers. It revolutionized how it trained soldiers, with far more realistic field exercises. It overhauled its doctrine of how to fight. It developed an array of new weapons. Almost everything about it changed but its concept of generalship.

CHAPTER 22
DePuy's great rebuilding

After the 1991 Gulf War, when Americans wanted to know how the U.S. Army had improved so radically in the sixteen years since the fall of Saigon, they were told about a quiet but sweeping rebuilding—of new weapons, better soldiers, and revamped thinking about how to fight. These accounts of that transformation were accurate—to a point. What was less noticed at the time was that the great rebuilding had also contained some shortcomings that would hobble the Army many years later in Iraq and Afghanistan.

In 1973, Creighton Abrams, who had led the relief of the besieged 101st Airborne Division during the Battle of the Bulge, again would ride to the rescue of his service when he replaced Westmoreland as Army chief of staff. It was not inevitable that Abrams would be picked to lead the Army. President Nixon did not like Abrams and in fact had discussed with Henry Kissinger whether to relieve him as commander in Vietnam, according to Nixon's chief of staff, H. R. Haldeman, and others. At one point in 1971, Nixon, upset with Abrams, had ordered Alexander Haig, then an Army brigadier general, to depart immediately for

Vietnam to replace him. The ambitious, self-confident Haig knew that the idea of a one-star general stepping in was ridiculous, but, being Haig, he still was tempted: "I had no doubt that I could do the job." However, the secretary of defense, Melvin Laird, admired Abrams, and Laird had won a promise from Nixon that he could make his own personnel decisions, so Abrams stayed in place. Still, the discussions about who would succeed Westmoreland dragged on, and Abrams was nominated just twelve days before Westmoreland was to step down.

As Abrams awaited confirmation, he had a conversation with Maj. Gen. Donn Starry, who warned him, "Your Army is on its ass." It was—and he was determined to change that. The Grant-like Abrams—compact, solid, thoughtful, cigar-smoking, hard-drinking, slouching, and grouchy—would initiate the rebuilding of the Army. The process began with the creation of an "expeditious discharge program" to try to clean the Army's ranks of drug addicts, gang members, and other troublemakers. Under this process, which sidestepped a court-martial, the U.S. Army in Europe ejected thirteen hundred soldiers in just four months. Barry McCaffrey, by then a battalion commander in Germany, would spend weekends with his company commanders assembling lists of "bad apple" soldiers. On Monday mornings, he would assemble the full battalion with a truck standing nearby. The names of those to be ejected would be read off, and those called out were put on the truck. When the loaded vehicle pulled out and headed to the discharge office, he said, "the full battalion would cheer to get rid of these bums."

In the following years, the Army also modernized its gear, made its training radically more realistic, and developed thoughtful new manuals for how to take on the Red Army in Central Europe, giving it a chance of prevailing even though it would fight the Russians outnumbered. Yet in the process of rebuilding,

Abrams and his subordinates appear to have planted some of the seeds of problems that would plague the Army in Iraq and Afghanistan thirty years later. "In 1973, I was present for a lecture by General Creighton Abrams," recalled a Marine officer who had served in Vietnam. "He declared that the Army was turning its back on counterinsurgency forever." That year the Army War College dropped its required five-week course in unconventional warfare. This officer concluded, "That was the decision that caused the Army to stumble so badly in Iraq for the first three years."

Abrams's influence over the Army's renewal, though positive, was limited. He soon was stricken with cancer, though he remained in office. Into the vacuum stepped William DePuy, who in the mid-1970s would become, in the assessment of one Army historian, "arguably, the most important general in the U.S. Army" and, in the view of another, "likely the most important figure in the recovery of the United States Army" from its collapse after the defeat in Vietnam. "What DePuy did was take a broken Army and fix it so it could fight in Europe under the conditions that prevailed," said Henry Gole, his biographer. For a spell, a fast-rising young officer, one Lt. Col. Colin Powell, worked for DePuy at the Pentagon. (In another sign of the extensive intergenerational connections in the Army, Powell reported in that post directly to Maj. Gen. Herbert McChrystal Jr., father of the general who would command in Afghanistan four decades later.)

On July 1, 1973, DePuy took command of the Army's Training and Doctrine Command (TRADOC). It was a newly created headquarters, designed by him to bring together, for the first time, the Army's efforts on training, research, and doctrine—the last of these being essentially how the service thinks about how to fight. The Army was out of Vietnam, and DePuy was focused on its future, which he saw as conventional, tank-heavy battles in Europe. When the fourth Arab-Israeli conflict (also known as the

Yom Kippur War, the Ramadan War, or the October War) broke out that fall, he made the lessons and implications of the Israeli counterattack the centerpiece of his efforts to modernize and refocus the Army. The Arab forces, Soviet-trained and equipped, were a reasonable facsimile of what the U.S. Army would face on the plains of Central Europe if the superpowers ever went to war. DePuy also radically improved the Army's training efforts, beginning by doing away with mind-numbing time-based training, in which a certain number of hours were to be spent on each basic task in a soldier's field, and replaced it with a competence-based system. "The soldier moved to the next sequential task only after he had demonstrated competence at the basic level," wrote Gole.

DePuy and his subordinates, most notably Starry and another rising general, Paul Gorman, studied the Navy's Fighter Weapons School, which had been established after the Navy calculated that 40 percent of its pilots flying over North Vietnam were lost during their first three hostile engagements and that 90 percent of those who made it through that first set of fights survived their entire tours of duty. The Navy had established the school, better known as Top Gun, in 1969, to better prepare new pilots by having them fly against experienced ones using Soviet-based tactics. Graduates of this Navy school, which was made famous by a 1986 Tom Cruise film, fared far better flying over North Vietnam, while Air Force pilots, many of them operating the same sort of aircraft but lacking this new training, continued to suffer the same loss ratios.

The Army set out to create its own version of this realistic training with the new National Training Center (NTC) at Fort Irwin, in the high Mojave Desert of California. The thousand-square-mile center, which would finally open in 1980, after DePuy retired, confronted visiting units with a smart, wily, live enemy, "the Opposition Force." Rather than have "who won" decided in arguments afterward, the forces were equipped with laser guns and receptors, which fairly accurately detected who had shot first and best, making the exercises more realistic. In addition, "observer-controllers" monitored the battlefield and gave commanders tough reviews after each round of maneuvers. By coincidence, the new training center opened just as the Army, after much hard work, began to attract smarter, more disciplined volunteers. Not only did the center improve the skills of soldiers, but the tough training gave platoons, companies, and battalions new confidence in themselves and their leaders. After the 1991 Gulf War, it would be commonplace for soldiers to report that the fighting they had seen had not been as hard as going through maneuvers at the National Training Center.

DePuy also correctly read the trend in military operations toward more sophisticated weaponry, and the implications of that for raising and training a force. This was not a foregone conclusion. At the time, there was a small but influential movement in Congress and among some defense intellectuals and journalists for equipping the military with large numbers of smaller, less expensive weapons. DePuy, seeming to anticipate the coming of computerized warfare, moved in the opposite direction. There would need to be a higher ratio of leaders to troops, he concluded, with smaller units and more intense training. "We cannot have the best man on a $200 typewriter while a less-qualified soldier operates a million-dollar tank," he wrote in 1978. He threw his institutional weight behind the development of five new weapons systems: the Abrams tank, the Bradley Fighting Vehicle, the Patriot antiaircraft system, the Apache attack helicopter, and the Black Hawk transport helicopter. They were accompanied by a revolution in the weapons used by the other services, with, among other advances, precision-guided munitions, stealthy fighters and bombers, and unmanned aircraft for both reconnaissance and strike missions. James Kitfield, author of the best book on the post-Vietnam military, also credits DePuy with helping to create the Army's semi-secret Delta Force, its elite Special Operations counterterror unit.

This is how David Barno, a general who served in the Army in the late twentieth century and commanded in the war in Afghanistan in 2004–5, summarized the post-Vietnam reconstruction of the Army:

> It not only ensured that the best weapons systems for conventional war against the Soviets got top priority, but it also matched them with organizational changes to optimize their performance in battle (a new infantry and armor battalion organization), a rigorous self-critical training methodology (including massive free-play armored force-on-force laser battles), advanced ranges and training simulators for mechanized warfare, and perhaps most importantly, the recruitment and leadership of extraordinarily high quality personnel who were bright, motivated, and superbly trained to make best use of the emerging new concepts and high-tech equipment being fielded. These innovations that grew out of the massive infusion of resources in the 1980s remain the cornerstone of the Army as an institution today. Their long-term influence on Army cultural and institutional preferences cannot be overstated.

Out at Fort Leavenworth, Maj. Gen. John Cushman also was thinking about rebuilding the Army. Cushman had grown up in the interwar Army: He was born in China in 1921 and lived there when his father was a captain in the 15th Infantry Regiment, serving as adjutant under the regimental executive officer, George Marshall, and also serving alongside another young officer, Matthew Ridgway.

In the early 1970s, Cushman commanded the 101st Division

when it came home from Vietnam. From that post he moved to take command at Leavenworth in 1973. There, he looked for ways to complement DePuy's tactical rebuilding with an ethical and intellectual rejuvenation. Despite the findings of the 1970 Army War College study that the Army's professional ethic had been badly eroded, ethics were still considered primarily the domain of the Army's Chaplain Corps, not an influential group. In leading the Army's Command and General Staff College at Leavenworth, Cushman was struck by how much students craved discussions of "basic questions such as honesty, candor, and the freedom to fail." His ensuing sessions with them only intensified their interest, so in March 1974 he held his first symposium on officer responsibility with students and about one hundred guests, including fifteen generals. He began by posing a series of questions about how to raise standards and create an environment of integrity, and the role of generals in making that environment routine. One of the speakers was Lt. Gen. Peers, who had investigated the leadership failures surrounding the My Lai massacre.

Generals who were accustomed to deference from officers far junior to them were taken aback at the free-flying atmosphere at the Leavenworth symposium. "It was tough, direct, and pointed and heated—and some of those generals got hurt—bad," recalled Col. Dandridge Malone.

One officer stood to talk about "dishonest demands coming down, dishonest reports going up."

"I never tolerated that in *my* division," responded one of the generals.

"I was *in* your division," the younger officer said.

"Lock your heels," the general said, using an abrupt phrase for ordering a subordinate to come to attention to prepare for an upbraiding.

Brig. Gen. Morris Brady, in a memorandum summarizing the

proceedings of the symposium, wrote that the feeling among the younger officers was that "the more senior an officer is, the more likely it is that he has compromised his integrity in order to achieve success. . . . From the students' perspective, we have created an environment that encourages professional immorality."

In the following days, Gen. Abrams began hearing complaints and sent a query: "What the hell happened out there at Leavenworth?" He eventually was persuaded that passion about ethics was a positive sign.

Others were even less enthusiastic about Cushman's initiative than Abrams, most notably William DePuy, to whom Cushman reported. Both men were described by others as stubborn and brilliant, but DePuy, by then one of the most powerful generals in the Army, also was described by some as determined to run things his way. He "did not want a dialogue he could not control," Maj. Paul Herbert concluded in an Army monograph. What's more, the two generals had differences dating back a decade, over the approach DePuy had devised to fight in Vietnam. As Cushman would put it,

> In 1964–67 I had taken exception to Bill DePuy's approach to fighting in Vietnam, having heard enough for me to believe that both as General Westmoreland's J-3 and then as division commander he had misunderstood the nature of the war, downrating pacification and emphasizing massive search and destroy operations by U.S. forces, while allowing those to shunt aside ARVN [Army of the Republic of Vietnam] troops and to take insufficient note of province and local forces and their advisors who were in the closest touch with the people.

In 1974, the fundamental difference between the two men, as Cushman saw it, was that DePuy was teaching the Army how to fight, while Cushman was complementing that work by teaching Army officers how to think about fighting. Both are necessary, but DePuy seemed to believe that he did not have the resources for both and that the first would have to take priority. He made it clear that he was not interested in sponsoring introspective studies of Army professional issues. He told his subordinate commanders that he had seen "the Army War College being thrown into lots of projects which really didn't inspire me much. These projects included surveys of what made lieutenant colonels unhappy, and others which I felt stirred up more bloody problems than they solved." When he visited Leavenworth, he undercut Cushman's educational efforts, telling the students at one point, "All I want from this class is ten battalion commanders."

DePuy was aware of his critics, who muttered that his reforms produced commanders who did not understand war. As the general himself later recalled, "They said that DePuy is going to cause a lacuna which is going to create a whole generation of idiots who all know how to clean a rifle but who don't know 'why' we have an Army. I didn't lose a lot of sleep over that because we do have a system that begins to answer the question of how to train an officer." This "lacuna" is, of course, close to what happened two decades later as the generation of astrategic officers trained under DePuy became the generals fighting in Iraq and Afghanistan—most notably Tommy R. Franks and Ricardo Sanchez—but no one could have known that back in the 1970s when DePuy mounted this defense of his efforts.

DePuy fired off a series of letters to Cushman, warning that he did not like Cushman's contemplative direction at Leavenworth. As Abrams succumbed to his cancer, he was less able to shield Cushman from DePuy, who did not have a lot of time for working out his differences with subordinates. "Nice warm human relationships are satisfying and fun, but they are not the purpose of an Army," he instructed other senior officers at Fort Benning the same year that he was confronting Cushman.

A year later, in April 1975, Cushman convened a second symposium on ethics and leadership. It was held at Leavenworth at an anguishing moment, just as the North Vietnamese tanks rolled into Saigon and the last American helicopters lifted off the roofs of U.S. government installations there. Cushman ended the symposium with a prayer for all those who had suffered in Vietnam. He asked that those present "be examples of the soldierly virtues." Then he looked up and said to the hundreds of assembled officers, "Now just go quietly out of here." It was a fitting emotional end to America's long, misbegotten war in Southeast Asia.

DePuy clashed even more with Cushman over the other part of his command: doctrine. Updating the Army's capstone manual, then known as "FM 100-5: Operations," was traditionally the job of the commander at Fort Leavenworth and the handful of trusted subordinates to whom he delegated the actual work of drafting.

Their fundamental philosophical differences made a clash between the two generals inevitable. It began during the drafting of the operations manual. "Major General Cushman believed that an organization worked best when liberated, to the degree possible, from the artificial constraints placed on the tremendous creative potential of the group," wrote Maj. Herbert in his history of the FM 100-5 manual during this time. "General DePuy believed that real initiative was rare in human beings and that an organization functioned best when its members were frequently told in simple terms what to do." DePuy's loyalists, such as Gen. Donn Starry, who would succeed him at TRADOC, thought Cushman was deeply in the wrong. "General Jack Cushman at Leavenworth led the surge of resentment about the 1976 edition of FM

100-5—Active Defense," Starry said in his oral history. "I have characterized that many times as probably the greatest act of institutional and individual disloyalty I have ever had the chance to observe."

As was probably also inevitable, DePuy rejected the draft Cushman had delivered and took over the job himself. DePuy was preparing for a big war. "Don't get too lofty or philosophical," he admonished the officers he picked to work with him on the manual. "Wars are won by draftees and reserve officers. Write so they can understand."

In 1976, DePuy published the edition of the manual that quickly became known as the "Active Defense" version. It provoked a huge and healthy debate inside the Army. While his version was eventually repudiated, and replaced in 1982 by the "AirLand Battle" edition of FM 100-5, he succeeded in elevating the role of doctrine itself and so revitalized thinking in the Army about its core missions. In the second half of the 1970s, *Military Review,* one of the Army's leading professional journals, would carry more than eighty articles on aspects of the new manual. DePuy made the drafting of doctrine—once considered drone work for second-rate midcareer staffers—a core function, the business of generals. This new emphasis made the Army, as an institution, mull basic strategic questions: *Who are we? What are we trying to do? How are we to do it—that is, how should we fight?* Ironically, while repudiating Cushman personally, DePuy had, to a degree, moved the Army into precisely the realm of thinking he had shunned but that Cushman had advocated.

By spotlighting doctrine, DePuy also helped wrest control of the strategic discussion back from civilians, who had become dominant in that sphere during the 1950s as nuclear weaponry grew to overshadow all other questions of warfare. As historian and strategic expert Hew Strachan later put it, in that difficult post-Vietnam recovery phase, "doctrine became one device by which it [the Army] sought to reassert its professional self-worth."

But the manual also contained deep flaws that resulted partly from DePuy's feud with Cushman. DePuy had emphasized the "synchronization" of military operations, which he saw as the temporal equivalent of concentrating forces physically. This would prove to be a mixed legacy. Overseen by a master of the battlefield, it was a useful tool, concluded his biographer, retired Army Col. Henry Gole. But in the hands of lesser officers, this approach tended to intensify the Army's inclination to follow cumbersome procedures that actually undercut combat effectiveness. In the 1991 Gulf War, wrote retired Army Col. Richard Swain, efforts to follow the idea of synchronization, of getting all the parts working together to greater effect, would become "the molasses in the system . . . a drag on opportunism."

More important, DePuy's manual was very much a product of the late Cold War. It emphasized training, which prepares soldiers for the known, far more than education, which prepares them to deal with the unknown. "DePuy wanted USACGSC [the Army's Command and General Staff College] to train its students to be experts at handling a division in combat," wrote Maj. Herbert. "Cushman wanted to educate students as well as to train them, to make them think, to enrich them personally and professionally, and to prepare them intellectually for all their years as field grade officers." DePuy readily conceded that he favored training over education. "We were tactical guys by self-definition and preference," he said later.

In truth, both DePuy and Cushman were correct about the necessary focus—DePuy in the short run and Cushman in the long one. DePuy's approach fit a time when the predictable enemy was the Soviet Union, when even the ground on which a confrontation with the forces of the Warsaw Pact would take place was well known. During the Cold War, some U.S. Army officers stationed in West Germany would take their families for Sunday picnics at the spots near Fulda where they expected to emplace their tanks to face the Red Army. There was little need for generals who were strategic thinkers, because the strategic threat at the time was obvious: It was the Soviet Union. The ways to deal with the Red Army remained fairly constant: Find ways to slow it down while fighting outnumbered, so that artillery, rockets, and aircraft could begin to even the balance by what was called, rather bizarrely, "servicing targets." "In a very real sense, it was a simple world model from the political-military point of view," Army Col. Donald Bletz noted in 1974. "The threat was clear, and not only the need for military force but also the nature of that force was clear and broadly accepted." DePuy's emphasis on tactical competence was necessary but not sufficient. His approach "courted the dangers of oversimplification, rigidity and impermanence," noted Herbert.

Be that as it may, he was in control—and intolerant of other approaches. "Dear Jack," DePuy wrote to Cushman in October 1975. "As you know, I am deeply concerned about the ability of our colonels and lieutenant colonels to lead their commands in the first battle of the next war." This was certainly his core concern, and he was determined to yank Cushman away from strategic thinking and ethical philosophizing. So he instructed Cushman to "design a refresher course in tactical leadership" for such officers headed to combat commands. It was as if DePuy had determined that future commanders, as well as Cushman, would take remedial instruction.

Cushman's approach to the manual was influenced by the Vietnam War, which was hardly mentioned in DePuy's 1976 edition of 100-5. His emphasis on strategic considerations was better for preparing officers for ambiguity, for handling crises involving a less understood foe, perhaps in parts of the world new to Americans and their Army. As Herbert notes, it would have been better if the two men had been able to resolve their differences and give Army officers both what they needed at the time and what they would need in the future. But DePuy and Cushman could not find such a compromise. The result was that, in the 1970s and 1980s, the Army for the most part neglected Cushman's approach and followed DePuy's. It produced a generation of officers who tended to be tactically adept, proficient as battalion commanders, but not prepared for senior generalship—especially when the Cold War ended and they faced a series of ambiguous crises. In its twenty-first-century wars, the Army would come to realize it needed leaders comfortable with vague situations, alien cultures, inadequate information, and ill-defined goals. It would have many such soldiers in its ranks, but few in key command positions at its top.

In the 1940s, Cushman would have likely been removed by DePuy. But this was the 1970s, and even DePuy had become shy of relief. At one point, DePuy told Starry that he had decided to fire Cushman and was traveling to Fort Leavenworth to do so, but, for reasons that are not known, he did not. Instead he gave Cushman a blistering performance review that criticized the Leavenworth commander for failing to follow DePuy's direction. "General Cushman is a very strong minded individual," it stated. "It is very difficult to make him truly responsive to guidance, to make him a true member of the team." But Fred Weyand, by now the Army chief of staff, liked and admired Cushman. Over DePuy's objection—expressed directly to Weyand—the chief of staff promoted Cushman and sent him to a top Army position in Korea. DePuy would have his revenge: Shortly after Cushman departed for Asia, DePuy canceled the third Leavenworth symposium on ethics, scheduled for April 1976. It is striking today to read the official histories of the early days of the Training and Doctrine

Command and see that DePuy looms large on nearly every page, while Cushman almost never appears.

The result of this feud between generals was that the Army's rejuvenation would be tactical, physical, and ethical but not particularly strategic or intellectual. The Army was concentrating on its soldiers, which generally is the correct approach, but appears to have done so at the cost of paying sufficient attention to generalship. The centerpiece of the training revolution of the late 1970s, the National Training Center, at Fort Irwin, California, along with two other centers that were established later, radically improved the tactical skills of soldiers and their leaders. But it also tended to focus the Army overmuch on battalion command. A successful tour leading a battalion had long been the beginning of the Army's path to becoming a general, but the training centers emphasized this even more. This new focus may have skewed Army views somewhat, leading officers to actually confuse battalion command with generalship. "From 1982 on, the National Training Center was the intellectual home of the Army, not the War College or West Point," observed Col. Paul Yingling. In its training revolution, the Army effectively built a new body but placed atop it an old head—a head that had not performed well in Vietnam. Battalion and brigade commanders knew how to conduct a blitzkrieg, but when they became generals, they did not know what to do once that speedy attack was concluded. Nor did they receive adequate political guidance from their civilian superiors, which would have underscored the need for better planning for war termination. And so four times—in 1989 in Panama, in 1991 and 2003 in Iraq, and in 2001 in Afghanistan—Army generals would lead swift attacks against enemy forces yet do so without a notion of what to do the day after their initial triumph, and in fact believing that it was not their job to consider the question. The military historian Brian Linn put it well: "The fixation on winning day-long battles in a two-week NTC rotation may well have distracted an entire generation of combat officers from learning, or even thinking about, how to turn short-term tactical victories into long-term strategic results."

However unevenly, the Army was recovering from Vietnam. One signal of this was the controversial testimony before a congressional committee by Gen. Edward Meyer, the relatively new chief of staff of the Army, in May 1980 that, "right now, . . . we have a hollow Army." The Army did not have enough recruits, and of those it did have coming in, only half were high school graduates. The Army also had huge budget problems, Meyer stated. His testimony made front-page headlines, but its meaning was missed. To outsiders, Meyer appeared to be admitting to failure. But to Meyer and those who understood what he was doing, it was rather that he was responding to the lack of integrity that had plagued the Army in the 1950s and even more in Vietnam, and that had come to be personified by William Westmoreland. Meyer was speaking truth to power. As James Kitfield perceptively wrote in describing the moment, "Meyer felt that lack of essential honesty and the breakdown in communication was exactly what had failed all of them—the civilian leadership, the military, the whole damn country—during Vietnam." Civilian leaders did not appreciate his effort. As Kitfield relates it, after returning to the Pentagon from Capitol Hill, Meyer was called into the office of the secretary of the Army, Clifford Alexander, and asked to disavow the "hollow Army" comment. Meyer declined to do so but instead offered to resign, a gesture that was rejected. In this instance, the Army's leadership was well ahead of its civilian overseers in shedding the lies and distrust that had so damaged discourse about the conduct of the Vietnam War.

The one thing that did not change much as the Army rebuilt was the sort of personality favored among those promoted to general officer rank. It remained, as it had for decades, the Omar

Bradley type: hardworking, determined, somewhat conformist, steady, prudent to a fault, and wary of innovation. In 1972, before the rebuilding, the Army sent twelve new brigadier generals to be evaluated by psychologists and others for two weeks. The experts found three managerial types among the twelve. Half were solidly in the mold of Bradley: "dependable, cautious, managerial type." Here is how one insightful Army expert outlined that sort of officer:

> He can be counted on to do what is expected of him. He is a highly capable, competent, very intelligent individual who enacts a standardized leadership role quite effectively. He has energy and drive. He is slightly introverted, not to the extent of being unsociable, but to the extent of being distant and somewhat removed. . . . He's trusting of others but not very flexible in his thinking and social behavior. . . . His weakness lies in his lack of innovativeness (in areas where innovativeness is appropriate but not organizationally required).

Another three of the new generals were of the "outgoing managerial type"—more prone to act quickly and less interested in details. Only three of the twelve were deemed to be of the "potentially creative managerial type." It was a small sample, but it appears to be representative.

In the 1980s, after the rebuilding was well under way, David Campbell, a psychologist specializing in leadership, administered another battery of personality and intelligence tests to new Army brigadier generals. His results were remarkably similar to those in the 1972 study. The generals were relatively intelligent (with an average IQ of at least 124), hardworking, responsible, and conformist. Like George Marshall, they were rather cold in personal relations, with almost half the brigadier generals scoring a zero on wanting to be included socially, a result that Campbell found "astonishing." But they were more rigid than Marshall had ever been in his professional thinking, scoring relatively low, Campbell found, "on the flexibility scale, which says something about their willingness, or lack thereof, to consider new, innovative solutions to problems." The result, concluded retired Army Col. Lloyd Matthews, was "a maladaptive Army senior officer corps." At just the time when the nation would need flexible generals, with the end of the Cold War and the emergence of a new set of problems and threats, the Army was selecting and developing the opposite type.

Nor were Army subordinates satisfied with this crop of generals. In 1983, an Army survey found that one-quarter of new brigadier generals were seen by officers who had commanded battalions under them as unqualified to be generals. In the survey, conducted by Lt. Col. Tilden Reid, an Army War College student, 110 battalion commanders reported that about one-third of the Army's new generals did not care about their soldiers, did not develop subordinates, and were more managers than leaders. Even more damning, the same percentage said that the new general they knew should not lead in combat and that they would not want to serve under that general again. Half the new generals were seen as micromanagers.

This was a damaged crop of generals.

An effort had been made to address these leadership flaws. In 1975, the Army established the Organizational Effectiveness Training Center, at Fort Ord, California. This was a radical departure for the service—a program that emphasized team building and adaptation. A study by the Army five years later found that the program had improved morale and the quality of leadership as judged by subordinates. Yet the program was always seen by many in the Army as suspiciously "touchy-feely," even "beads and sandals." Nor was it clear where it belonged in the Army: Was it a personnel function, or, as a leadership issue, should its command-ers report directly to the chief of staff?

In 1985, with its post-Vietnam reconstruction well under way, the Army terminated the program. In other words, as soon as the crisis was perceived to have passed, the Army's leadership went back to the old ways. Army chief of staff Gen. John Wickham and Secretary of the Army John Marsh said as much in a statement to Wickham's predecessor, Gen. Bernard Rogers, who had protested the closure. "While organizational effectiveness has served the Army well since the mid-seventies, the environment we find our-selves in today is different than when we took advantage of emerg-ing behavioral science initiatives to help the chain of command solve tough issues," they wrote. "Today, as you know, we are pro-viding much better preparation for leaders prior to their assump-tion of command." The official reason given was that leadership would be taught at the new Joint Readiness Training Center, which, as Col. Peter Varljen pointed out, really represented a reversion to the old development of leadership skills "that could easily be measured in terms of mission accomplishment."

CHAPTER 23
"How to teach judgment"

The struggle over the future of the force continued in other arenas. Almost as soon as DePuy and his principal allies had retired, new steps were taken to deal with the vacuum in the Army's strategic education and thinking. DePuy's 1976 edition of 100-5, the key Army manual, "was confined to the science of tactical engagements only," noted Col. Huba Wass de Czege, an Army officer descended, unusually enough, from Transylvanian nobility. What the Army was teaching its captains and majors, he observed, was "all method—you know, here's how you do a movement to contact. They had not been taught why you organize for a movement to contact the way the method prescribes. Why the prescribed distribution of forces and assignments? What's the theory behind what it is you're trying to do?" Wass de Czege had been pondering the Army's lack of strategic ability for more than a decade, since he was a young Army officer "on a hill in Vietnam wondering why all the field grade officers above me hadn't a clue about what they were sending me out to do." He returned to the subject in the early 1980s, when Lt. Gen. William Richardson appointed him to a group at the Command and General Staff College that was asked to study "how to teach judgment."

Wass de Czege developed an idea about how to do just that. Knowing that his immediate superiors would oppose the idea, Wass de Czege waited until he knew he could get Gen. Richardson alone, which, as it happened, was during the first peaceful military-to-military exchange between the People's Liberation Army of China and the American military. In June 1981, Wass de Czege buttonholed Richardson on the fantail of a boat on the Yangtze River and talked to him for an hour. What the Army needed, he said, was a new school that would teach an elite group of officers how to get beyond tactical thinking.

Wass de Czege's plea in China for educating officers was a sign that, with DePuy out of the way, Cushman's opinions about doctrine were returning with renewed vigor. Richardson and others around him were admirers of DePuy, and Richardson, in fact, had been the general's executive assistant at the Pentagon in 1968–69. Even so, they saw a need to balance DePuy's rebuilding of the Army. "A system of officer education which emphasizes 'how-to' *training* applicable only to the present will fail to provide the needed *education* the US Army officer corps will need to be adaptive in the uncertain future," Wass de Czege wrote in a 1983 study that offered a blueprint for the new school. "More officers must be educated in theories and principles which will make them adaptive and innovative." The problem as he saw it was that Army officers were being trained by "marginally qualified," "defensive and dogmatic" teachers at the Command and General Staff College who gave them the false hope of "formulas, recipes, and safe engineering solutions to make order of potential chaos." The solution, he wrote, was that "a key segment of our officer corps must know *how to think* and not only *what to think* about war." The Army could develop such officers by teaching them "better military judgment." If there was, in fact, a science to warfare, he thought, then some small portion of its professionals needed to understand the theoretical basis of that science.

Just two years after the conversation on the Yangtze, the Army launched a pilot program at Fort Leavenworth to do just that. The Department of Advanced Military Studies was an intellectual version of the Army's Ranger School, which is legendary for pushing its participants to their physical limits. As Lt. Col. Harold R. Winton, the school's first faculty member, put it, "The Army gave them the opportunity of a lifetime to study their profession in depth, in a no-holds-barred arena where their best ideas were put up against the best ideas of other people, and where they were used to winning arguments, they were now losing arguments."

The faculty was also selected differently than at most Army schools. Wass de Czege required that they have teaching experience and at least a master's degree at a first-rank university (the first three professors had advanced degrees from Stanford, Harvard, and the University of Michigan), and in addition they had to have demonstrated the ability to command military units, which was important for winning the respect of their students. The new effort had an independent spirit that was consistent with its mission of teaching thinking and judgment, but it stood out in the hierarchical Army. For example, its second director, Col. Richard Sinnreich, without seeking clearance from the leadership of the Command and General Staff College, changed the program's name, making it the School of Advanced Military Studies (SAMS). Sinnreich also flatly stated that the school was intended to address the mistakes of Vietnam and also of DePuy's version of the 100-5 manual. "I came out of that war really unhappy. Something was broken. . . . [There was] a big huge intellectual hole in the Army's understanding of how you go to war," he said. In addition, the DePuy 100-5 made him worry that "here we were going right back to where we had been before, tactical as hell but not operational content at all. We'd win the first battle, but what about the war?" It was a legitimate concern, as subsequent American wars would demonstrate.

The first class of thirteen students graduated in June 1984. In a farewell talk, Wass de Czege admonished them not to be intellectual show-offs. "When you get to the unit the one thing you absolutely do not want to do is talk about and quote Clausewitz and Sun Tzu. What you have to do is max the PT [physical training] test and get your hands dirty in the motor pool. You will succeed if you do those things and heed the motto of the German general staff to 'be more than you appear to be.'"

Word quickly got out that the new school at Leavenworth was producing a valuable new kind of officer. "Getting these guys was like gold," recalled Robert Killebrew, chief of planning for the XVIII Airborne Corps in the late 1980s. "They came with missionary zeal and had been issued notebook computers—then rare—and were encouraged to network with their fellow graduates around the Army, all of whom went to pinpoint assignments in critical plans and ops jobs in divisions and corps." A bonus, he recalled, was that they had the inside line on upcoming personnel moves and other inside knowledge. "They knew more about what was going on around the Army than anybody." It also helped that Gen. Richardson, who had approved the idea, became the Army's deputy chief of staff for operations, a position in which he could strongly encourage personnel managers to allow good officers to apply to the new program. After that, Richardson took over as the head of the Training and Doctrine Command, with Leavenworth under his purview, which meant he could continue to protect and nurture the new school.

In his 1983 study, Wass de Czege had predicted that if a school for advanced studies was established, it "would make a tremendous impact on the US Army by the year 2000." He probably was overoptimistic by about five or six years. Over the years, some seventy-seven graduates of the new institution would join the ranks of the Army's general officers. The first SAMS general was Charles Cannon, in October 1992, and the second, Robert St.

Onge Jr., was promoted three years later. By 2000 there were a total of fourteen. In overseeing Army war games, Wass de Czege found he could spot the SAMS graduates even without knowing the background of the officers he was mentoring. They were the ones, he noted, who "just seemed to approach the issues at a higher cognitive level first and then to work from there to the practical level. They were able to make sense of complexity far easier than their peers." Over the following decade, an additional fifty-five SAMS alumni became generals. All had taken away at least a bit of what one officer in the second class recalled learning at SAMS: "War is much more than a tactical battle of attrition." No surprise nowadays, but a departure from what DePuy had practiced in Vietnam and taught for many years afterward.

But however bright it was, the strategic lamp lit at Leavenworth was a small one—by design, because it was envisioned as an institution to find and polish an elite. It would take many years for the officers receiving this new level of education to develop into a critical mass. In the meantime, Army generalship would change very little. In fact, in the short run, the addition of SAMS graduates to the ranks of lieutenant colonels and colonels may have reinforced the trend among generals toward tactical orientation, by making the senior officers believe—falsely—that they did not need to think and read deeply about their profession, because the Army was producing officers who could do that for them.

SAMS-trained planners first came to the forefront in the 1991 Gulf War, when Gen. Schwarzkopf employed eighty-two of them—if somewhat shortsightedly, using all of them for the attack and none for what followed. For the most part, the Army would be led in that war by DePuy-shaped men who, unfortunately, embodied Wass de Czege's warning of 1983 about training rather than educating officers: "For nearly ten years we have attempted to train CGSC [Command and General Staff College] graduates for the 'First Battle' and for virtually nothing beyond that yet-to-occur confrontation."

Gen. Tommy R. Franks would use SAMS graduates even less effectively twelve years later, in the 2003 invasion of Iraq, when a plan developed by "SAMSters" for the occupation of Iraq was only partially executed before being discarded. Most notably, that plan called for keeping the Iraqi army whole and assigning it to reconstruction tasks, rather than sending it home in disgrace, as would happen in mid-2003. By 2009, a SAMS brochure read like a critique of the shortcomings of non-SAMS Army generals: SAMS graduates, it said, "are innovative leaders, willing to accept risk and experiment; are adaptive leaders who excel at the art of command; anticipate future operational environments; apply critical and creative thinking skills in order to solve complex problems."

The recovery falls short

Despite the existence of SAMS, the flaws of Army generalship tended to remain the same in the 1980s and '90s as in earlier decades. Most notably, the complaints about micromanagement by senior officers that plagued the Army in the 1950s and '60s would continue into the rebuilt Army of the 1980s and '90s.

Numerous internal Army studies dissected the institution's problems, but the Army's leaders seemed incapable of responding effectively to these findings. In 1984, an Army survey found that leadership skills were the second greatest weakness in officer development, following operational skills. In 1985, officers reported broad dissatisfaction with a culture of careerism. An internal survey conducted at about the same time found a consensus opinion that bold and creative officers could not survive in the Army and that it was led by generals who behaved more like corporate managers than leaders. In 1987, a survey of 141 senior Army sergeants produced a startling profile of Army officership of the day. Some 57 percent of the NCOs reported that officers showed slight or no loyalty downward, while only 8 percent felt that officers would stand up to superiors on their behalf. More than 43 percent thought officers lacked flexibility. In perhaps the greatest departure from the old Marshall template, exactly 50 percent said officers had a slight or no sense of team play, and slightly more said that officers cared more about staying ahead of their peers than they did about their soldiers. Forty-eight percent said that officers did not inspire trust and confidence. The sergeants graded officers most harshly on integrity, with 62 percent stating that officers to a great extent tended to cover up incidents that made them look bad.

There is an inverse relationship between trust and micromanagement. The more one trusts subordinates, even to the point of allowing them to make their own corrections after erring, the less necessary it is to hover over them. Lack of trust has corrosive effects within organizations, slowing them down and cramping their ability to move information quickly, adjust to new circumstances, or engage in prudent risk taking. "Not trusting people is an invitation to organizational disaster," Lt. Gen. Walter Ulmer Jr., the Army's foremost expert on leadership at the time, warned in 1986. A significant portion of the Army did not trust its superiors, according to another 1987 survey, done at the Army War College, in which 30 percent of respondents said their leaders did not live up to ethical standards.

When the rare public relief occurred, it was almost always in order to punish personal indiscretion rather than professional incompetence. Indeed, despite all the complaints about micromanagement, with its presumption of close oversight and swift correction, the Army seemed to tolerate ineffectiveness—which is surprising, because in combat, ineptitude gets soldiers killed unnecessarily. In 1985, Maj. Gen. Clay Buckingham would look at the state of the Army and conclude, "As a rule . . . general officers do not get relieved for incompetence." No generals were fired after the "Desert One" hostage rescue debacle in Iran in April 1980, nor after the Beirut barracks bombing in 1983. When reliefs did occur, they were carried out very quietly, with little public disclosure.

Donn Starry, a thoughtful general who had the courage to act on his convictions, actually came to the conclusion that the Marshall approach of swift but nonterminal relief was the correct one. The way to do this, he thought, was to give new commanders an initial probationary period in which they could be tested and, if necessary, removed without much harm to their careers. "It would be much better if we had a system in which we said, 'All right, we're going to put this guy in command,' and then six or eight months later, you say, 'I don't think old George is going to make it,' so we take old George out without any retribution or black mark on his record." But Starry finally decided that it was beyond the Army's ability to be so innovative in its approach to leadership. "That required a cultural change that I just think is beyond our scope."

Coda: The end of DePuy

DePuy's rebuilding of the Army had been necessary and magnificent—but insufficient. As Lt. Col. Suzanne Nielsen wrote in a 2010 assessment, "The Army gained tactical and operational excellence but failed to develop leaders well-suited to helping political leaders attain strategic success." That is a devastating critique, because it charges that the Army, despite all the self-congratulation about its rebuilding, was failing to carry out its core function as a servant of the nation. It is perhaps the best epitaph for the Army's performances in Iraq and Afghanistan.

Some insiders understood the shortfall. "We were trying to change the Army," Richard Sinnreich, one of the founders of the School of Advanced Military Studies, would conclude. "We have been a failure." But such statements were rare.

William DePuy's legacy lived on in the Army in other ways. In the early 1980s, one his followers, Maxwell Thurman, revitalized Army recruiting and, in the process, perhaps saved the concept of the all-volunteer force. Thurman would rise even higher a few years later, in mid-1989, when Defense Secretary Dick Cheney, contemplating launching an attack on Panama to oust Manuel Noriega, decided that Gen. Frederick Woerner, the senior American officer in Panama, was not up to the job. Cheney fired Woerner and replaced him with Thurman, who was just a month away from retiring. "I figured it was my obligation to make certain I had somebody there that I had confidence in and who I trusted," Cheney explained later, in a clear formulation of the proper relationship between civilian leadership and senior officers. Again the new pattern asserted itself: When the military stopped relieving senior generals, civilians started doing so.

Gen. DePuy's last major public appearance came on the eve of the Gulf War, when the formidable Army he had played such a large role in creating was deploying to fight in the Middle East. It was December 1990, and he was nearing the end of his life. The old general was asked by members of the House Armed Services Committee to discuss what war against Saddam Hussein's Iraq, then occupying Kuwait, might be like. He would end with his beginning, reaching back to his time as a young officer in the hard summer after the D-Day invasion of France, in June 1944. "Let me use the example first of Normandy," he told the committee. He focused on "the Falaise pocket," in which some ten thousand German soldiers were killed and perhaps another fifty thousand taken prisoner as they tried to flee eastward. "They were moving over essentially one road," he noted—an eerie fore-shadowing of how the Gulf War would end a few months later, with a "highway of death" for Iraqi soldiers fleeing northward. In the following year, DePuy would deteriorate rapidly into dementia. He died in September 1992. But by then he had seen the Army he had rebuilt demonstrate its tactical prowess to the world.

PART V

IRAQ AND THE HIDDEN COSTS OF REBUILDING

The Army in 1991, on the eve of the Gulf War, had 710,000 soldiers, which was 80,000 fewer than the Army that had come out of Vietnam. But it was more effective in almost every way: better trained, better equipped, and better led—at least at the tactical and operational levels of war.

CHAPTER 24

Colin Powell, Norman Schwarzkopf, and the empty triumph of the 1991 war

The two generals who dominated the public image of the Army of the early 1990s—what might be called the newly vigorous, actively deployed, post-post-Vietnam force—were Colin Powell and, joining him but not supplanting him, H. Norman Schwarzkopf. They were oddly similar men, near contemporaries with parallel experiences in the military: Both were commissioned in the late 1950s and served two tours in Vietnam, first as advisers and then with the bottom-scraping Americal Division. Despite those demoralizing assignments, both stayed in the Army through its post-Vietnam crisis of confidence and labored to rebuild it. In background, both also were somewhat outliers for the Army—Schwarzkopf being a liberal intellectual from New Jersey, Powell a black inner-city New Yorker, also generally liberal but less of an intellectual.

Yet there was one major difference between the two: Schwarzkopf, who had grown up partly in Iran, was more sophisticated, but it was Powell, a son of the South Bronx, who proved more adroit in working in the political world of Washington. The experience that formed Powell, and perhaps resulted in his elevation beyond four-star generalship to become chairman of the Joint Chiefs and then secretary of state, likely was not his service in uniform but rather his time as a White House Fellow.

Schwarzkopf never had any such assignment, and his lack of exposure to the world of politics would show in his contentious dealings with Washington during the 1991 Gulf War. He had the opposite experience: In an early brush with Washington seventeen years before that war, he had been part of a team that labored to develop a list of suggested installations for the Army to shutter as part of its budget cutting. "We were confident that this was the best and fairest base-closure list in military history," he remembered. What he meant by that was that it was based on the Army's assessment of what fit the needs of the Army and of the likely impacts on the economy and the environment. When Congress rejected the proposal, Schwarzkopf concluded that there was something wrong not with his thinking but with the political system: "Eighteen months of hard work counted for nothing. . . . To accomplish anything in Washington meant having to compromise, manipulate, and put in the fix behind the scenes." Schwarzkopf did not pause here to consider his own blindness. He had spent more than a year on a project that would deeply concern hundreds of members of Congress, who would have to approve the proposed closures, but he had not taken that into account before coming to his conclusions. In addition, the Army's views on base closures would ultimately prove to be hardly "the best" course for the nation, nor even for the Army. Left to its own devices, the Army, in subsequent rounds of closings, tended to shutter installations on the coasts and leave open those in economically depressed sections of the rural South, which, among other drawbacks, was discouraging to military spouses looking to find work. Congress was more attuned to changes in the population than the Army was.

Going along to get along

Colin Powell, by contrast, learned early on not to reject how Washington works but to study it. "Democracy did not always function well in the light of day," he would remember being advised during his time as a White House Fellow, part of an idealistic program that introduces small numbers of highly promising young Americans to the workings of government. "People have to trade, change, deal, retreat, bend, compromise, as they move from the ideal to the possible. To the uninitiated, the process can be messy, disappointing, even shocking. Compromise can make the participants look manipulative, unprincipled, two-faced." Powell thrived in this environment, attracting the notice of rising Republican officials such as Caspar Weinberger and Frank Carlucci.

Powell was, in many ways, exactly what the Army needed after Vietnam, to repair its relationship with Washington. Political leaders respect political power, and Powell developed an independent political base. He was a general the American people felt they could trust. He brought to his positions not just a political savviness but also a personal history that appealed to the public. He was black, from a working-class background, and also was a graduate of City College of New York, carrying none of the Westmorelandesque odor of West Point. His combination of an easygoing public persona and an intense work ethic resembled Eisenhower's, for whom he "always felt a special affinity. . . . I admired him as a soldier, a President, and a man." Like that earlier officer, he believed in maintaining an atmosphere of "perpetual optimism." Also like Ike, he brought to the Army a knack for geniality, a trait that might stem from the fact that both men had become powerfully ambitious relatively late in life, after their military careers had begun and their personalities largely had been formed.

That appearance of easygoing motivation might have enabled both men to be involved in troubling episodes without being tainted by them. Ike's military and political careers were not damaged by his being present during MacArthur's 1932 attack on the Bonus Marchers. Nor was Powell much hurt by being on the staff of the American Division during the attempted cover-up of the My Lai massacre, or by being brushed by the Reagan Administration's bizarre attempt to illegally fund the Nicaraguan contras by selling weapons to Iran. (In fact, Powell once observed that the latter scandal helped his career, by creating a vacancy in the post of national security adviser to President Reagan in 1987, when he was the deputy adviser. "If it hadn't been for Iran-Contra," he once cracked to Harvard professor Henry Louis Gates Jr., "I'd still be an obscure general somewhere. Retired, never heard of.") Also like Eisenhower, Powell enjoyed solving problems. But while Ike was drawn to human puzzles, Powell preferred to relax with the more predictable mechanical issues offered by automobile engines, making a hobby of rehabilitating old Volvos. "Cars, unlike people, lack temperament," he once explained. "When working on them, I was dealing not with the gods of the unknown, but the gods of the certain."

Even more than Eisenhower, Powell seemed to attract, or locate, the right sort of mentors, and, better than most officers, he learned how to advance. He worked briefly for Gen. DePuy, that most influential of officers inside the post-Vietnam Army, and in his memoir he labels himself a "DePuy alumnus." After his White House felowship, he moved to Korea to take command of the 1st Battalion of the 32nd Infantry Regiment, the same unit Lt. Col. Don Faith had led so tragically on the east side of the Chosin Reservoir in 1950.

But it was command of a brigade that seems to have been more significant for Powell's career and his approach to generalship. Successful brigade leadership as a colonel is an essential hurdle to clear before promotion to one-star general. In his memoir, as he recalls his time in brigade command, Powell offers an odd little sermon about going along to get along. There is an element of defensiveness in it, but there is also pride, perhaps that of a triple outsider—an African American and New Yorker with an ROTC commission—who learned how to play the Army's game. "I had long since learned to cope with Army management fashions. You pay the king his shilling, get him off your back, and then go about what you consider important." He was not inclined to become one of those irritating Army dissidents, he says, in a sentence burdened by three metaphors: "I detected a common thread running through the careers of officers who ran aground even though they were clearly able—a stubbornness about coughing up that shilling. They fought what they found foolish or irrelevant, and consequently did not survive to do what they considered vital." This willingness to cope was a recipe for getting ahead, as Powell's subsequent career would demonstrate. It was a trait that would serve him well for decades—but ultimately might have led to his undoing. Powell might have been training himself to kowtow just when he was reaching the age and rank at which he should have been starting to shake off such deferential habits. Retired Army Lt. Gen. David Barno, looking back on his Army career, observed that "the higher you rise, the more pressure there is to conform and to be a loyal team player. The phrase I kept hearing was, 'stay in your lane.'" This meant, he said, that one should keep quiet and not comment on anything other than one's own duties: "When we want your opinion, we'll beat it out of you." In 1991, Powell, having risen to become chairman of the Joint Chiefs of Staff, would prove to be an Eisenhower without a Marshall—that is, a master implementer lacking a real strategy to implement. His efforts to prod Cheney and his other superiors into mulling the strategic questions would be rebuffed: Cheney would effectively tell him to stay in his lane.

The empty triumph of the 1991 Gulf War

Norman Schwarzkopf also benefited from Colin Powell's growing influence in Washington. He held his position as commander of

American forces in the Gulf War because of Powell. When the post of commander of Central Command (Centcom), the American military headquarters for the Middle East, opened up in 1988, it was, according to a fairly recent tradition, the Navy's "turn" to fill it. But Powell, by then Ronald Reagan's national security adviser, believed that the position should go to someone familiar with ground forces—that is, from the Army or Marine Corps—rather than an admiral. He intervened with his old friend and mentor Frank Carlucci, then secretary of defense. "And that," Powell stated, "is how Norm Schwarzkopf came to obtain the command that would propel him into history."

On the ground, in the air, and even in diplomacy, the Gulf War of 1991 was designed as the anti-Vietnam. When Iraq invaded Kuwait in the summer of 1990, Powell already had moved from the White House back to the military and had become chairman of the Joint Chiefs of Staff. A major factor driving both Schwarzkopf and Powell as they prepared the American response to Saddam Hussein's attack was a determination not to repeat the mistakes of the war in Indochina. Looming over all discussions was the Weinberger Doctrine, which Powell had helped develop and which held that America should never go to war again half-heartedly and without the support of its people.

At White House meetings during the run-up to the American intervention to oust Iraqi forces from Kuwait, Powell kept in mind his dismay at the men who had constituted the Joint Chiefs of Staff in the 1960s, "fighting the war in Vietnam without ever pressing the political leaders to lay out clear objectives for them." His determination to do so led him to raise the question, at a White House meeting, of "if it was worth going to war to liberate Kuwait"—a query that provoked Defense Secretary Dick Cheney to lecture him later that day, saying, "You're not Secretary of State. You're not the National Security Advisor anymore. And you're not Secretary of Defense. So stick to military matters." Nevertheless,

Powell pointedly would flag the need to call up the Army and Marine Reserves, a major stumbling point in the earlier war.

Schwarzkopf likewise invoked Vietnam when discussing military personnel policies. According to a staff log he quotes in his memoir, in October 1990 Schwarzkopf proposed a plan not to have individual soldiers rotate but instead to switch out ground combat units every six to eight months. But Cheney decided that there would be no rotation at all and that soldiers would remain in the war "for the duration"—a sign that the administration of George H. W. Bush would act sooner rather than later and that the duration would simply not be that long, because the president would not let troops sit in the desert waiting endlessly for economic sanctions to change Saddam Hussein's mind. When briefing his subordinates on his war plan, Schwarzkopf wrote, "For the benefit of the Vietnam vets—practically the whole room—I emphasized that, 'we're not going into this with one arm tied behind our backs.'" Unlike in Vietnam, where the American presence increased incrementally to a half-million troops, Schwarzkopf would begin his counteroffensive with that number in place. Likewise, the air campaign was dubbed "Instant Thunder," specifically to contrast it with the gradualism of the Vietnam War's bombing campaign, which had been code-named "Rolling Thunder." In their tense face-to-face meeting in Geneva, Switzerland, on the eve of the war, Secretary of State James Baker would warn his Iraqi counterpart, Tariq Aziz, that if it came to an American assault, "It will be massive. This will not be another Vietnam. It will be fought to a quick and decisive end."

Schwarzkopf's determination not to be a Vietnam-style general might have blinded him to his own shortcomings. In October 1990, Schwarzkopf dispatched a group of his planners to brief the Bush Administration's national security leadership on his tentative plans to oust Iraq's military from Kuwait. The reception in Washington from the civilian officials to his proposed head-on assault was chilly. "I found the plan unimaginative," Cheney would recall drily. One of Cheney's subordinates, Henry Rowen, mocked it as "the charge of the light brigade into the *wadi* of death." Others summarized the Centcom plan as "hey diddle diddle, straight up the middle." Brent Scowcroft, the soft-spoken national security adviser, was even harsher than Cheney. "I was pretty appalled," he said years later. "It sounded to me like a briefing by people who didn't want to do it. . . . The preferred option that they presented was frankly a poor option and my first question is, 'Why don't you go round to the west?,' and the answer was, 'Well, we don't have enough gas trucks for it.'" In the wake of that head-slapper, Cheney established his own competing planning operation. Doing so, he said, "sent the signal to everybody, the Joint Staff, out in the field and Central Command: 'Guys, get your act together and produce a plan, because if you don't produce one that I'm comfortable with, I'll impose one.'"

Despite that disastrous briefing, Schwarzkopf held on to his post. Not all senior officers were so lucky. The Gulf War would be marked near its outset by the relief of a top general, but, in keeping with the new pattern, the firing was conducted by a civilian. In this case, Gen. Michael Dugan, the Air Force chief of staff, angered Powell and Cheney by touting, in a newspaper interview, the role airpower would play in the impending war. Powell's lingering indignation was evident in his summary of that *Washington Post* article: "In a single story, Dugan made the Iraqis look like a pushover; suggested that American commanders were taking their cue from Israel . . . suggested political assassination . . . claimed that airpower was the only option." The next day, Cheney relieved Dugan.

January 17, 1991, brought the first night of the air war against Iraq. It marked the moment it became undeniable that the U.S. military had successfully overhauled itself in the sixteen years since the fall of Saigon. As the air strikes began, even inside the military there was a lingering skepticism about the reliability of America's new high-tech arsenal, which bristled with largely untried weaponry such as precision-guided bombs and radar-evading "stealth" aircraft. "I don't give a damn if you shoot every TLAM the Navy's got, they're still not worth a shit," Powell supposedly said about Tomahawk land attack cruise missiles before the war began. As it happened, he was wrong; they worked well. At the Pentagon, Powell and Cheney braced themselves. "We assumed with respect to the air war that our worst night would be the first night," Cheney recalled. He spent the night at his Pentagon office and was surprised when he was told that out of nearly seven hundred aircraft that flew that night, only one had been lost. "It was just a phenomenal result. I could not believe that we'd done that well."

On the second night of the war, there were warning signs that the civil-military discourse, so essential to the healthy conduct of a war, had hit a sticking point. Iraq began its major political gambit of the war, a campaign to draw Israel into the conflict, by firing seven Scud missiles across the border. This was a tactically insignificant move, but it had the strategic aim of provoking Israel to retaliate, which would embarrass other Arab states into leaving the American-led coalition. Schwarzkopf, unattuned to politics, was obtuse about this danger, believing that dealing with the problem was somehow unrelated to his job. In his view, the small, inaccurate Iraqi missiles, which were being pushed to carry warheads far beyond their effective range, posed no military threat, and so the issue was not on his turf. Defense Secretary Cheney, who had pushed Powell away from discussing political considerations, came away from talks with Schwarzkopf doubting that he "fully understood the importance of dedicating assets to hunting Scuds." Schwarzkopf's stance provoked Paul Wolfowitz, then a Pentagon policy official, to crack, "The guy supposedly has read Clausewitz and knows wars are political, right?" In fact, Schwarzkopf simply was following both Cheney's direction and the lessons he had learned in Gen. DePuy's post-Vietnam Army: Decouple the fighting from the strategy and focus on the tactical level of war.

To remedy the situation, Cheney ultimately had to intervene. He ordered Schwarzkopf to divert aircraft from planned missions around Baghdad and instead assign them to try to destroy mobile Scud launchers in the vast western Iraqi desert. Even if the anti-launcher effort proved ineffective, Cheney recalled, "I needed to be able to say [to the Israeli government], 'Look, last night we flew fifty sorties over western Iraq dealing with this and here are the results we got.' That's the one place where I intervened really in the conduct of the war. . . . Didn't kill many Scuds. . . . But it was very important that we tried, that we were perceived as doing everything we could." Cheney was thinking strategically, but Schwarzkopf was not. Cheney, Powell, and Schwarzkopf all were at fault for not pausing at this point to focus on repairing the quality and clarity of their discourse.

Instead, Schwarzkopf would blunder on. He failed to consider that in order to find and destroy Scud launchers, it likely would be necessary to insert Special Operations troops as surreptitious observers on the ground in western Iraq.

He also would prove slow to grasp the implications of early ground actions in the war. At the end of January 1991, the Iraqi army launched a surprise assault into Saudi Arabia. This offensive, now known as the Battle of Khafji, was little understood at the time and is less remembered now. As two of the best analysts of the 1991 war, military journalist Michael Gordon and retired Marine Lt. Gen. Bernard Trainor, put it in their study, this was a well-planned offensive involving three Iraqi armored divisions, "designed to humiliate the Saudi army, start the ground war, and begin to bleed the Americans." The Iraqis fought as they had against Iran a few years earlier, punching a hole into the enemy line and then sending in reinforcements. But there was a crucial difference in this battle: Iraqi antiair defenses proved ineffective against American attack aircraft, which were able to severely weaken the Iraqi forces, especially by hitting the armored vehicles in massed columns and the supply trucks bringing in ammunition and fuel. The Iraqis were stunned. We know now that Iraqi commanders were surprised by the vigor and precision of the American counterattack. One rattled member of Iraq's 5th Mechanized Division, it was reported, said that American airpower had done more damage to his brigade in half an hour than it had suffered in eight years of fighting the Iranians. Senior Iraqi commanders agreed. In a tape captured after the 2003 American invasion, Saddam Hussein was heard telling his advisers, "After the operations of al Khafji, some of the commanders said to me, 'Sir, we think there has been a mistake. It means all our assessments about the American army were wrong.'"

Yet neither Schwarzkopf nor Powell appreciated the meaning of the Khafji encounter. Schwarzkopf airily dismissed the three-day battle of Khafji as "about as significant as a mosquito on an elephant." This was a failure of generalship, of mulling battlefield events and adjusting one's plans in light of fresh information. Khafji should have made it clear to Schwarzkopf that the Iraqi army was not as formidable as he believed and that it could be defeated more quickly than he thought, but Schwarzkopf did not grasp this message. His failure would have major implications for his handling of the American ground offensive into Kuwait several weeks later.

The lingering differences between Powell and Schwarzkopf came to a head several weeks later, in mid-February 1991, on the eve of the ground attack. Schwarzkopf remained hesitant to begin. Powell confronted him in a heated telephone call, saying to Schwarzkopf, "Look, ten days ago you told me the 21st. Then you wanted the 24th. Now you're asking for the 26th. I've got a president and a secretary of Defense on my back. They've got a bad Russian peace proposal they're trying to dodge. You've got to give me a better case for postponement. I don't think you understand the pressure I'm under." (That last comment is striking in its pleading tone. It is hard to imagine George Marshall beseeching Eisenhower in such a manner.)

Schwarzkopf roared back angrily, "My responsibility is the lives of my soldiers. This is all political." He continued: "My Marine commander says we need to wait. We're talking about Marines' lives."

Powell probably should have responded coolly that as chairman of the Joint Chiefs it was his job—his obligation—to ensure that politics were connected to military operations. After all, the best-known observation of Clausewitz, the great Prussian theorist of war, is that war is the continuation of politics by other means. A war not fought for political ends is simply mindless bloodshed. Yet Powell did not say any of that. Rather, he responded with full-throated emotion. "Don't you pull that on me," he shouted back at his fellow Vietnam veteran. "Don't you try to lay a patronizing guilt trip on me! Don't tell me I don't care about casualties!"

Schwarzkopf backed down a bit. "You're pressuring me to put aside my military judgment out of political expediency," he pleaded. All in all, it was a remarkably revealing exchange, showing neither general in a good light. Schwarzkopf's unreflective insistence on some sort of separation between war and politics foreshadowed the indeterminate conclusion toward which the two men would steer their campaign.

CHAPTER 25

The ground war

Schwarzkopf vs. Frederick Franks

The ground assault brought swift and deadly confirmation of the reemergence of the American ground forces. On the afternoon of February 26, in a half-hour encounter dubbed the Battle of 73 Easting, for its location on the map of the featureless desert just west of Kuwait, a handful of American tanks and Bradley Fighting Vehicles from the 2nd Armored Cavalry Regiment destroyed roughly 30 Iraqi tanks, 20 other armored vehicles, and 30 trucks. The Americans lost one soldier and one Bradley. At the Battle of Medina Ridge, the following day, the Americans would post similarly lopsided results, with the 1st Armored Division destroying 186 Iraqi tanks and a similar number of armored vehicles. It was, in historian Rick Atkinson's phrase, "a brilliant slaughter."

But today, the four-day-long ground campaign against the Iraqis in February 1991 is perhaps best remembered inside the U.S. Army for the squabbling it provoked among American generals. For all their insistence on heeding the lessons of Vietnam, the one that seems to have escaped Schwarzkopf and Powell was one of the most important: the need to relieve subordinates.

Schwarzkopf's memoir of the war is scathing in its portrayal of
Lt. Gen. Frederick Franks, a popular one-footed Vietnam veteran
who led the Army's heavy VII Corps, with five divisions and sixteen hundred tanks, through the desert west of Kuwait. Schwarzkopf depicts Franks as jittery and wheedling, misunderstanding
the fight he is in, being overcautious, wanting to turn south to
clean up some bypassed Iraqi elements before proceeding east
with the main attack into Kuwait. "What the hell's going on with
VII Corps?" Schwarzkopf exclaimed at one point to his staff. "Did
VII Corps stop for the night?"

Franks's own explanation, when he had a chance to offer it
much later to a documentary filmmaker, was "I was thinking
forty-eight hours ahead. I wanted to be in a posture that when we
hit the Republican Guards, that we would hit them with a fist
massed from an unexpected direction at full speed, and so what I
needed to do was get the corps in a posture that would allow that
to happen." He also worried, legitimately, about fratricidal fire,
which is a danger especially at night and in the fluid opening
phase of ground operations. In his memoir, Franks would criticize Schwarzkopf as a career infantryman who had little feel for
the maneuvering of armored formations and compounded his
misunderstanding by being a foul-tempered "chateau general"
trying to run the war from an underground bunker four hundred
miles to the south in Riyadh. "Since General Schwarzkopf never
called me directly or came out to see for himself, he did not have
a complete picture of the VII Corps situation," Franks wrote. He
also stated that Schwarzkopf simply was wrong about Franks's
intention to turn south.

Gordon and Trainor, in their own astute analysis, concluded
that Franks, like Schwarzkopf, was wedded to an existing campaign plan, in this case an "overly elaborate plan for a two-
pronged attack that could not be easily adapted"—that is, a poor

form of DePuy's synchronization. The friction between Franks and Schwarzkopf intensified, they added, because Schwarzkopf sentimentally left in place as an intermediary Army Lt. Gen. John Yeosock, a diffident man then recovering from an emergency gallbladder operation. Still weak when the land war began, Yeosock was described by one officer as looking "more like he belonged in a morgue than in a war room." After the war, Schwarzkopf would blame Franks for the Army's failure to destroy the Republican Guard. In fact, Gordon and Trainor concluded, it was Schwarzkopf's own war plan that was at fault, by having an all-out Marine attack commence against southern Iraq before the Army had the chance to move in from the west and close the Iraqis' exit door in northern Kuwait. Thus, instead of penning in Iraqi forces, Schwarzkopf's war plan pushed them out, like a cork popped from a bottle.

In his determination not to repeat the mistake in Vietnam of underestimating the enemy, Schwarzkopf had gone to the opposite extreme. "Schwarzkopf's great shortcoming was his inability to take an elevated view of the battlefield, to recognize and accept the presence of friction in execution and 'noise' in the information system," wrote Richard Swain, an Army historian. "Increasingly behind events, he could neither influence nor understand the limitations on the maneuver of massive armored forces in the field."

As a matter of top command, Schwarzkopf failed to handle Franks properly. In World War II, a corps or division commander perceived by his superiors to be suffering from a case of "the slows," who seemed so resistant to his commander's direction, almost certainly would have been removed, as happened with Maj. Gen. John Lucas at Anzio and with Maj. Gen. Fay Prickett, commander of the 75th Infantry Division, after the Battle of the Bulge. It almost would have been kinder to relieve Franks than to leave him in place and then pound him in a memoir. In any event, no World War II commander would have pleaded, as Schwarzkopf did in that memoir, that the war would have gone better if only his subordinates had been more responsive. It is not difficult to imagine how George Marshall, Dwight Eisenhower, or Omar Bradley would have responded to such an alibi.

Another Vietnam-influenced impulse, the distancing of military operations from political considerations, led Schwarzkopf to his worst moment, which came at the end of the war. Refusing to think politically was, after all, a quixotic, unreasonable approach, because war ultimately must be about achieving political aims. Yet in the war's final days, Schwarzkopf acted as if he had done no planning or even vague thinking about war termination. He misleadingly told the world in a press conference that "the gates are closed" to a Republican Guard retreat from Kuwait, even as the Guard was escaping. "They have few options other than surrender or destruction." He was wrong: The Army would conclude that, ultimately, between one-third and one-half of the Republican Guard's tanks left Kuwait unscathed. Even more remarkably, of the tens of thousands of Iraqi troops taken prisoner, only one was a senior officer of the Guard.

He did not consult with his superiors before sitting down to parley with the Iraqis. On March 3, 1991, he brought almost no advisers to his cease-fire discussion with Iraqi generals in Safwan, Iraq—no senior civilian officials, nor even someone from the Air Force. He did not know it, but he was flying blind. The nadir of the discussion came when the Iraqi generals asked permission to fly helicopters. "As long as it is not over the part we are in, that is absolutely no problem," Schwarzkopf responded, according to a transcript of the meeting later published in an Iraqi newspaper. "So we will let the helicopters, and that is a very important point, and I want to make sure that's recorded, that military helicopters can fly over Iraq. Not fighters, not bombers."

Perhaps surprised at this munificence, the Iraqi general sought to confirm the meaning of Schwarzkopf's statement. "So you mean that even the helicopters that is armed in the Iraqi sky can fly, but not the fighters?"

"Yeah," Schwarzkopf said. "I will instruct our Air Force not to shoot any helicopters that are flying over the territory of Iraq where we are not located." With that exchange, he helped seal the fate of southern Iraq's Shiites, who, encouraged by the U.S. government, were then beginning to rise up against Saddam Hussein. In the following days, Iraqi army attack helicopters would fly over alleys and cities, machine-gunning rebels. This fact would be remembered bitterly by Iraqis when Americans returned to Iraq twelve years later.

The failure to consider the conditions of the end of the war was hardly Schwarzkopf's alone, of course. Rather, it indicates that there was a lack of guidance from Washington. Ultimately, this was a failure of civilian leadership, and it suggests that during the 1991 war, civil-military discourse was not as healthy as was depicted at the time. Military historian Robert Goldich noted that this failure is particularly interesting because Bush Administration officials were so deft in organizing and sustaining the coalition, and also in winning political support at home. Yet they had a blind spot when it came to war termination. "They fell down on their job a lot more than Schwarzkopf did on his," Goldich concluded.

Reviewing the Bush Administration's handling of the end of the war, Gideon Rose, now the editor of *Foreign Affairs* magazine, concluded that "the U.S. war effort split open at its politico-military seam." The lesson here is that simply getting along should not be the goal for civilian and military leaders. Healthy discussions sometimes become heated, especially when assumptions, failures, and omissions are examined. Nonetheless, they must be encouraged, and the occasional flare of a temper must be expected and tolerated.

After the war ended, both Schwarzkopf and Powell also brought a poor sense of history to their judgment of its significance. They viewed it through the prism of the Vietnam War, and in that context it undeniably was impressive: In less than two months, the U.S. military and its allies defeated a large Middle Eastern army that had forty-three fielded divisions. In just four days of ground combat, American forces had destroyed or captured 3,000 tanks, 1,400 armored vehicles, and 2,200 artillery pieces, with a loss of just 240 soldiers. Yet the two generals came to believe that their short war's conclusion marked a terminus in history akin to World War II. At one point, Powell and Schwarzkopf even discussed the feasibility of holding the cease-fire ceremony aboard the USS *Missouri,* to evoke MacArthur's acceptance of the Japanese surrender aboard that ship in 1945. That idea was put aside only for logistical reasons, and instead the ceremony was held in a tent. The table used for the signing of papers was slated for donation to the Smithsonian Institution, "in case they ever wanted to recreate the Safwan negotiation scene."

Powell is a puzzle here. He had become almost the opposite of MacArthur, a general who might have been too sensitive to politics. Defending his thinking about ending the war perhaps before it was over, with Saddam Hussein still in power and the Republican Guard intact enough to suppress the Iraqi uprising, he wrote, "We were fighting a limited war under a limited mandate for a limited purpose." Schwarzkopf was more self-congratulatory: "For once," he concluded, "we were strategically smart enough to win the war and the peace."

But with the passage of time, the 1991 war looks increasingly like a tactical triumph but a strategic draw at best. As such, it foreshadowed the American experience in the Iraq of the early twenty-first century. Schwarzkopf, in both good and bad ways, embodied DePuy's post-Vietnam Army: He knew how to fight a war, but not to what end. He had realized DePuy's dream of winning the first battle of a war—almost for the first time in American history—but he called off the fighting prematurely. In other words, his "victory" came at the high but undisclosed price of not being attached to any stated strategic objectives. He personified what Lt. Col. Antulio Echevarria later would outline in an Army War College monograph as the contemporary American way of war:

> Its underlying concepts—a polyglot of information-centric theories such as network-centric warfare, rapid decisive operations, and shock and awe—center on "taking down" an opponent quickly, rather than finding ways to apply military force in the pursuit of broader political aims. . . . [It] is about winning battles—not wars—in the Information Age.

Schwarzkopf had done passably well in tactical operations, but he had been flummoxed—even angered—when asked to connect those operations to strategy. A critique by two Australian defense experts put an even sharper point on it: "The confusion surrounding the termination of the operation, the negotiation of a ceasefire by General Norman Schwarzkopf in the apparent absence of any guidance from above, and the litany of strategic opportunities thereby foregone . . . all indicate a surfeit of attention being paid to a single operation and a failure to ensure that the campaign fitted into a strategy."

So, despite all the efforts not to repeat the mistakes of Vietnam, in the muddled ending of the 1991 war there was a disconcerting echo of the earlier war. Just as the Vietnam War had been waged on the unexamined and flawed assumption that a strategy of attrition eventually would lead Hanoi to a breaking point, so was the 1991 war fought on the unexamined and flawed assumption that a decisive battlefield defeat would cripple Saddam Hussein and lead to his downfall. As Cheney had put it, "The assumption was that Saddam would never survive the defeat, that you could not impose this sort of battering on Iraq and Iraqi armed forces and have Saddam stay in power."

Saddam Hussein's view of the ending of the war was very different from Schwarzkopf's. Tapes captured after the American invasion of 2003 would show he was a bit perplexed about why the Americans had given him what he called "a unilateral ceasefire." But he had no doubt about the major lesson of the war: Less than two years after it ended, he observed, George H. W. Bush was out of office, but Saddam himself was still in power. "Bush fell and Iraq lasted," he told aides. Despite some hard hits, the war, he concluded, was "a victory for us, one way or the other." He had taken on the combined might of the Americans, the British, and their allies and survived. In the Arab world, that was quite a victory.

As the Gulf War ended, it was difficult amid all the hoopla to discern the echo of the Vietnam War, but some perceptive observers, such as retired Army Col. Andrew Bacevich, heard it. "As a mechanism to advance the cause of global peace and harmony the war proved a total bust," he wrote. "Apart from restoring Kuwaiti sovereignty, Operation Desert Storm solved remarkably little." In fact, noted Bacevich, the effect of the 1991 campaign might have been pernicious, in that it led American leaders to believe that they could use their military might to remake the Middle East in a manner more consistent with American interests.

The most important aspect of the ending of the 1991 Gulf War is that it really never ended. Rather, it marked the beginning of two decades of low-level hostilities—punctuated by several rounds of intense violence—between Americans and Iraqis. For the following twelve years, during the containment phase, America would be involved in Iraq mainly in the air but occasionally on the ground. It was not a full-blown war, but it certainly was not a state of peace. First, in April 1991, not long after Schwarzkopf's ceremony at Safwan, the United States imposed a no-fly zone, covering all Iraqi aircraft, including helicopters, in the north of Iraq in order to protect Kurds fleeing an Iraqi offensive. Then, to ensure that the refugees did not settle in Turkey, it sent in Army and Marine units to protect them as they returned to Iraq. In August 1992, the United States declared a similar but far larger no-fly zone for southern Iraq. It conducted air strikes in January and June 1993 in response to actions by Saddam Hussein. It deployed troops to Kuwait in 1994 when he appeared to be threatening to invade again. The biggest round of air strikes came over four nights in December 1998, when the U.S. military fired 415 cruise missiles, more than it had expended during the 1991 war. The missiles, as well as 600 bombs, hit 97 sites, mainly weapons production facilities and military headquarters, and appear to have had a devastating effect on the efforts and morale of Iraqi weapons scientists. In the 1991 war, American aircraft had flown a total of 110,000 sorties; in the subsequent decade, they would average 34,000 sorties a year over Iraq—that is, nearly one-third of a Desert Storm every year.

Finally, in 2003, American ground forces would again fight Iraq, and this time occupy it.

CHAPTER 26
The post–Gulf War military

The Army, like the country as a whole, emerged from the 1991 Gulf War understandably relieved, and also very pleased with itself—probably too much so. The American military of that time may or may not have been the best the nation ever fielded, but it certainly was among the most self-satisfied. In a Fort Leavenworth course on the combat operations of corps and divisions, the Army gave 99.5 percent of the officers an "above average" score. "Basking in the glow of victory in Gulf War I, we became complacent . . . 'the best trained, best equipped, and best Army in the world!'" recalled Maj. Chad Foster. "We spoke of ourselves only in the superlative."

Nearly twenty years later, after the Army's missteps and failures in occupying Iraq, retired Army Gen. Jack Keane, a former vice chief of staff, concluded that the problems had begun in the Gulf War: "The thing that killed us was the 1991 Gulf War. Intellectually, it bankrupted us for the rest of the decade." Partly as a result of its overestimation of its victory in the Gulf, the Army failed to continue to build on its success in the 1980s, when it had been rebuilt and reequipped. Gen. Huba Wass de Czege, who had helped build this Army, worried that in the aftermath of the victory in Kuwait, "shallow 'bumper sticker' concepts captured the imagination of DoD officials and the public—'Shock and Awe,' 'Global Reach—Global Power,' 'Operational Maneuver from the Sea,' 'Rapid Decisive Operations.'" Just as the Army had abandoned "organizational effectiveness" programs in the 1980s as soon as it was on the road to recovery, so, too, in the 1990s were intellectually oriented programs like the School for Advanced Military Studies given less priority, and instead the Army placed a new emphasis on "digitization" and other Information Age technologies. Applications to the school began to decline, and the quality and influence of its graduates likely did as well.

To be fair to Army leaders of the time, it was an odd, unsettled period. The Cold War was over. It wasn't clear what would come next, but there was a feeling in political Washington in the early 1990s that the military was facing a period of dormancy. Bill Clinton ran for president in 1992 on a platform that emphasized, among other things, "defense conversion," or redirecting Cold War defense assets toward peaceful, domestic purposes. Trimming the defense budget produced what was called at the time "the peace dividend." Reflecting this assumption, the size of the Army was cut by nearly 40 percent, from 749,000 soldiers in 1989 to 462,000 a decade later. Few observers realized that superpower competition had kept a lid on many conflicts and that without the presence of the Soviet threat, it would be far easier (and less strategically risky) for the United States to use force abroad—as it would do in Somalia, Haiti, Bosnia, Kosovo, and, most of all, the Middle East.

There has never been a truly successful drawdown of American military forces after a war. Marshall, Eisenhower, and Bradley were inspired by the troubles of the post–World War I reduction to try to do better after World War II, but they failed and did worse, creating an undertrained, underequipped, out-of-shape force that would be sent to Korea in the summer of 1950. The American military was flat on its back after Vietnam. If there ever was a reduction that came close to success, it likely was the post–Cold War drawdown of the 1990s. That most recent reduction is hardly remembered today, and this is one measure of its achievement. Even as the Army shrank, it managed to conduct some innovative experiments, such as creating a new, faster, lighter type of unit built around wheeled (rather than tracked) armored vehicles called Strykers. "Not all went right, but a lot did," commented Lt. Gen. James Dubik, now retired but at the time involved in designing and training the first Stryker battalions.

Yet even that reduction in the force had its flaws, most notably that it reinforced existing trends toward intellectual conformity and complacency in the Army. "It only took one boss to say something not nice [in a performance review] and that was it," recalled Col. John Ferrari, whose career survived that era. He continued: "The nail that sticks up gets whacked. The Army whacked everyone who wasn't on track for battalion command. To be that, you had to be the S-3, the XO, and then battalion command. And one day we woke up and looked for a Spanish-speaking officer to be a defense attaché, and they were all gone."

The Army was so pressed to keep its combat units filled that it turned to the private sector for some of its intellectual functions, Ferrari explained: "We outsourced our thinking. We had MPRI [a consulting company led by retired Army generals] to write our doctrine, we had retired colonels as instructors, and we didn't have battlefield feedback shaping doctrine. . . . It cost us in the decade of war."

The Army's nagging leadership problems persisted. When the Army Command and General Staff College surveyed officers in 1995, it found the same concerns that had been reported in the Army War College's 1970 *Study on Military Professionalism*. "The overcontrolling leader and the micromanager remain alive and well in the Army today," retired Army Col. Lloyd Matthews wrote in 1996, in a statement that was greeted as uncontroversial. A year later, retired Maj. Gen. John Faith wrote an article bewailing military micromanagement that was essentially no different from the articles in *Military Review* four decades earlier. He also noted that there seemed to have been no attempt by anyone to refute Matthews's charge.

A study done at West Point as the century ended came to several startling conclusions about the state of the Army:

- The Army was "more bureaucracy than profession"—that is, officers didn't look at it as a profession, and saw themselves as time-serving employees of a highly centralized organization.
- While there have always been tensions between junior officers and senior ones, there had also grown a gap between them that had eroded trust: "Unless commanders establish a culture of trust within Army units, soldiers will not feel free to tell the truth, and without transparent honesty in interpersonal relations and official reporting systems, effectiveness suffers. This downward spiral induces micromanagement on the part of leaders."
- By increasingly relying on retired officers to help write doctrine and teach and train troops, the Army was contributing to its own de-professionalization, because the retirees were working not for the Army but for for-profit companies.

A paper written at about the same time by Col. Michael Cody at the Army War College accused the Army of institutionalized hypocrisy, preaching a doctrine of innovation while actually awarding risk-averse behavior:

Departing from the tried and proven solution to problems or recurring situations is in fact discouraged in a number of different ways by senior leaders, for lots of different reasons, despite the brave rhetoric to the contrary suggested on the appraisal forms. The message received by the junior officer is: don't take risks, don't depart from the norm, and don't dare be less than successful in using a new approach.

The Army had developed a set of code words to ostracize those who departed, Cody noted: "irresponsible, maverick, immature, reckless."

The plague of micromanagement appeared to be worse than ever in the Army, despite periodic attempts to tamp it down. In 2000, Lt. Col. Lee Staab surveyed fifty people who had left the Army as junior officers and found that every one of them "felt that there was a high degree of micro-management within their final assignments on active duty." Maj. Anneliese Steele concluded in a monograph done at the School of Advanced Military Studies that "relationships between junior and senior leaders tend to be dysfunctional." Even as the Army and Marines were invading Iraq in the spring of 2003, *Military Review* carried yet another article worrying that Army leadership was perceived, in the words of Col. Peter Varljen, as "self-serving, short-sighted, out-of-touch, unethical, and averse to risk." The Army was led by managers and "performers" rather than by leaders. These men focused more on "short-term mission accomplishment" than on "developing effective organizations," concluded a study by Col. Steven Jones at the Army War College the same year. Senior officers were skilled at following rules but not in inspiring subordinates or rewriting the rules when necessary.

Despite these persistent problems with leadership, one of the obvious remedies—relief of poor commanders—remained exceedingly rare. Two prominent generals, Walter Ulmer and Montgomery Meigs, published essays about generalship in *Parameters,* the journal of the Army War College—the former in 1998, the latter in 2001. Both were candid and offered a variety of thoughts. Ulmer argued that the Army could do better in selecting its senior leaders. Yet neither suggested that relief could be a viable solution to the problem. Dismissal, a basic tool of Army officer management in the 1940s, was beyond the realm of conception sixty years later. The vocabulary of relief had been lost.

The post–Cold War era, with its unpredictability in battles and even in foes, would demand a new flexibility in military leadership. Yet it appeared as if adaptability and risk taking largely had been bred out of American generals.

Meanwhile, as a result of the DePuy-era reforms, the Army continued to improve tactically. The all-volunteer force had come into its own. Everyone who was in the military had asked to be there, and most had learned a lot. It was a well-trained, professional, competent force. But the soldiers often were better at their tasks than the generals leading them were at theirs. In Iraq, the U.S. Army would illustrate the danger of viewing war too narrowly. "When war is reduced to fighting," strategic expert Colin Gray once warned,

> the logistic, economic, political and diplomatic, and sociocultural contexts are likely to be neglected. Any of those dimensions, singly or in malign combination, can carry the virus of eventual defeat, virtually no matter how an army performs on the battlefield. . . . When a belligerent approaches war almost exclusively as warfare, it is all but asking to be out-generalled by an enemy who fights smarter.

That troubling thought set the stage for the American invasion of Iraq in 2003 and its aftermath, when the American military would be "out-generalled," to use Gray's term, by an insurgency that appeared to have few if any generals—but had a better conception of how to wage war in Iraq.

Coda: Powell stays on too long

Colin Powell's last memorable act in government was to clear the way politically for that invasion of Iraq, with a speech at the United Nations early in 2003. Just eight years after writing his Horatio Alger–like memoir, the decent, go-along-to-get-along general would go along one more time, this time with catastrophic results for his reputation.

For several years, Powell had tried to turn a blind eye to the growing split between his beliefs and those of the Republican Party. After retiring as chairman of the Joint Chiefs of Staff in September 1993, he had veered onto the thin ice of an old general involved in politics. Like Douglas MacArthur, he delivered the keynote address at a Republican National Convention. Just as the Chicago convention of 1952 had soured on MacArthur in response to his talk, the San Diego convention of 1996 was unhappy with Powell's speech, in which he emphatically supported affirmative action and abortion rights. (In another odd parallel, the 1952 Republican convention had been the first to nominate a World War II vet, Eisenhower, while the 1996 convention would be the last, selecting another Kansan, Sen. Bob Dole.) Had Powell left for private life at that point, his reputation would have remained unblemished. But late in his career, his exquisite sense of timing deserted him. He stayed in power too long, becoming secretary of state in 2001 for George W. Bush and Dick Cheney, men whose views were strongly at odds with his. They were willing to let him be secretary of state but not to make policy, and Powell was slow to grasp the nature and extent of his isolation.

Again there was a failure of discourse at the top. Like Mac-

Arthur in Korea, Powell was an old general at odds with his president. He thought he could bring his chief around and remained unwilling to face the fact that he could not and rather needed simply to get out of the way. Unlike MacArthur's, Powell's disagreements with his command in chief were grounded in loyalty. He remained a good, obedient soldier—and that would be his undoing, in part because he now was supposed to be acting as a civilian official. In his tragic final act, he dutifully carried water for the Bush Administration, traveling to the United Nations in February 2003 to deliver the speech that laid the diplomatic groundwork for the American invasion of Iraq. It was a bravura performance, in which Powell played on all the credibility he had developed during three decades of public service. "My colleagues, every statement I make today is backed up by sources, solid sources," he said early on, with CIA director George Tenet sitting behind him, literally backing him up. "These are not assertions. What we are giving you are facts and conclusions based on solid intelligence." He then appeared to divulge intercepted communications—an extraordinary act, given that those are usually the most classified sort of intelligence. He discussed with great confidence Iraq's biological weapons factories, its stockpile of chemical weapons, its intentions to acquire nuclear weapons.

We now know that almost every single assertion he made in that speech was questionable and that, in fact, much of it was doubted at the time by experts in the intelligence community. Most embarrassingly, his claims about Iraq's biological weapons turned out to have been based mainly on the statements of one Iraqi defector, code-named Curveball, whose allegations had been discredited even before Powell presented them to the world. In May 2004, long after the damage had been done by his speech and the United States was mired in Iraq, the CIA would officially recant everything Curveball had asserted, spurred perhaps by having learned that Curveball had not even been in Iraq during some of the time when he claimed to have witnessed important developments. Powell's UN speech also relied on a second informant on biological weapons, but that source had been formally declared a fabricator months earlier by the Defense Intelligence Agency, and no one had informed Powell about that fabrication notice. The UN speech, unfortunately, would become the epitaph to Powell's long career. "Who went to the United Nations and, regrettably, with a lot of false information?" he said in 2011. "It was me." In another interview, he lamented, "I will forever be known as the one who made the case."

In 2003, Powell did the job the Bush Administration needed him to do, putting war skeptics on the defensive. Powell "presented not opinions, not conjecture, but facts," Defense Secretary Donald Rumsfeld stated to a gathering of European allies not long afterward. He continued, "It is difficult to believe that there still could be question in the minds of reasonable people open to the facts before them."

Yet behind closed doors, Powell still had doubts. Shortly before the invasion of Iraq, he called Gen. Tommy R. Franks to ask him whether he was sure he had enough troops in his war plan. Powell thought there were sufficient troops to get to Baghdad but was concerned about what would happen after that. "But Tommy was confident," Powell said ruefully. "They had enough to get to Baghdad, and it fell beautifully, but then the fun started."

CHAPTER 27

Tommy R. Franks

Two-time loser

After the surprise attack on Pearl Harbor in 1941, the top American military officers in Hawaii were drummed out of the military. After the surprise attacks on 9/11, no one was fired or took responsibility. Nor were subsequent setbacks punished.

The representative general of the post-9/11 era was Tommy R. Franks. If Norman Schwarzkopf embodied both the qualities and the limitations of the post-Vietnam military, Tommy Franks was the apotheosis of the hubristic post–Gulf War force. Like Schwarzkopf, Franks refused to think seriously about what would happen after his forces attacked. One lesson of Vietnam, he had concluded, quite mistakenly, was that such political issues simply were someone's else's job. "During the Vietnam War, Defense Secretary Robert McNamara and his Whiz Kids had repeatedly picked individual bombing targets and approved battalion-size maneuvers," he wrote in his memoirs. Then, in an intellectual non sequitur, he continued, "I knew the President and Don Rumsfeld would back me up, so I felt free to pass the message along to the bureaucracy beneath them: *You pay attention to the day* after *and I'll pay attention to the day* of."

This is not all the fault of Franks. He is best understood as exactly what the post-Vietnam Army was trying to create, the natural and desired outcome of Gen. DePuy's insistence on a tactical focus and the parallel repudiation of Gen. Cushman's call for a broader-minded, deeper-thinking sort of senior officer. As Cushman later observed of Franks, "His development approached the ideal career pattern of senior officer development at the time."

Most generals, at worst, get the opportunity to lose one war. Franks bungled two in just three years, and in both he would illustrate the shortcomings of the force built by DePuy. The post-Vietnam tendency of the American military to decouple political questions from military operations, and the willingness of their civilian superiors to go along with that approach, were damaging in the 1991 war, which was a conventional conflict. But it became lethal to the American cause in the counterinsurgency campaigns in Afghanistan, starting in September 2001, and in Iraq, starting in March 2003. Army Maj. William Taylor would write years later from Afghanistan, "The American military is simply uncomfortable and weak at linking political repercussions to military action. In stark contrast, the insurgents see military and political action as one in the same, and consequently are quite effective in shaping their violence to send a message."

The warning signs about Franks began flashing in late 2001, with his bumbling effort to capture Osama bin Laden in Tora Bora, along the Afghan-Pakistani border, about ninety miles southeast of the Afghan capital, Kabul. Coming just three months after the stunning attacks of 9/11, the Tora Bora fight provided the best chance American forces had to kill or capture the al-Qaeda leader. Yet Franks seemed inattentive, almost as if the battle were someone else's problem. Like Schwarzkopf with Scuds in 1991, he did not see bin Laden's capture as crucial to his campaign, a goal for which he should risk casualties and a messy fight.

Unlike Schwarzkopf, he was content to provide airpower, with 700,000 pounds of bombs being dropped in the area of Tora Bora during just a few days in December 2001.

The CIA officer in charge at Tora Bora was certain he had bin Laden cornered, though his team remained outnumbered on the ground. He repeatedly requested a battalion of Army Rangers to help press the attack and seal the escape routes into Pakistan. This could have been done by airlifting the Rangers into Pakistan, where the United States had forward bases at the time, and then flying them by helicopter into the relatively low-altitude areas north and southeast of Tora Bora, where they could establish blocking positions. But Franks, perhaps acting under the direction of Defense Secretary Rumsfeld, declined the request. He cited several reasons in his response, among them his desire not to inject more troops, the time it would take to send them, and his sense that the intelligence on bin Laden's location was less reliable than the CIA believed. The best evidence indicates that bin Laden walked out of Afghanistan and south into Pakistan in mid-December 2001, perhaps wounded in the shoulder.

Four months later, Franks would make a similar mistake during Operation Anaconda, declining to provide adequate artillery support to light infantry units that had pinned down several hundred al-Qaeda fighters in the Shah-i-Kot Valley, south of Kabul. Franks explained this refusal in political terms: He was trying to follow the limitations on troop numbers imposed by Rumsfeld. Again, the al-Qaeda men escaped into Pakistan. "I thought it was a very successful operation," the general said afterward. "I thought the planning that was done was very good planning, and I think the result of the operation was also outstanding." He somehow seemed to believe that it was a net strategic gain to push the Islamic extremists from Afghanistan into neighboring Pakistan, a far more populous country that suffered from a shaky security situation—and possessed a nuclear arsenal estimated to contain at least one hundred warheads. One could believe such a course was wise only if one were failing to think strategically. This was a failure of both Franks and his civilian overseers—Rumsfeld and President George W. Bush. Rather than check one another's thinking, the civilian and military sides were reinforcing one another's shortcomings.

Not long after the Anaconda battle, Franks spoke at the Naval War College, in Newport, Rhode Island. A student heard his talk and then posed the most basic but most important sort of question: *What is the nature of the war you are fighting in Afghanistan?* Franks, in his answer, indicated that he did not have a clue. "That's a great question for historians," Franks said. He then answered in a wholly tactical manner, discussing how U.S. troops cleared cave complexes in Afghanistan. It was a sergeant's answer, not a general's. He was repeating Westmoreland's episode in Vietnam in which that commander told senior officers he would share with them the principles of war, then proceeded to tell them how to care for a squad. Franks "really was comfortable at the tactical level," concluded an officer who was in the audience that day.

Privately, Army strategists agreed with that verdict, according to an after-action review of the first part of the Afghan war completed at the Army War College the following summer by fifty-one Army officers and civilian officials from the Army staff and its major commands, including Army Special Operations Command and Central Command. The report is especially striking in that it is not the work of the media or academic specialists but of Army insiders writing for internal consumption. These military professionals explicitly faulted both Franks and Rumsfeld for their decisions as well as for their style of leadership. A document prepared for public release played down the problems caused by the two men, but an internal memorandum on that subject was scathing.

"The lack of a war plan or theater campaign plan has hindered operations and led to a tactical focus that ignores long-term objectives," it stated in regard to Franks's efforts. It found that his headquarters suffered from "many disturbing trends including a short-term focus." But, nodding at Rumsfeld's failings, it went on to say that "all participants at the conference from all commands complained about the problems caused by a lack of clear higher direction." It particularly faulted the limitations on troop numbers imposed by Rumsfeld and enforced by Franks, saying that they "have had a significant negative impact on operations." Unfortunately for Franks and for the war effort, Rumsfeld proved to be the worst sort of micromanager, one who interfered incessantly but did so without providing clear overarching direction. In other words, this was both a failure of generalship and a failure of civil-military discourse. It was an important warning sign: Under Rumsfeld, the quality of civil-military discourse would further erode, eventually coming to resemble the days during the Vietnam War when Lyndon Johnson became estranged from his Joint Chiefs of Staff.

The failures in Afghanistan in 2001–2 probably did not get as much attention as they normally would have, because by the spring of 2002 Franks and many of the other leaders of the American military establishment already were shifting attention and resources away from the Afghan war, which for another six years would become a kind of stepchild of conflicts. It would not thrive on neglect.

If Afghanistan hinted at Franks's shortcomings, Iraq would reveal them in full, painful display. Historically, thinking about war and then arriving at conclusions that can be implemented has been the core task of generals. Yet, in a bizarre mutation of military thought, Franks seemed to believe—and to have been taught by the Army—that thinking was something others did for generals.

In his autobiography he referred to his military planners, with a whiff of good ol' boy contempt, as "the fifty-pound brains."

Part of the problem was Franks's personality. He was that most graceless sort of leader, both dull and arrogant. His memoir, while often evoking Tom Clancy's adventure novels, still revealed the man well, sometimes inadvertently, in its evasions and omissions. He opened the book with his recollection of the time his father placed him in the electric chair at a Texas state prison, expressing the warning that "this is the ultimate consequence for the ultimate act of evil."

On larger questions, the memoir is not reliable as a historical record. For example, he claimed in it that the aftermath of the Iraq invasion "actually was going as I had expected—not as I had hoped, but as I had expected." If he really had held such grim expectations, he should have shared the thought with his headquarters before the invasion. In fact, his assertion contradicted the formal planning documents produced by his subordinates. For example, one classified PowerPoint briefing given shortly before the invasion of Iraq stated, under the heading "What to Expect After Regime Change," that

> most tribesmen, including Sunni loyalists, will realize that their lives will be better once Saddam is gone for good. Reporting indicates a growing sense of fatalism, and accepting their fate, among Sunnis. There may be a small group of die hard supporters that willing [*sic*] to rally in the regime's heartland near Tikrit—but they won't last long without support.

In addition, Lt. Gen. Ricardo Sanchez, who took over the Iraq war from him, stated in his own memoirs, which are angrier but more accurate than Franks's, that Franks had told him in June 2003 that American forces would be out of Iraq later that year.

Again, Franks resembled Westmoreland, making statements in a memoir that made him look good but were easily shown to be false.

Although Franks in his memoir depicted himself as a maverick who wrote poetry and read "Bertram Russell," he failed to offer an example of fresh or even mildly offbeat military thinking. He apparently had nothing to remember about his time at the Army's schools. Judging by his lack of comment, the Army War College, where he might have learned about connecting operations to national strategy, had absolutely no impact on him. Nor did he have anything of substance to say about the pivotal Tora Bora battle, which he mentioned only in passing.

Not long before the invasion began, Gen. Eric Shinseki, the Army chief of staff, expressed concern that the force lacked sufficient troops for occupying Iraq. For his pains, Shinseki was effectively ostracized inside the Rumsfeld Pentagon. It was a low point in civil-military discourse. "The treatment of Army General Eric Shinseki after testifying honestly (and, as it turns out, accurately) . . . is widely viewed as an object lesson of the most negative type," wrote Air Force Maj. Gen. Charles Dunlap Jr. Franks said nothing about that in his book. When asked about Shinseki's concerns in an interview, he dismissed the question, saying that Shinseki "didn't provide anything that all of us didn't already know." Franks also dwelled in his book on the variety of ways he had devised to start the Iraq war ("Generated," "Running Start," and "Hybrid") but had little to say about how he thought it should end and what steps he took to bring that about. He insisted that he did a lot of hard thinking about postwar Iraq, but in a chart he proudly reproduced in the book, outlining his "basic grand strategy" for the war, there was nothing to support that claim—it was all about attacking. In fact, his chart represented not a strategy but a disparate collection of tactical approaches.

Two thorough reviews conducted in subsequent years found overwhelming evidence that Franks and his staff devoted almost all of their energies to the mission of removing a weak regime and almost none to the more difficult task of replacing it. This omission on his part became disastrous, because no one above him in the Bush Administration was focusing on the problem, either. In 2004, an official Pentagon review led by two former defense secretaries, James Schlesinger and Harold Brown, unambiguously concluded, "The October 2002 Centcom war plan presupposed that relatively benign stability and security operations would precede a handover to Iraq's authorities." The following year, the head of the RAND Corporation, hardly a hostile observer, would send a memorandum to Defense Secretary Rumsfeld stating that after extensive review of internal documents, his researchers had found that "post conflict stabilization and reconstruction were addressed only very generally, largely because of the prevailing view that the task would not be difficult."

At times, Franks's account of his wars was just stunning. "There's never been a combat operation as successful as Iraqi Freedom," he asserted. In August 2004, as the American war in Iraq was just settling into a long, hard grind, he pushed back against interviewers' questions, responding, "I just think it's interesting that while we are concerned with what many would describe as the failures of Phase Four operations in Iraq we actually have so many just tremendous successes." This was the optimism of the Marshall template degraded into low-grade boosterism.

But the mistakes made in Afghanistan and Iraq were hardly the fault of one general. Nor were they simply military mistakes. Franks was operating in a military and civilian system that was not working well. Led by Rumsfeld, top civilian leaders focused not on the big questions but on the picayune.

Nor was there much relationship between an officer's battlefield performance and his subsequent promotions. As an American civilian official then based in Afghanistan put it, "The guys who did well didn't get treated well, and the guys who did badly didn't get treated badly."

Coda: The sole relief of the 2003 invasion

One chilly night in Afghanistan late in 2001, Nathaniel Fick, a young Marine officer, was checking on the sentries in his outposts when, after midnight, he spotted three heads in a fighting hole when there should have been just two. He slid down into the hole to find that the third man was Brig. Gen. James Mattis, leaning against some sandbags, talking with a sergeant and a lance corporal. "This was real leadership," Fick later reflected. "No one would have questioned Mattis if he'd slept eight hours each night in a private room, to be woken each morning by an aide who ironed his uniforms and heated his MREs. But there he was, in the middle of a freezing night, out on the lines with his Marines."

It is no accident that, two years later, this general who cared about his men in Afghanistan would carry out the only high-profile relief that occurred during the American invasion of Iraq. The officer removed was not a general but a colonel. At the time, relief was so unusual that even this firing—of Col. Joe D. Dowdy, a regimental commander—made page-one news. Mattis has never publicly spoken about the relief, and in fact, in an oral history interview with an official Marine Corps historian, he declined to discuss it. However, in an interview on strategic issues, he did say in an aside that the practice of relief remains alive in his service: "We're doing it in the Marines. Even Jesus of Nazareth had one out of twelve turn to mud on him."

It is worth looking at the incident to understand what relief of generals might look like in our own era's wars had the tradition not been lost. Col. Dowdy, in his oral history interview with a Marine Corps historian, blamed the situation largely on Mattis's assistant division commander, Brig. Gen. John Kelly, who he said had nagged him about not moving fast enough, especially after Dowdy's regiment had stopped for twenty-four hours outside the city of Nasiriyah, about 190 miles southeast of Baghdad, where both the Army and the Marines had run into stiffer resistance than they had expected. "Are you attacking?" Kelly said to him in a radio exchange during the invasion, according to Dowdy. Yes, Dowdy said, but "we're still shaping"—meaning that he was in the initial stage of an attack, using artillery fire and maneuvering of units before directly engaging the enemy.

"Why don't you drive through al-Kut?" Kelly said, pushing him again. Dowdy, who originally had been told to bypass that city via a roundabout route, asked why that was necessarily the best way to go, especially because he had reports of Iraqi minefields along the more direct route. He did not want to run another gauntlet like Nasiriyah, where an Army convoy had gotten lost, resulting in the deaths of eleven Army soldiers and the capture of several others, including two women, Pvt. Jessica Lynch and Spec. Shoshana Johnson. His view was that he was the commander in place and thus the officer best equipped to decide how and when to attack.

Not satisfied, Gen. Kelly called him again at one or two o'clock the following morning. "What's wrong with you?" Kelly asked.

"There's nothing wrong," Dowdy replied.

Kelly said he did not want to hear excuses.

"They're not excuses," Dowdy responded. "I'm the commander on the ground."

Kelly told him that he was tired of the 1st Regiment "sitting on its ass" and planned to recommend that Mattis relieve Dowdy. "Maybe General Mattis won't do it. Maybe he'll decide he can get along with a regiment that isn't worth a shit. But that's what I'm going to recommend."

Dowdy bypassed al-Kut and by morning had seized the bridges beyond the city that were his next objective. He felt "euphoric," explaining that "we'd done what we needed to do, despite . . . the threat of being relieved." He sensed that his unit was maturing and getting stronger, which he believed made it ready for the big fight he expected in Baghdad.

Then he got a message telling him to fly to the division's forward headquarters. After he landed in a farm field and was walking to the tents where the division headquarters was set up, a dog leaped out and attacked him, "which you know kind of seemed symbolic." Next he encountered Gen. Kelly, who told him that he had lost the trust of his superiors. Dowdy reeled at this, feeling that his twenty-four years of service in the Marines were going down the drain.

He walked inside the command post and saw the division chief of staff. "You're doing great," the officer said.

"I think I'm being relieved," Dowdy responded.

"Nah, that's bullshit," the officer said.

Dowdy went in to see Gen. Mattis, a quiet but intense officer with a reputation for favoring fiercely aggressive tactics. They were so near the front that artillery shells were passing overhead and tanks were rolling by the tent, creating what Dowdy heard as a whirlwind of noise. Mattis began asking questions that indicated to Dowdy that he would be removed on the grounds of fatigue. Dowdy had not slept for two days and felt that Kelly had just crushed his spirit. "I didn't give a very good account of myself," he told the Marine historian when he recounted his relief.

"What's wrong?" Mattis gently and repeatedly asked him. "Why aren't you pressing in the cities more?"

Dowdy, fatigued and confused, said that he was attacking but that "I love my Marines, and I don't want to waste their lives." By his own account, he then babbled a bit about his "lack of self-esteem" when he was younger. Even he recognized that such talk was a fatal misstep. At that point, he said, "I knew I was screwed."

Mattis asked him about his combat experience. "We'll do better," Dowdy responded.

"No, no, no," Mattis said. He stepped out of the tent, clearly wanting to think over his decision. Then he came back in and told Dowdy that he was being relieved and would be replaced by Col. John Toolan, who by chance had been Dowdy's neighbor at one point. Dowdy first asked him to reconsider, citing the effect on him and his family. Mattis declined to do so. Dowdy then accepted the judgment and asked if he could work as a watch officer on the division staff, but Mattis told him that he "needed to go away."

Dowdy left the tent and helicoptered south to a Marine C-130 aircraft, which then took him to a rear base in Kuwait. He took a shower and called his wife. "She already knew," he recalled. He had become the only senior officer to be relieved in the entire invasion.

His conclusion about the affair was that relief should never be taken lightly. "It has such an adverse impact on someone, it's very difficult to describe. But the whole world that you've built comes crumbling down. . . . And then to end it, to be subject to international humiliation. . . . To be the only commander in the whole war to be relieved, it's very difficult to deal with that." He left the Marines the following year and eventually went to work for NASA.

Mattis, by contrast, would rise swiftly through the military hierarchy, eventually succeeding David Petraeus as head of Central Command, a four-star post. He remains one of the most clear-thinking of American generals today, with a pungency in his speech that sometimes gets him into trouble but always seems to make an impression on young soldiers and Marines. "If we are to keep this great big experiment called America alive—and that's all it is, an experiment—we need cocky, macho, unselfish, and morally very straight young men and women to lead our forces against the enemy," he said to a group of midshipmen at the Naval Academy eighteen months after he fired Dowdy. He continued:

> Okay, it's not a perfect world, but America is worth fighting for on its worst day. So, if you have got the guts to step across that line, as each of you have, then just go out and enjoy the brawl. Just have a damn good time. Train your men well. Go beat the crap out of people who deserve it, and when they throw down their gun, then you have won.

CHAPTER 28
Ricardo Sanchez
Over his head

Many Americans now remember the Iraq war simply as a string of mistakes by the Bush Administration—from overestimating the threat posed by Saddam Hussein to underestimating the difficulty of occupying the country.

While that is correct, it hardly tells the entire story. Less remembered are the errors committed by the military. One dissent to this narrative of solely civilian fault has come from Philip Zelikow, who became the State Department's counselor as the war in Iraq descended into chaos. "I think the situation is worse than people realize, and the problems are primarily with the military," he said. Discussing American generalship in Iraq over the course of the war, he added: "I don't think people realized how bad this was. . . . The American people believe the problem is the civilians didn't listen to the generals. This is very unhealthy for the Army." In fact, he argued, the civilians were wrong, but so was the Army, because neither group was thinking clearly about Iraq. The U.S. Army in Iraq, Zelikow added, reminded him of the French army before World War I. "The military is venerated. It is the inheritor of Napoleon. The general is decorated with gold braid—but there's no 'there' there. There is an aversion to deep thinking."

American generalship in Iraq in 2003 and the following years is too often a tale of ineptitude exacerbated by a wholesale failure of accountability. The war began badly, with Tommy R. Franks failing to understand the war he was fighting. Why did Franks appear to be strategically illiterate, and why was he allowed to guide the initial stages of two wars, each time with large strategic costs? Franks retired not long after the fall of Baghdad and took off to enjoy the American version of a Roman triumph, going on the road to make speeches for large sums and issuing a quick memoir.

Franks passed command of the Iraq war to another Texan, Ricardo Sanchez, the newest lieutenant general in the Army, who resembled Franks but understood the conflict perhaps even less. "I came away from my first meeting with him saying this guy doesn't get it," said Richard Armitage, who was the deputy secretary of state at the time. Sanchez was a tragic figure, a mediocre officer placed in an impossible situation. Iraq was boiling over, the Pentagon and the Bush Administration were in denial, and he was trying to deal with this while operating in a confused command structure that generated constant friction between him and L. Paul Bremer III, the top American civilian in Iraq. Sanchez held the manpower, money, and machines, but Bremer believed he outranked him. Relations between the two deteriorated to the point that, in the spring of 2004, when Bremer asked Sanchez to tell him about the American plan to attack Shiite militias in Najaf, Sanchez refused. In his memoir, Sanchez appears proud of this:

> "I'm not going to do it," I said. "I guarantee you that we have a tactical plan. I am comfortable with it and have reviewed it with the division commander. I know he can execute the orders he's been assigned.
>
> "Well, we need to know . . . "

"Stop right there, sir. I am not going to give you the details of our tactical plan."

Sanchez did not explain why he would so refuse to brief the senior American official in Iraq.

This exchange was more than just an indication of personal enmity. It was a flashing warning sign that civil-military discourse over the conduct of the war had broken down. At this point, one of the two should have stepped aside or demanded that the other do so. Another officer might have risen to the occasion. Sanchez, an inveterate micromanager, instead sank into the details, correcting subordinates constantly but failing to provide overarching guidance. Like the worst generals of the Vietnam era, he tended to descend into the weeds, where he was comfortable, ignoring the larger situation—which, after all, was his job. Like many micromanagers, Sanchez also tended to criticize harshly in public. "He would rip generals apart on the tacsat"—the military's tactical, satellite-based communications network—"with everybody in the country listening," recalled an officer who served on his staff.

To be sure, the primary errors in Iraq should not be laid at Sanchez's feet, because they were made well above his level. The original sin was President Bush's decision to go to war preemptively on information that would prove false. The second major mistake was the failure of the Joint Chiefs of Staff to point out the fundamental contradiction between the civilian view of the mission in Iraq and the military's view. The mission was never defined—a sin of omission committed by both the military and the civilians. The Bush Administration wanted to transform Iraq into a beacon of free-market democracy for the Middle East. The American military never said so publicly, but in its actions it rejected that revolutionary mission and instead stated that its goal was to stabilize Iraq—which was almost the opposite of the president's intent. That was the root cause of much of the friction between civil and military authority in the first three years of the American occupation of Iraq.

Because this basic contradiction was left unexamined, Sanchez really had no strategy to implement. That lack manifested itself in the radically different approaches taken by different Army divisions in the war. Observers moving from one part of Iraq to another often were struck by how each division was fighting its own war, with its own assessment of the threat, its own solutions, and its own rules of engagement. It was as if there were four separate wars under way. In western Iraq's Anbar Province, the 82nd Airborne and the 3rd Armored Cavalry Regiment got tough fast. The 4th Infantry Division, based in Tikrit, in north-central Iraq, operated even more harshly, rounding up thousands of "military age males" and probably turning many of them into insurgents in the process. Baghdad was its own separate situation, exceedingly complex and changing from block to block. Meanwhile, in far northern Iraq, Maj. Gen. David Petraeus and the 101st Airborne Division made a separate peace, to the extent of ignoring many of the anti-Baathist rules coming out of Baghdad and conducting negotiations with the government of Syria to provide energy to Mosul. One reason for such distinctly diverse approaches was that conditions were very different in each of these areas. But another reason was that each division commander more or less went his own way, with little guidance from Sanchez. Jeffrey White, a veteran analyst of Middle Eastern affairs for the Defense Intelligence Agency, wrote early in 2004, "Some observers feel that the various U.S. divisions in Iraq have thus far waged more or less independent campaigns."

Yet Sanchez compounded the problem through smallness of mind and inflexibility in approach. He did not seem willing to learn and adapt. Some commanders at the tactical level took effective approaches, but these were ignored or even discouraged by Sanchez. For example, a Florida National Guard battalion stationed in Ramadi in 2003 was more adept at police work than most military units, having many members of the Miami-Dade police force in its ranks. It emphasized local policing, setting up an academy and an Iraqi force, and also helped cooperative sheikhs win contracts for reconstruction projects, remembered an Army intelligence officer who served in Iraq. But, he noted, "The efforts of 1-124 [the Guard unit] were consistently undermined at the theater level by military leadership that lacked a campaign plan," as well as by the failings of the Civilian Provisional Authority and other civilians. When Gen. John Abizaid, who had replaced Franks as chief of Central Command, visited Ramadi, he was so impressed with operations there that he told Sanchez to go there and get the same briefing. Sanchez did so, apparently rather unhappily. "Sanchez came in pissed off that he'd been ordered to get a clue from O-6s and below in the hinterland and was in full attack mode," the officer recalled. "He lit up the staff, told us we didn't know what we were doing, and went back to Baghdad having learned nothing."

But Sanchez's biggest failure as commander was that on his watch, some units acted in ways that were not only counterproductive but illegal. Not knowing how else to put down an insurgency, some divisions indiscriminately detained thousands of Iraqis and shipped them off to Abu Ghraib prison and other detention centers, where the Army lacked sufficient guards and interrogators to hold and sort them. Another, less noticed reason for these big roundups was that American soldiers expected to leave Iraq before long, either as part of a withdrawal or by way of troop rotation. "In the summer of '03, we all thought we were going home by Christmas, so there was no consideration for the long-term consequences of locking up the wrong guys," recalled Lt. Col. Russell Godsil, the senior intelligence officer for the 1st

Brigade of the 1st Armored Division. "Commanders just wanted all the 'possible' bad guys out of their neighborhoods until they left." Where those Iraqis wound up was someone else's problem.

When the world learned in the spring of 2004 that American soldiers had sadistically abused prisoners at Abu Ghraib, Sanchez treated the scandal as a breakdown of discipline among a few enlisted soldiers, rather than a problem caused by a series of leadership failures, most notably his tolerance of massive roundups by some divisions. An Army intelligence expert later estimated that more than 85 percent of the detainees had no intelligence value. Even if it had been the right approach—and even now, some Army officers maintain that it was—Sanchez had failed to ensure that he had a back office capable of processing what the frontline force collected. Not only were more than ten thousand Iraqis imprisoned, but, because prisoners were not sorted by political orientation, hard-core insurgents and al-Qaeda terrorists were able to use the prisons as recruiting and training centers. Worst of all, the Abu Ghraib prison was run by a small, undertrained, poorly led Army Reserve military police unit that amused itself by playing brutal games with prisoners. One detainee, for example, later told Army investigators of being made to "bark like a dog, being forced to crawl on his stomach while MPs spit and urinated on him, and being struck causing unconsciousness." The revelation of their crimes was the biggest setback of Sanchez's year of command in Iraq, a black eye for the American military and the United States, and a major boost for the insurgency.

It is telling that, even as some senior officers were wondering whether to relieve Sanchez, he was contemplating relieving Brig. Gen. Janis Karpinski, the commander of the American jailers at Abu Ghraib. He did not do so, he said, because she was due to rotate home in less than two months. Once again, rotation was the enemy of competence and accountability.

Gen. John Cushman, the long-retired commander at Leaven-

worth, could not believe that the Army he had helped rebuild after Vietnam was so lacking in general officer supervision in Iraq.
In a privately circulated essay on American generalship in Iraq, he
concluded that Sanchez should have been relieved and that Gen.
Abizaid, Sanchez's immediate superior at Central Command, was
derelict in duty for not acting at once to do so.

As it became mired in Iraq, the Army began to hear echoes
from earlier wars. In his farewell speech as Army chief of staff in
mid-2003, Gen. Eric Shinseki, who frequently had been at odds
with Rumsfeld, told the assembled crowd—which pointedly did
not include Rumsfeld—that "the current war brings me full circle
to where I began my journey as a soldier. The lessons that I
learned in Vietnam are always with me." In Vietnam, the American military had gone to war under the Johnson Administration's
unexamined and false assumption that Hanoi and its forces had a
breaking point that could be reached fairly quickly. In Iraq, the
military went to war under the Bush Administration's unexamined and false assumption that occupation of the country would
be relatively easy. Making the same mistake is a signal that our
leaders were not thinking strategically in either 1991 or 2003, and
in particular they were not unearthing and dissecting differences
and assumptions.

In addition, the American generals in Iraq were burdened
with a defense secretary who, like McNamara with Vietnam, frequently thought he knew better than they did. Further complicating the Iraqi situation, of course, was a factor unique to Iraq: the
Bush Administration's unfounded belief that the Arab state possessed an arsenal of chemical and biological weapons.

Of all the commanders Ricardo Sanchez resembled, perhaps the
best precedent was not any of the Vietnam-era generals but

William Dean, the ill-fated commander at the outset of the Korean War. Like Dean, Sanchez led a force unprepared for what it faced. The troops sent to Korea were simply ill-equipped and undertrained. The force sent to Iraq was much more tactically competent, but it was led by officers who did not know how to deal with an insurgency. Sanchez was never captured, but, as with Dean, his reputation would be all but destroyed by his war experience. Andrew Bacevich's verdict on Sanchez's performance in Iraq is harsh but fair:

> When Lieutenant General Ricardo S. Sanchez assumed command of coalition forces in Iraq in 2003, the first stirrings of an insurgency had begun to appear; his job was to snuff out that insurgency and establish a secure environment. When Sanchez gave up command a year later, Iraq was all but coming apart at the seams. Security had deteriorated appreciably. The general failed to accomplish his mission, egregiously so. Yet amidst all of the endless commentary and chatter about Iraq, that failure of command has gone all but unnoted, as if for outsiders to evaluate senior officer performance qualifies as bad form. Had Sanchez been a head coach or CEO, he'd likely have been cashiered.

Given that dismal record, it is startling that one of the preoccupations of Sanchez's memoir was how the Bush Administration had failed to elevate him to four-star rank. The end of his memoir dwelled not on the mess he had helped make of Iraq, nor on the American troops who were stuck there, nor on the American and Iraqi dead—thousands of them, perhaps unnecessarily—but on how he did not get a promotion he believed he had been promised. When the chairman of the Joint Chiefs called him to inform him that he instead would be retired, he lashed out: "You all have betrayed me." As he was trying to salvage his promotion,

Sanchez turned to an aide and uttered that most tired of Army lines: "Boy, am I glad to be leaving Washington. At least in Iraq I know who my enemies are and what to do about them." Sadly, even this military cliché was false: In Iraq, Sanchez was even more out of his depth than he was in Washington. In the spreading war in Mesopotamia, he had only a dim idea of who his foes were, and even less sense of how to deal with them.

In a 2009 study, a veteran Army intelligence officer, Maj. Douglas Pryer, reviewed Sanchez's performance. In his report, Pryer acknowledged that Sanchez was the victim of neglect by the Pentagon, but he still faulted him for poor leadership. "Perhaps most unforgivably, based on his staff's recommendations, Lt. Gen. Sanchez approved two interrogation policy memoranda that were, at best, poorly considered and poorly written," Pryer wrote. It was not lack of resources or training that was the basic cause of the Abu Ghraib scandal, he concluded; it was lack of ethical leadership. "The fundamental reason why interrogation abuse in Iraq occurred was a failure in leadership. The answer is that simple."

The behavior of both Franks and Sanchez after they left the military may be seen as confirmation of Zelikow's suspicions about their talents. Franks made news in 2008 when it was revealed that he had been paid $100,000 to endorse two veterans' charities that, it turned out, used only a small portion of the money they raised to help veterans. The charities had been graded "F" by the American Institute of Philanthropy. Sanchez, for his part, reemerged in November 2007, delivering the Democratic Party's radio response to the president's weekly statement. He began disingenuously: "I speak to you today not as a representative of the Democratic Party, but as a retired military officer who is a former commander of Multi-National Force-Iraq." Without skipping a beat, he proceeded to blast the Bush Administration: "In that capacity, I saw firsthand the administration's failure to devise a strategy for victory in Iraq that employed, in a coordinated manner, the political, economic, diplomatic and military power of the United States. That failure continues today." It was, noted one Marine colonel who had served in Iraq, like listening to George Custer lecture on Indian affairs. In 2011, Sanchez announced that he would seek the Democratic Party's nomination for U.S. senator from Texas, only to withdraw at the end of the year after his fund-raising efforts fizzled.

Together, Franks and Sanchez proved just how much American generalship had abandoned the model of George Marshall. Marshall consistently turned down lucrative business offers and always distanced himself as much as possible from politics. The activities of both of these Texan generals were damaging to future generals, because they undercut trust in the military profession. Franks fundamentally misconceived his war, leading to the deaths of thousands of Americans and an untold number of Iraqis. This eroded civilian confidence in the military and may help explain President Barack Obama's skepticism about military advice. Sanchez's venture into politics also was damaging. When generals engage in partisan politics, they venture into an area where they are amateurs and so are unlikely to operate effectively. But by doing so, they could make future politicians take politics into consideration when choosing and working with generals. Politicians might select a lesser officer for a command because he was seen as less of a possible political threat. Such thinking by civilian leaders would result in reduced military effectiveness.

The troops: Lions often led by donkeys

Under both Franks and Sanchez, the failures of the American military in Iraq were not those of frontline soldiers. American troops deployed to Iraq fit and well trained. However, training tends to prepare one for known problems, while education better prepares one for the unknown, the unpredictable, and the unexpected. Like their civilian overseers, the generals leading the Army in Iraq had a major gap in their educations. They were not mentally prepared for the war they encountered in Iraq. "The troops were good at what they were told to do, from day one," observed retired Army Col. Robert Killebrew, a longtime student of strategy and leadership. It was the generals who were unable to tell their soldiers how to counter an insurgency. "Had counterinsurgency been invoked on day two, [the soldiers] would have adapted." As an exception, Killebrew pointed to the 101st Airborne Division in Mosul, which in 2003, under Gen. David Petraeus, moved quickly to a counterinsurgency strategy and kept Mosul surprisingly quiet for almost a year. The problem, Killebrew continued, was not the troops but the senior leaders. "As is often the case in war, the question is not whether the troops can adapt, but whether the leaders can. The troops, as always, paid the price of educating their leaders." It would take more than three years for Army leaders simply to begin listening—that is, about as much time as the U.S. military spent altogether in World War II.

The result of being tactically proficient but strategically inept was that the American Army in Iraq was powerful but poorly led. The warning Huba Wass de Czege had issued in 1984 was, despite his best efforts in creating the School of Advanced Military Studies, coming back to haunt the Army: "A system of officer education which emphasizes how-to training applicable only to present methods, means and conditions will fail to provide the needed education the Army officer corps will need to be adaptive in the uncertain future."

Tactical excellence may in fact have enabled strategic incompetence. The irony of the DePuy model of the U.S. Army was that its combat effectiveness allowed its generals to dither for much longer than if the Army had been suffering clear tactical setbacks. Competent tactical leadership bought time for the generals to adjust. That is the way it always goes in war, because the shock of reality that wakes generals up and forces them to adjust tends to hit first at the tactical level. Good generalship is measured by the time it takes from first contact with the enemy for the generals to readjust their thinking to the actual conditions they face. In Iraq, it took far too long for the Army's senior officers to make that adjustment. "One of the reasons we were able to hold on despite a failing strategy and then turn the situation around was that our soldiers continued to be led by highly competent, professional junior officers and non-commissioned officers whom they respected," concluded Sean MacFarland, who as a brigade commander in Ramadi in 2006 would be responsible for a major counterinsurgency success. "And they gave us senior officers the breathing space that we needed, but probably didn't deserve, to properly understand the fight we were in." MacFarland's point is one not often made, but worth pausing over, because its implications are far-reaching. Imagine a U.S. military at the other extreme—tactically mediocre and manned with draftees. In such a circumstance, it is hard to imagine the wars in Iraq and Afghanistan being allowed to meander for years without serious strategic direction.

A few reliefs might have broken the strategic logjam, but the vocabulary of accountability had been lost. In 2005, a RAND Corporation study of Army generalship referred not to "firings" or "relief for cause" but, vaguely, to "performance departures"—which could mean leaving voluntarily or not. Similarly, a fine essay by Col. George Reed on "toxic leadership" in the military analyzed the problem bravely but tiptoed around the obvious solution, saying only, rather tentatively, "If the behavior does not change, there are many administrative remedies available." And a study done at the Army War College by Col. Steven Jones at about the same time again pointed to persistent problems with rotation and unaccountability of officers, as well as an Army system of assessing officers that tended to reward abusive leadership—but, again, it never could quite mention the need for firing such leaders.

Coda: Lieutenant Colonel Sassaman's breakdown

Relief, if done early enough, might even save an officer's career. For example, had Maj. Gen. Raymond Odierno, commander of the 4th Infantry Division and now the Army chief of staff, removed Lt. Col. Nathan Sassaman from battalion command back in late 2003, Sassaman probably would still be in the Army today. Given his track record before he went to Iraq, he might even be a general now.

Sassaman deployed to Iraq in 2003 as one of the highest-profile officers of his generation. Standing six feet seven inches, he had been a star quarterback at West Point, leading its football team to its first bowl game ever, the 1984 Cherry Bowl, at which it beat Michigan State University, 10–6. Sassaman played much of the season with three cracked ribs and, being a successful player, became a symbol of the rejuvenation of the Army. "I was with Nate at West Point," recalled Conrad Crane, a military officer turned historian who taught there when Sassaman was assigned to the admissions office. The two sometimes played basketball. "He had the most intense desire to win of anyone I've ever seen," Crane said. In Iraq, Sassaman continued to make a striking first impression. "In person, the ruggedly handsome commander crackled with competence and charisma," observed Capt. Vivian Gembara, a legal officer. "Few who met him doubted that this was the sort of man soldiers would follow anywhere."

Sassaman went into Iraq cocky, a believer in the efficacy of the pre-9/11 Army's three "Fs"—fear, firepower, and force protection. "With a heavy dose of fear and violence, and a lot of money for projects, I think we can convince these people we are here to help them," he told Dexter Filkins, of the *New York Times,* late in 2003. Contrary to the experience of many commanders, his time in Iraq only confirmed his belief in this approach. "The simple, somewhat barbaric truth is that we had to convince the Iraqi people that they should fear us more than they feared the insurgents," he would still believe years later.

But during his year in Iraq, Sassaman appears to have cracked, especially after one of his favorite subordinate officers was killed. Complicating matters, Sassaman was constantly at odds with his immediate superior, Col. Frederick Rudesheim, who was following a softer, more nuanced approach toward the Iraqis. "I neither trusted nor respected him," Sassaman wrote of his commander, in a bitter memoir. When Rudesheim directed him to seek clearance for any use of indirect fire—that is, mortars and artillery—Sassaman told his soldiers to ignore the order. "Screw brigade," he instructed them.

So it went between me and Colonel Rudesheim—a pattern of disrespect and disobedience having now been established, I gave orders based on instinct and experience, rather than on consideration for the chain of command and traditional army protocol. I had crossed a line, and I knew it, but I didn't care. By now it was apparent that in my one year of combat duty, as a battalion commander, I was going to be working for a man who did not believe in fighting; who felt that we should be prosecuting the war with a policy of appeasement—where we paid people to stop attacking us, instead of just eliminating the attackers. I couldn't do that.

The approach Sassaman denounced, that of paying off insurgents and finding other nonviolent ways of getting them to stop attacking Americans, became official American policy four years later and would be key to the success of the "surge" that helped the United States withdraw from the war. Had Sassaman been relieved at this point, when it was clear that he had developed a spectacularly bad relationship with his commander and was fomenting indiscipline, it would have been better not only for him but for the soldiers in his unit and for Iraqis in his area of operations. For example, Odierno could have ordered him to switch jobs with an officer on the division staff. But he was not removed, and his unit began to slide insidiously from indiscipline to criminality. Capt. Gembara, the legal officer who had been so impressed by Sassaman at first, developed second thoughts. "First Battalion, 8th Infantry Regiment was a world unto itself, one where unlawful, even brutal, acts were, at best, condoned and, at worst, explicitly ordered," she wrote.

One night in January 2004, some of Sassaman's soldiers forced two handcuffed detainees to jump into the Tigris River. One was reported to have drowned. Sassaman obstructed the subsequent investigation, instructing his soldiers to lie and say that they had dropped the Iraqis at the side of the road. One officer, Lt. Jack Saville, later testified, in his own court-martial trial, that he had discussed with Sassaman how to mislead the Army investigators. This time Gen. Odierno gave Sassaman a written reprimand. "Your conduct was wrongful, criminal, and will not be tolerated," Odierno stated. Yet in fact it *was* tolerated, by Odierno and by the Army. Official disinclination to relieve commanders had grown so intense that even at that point Odierno did not relieve Sassaman. Lt. Col. David Poirier, an MP battalion commander who witnessed the affair, was astounded: "When you have a battalion commander who leads a staff in rehearsing a story about murder—and he's still in command?" Sassaman was allowed to retire quietly after his time in command.

It all sounded a bit like the U.S. Army in Vietnam, echoing Gen. Koster's own letter of reprimand after My Lai. The biggest difference was that, four decades after the Indochina war, the American public was less critical of its military—and so the military was not forced to conduct the kind of self-examination that could have helped it correct its course.

CHAPTER 29

George Casey

Trying but treading water

Sanchez was replaced in Iraq in mid-2004 by Gen. George Casey, a deeply conventional man who tried to convince the Army to operate unconventionally.

Casey was an Army insider—a four-star general and, in fact, the son of the highest-ranking American casualty of the Vietnam War, a division commander who was killed in a July 1970 helicopter crash. He knew the Army needed to start operating differently in Iraq. He developed a formal campaign plan, something Sanchez had never actually done. More significantly, he asked two counterinsurgency experts, Col. Bill Hix and retired Lt. Col. Kalev Sepp, to review what units were doing and make suggestions. Sepp, a Special Forces veteran of El Salvador with a doctorate from Harvard, reviewed every battalion, regimental, and brigade commander in Iraq and concluded that 20 percent of them understood how to conduct counterinsurgency operations, 60 percent were struggling to do so, and 20 percent were not interested in changing and were fighting conventionally, "oblivious to the inefficacy and counterproductivity of their operations." In other words, the majority of U.S. units were not operating effectively.

Casey—his misgivings confirmed by that review, and despairing of the Army being able to train officers in counterinsurgency before they deployed to Iraq—started the Counterinsurgency (COIN) Academy at the big military base in Taji, just north of Baghdad. There, he gave newcomers one-week courses in the basics. "Because the Army won't change itself, I'm going to change the Army here in Iraq," he told subordinates. Just capturing a known insurgent is not necessarily a tactical gain, the academy taught the students, if it is done in such a way that it creates new enemies. As the course's textbook put it, "The potential second- and third-order effects . . . can turn it into a long-term defeat if our actions humiliate the family, needlessly destroy property, or alienate the local population from our goals." Even so, both Casey and the Army were slow to adjust and had a difficult time doing so. For example, a key tenet of classic counterinsurgency theory is that troops should live in small outposts among the people, to better understand them and to deter the enemy from controlling them. Yet Casey, in 2006, was determined to close smaller outposts and move his troops onto a bunch of very big bases. "By and large," concluded Francis West, a counterinsurgency expert and Vietnam veteran who studied American military operations in Iraq, "the battalions continued to do what they knew best: conduct sweeps and mounted patrols during the day and targeted raids by night."

Many units simply did not follow Casey's lead. If Sanchez's time in Iraq was colored by the Abu Ghraib scandal of 2004, the Casey phase would be characterized by two outrages committed by American forces. The first was the Haditha massacre of November 19, 2005. This killing of a score of Iraqi civilians by Marines lashing out after being bombed showed the essential bankruptcy of the way the Americans were fighting the war: You cannot protect people by killing them.

A second incident, a few months later, demonstrated even more clearly the basic failure of the American approach in Iraq.

In March 2006, in what would come to be known as the Black Hearts incident, a group of four soldiers from 1st Platoon, Bravo Company, 1st Battalion, 502nd Infantry Regiment, 101st Airborne Division, got drunk in their outpost a few miles southwest of Baghdad, then went to a nearby house and gang-raped and killed a fourteen-year-old girl and murdered her parents and her six-year-old sister. After this they walked back to their outpost, where some slept while others grilled chicken wings. An investigation by journalist Jim Frederick provided overwhelming evidence that, while the unit was poorly led, the fundamental problem was that the unit was badly overstretched, with squads coming in from one mission and immediately going out on another, for days at a time. "There was no downtime," said one soldier. Squads were doing the jobs of platoons, platoons of companies, companies of battalions. One squad in particular felt strained, in part because of poisonous relationships in its chain of command, most notably with its company commander and his battalion commander, who was fond of telling captains that they were "shitbags" who constantly "fucked up." The captains often told him they needed more men, and he would respond that they simply needed to operate more effectively. Bravo Company's commander, in turn, felt he had to stay on the radio in his command post around the clock, catnapping in his chair under a poncho when he could.

In a representative moment, Lt. Col. Tom Kunk, the battalion commander, chewed out Sgt. Daniel Carrick for nearly being killed while on a patrol to search for roadside bombs. "You are getting blown up because you are not following the proper procedures," he told Carrick and other soldiers. "What the fuck happened to you today? What the fuck were you doing? Probably just walking down the fucking street not paying attention."

Carrick resented the charge that he was careless. He actually had approached the bomb because the specialized Explosive

Ordnance Disposal (EOD) unit would not come to detonate it unless he could get additional visual confirmation. "I did everything by the book. EOD told me to get closer."

"Bullshit," Kunk said. "You were not following the proper tactics, the proper methods."

"Fuck you, sir," the sergeant told the lieutenant colonel, and walked away.

Gen. Cushman, who had clashed with Gen. DePuy decades earlier, read about the Black Hearts war crime and was horrified. He sat down to explore in writing his growing feeling that American generals in Iraq were not doing their jobs. The powerful essay that resulted circulated at West Point and elsewhere in the Army. In it, Cushman faulted the chain of command above the battalion for not being aware earlier of the months-long deterioration in Bravo Company. Here, as with Abu Ghraib, he argued, there was a problem of generals not knowing what was going on in a troubled unit when it was their responsibility—and they had the means—to do so. Here, as with Abu Ghraib, he argued, there was a problem of "general officer command responsibility," of commanders burdening units with more tasks than it was possible for them to do, of not understanding what was happening in the field. The issue was personal for Cushman: The Army in Iraq was not just part of the Army he had helped rebuild; the "Black Hearts" battalion was part of the same brigade of the 101st Airborne that he had commanded four decades earlier in Vietnam, during the Tet Offensive.

Torn and confused, trying to change course while under assault by a sophisticated group of enemies who adapted constantly, the American military under Casey did not make progress in Iraq. In 2004, it recorded 26,496 insurgent attacks. In 2005, that number increased to 34,131. Casey hopefully announced that 2006 would be "the Year of the Police," but it turned out to be the year of bitter urban fighting as Baghdad was consumed by a small-scale civil war. Fighting intensified in July 2006, especially in and around the capital. Every day that summer, there were fifty insurgent attacks just in Anbar Province, west of the capital. By the end of the summer, Baghdad had been largely ethnically cleansed, with Sunnis reduced to a few embattled enclaves on its western side. Insurgents were detonating about a thousand roadside bombs a week. An estimated two million Iraqis had fled the country, most of them Sunni, and an equal number were classified as internally displaced.

Casey and those around him did not seem to grasp how quickly the situation was deteriorating. Adm. William Fallon, the American military commander for the Pacific, visited Baghdad in midsummer and then, when back home, telephoned retired Army Gen. Jack Keane, an influential figure behind the scenes in Washington. "Jack, I just came out of Iraq," Fallon began. "Could you help me to understand what the fuck is going on? . . . Casey is up to his ears in quicksand and he doesn't even know it. This thing is going down around him." The following year, Fallon would be reassigned to run Central Command, overseeing the wars in Iraq and Afghanistan, but he was forced by Defense Secretary Robert Gates to step down early in 2008, after making disparaging comments to a journalist about Bush Administration policy in the Middle East.

Casey's lack of awareness began to undercut his support at the top of the Bush Administration. He did not seem to realize that by the late summer of 2006 he was losing not only Baghdad but also the support of the White House. "I didn't see that at the time," he confessed in a subsequent interview. On August 17, in a briefing to top national security officials through a video link, he said he wanted to stick with his plan to turn over Baghdad to Iraqi security forces by the end of the year. Vice President Cheney, watching from Wyoming, was troubled by that comment. "I respected General Casey, but I couldn't see a basis for his optimism," Cheney wrote later.

In the wake of that briefing, the vice president began poking around for a different strategy—and different generals to lead it. Among those he would meet with was Col. H. R. McMaster, the author of *Dereliction of Duty,* about the failures of top American generals in Vietnam. The colonel told Cheney that the U.S. government should abandon the view, held by Casey, that the American goal was to turn over control to Iraqis as soon as possible.

In the first week of October 2006, some twenty-four American service members were killed in Iraq, and nearly three hundred more were wounded. Bush had tended to be "upbeat" in his frequent video teleconferences with commanders in Iraq, but in November, Casey would recall, that changed, and "the president was noticeably cold." Casey was being relieved but did not quite recognize it, because it was happening in slow motion. In December he was told to leave Iraq within a few weeks rather than in the spring of 2007, as he had planned. "I left not really understanding what the hell had happened," Casey said.

Ultimately, Casey's record in Iraq was mixed. He did not succeed, but he probably deserves more credit than he has been given. In this way he resembles Gen. Walton Walker in Korea, doggedly fighting but skating near relief without realizing it. It is the fate of some generals simply to stave off defeat. Both Walker and Casey held on long enough in their wars for their successors to be able to act quickly and reap much credit in the process.

CHAPTER 30
David Petraeus
An outlier moves in, then leaves

If George Casey was the Walton Walker of the Iraq war, Gen. David Petraeus would be its Matthew Ridgway, arriving and soberly reassessing the situation and then, through clear thinking and impressive willpower, as well as taking advantage of changes on the ground, putting a new face on it.

Behind him, and enabling him to act, was a major improvement in civil-military discourse. The American position in Iraq began to improve only after President Bush turned away from Casey and his other senior generals and sought the advice of others, asking some hard questions that had been deflected for years. Taken aback by the setbacks suffered by Republican candidates in the midterm elections of 2006, President Bush asked outside experts to come to the White House. It is significant that at his meeting with several strategic thinkers on December 11, 2006, one of the major subjects was accountability and generalship. It is not enough that your generals are good men, advised Eliot Cohen, of Johns Hopkins University; they also must be competent commanders. "Not a single general has been removed for ineffectiveness during the course of this war," Cohen gently scolded Bush.

The foremost result of that December meeting was that Gen. Petraeus would be selected to replace Casey as the new American commander in Iraq. It is significant that Petraeus was suggested by outsiders and picked by the president. He expressly was not the choice of the military. He was regarded by many of his peers as something of a thrice-cursed outlier—an officer with a doctorate from Princeton who also seemed to enjoy talking to reporters and even to politicians and who had made his peers look bad with his success leading the 101st Airborne Division in Mosul in 2003–4.

Together with Lt. Gen. Raymond Odierno, Petraeus revamped the American approach in Iraq, taking more risks, moving more aggressively, and, despite suffering an increase in casualties, radically improving the morale of American troops. Petraeus and Odierno also brought in like-minded officers, such as Lt. Gen. James Dubik, another outlying intellectual the Army seemed puzzled by. The common trait in all these officers was the ability to think critically, enabling them to arrive at new solutions when their Army training proved insufficient. Like other successful post-9/11 generals, such as Martin Dempsey (who became chairman of the Joint Chiefs of Staff in 2011) and James Mattis (who became chief of Central Command in 2010), these were not officers who fit the relentlessly tactical mode developed by DePuy but rather men who had, on their own, found the alternative mode supported by Gen. Cushman in the 1970s and '80s: flexible commanders able to think independently. It is typical of Dubik that, upon retiring a few years later, he decided to pursue a doctorate in philosophy at Johns Hopkins University.

Petraeus and Odierno reversed some of Casey's directives. They ordered their troops off the big bases where Casey had consolidated them and organized scores of small outposts, "patrol bases," where groups of perhaps thirty-five to seventy-five soldiers would live near and even among the Iraqi people. They also told subordinates that it was not just acceptable but necessary to begin negotiating with insurgent groups. The biggest change was the hardest to see: They formally demoted "transitioning" to Iraqi security forces from the top American priority to number seven on their mission list. Replacing it as the number-one task was the mission of protecting the Iraqi people.

Equally significantly, Petraeus worked to repair the civil-military relationship at his level. He and the new American ambassador, Ryan Crocker, made it clear that they would work relentlessly closely and expected the same "unity of effort" from their subordinates.

Casey was in the dark about the coming changes. He learned only belatedly that retired Gen. Keane, a former vice chief of staff of the Army, had been bypassing the chain of command and communicating directly with Odierno, a former subordinate of his, and even carrying messages between the White House and Odierno, as well as to Petraeus. Not long after returning to the United States, Casey—kicked upstairs to Army chief of staff, as Westmoreland had been during the Vietnam War—ran into Keane at the Walter Reed Army Medical Center and angrily braced him. "We feel—the Chiefs feel—you are way too out in front in advocating a policy for which you are not accountable," Casey said. "We're accountable. You're not accountable. And that's a problem." Asked about this in an interview, Casey confirmed the exchange, saying, "I always felt that as a professional military officer if he felt that he had something he thought that he could offer to the mission he ought to have called me or sent it to me or contacted me in some way. And he never did." Casey's reasoning was dead wrong. Keane was in fact injecting accountability into the system. He was repairing civil-military discourse by helping civilians ask tough questions about the conduct of the war. Keane's intervention might superficially resemble the role played by Maxwell Taylor in the early 1960s, but actually it was radically different. Both retired generals alienated the Joint Chiefs of Staff of their time. But Taylor's actions diminished the quality of civil-military interactions, while Keane's improved them.

Unlike Ridgway, Petraeus already had served in the war he would transform, with two previous tours in Iraq, the first as commander of the 101st Airborne Division in northern Iraq, in 2003–4. It had not been inevitable that Mosul and the rest of the north would be relatively quiet. Some intelligence analysts had predicted that it would likely be one of the more violent parts of the country, because over 100,000 former Iraqi officers and soldiers lived there, including more than 1,000 retired generals. Nearby were 20,000 Kurdish militiamen, backing conflicting claims to various parts of the region. The city contained so many opponents of the American occupation that Saddam Hussein's sons, Uday and Qusay, chose to hide there. Yet on Petraeus's watch, Mosul and the surrounding area remained relatively calm. This was in part because Petraeus, operating so far from Baghdad and under the uncertain command of Ricardo Sanchez, was able to run his own operation with his own policies. For example, he was notably more forgiving of former Baathists than was official American policy. As he said in 2004, when he had all but split from Rumsfeld and other Pentagon officials, "It is not possible to fire all former Baathists and expect them to become anything other than enemies."

In many ways, Petraeus in Iraq in 2007 was running higher risks than Ridgway had when he took command in Korea at the end of 1950. Unlike Ridgway, Petraeus did not have the military establishment backing his new direction. Rather, it is striking how many senior officials opposed the changes he and Odierno proposed to make: The chairman of the Joint Chiefs, the chief of staff of the Army, and the head of Central Command all spoke out against the new course. (Marine Gen. Peter Pace, the chairman of the Joint Chiefs, would be ousted by Defense Secretary Gates in mid-2007, having served just two years in the job, half the normal tenure.) There also was opposition in Congress to Petraeus's changes, although that was not expressed with any kind of determination.

But Petraeus and Odierno enjoyed a kind of secret source of support: After four years of often fruitless combat, lower echelons of the American military were receptive to trying a new course. As Petraeus's executive officer, Col. Peter Mansoor, would observe, "By the beginning of the surge in early 2007, the military had undergone a renaissance in its ability to connect with the Iraqi people, an adaptation that greatly assisted its ability to conduct counterinsurgency operations."

Although this phase of the war, beginning in early 2007, became known as the surge—with 30,000 additional troops ultimately sent to Iraq, for a peak strength of about 166,000—the number of troops was far less meaningful than how they were employed. The measure of their success, American soldiers were told, was not trends in American casualties but trends in Iraqi civilian losses. Despite their lack of backing from their superiors, Petraeus and Odierno were effective in conveying this message down through the echelons of their command, from corps to divisions to brigades, battalions, companies, and platoons. "Our mindset was not to kill, it was to win," said Lt. John Burns, leader of a scout platoon in Baghdad during the Petraeus counteroffensive. "We constantly evaluated our situation and made certain we were fighting the war we had and not necessarily the one we wanted." The time also was ripe for a different American approach. Sunnis had lost control of western Baghdad to Shiite militias, and their backs were to the wall. In Anbar Province, sheikhs were angry with al-Qaeda for muscling in on their cross-border smuggling operations.

Success often looks inevitable in retrospect. But at the time in Iraq, the changes Petraeus and Odierno had implemented looked very risky—and indeed they were. Petraeus's biggest risk was reaching out to the Sunni insurgents and offering them money to turn sides. He did not clear this move with President Bush. "I don't think it was something that we needed to ask permission for," he would say in an interview, but he probably had realized that the best course was not to put the president in a box, but instead to take action first and seek approval afterward.

When Petraeus arrived in Iraq in February 2007, said Philip Zelikow, the State Department strategist, "he basically inherited a strategic void." It was a surprisingly tough time. In the first days of the surge, there was an average of almost 180 attacks a day on American forces. For several months, through the entire spring of 2007, there was almost no sign that the changes were working. April was ghastly, with Baghdad feeling like a dying city under siege. May was worse, with 126 U.S. combat deaths, the worst month for American troops that year. Petraeus later would call this time "almost an excruciating period . . . [a] horrific nightmare." In June, a smart colonel who knew Iraq well concluded that Petraeus had lost: "I think he had one shot at winning. Frankly, I think he's past that point."

Yet even as that officer spoke, a major shift was under way. It was difficult to perceive and took months to fully emerge. The wide-ranging battle for control of Baghdad, a sprawling metropolis of about five million people, reached its climax in late spring and early summer. By June 2007 the new approach had begun to show results. As summer began, Sunni insurgents began coming over to the American side—not surrendering, but keeping their weapons and going on the American payroll in return for agreeing to cease their attacks on Americans. Eventually, more than 100,000 insurgents would turn. As they did, the sanctuaries of their more hard-core former comrades began evaporating, Petraeus recalled: "We were literally over-running their support zones, if you will, their command and control facilities." There were ninety-three Americans killed in action in June 2007, then sixty-six in July, fifty-five in August, and, as the changes spread, just fourteen in December. The American role in the war in Iraq began to diminish.

The following year, Petraeus would be promoted to take over Central Command. It looked as if he and those around him were successfully conducting a campaign not just in Iraq but inside the U.S. Army. Underscoring his newfound influence, he had been called back from Iraq to Washington to lead a promotion board to pick the Army's new class of brigadier generals—an unprecedented assignment for a theater commander in the midst of a war. He appeared to try to push the selection of brigadier generals back toward the Marshall template, picking a slate notably heavy in officers with successful combat commands, especially leading infantry and Special Operations units. Among the colonels picked for promotion was H. R. McMaster, not only author of one of the best studies of senior generalship in the Vietnam War but also leader of one of the first successful counterinsurgency campaigns in northwestern Iraq.

Afghanistan deteriorates

Meanwhile, the other American war, in Afghanistan, was meandering without much strategic direction—which had implications for Petraeus's future. The Afghan war was treated by American policymakers as a sideshow. The job of American gen-

David Petraeus | 439

erals in Afghanistan seemed to be, foremost, not to bother the
Pentagon. "We were really an orphan headquarters, in many re-
spects," recalled retired Lt. Gen. David Barno, the U.S. commander
in Afghanistan in 2004–5. He found it difficult simply to get the
Army to send him officers for his staff: "They clearly had Iraq on
their minds, but there was no interest whatsoever in providing us
with anything but the absolute minimum level of support." He
eventually filled out his staff with aging reservists, leading to the
joke that his headquarters represented "the world's most forward
deployed AARP chapter."

The Afghan war did not thrive on neglect. From 2004 to 2009,
the number of reported security problems increased ninefold,
with an even sharper rise in suicide bombings. The turning point
in the war came in 2005, when the U.S. government repeatedly
signaled disengagement from the war, first by calling for NATO
to take it over and later by publicly stating that it planned to
reduce its combat strength by 2,500 troops. Perhaps as a result,
the government of Pakistan in 2005 seemed to go into opposition
against the American presence in Afghanistan, its military intelligence agency again coming to the aid of the Taliban and other
Afghan allies. There were even a number of incidents in which
Pakistani border posts fired heavy machine guns in support of
Taliban attacks.

Even as Afghanistan became more dangerous, American attention remained riveted on Iraq. The Afghan war did not really
come back into focus for Washington policymakers until 2009. As
the Obama Administration began to pay attention to the Afghan
war, its officials grew unhappy with its military leadership, especially Army Gen. David McKiernan, whom they saw as unable to
adjust from a conventional approach to more of a counterinsurgency approach.

What followed fit the post-Marshall model of top generals

being removed by civilians. First McKiernan was relieved as the commander in Afghanistan in May 2009, on the general feeling of Defense Secretary Gates and other officials that a new leader was needed to take the war in a new direction. This was a reasonable position, and McKiernan in turn acted reasonably, retiring quietly and with dignity. As an Air Force officer and a retired Army officer wrote together, "The replacement of McKiernan reminds us that senior leaders have prerogative to build the team they feel is best suited to execute the selected strategy." One could almost see the ghost of George Marshall nodding in approval.

The next American commander in Afghanistan was Gen. Stanley McChrystal. It was only in May 2010 that the Afghan war became the "larger" of the two wars for the United States, in the sense that there were more American troops there than in Iraq. A month later, McChrystal was fired and forced into retirement by President Obama after members of his traveling party unwisely—and inexplicably—made comments critical of the Obama Administration to a reporter for *Rolling Stone*. McChrystal was succeeded by Petraeus. For the second time, Petraeus had been assigned the task of trying to right a war that initially had been mishandled by Tommy Franks. Petraeus would serve in Afghanistan for a year before turning the war over to Marine Gen. John Allen, whom he had come to know through the recommendation of Gen. Mattis. It is difficult at this point to see whether Allen will have the same success in Afghanistan that Petraeus had in Iraq in finding a way to extricate the Americans from a war.

Since 2003, the overseers of the Afghan war have been Tommy Franks, Paul Mikolashek, Dan McNeill, John Vines, David Barno, Karl Eikenberry, McNeill on a second tour, David McKiernan, Stanley McChrystal, David Petraeus, and John Allen. In an interview, Gen. Barno said the biggest problem with American generalship was rapid turnover. "You have ten commanders in ten years, which is horrifically bad, and seven U.S. ambassadors, too," he said. "So what you are going to have is chaos, no matter what your plan is."

Coda: A lieutenant colonel denounces today's generals

One day in late 2006, Lt. Col. Paul Yingling, deputy commander of H. R. McMaster's 3rd Armored Cavalry Regiment, attended a ceremony awarding the Purple Heart to soldiers in his unit who had been wounded in Iraq. It had been his second tour of duty there. Yingling, a 2002 graduate of the School of Advanced Military Studies who had earned another master's degree—in political science, at the University of Chicago—went home filled with emotion and began to write. From his computer emerged a blast at Army leadership that would be published in the spring of 2007.

"America's generals have failed to prepare our armed forces for war and advise civilian authorities on the application of force to achieve the aims of policy," Yingling charged. It was the responsibility of a nation's generals to calculate and explain how force would be used: "If the policymaker desires ends for which the means he provides are insufficient, the general is responsible for advising the statesman of this incongruence." This, of course, was exactly what the generals had not done with the Bush Administration in considering Iraq. Nor, Yingling continued, had the generals understood the war they were fighting or been candid about it with the American people. "After going into Iraq with too few troops and no coherent plan for postwar stabilization, America's general officer corps did not accurately portray the intensity of the insurgency to the American public." For more than three years, they had told the American public that they were making progress when they were not.

But it was too much to expect the generals to suddenly wake up and start thinking differently, he added, because they were products of a system. That system, he said, "does little to reward creativity and moral courage." Given that, he wrote, "it is unreasonable to expect that an officer who spends 25 years conforming to institutional expectations will emerge as an innovator in his late forties."

To change the nature of American generals, Yingling called on the Army to use 360-degree reviews of officers and on the Congress to hold commanders accountable for failure:

> A general who presides over a massive human rights scandal or a substantial deterioration in security ought to be retired at a lower rank than one who serves with distinction. A general who fails to provide Congress with an accurate and candid assessment of strategic probabilities ought to suffer the same penalty. As matters stand now, a private who loses a rifle suffers far greater consequences than a general who loses a war.

Perhaps most provocative—and most painful of all for the post-Vietnam generation of generals—was Yingling's charge that the generals of 2006 were repeating the mistakes of Vietnam, having failed to prepare their forces for the war they fought or to provide Congress and the American people with "an accurate assessment" of the Iraq war.

One of Yingling's closest friends, another Army lieutenant colonel, John Nagl, who had combat experience and a Ph.D. from Oxford, advised him to publish the essay anonymously. The two had been assigned adjacent offices when both were teaching at West Point in the late 1990s and then had been classmates at the Command and General Staff College together. Yingling declined to follow his friend's advice and signed his name to the open letter—"which," Nagl recalled, "I thought was a measure of poor judgment and strong character."

Unsurprisingly, Army generals spoke out against the article. At

Fort Hood, Texas, where Yingling was stationed, Maj. Gen. Jeffery Hammond, commander of the 4th Infantry Division, assembled about two hundred captains in the base chapel to hear his response to Yingling's charges. "I believe in our generals. They are dedicated, selfless servants," Hammond said. At any rate, he added, Yingling "has never worn the shoes of a general." In other words, only other generals were qualified to judge the performance of Army generals. To emphasize the point, he gave Yingling a mediocre performance evaluation.

Later that summer, a higher-ranking general, Richard Cody, the vice chief of staff of the Army, was speaking to a group of captains at Fort Knox, Kentucky, when one inquired about the Yingling article. Gen. Cody responded by asking the assembled captains for their opinion of the Army's generals. He got an earful, including a follow-up question from Capt. Justin Rosenbaum, who had read H. R. McMaster's *Dereliction of Duty*, about whether any Army generals should be held accountable for the mess in Iraq. That was enough for Cody. "I think we've got great general officers that are meeting tough demands," he said. As for Rosenbaum's query, he said that the people to blame were the politicians who had trimmed the size of the military during the post–Cold War reductions of the 1990s: "Those are the people who ought to be held accountable."

Despite being rejected publicly by Army leaders such as Hammond and Cody, Yingling's article went on to be cited in speeches by Defense Secretary Gates and other senior officials. It also appeared in the curricula of some of the military war colleges. Yingling stuck to his guns and elaborated on his indictment. Early in 2011, he delivered a lecture at a Department of Defense school that found today's generals "guilty of three important failures": to prepare their troops for irregular warfare, to develop war plans that achieved the aims of policy, and to provide candid advice to civilian leaders. Later that year, he commented that "officers have ceased to police our own ranks, especially at the field grade and flag levels." Asked whether contemporary U.S. Army leaders reminded him of World War I's British army supposedly being "lions led by donkeys," he responded, "There's a good case to be made that we are less adaptive than the generals of World War I."

Yet the Army would have its revenge. Yingling was promoted to colonel, supposedly by the skin of his teeth and only after the direct intervention of the vice chief of staff of the Army, Peter Chiarelli. He wound up teaching at the George C. Marshall European Center for Security Studies, a joint effort of the American and German governments. It was not a bad place to land. But in the summer of 2011, Yingling was informed that he had not been selected to be a student at the Army War College, even though his own writings were being studied there. He decided to retire and move to Colorado to teach high school social science.

None of these developments indicate that the Army has refused to change in recent years or that its generals are always inflexible or that no accountability exists. The wars in Iraq and Afghanistan saw some improvement, but it was uneven and took far longer than it had in World War II. "I would say most of the current GO [general officer] crop, from a junior view, is the best I have seen since I was commissioned," Maj. Neil Smith wrote from Afghanistan early in 2011. He went on:

> War has a way, like it did in WWII, of bringing the true performers [instead of] the garrison performers to the top. You see much less of the very hierarchical/domineering personality sets in the recently promoted general officers. This mission set in particular has rewarded those with interpersonal skills capable of synchronizing and working across the joint force, U.S. government agencies, and foreign partners versus simply being able to lead a military-dominated hierarchy.

Yet it is unclear how deep the changes go, or how long they will last as the wars in Iraq and Afghanistan wind down and the American military establishment shifts back to peacetime mode. It is not difficult to find experienced officers who are uneasy with how today's generals operate. "They have somewhat abdicated their role in developing their intent or guidance, their vision," concluded Army Col. Dale Eikmeier, who served as a strategic planner in Iraq. "They've subcontracted that out to staff officers to come up with an intent or guidance for them." To Eikmeier, this meant that "they're not really showing leadership."

As defense secretary, Donald Rumsfeld did a poor job at many things, including enforcing accountability. He was wont to loudly criticize and abuse subordinates, but he rarely actually fired them. His successor, Robert Gates, did an admirable job of restoring accountability. Gates was far quicker to react to failure, and he did it with a minimum of emotion. "With Gates, it is not to destroy people," commented Gen. Mattis, who succeeded Petraeus as head of Central Command in 2010. "It is not vicious. It is just pure accountability."

Gates moved on from the Pentagon in July 2011, replaced by Leon Panetta. But whoever holds this position, it is difficult for civilian officials to reach below the highest levels. That means the job of enforcing accountability at all but the top level of the military must be done by the generals themselves. When Gen. Martin Dempsey took over as chairman of the Joint Chiefs of Staff in the fall of 2011, he was the first Army officer to hold the job in a decade. Reporters were told of two changes in his office furnishings, each representing a major figure in Army history. Dempsey displayed in his office a portrait of George C. Marshall, but he chose to use the desk of Douglas MacArthur. It was a mixed signal. In addition, David Petraeus, who had seemed to promise a new direction for the Army, retired in the summer of 2011 to become director of the CIA. It seems his influence on the Army will be limited. It is possible that he might be brought back on active duty, but it seems a good bet that there will not be a "Petraeus generation" of generals. Indeed, even as Petraeus was leaving the Army, the service seemed to be edging toward burying the entire experience of counterinsurgency as a failed experiment. Dempsey stated early in 2012 that the Army was moving away "from counterinsurgency as kind of our central organizing principle" and instead would adopt "a global networked approach to warfare." The commander of one of the Army's most important training centers, Brig. Gen. Clarence Chinn, was even more emphatic, stating at about the same time, "We're going to go back and make sure we're well-grounded in the basics and fundamentals of war fighting." In this reflex the Army of today resembles the Army of the 1970s, which turned away from Vietnam and refocused on conventional warfare skills. The problem with this, of course, is that it is more likely to be dispatched to fight messy small wars than conventional state-on-state battles featuring tanks and fighter aircraft. One of the lessons of the Iraq and Afghanistan wars for potential adversaries is that it is difficult to wage conventional warfare against the Americans, and far more effective to hide in the population and employ guerrilla techniques.

Most notably, the American military, as of mid-2012, has not steeled itself and launched a soul-searching review of its performance in Iraq and Afghanistan. Without such a no-holds-barred examination, akin to the Army review of the state of its officer corps conducted as the Vietnam War wound down, it might not do much better the next time it goes to war. But as long as it cares more about not embarrassing generals than it does about taking care of soldiers, it is unlikely to undertake such a review.

EPILOGUE

Restoring American military leadership

The American ground force today is a long way from being George Marshall's Army, but it is not clear whose Army it has become. The post-Vietnam Army was created in large part by Creighton Abrams, William DePuy, Donn Starry, Maxwell Thurman, and Paul Gorman, but even their far-reaching influence is fading. It did not become the Army of David Petraeus—but nor is it, thankfully, the Army of Tommy R. Franks. Today's Army is deeply strained, having fought for more than ten years since 9/11, with soldiers serving multiple combat tours while 99 percent of the American population has been asked to sacrifice nothing except its time and privacy when going through airport security checkpoints. Now the Army and the other services are facing a decade or more of budget cuts. The Army will be shaped by young officers, likely veterans of Iraq and Afghanistan, who in the coming years will rise to command the force.

What would George Marshall do if he could come back and fix things?

First, I think that he would instruct his senior generals in how to interact with civilian leadership. He likely would tell the Joint

Chiefs of Staff and other top officers also to keep their social distance from the president, as he had with Franklin Roosevelt. At the same time, he would tell the generals to insist on being heard out by the president and his advisers—and to be candid when doing so, in a continual and vigorous dialogue. All too often in recent decades, our generals have believed that politicians should get out of the way once a war has begun. That is wrong. Rather, generals and politicians must, in the American system, collaborate in all three phases—entering a war, executing it, and ending it. In *Supreme Command*, the best book ever written about how presidents should oversee generals, military historian Eliot Cohen, who succeeded Philip Zelikow as counselor at the State Department, recommended a far more engaged approach. We do not need presidents to get out of the way of generals. Rather, we need presidents who are willing, when necessary, to push generals out of their own way if they do not succeed:

> Generals are, or should be, disposable. Statesmen should not, of course, discard them thoughtlessly, nor should they treat them discourteously. Yet all four of these statesmen [Lincoln, Clemenceau, Churchill, and Ben-Gurion] showed themselves able to treat generals in line with Gladstone's first requirement for success as a prime minister: "One must be a good butcher." Indeed, it was the most mild-mannered of the four, Lincoln, who relieved commanders the most frequently.

This is a good summary of how the system should work, with superiors, both military and civilian, rewarding those who succeed and removing those who fail. In wartime especially, this approach promotes to senior ranks those officers who tend to be younger and more energetic and so better able to adapt to the situation at hand.

When civilians do not intervene, they add inertia to a military incentive structure that already tends, in its current form, to reward inaction. All too often, it is easy for civilians and military superiors to back away and to defer to the excuses of commanders at the front, which in recent years has proven to be a recipe for risk-averse approaches. As one battalion commander said about his captains in Afghanistan, "For a number of my officers, success equaled nothing that made them stand out for a year. So the fewer times you left the FOB [forward operating base], the fewer times you interacted with the locals, the fewer times you did anything—that was success." This was a rational choice on the part of his subordinates, because in today's Army, he said, the "B minus and C plus" officer fares better than the "A performer" who occasionally takes risks and fails.

Second, in assessing the strategic situation today, Marshall might conclude that having adaptive, flexible military leaders who also are energetic, determined, cooperative, and trustworthy is probably more important now than it has been at any time since he was chief of staff. For most of the time since then, the primary task of the American military establishment was to deter or counter the might of the Soviet Union. The tasks were known and the strategy was set, so not much change or strategic revision was required. When other missions surfaced—most notably the wars in Korea and Vietnam and, as the Cold War ended, dealing with Iraq—the military proved less successful and perhaps prone to stalemates, which generals then blamed on politicians.

Tolerance of below-average performance has a corrosive effect on the quality of leadership. Brig. Gen. Mark Arnold, an Army Reserve commander who in his civilian career was, among other things, an executive at General Electric, wrote that in one recent year, 94 percent of Army lieutenant colonels were promoted. That rate, he observed, "rings loudly of institutionalizing mediocrity." The personnel equivalent of Gresham's Law is that bad leaders drive out good ones. Indeed, Arnold noted that a study in 2010 by the Army Research Institute concluded that "the main reason talented people leave is not the lure of a lucrative civilian career, but because mediocre people stay in and get promoted."

The Army has been far better at improving tactically than it has been at improving strategically. That is worrisome, because we now are living in an era of strategic uncertainty, just as Marshall was in his first years as chief of staff, between September 1939 and December 7, 1941. Old adversaries have disappeared or are diminishing, and new ones may be emerging. In addition, nonstate foes, such as terrorists, loom much larger in American calculations than ever before. Thus, we have a strong need for leaders, both military and civilian, who not only can handle old tasks in better and more efficient ways but also can address new and different tasks. Civilian leaders should signal the military that they will tolerate robust debate with energetic military leaders, even when such discussions become uncomfortable. Sometimes contentious dialogue is a sign of healthy discourse. In exchange, military leaders should make it clear that when decisions are made, they will execute their orders vigorously—and will not share their dissenting positions with reporters.

Usually, everyone gets it wrong at the beginning of a war, military historian Sir Michael Howard once observed: "In 1914 every army of all the belligerent powers shared a common doctrine of the dominance of the offensive and the inevitability of rapid and decisive campaigns. All navies believed in the dominant role of the capital ship." The point, Howard continued, is not to be right at the outset—an almost impossible task—but to be able to change as a war unfolds. "In these circumstances when everybody starts wrong, the advantage goes to the side which can most quickly adjust itself to the new and unfamiliar environment and learn from its mistakes." So, he said, the goal is to develop the "capacity to get it right quickly when the moment arrives."

How might such capacity be developed? If the Army is serious about having an officer corps that is adaptive, it needs to try to carry out a major cultural shift that enables it to embrace accountability, rather than shun it. This is not as difficult as it might sound. Generals should be relieved not just for personal foibles but for poor performance in command. A few such actions would send signals that would rapidly change the culture. As Col. Steven Jones wrote, "Accountability provides the motivation for change." Put another way, accountability is the engine that drives adapability.

Marshall would know, of course, that the first step toward improving the capacity of leadership is to reinstate his policy of swift relief, with the option of forgiveness. This policy itself must be flexible, letting senior leaders err and learn. Yet persistent failure should lead to relief—which actually can benefit an officer if it stops him before he moves from small but serious failures to unredeemable, catastrophic ones. And it certainly helps soldiers who have been suffering under an inept commander. Also, success rarely can be rewarded adequately if failure carries little or no consequence. Nor will the standout officer be watched and imitated as he or she should be.

Also, there should be second and even third chances. It is essential to follow a policy under which relief from command does not terminate an officer's career. In cases in which the firing was not caused by a character flaw or an unredeemable pattern of poor judgment, relieved officers should be assigned to good posts that carry the possibility of additional promotions and even a return to combat commands. Relief then could be seen as it was in World War II—not as a sign of the system failing but rather as a sign that the system is working.

Marshall would remind top civilian and military officials to be poised to relieve commanders especially at the beginnings of wars. Yes, moving people causes turbulence, but it is better to endure friction in the personnel system than it is to unnecessarily lose people and battles. Also, when making such reliefs, it probably is better to announce them, in order to remove the mystery and dispel rumors, and also to make it clear that the removals are not punitive and might simply be a matter of bad luck or of being in the wrong place at the wrong time. Hiding firings only feeds the rumor mills and so unnecessarily increases uncertainty. A relieved commander's peers and subordinates need to be informed about why something has happened so they can learn from it. There is so much uncertainty in war that what simple steps can be taken to reduce it should be used when possible.

Reliefs should also be disclosed to the public. The Army's leadership should place its duty to the nation over the perceived privacy rights of generals, or else it risks damaging the faith and trust of the people. Failure to relieve is sometimes a form of leadership indiscipline, and failure to disclose reliefs sometimes is an abuse of the stewardship role of Army leaders.

In relieving leaders, the Army can learn from the Navy, which has maintained the practice of relief even as the Army has lost it, with more than 120 commanding officers relieved from 2000 through 2011. This parade of dismissals might occur, in part, because the Navy does not screen junior officers adequately and so only ousts them later in their careers. But the Navy also operates in this way in part because the sea service still steers by the approach Adm. Arleigh Burke summarized with his comment that "the first thing that a commander must learn is not to tolerate incompetence. As soon as you tolerate incompetence . . . you have an incompetent organization." What the Army should avoid is the unforgiving approach the Navy takes, in which relief from command usually results in leaving the service and often a kind of isolation and disgrace.

Implementation of the changes would require top-level attention and coordination for several years. In order for a policy of swift yet forgiving relief to succeed, it would need to be employed frequently enough to eventually be perceived as unexceptional. That is not the case now. One day in 2010, while on a research trip, I was discussing this book with a smart retired Army colonel near the Army War College, in Carlisle, Pennsylvania. When I said I would recommend in it that the Army restore the tradition of relieving unsuccessful generals, this officer, though steeped in military history, muttered, "Why not just court-martial them?" and then walked away, cutting off the conversation. If relief continues to be seen in that way, as an extreme move tantamount to bringing legal charges, then we will not be able to revive the Marshall approach to relief.

Marshall might then consider several smaller, somewhat tactical steps. One possibility to ease the transition to restoring the practice of relief would be to reexamine Gen. Starry's proposal to make all command positions, from platoon leader to four-star general, probationary for their first six months. "There's no way to tell whether you've picked good commanders until you put them in the job," he observed. He suggested that the Army have a system under which a new commander who was not working out, for whatever reason, could be removed without detriment to his career. "The system should be willing, under a least-retribution or no-retribution policy, to say that this sort of work isn't for that fellow, and in the first six months or so take him out if he doesn't meet the standards." However, it is unlikely that Marshall would endorse such a move, because it would inject the friction of uncertainty, especially in wartime.

As a side benefit, a policy that punished failure and rewarded success that was implemented with integrity and care for the institution and its people likely would increase the retention of talented junior officers. A 2011 study at Harvard's Kennedy School of Government of young officers who had left the military found that their top reasons for doing so were not the high operating tempo or the chance of being maimed but rather two other factors: "limited ability to control their own careers" and "frustration with military bureaucracy." The former officers overwhelmingly believed that the Army did not reward talent with faster promotions and did not do a good job of matching talent to jobs. The authors of the paper noted that an exodus of talented young officers is not just a problem in itself but also "a symptom of larger underlying institutional challenges." Among the recommendations made by these departed soldiers was "Be willing to fire people for poor performance (not just send them to another unit or higher echelon where they will do less work, which actually exacerbates the problem by giving them a more impressive resume)." What the Army system valued more than talent was the ability to not "rock the boat," another commented.

Marshall also would consider updating personnel policies, something he actually spent a good deal of energy on as Army chief of staff before the United States entered World War II. He might even consider serious "360-degree" evaluations, in which superiors, peers, and subordinates would all assess the strengths and weaknesses of military leaders. The Army has tiptoed toward this for years. As it currently stands, such evaluations are available but only on a semivoluntary basis, with officers required to seek one such review every three years. However, the results of these evaluations are not included in officers' performance reviews. As retired Sgt. Maj. Erik Wilson put it, this means that the voluntary reviews likely "will have minimal impact in ridding the Army of toxic leaders, but it will help the good leaders get better." This sort of half measure only makes the Army look weak on the core issue of accountability. However, in considering 360s, it is also important to ensure that they do not reward the pleasant conformists and punish the brilliant outliers. All too often, an officer is promoted not for professional competence but because he has been deemed "a good guy" or, even more euphemistically, "a great American." Both are essentially code words for being members of the club. Hence, the use of 360-disgree reviews will make much difference only if it is part of a larger set of changes that introduces consequences for performance, making managers want to search for the effective activist and to avoid those geared for risk avoidance and inaction. Remember Marshall's prewar letter about Terry Allen and some other atypical officers: "There are very few of them, [who] are of that unusual type who enthuse all of their subordinates and carry through almost impossible tasks."

Marshall, alert to new technologies, would recognize that Information Age equipment can help the Army become more agile in personnel policy, such as by letting officers take leaves of absence from the service. Additional flexibility should be concentrated especially in the handling of leadership, regarding questions such as the duration of command tours. Successful senior commanders who have not burned out and wish to remain in place should be allowed to do so until good replacements become available. This would vastly increase the difficulty of managing general officers but would likely increase military effectiveness even more. And that goal, not predictability or making the manager's life easy, is the real task of military personnel management. "Too hard for the personnel guys" should not be the Army's default position.

The Army also needs to engage in an introspective study of its performance in the post-9/11 wars. It should examine the good and the bad at both tactical and strategic levels. It should ask whether leaders at each level were held accountable and, if not, why not. The fact that such a wide-ranging review, akin to the study on professionalism done in 1970 as the Vietnam War wound down, has not been conducted is not a good sign.

As part of any such review, personnel policy should be scrutinized, especially the policy of troop rotation. This is a difficult issue for which no good answers exist, and even Marshall might despair of solving it. Even so, the policy should be reviewed with an eye to better grasping the damage it does to American combat effectiveness—and especially to military leadership. The unit approach to rotation used in Iraq almost certainly was better than individual rotations, which in Vietnam were shown to be demoralizing and damaging to cohesion. Even so, the problems associated with unit rotation remain all but unexamined—and there are many, even if the Army does not wish to examine them. In Iraq, as each unit left, the successor unit tended to pronounce the situation a mess—and then announce twelve months later that it had solved the problem, only to have the next unit go through the same sequence. Also, Iraqis soon learned how to manipulate the rotation cycle. This was not just a matter of insurgents becoming increasingly sophisticated, and so having a better learning curve than the rotating Americans did, but also of local allies using the twelve-month horizon of American commanders to suit their own ends. An Iraqi general once related how it was easy to handle a new American commander working on a one-year timeline. First, he said, you would decline to meet with him, or simply not show up. Next you could have a series of sessions at which you resisted the changes he was recommending. In the third phase, you would begin to agree but argue over implementation. Finally, about eight months into the talks, you would slowly begin making his desired changes. By month ten, he noted, the American commander's focus would shift to his impending redeployment, and the pressure was off. And then, at month thirteen, the American commander's successor would sit down for a cup of tea, and the cycle would begin again. In order to deal with this problem, the Army and the Marine Corps should examine the possibility of keeping division and brigade commanders and staffs in place and rotating individual battalions and companies underneath them. Here again, such an approach would be difficult to manage and would introduce new problems, but it would likely be more effective in combat and other operations in the long term.

In another personnel matter, the military should recognize changes in the health of middle-aged officers and stop retiring them after twenty years of service. Senior sergeants, especially infantrymen, often do need to retire after twenty years in the field, but officers alternate tours in the field with desk jobs and therefore tend to suffer less damage to their knees and spines. Today, many forty-three-year-old lieutenant colonels who retire on the full pension to which they are entitled after twenty years of service look like relatively young men, not even middle-aged. They have many years of good service left in them, and many would be willing to provide it.

To implement such changes and make them work, the military would need a major shift in its attitudes, beginning at the top with the chairman of the Joint Chiefs of Staff, the Army chief of staff, and the rest of the Army's senior generals. Leadership should not be seen as a matter of officers taking turns or waiting in line, as sometimes seems to be the case in the Army. Leading soldiers is a privilege, not a right. Just as getting that position is earned, so should keeping it be. The other side of the coin is that, if failure is punished with relief, success can be rewarded with fast promotions. A colonel who has notably thrived in leading a brigade or regiment in combat should not be shuffled off to an obscure one-star apprenticeship in the backwaters of the Army but instead should be considered immediately for a top post in a division—as either its commander or its assistant commander. This notably was not the case in the first years of the Iraq war, when one's performance as a combat commander seemed to have little or no bearing on subsequent posts. Simply comparing the performances of different commanders was treated as an act of questionable taste.

In the same vein, how officers are prepared and selected should be examined. Are we picking determined, dedicated, flexible team players in the Marshall mold? If not, why not?

In an environment where success and failure actually are noticed and acted upon, it would be good to help more general officers succeed. To do this, commanders need to be educated less on what to think and more on how to think—and also on how to adapt. They need to learn how to learn. All too often, our generals think like jumped-up battalion commanders—that is, lieutenant colonels. "We don't educate [our officers] to be generals," a Special Operations colonel told researchers from the RAND Corporation a few years ago. This can be remedied, and should be, because critical thinking is an essential tool of top command. Some people have the ability instinctively, while others have cultivated it on their own by closely studying military and cultural history, but it also can be taught, especially by sending rising officers to pursue advanced degrees at elite civilian institutions, where many of their basic assumptions will be challenged. As an added benefit, many would learn to write clearly, a skill notably lacking in many American generals in this era of PowerPoint bullet-point briefings that lack verbs and causal thinking and all too often confuse a statement of goals with a strategy for actually achieving them. Along the same lines, parts of American military culture sometimes take a dim view of writing for professional journals. This should be changed, and can be, if credit is given by promotion boards for publishing notable and influential articles.

We also should consider new programs for generals, tailored to their needs. A one-year course of preparation might aid new brigadiers in their duties. Another possibility would be to send them to live overseas in third-world countries for a "sabbatical" year of broadening. These officers could study at a university, train with a foreign military, or even do Peace Corps–style work. While this would be difficult to fit into the current military career pattern, there is no good reason, in an era when senior officers tend to be far healthier than they were decades ago, to force people to retire after thirty or even thirty-five years of service.

Yet such unconventional career moves will have a long-term beneficial effect only if they are seen not as distractions but as stepping-stones to promotion and choice assignments. To improve the crop of officers contending to become generals, we also should make intermediate-level military education—the mid-career schooling given to majors and lieutenant commanders—more rigorous. Right now, some U.S. military staff colleges seem to operate as disguised yearlong bonding-and-relaxation sessions. One of them has become so lax and uncompetitive that rules were instituted to prevent more than half the students in certain courses from receiving A's, leading to jokes about "no major left behind." Selective entrance examinations, frequent paper-writing assignments, and reading loads equivalent to those at civilian graduate schools should be adopted, except when there is a clear and compelling reason not to do so. The taxpayer is entitled to nothing less, especially in an era of tightening defense budgets.

Again and again, Marshall likely would return to the theme that when choosing senior leaders, the needs of the nation should come before the needs of the individual or even the service. Do not just assign to a mission the next available officer of appropriate rank, as the Army seems so often to do. "It is depressing how so many of our senior officers and officials in Vietnam, especially at the middle levels, were picked on the basis of normal institutional criteria or even the convenience of the institution rather than because they were regarded as particularly qualified for the job," Robert Komer wrote in his clear-sighted autopsy of why the U.S. government failed in the Vietnam War. Similarly, in the summer of 2003, when the Army made Lt. Gen. Ricardo Sanchez the commander of U.S. military operations in Iraq, it did so essentially because he happened to be on hand. That is a negligent, even reckless way to handle the national interest. Marshall spent much of his energy studying the jobs he had to fill and picking the right people for them. He selected Eisenhower for supreme command in Europe not because he thought Ike was a fine fellow but because he believed Ike possessed the specific combination of ambition, steel, and cooperativeness that was needed for leading a coalition effort. Ike, in turn, kept Patton viable because he knew that at some point in the war the Americans would be chasing the Germans across northern Europe, and he calculated that Patton was temperamentally perfect for leading such a grand pursuit.

We also should reward commanders who cultivate and maintain cultures in which their subordinates feel free to exercise initiative and speak their minds freely. Gen. Petraeus was fond of quoting a sign put up by a company commander in western Baghdad: "In the absence of orders and guidance, figure out what they should have been and exercise vigorously."

As a fallback position, military leaders should at least consider ways to keep alive the careers of outliers and innovators such as David Petraeus and Paul Yingling. It is probably asking too much that such types, who make many officers uneasy, become generals during peacetime. But there should be ways to keep them in the military so that they can be called upon during a crisis. The thought was put best by Yingling: "Intellectuals are most valued when the dominant paradigm begins to break down. In this moment of crisis, the heretics become the heroes, as they have already constructed alternative paradigms that others haven't considered." So, he concluded, "in large organizations, the challenge is to keep the skeptics from becoming extinct."

It is easier to prescribe all these changes than to foresee how they might be implemented. We should not look to Congress for legislative remedies. There has been a steady decline in the number of members of Congress who understand the military, especially the intricacies of the internal workings of personnel policies. In 1969, there were 398 military veterans in the House and Senate; a decade later there were 298. At the beginning of the 112th Congress, in 2011, there were 118. Congress should be asked to do more, but realistically, the best that can be expected is that some of its members might support and protect efforts by civilians in the executive branch—or dissidents inside the military—to initiate needed reforms.

Any attempt to make such reforms likely will be attacked by the military bureaucracy. The Army's civilian overseers, both in the Pentagon and in the Congress, should be wary when the Army rejects suggested changes and defends current personnel policies on the grounds of "fairness." This tends, in reality, to be code for placing the interests of officers and the institutional Army above the interests of the rank-and-file or of the nation as a whole. The foremost example of an abusive policy being promulgated in the name of fairness was the six-month command tour in the Vietnam War, which spread the burden of combat among officers but without a doubt resulted in more soldiers being killed and the war being prosecuted less capably—and so did not serve the nation. If self-sacrifice is in fact an Army virtue, then the officer corps must sometimes practice it as a matter of policy. There is no clear way to formalize this warning, but one informal way is to keep in mind this question: *Fair to whom—the officer corps or the soldier and the nation?*

This leads to the final and most important step, which is to abide by the belief that the lives of soldiers are more important than the careers of officers—and that winning wars is more important than either. This is both fundamental and all that needs to be said to justify the previous steps. As Marshall understood during World War II, instilling that attitude is healthy for a military that protects a great democracy.

If the military declines to follow this course and fails to restore the traditions of accountability, then it seems likely that the current trend will continue: When generals don't fire generals, civilians will. Thus it is really not a question of *whether* to relieve generals but of *who* will relieve them. As unhappiness with the conduct of a war increases, pressure will build to get rid of someone. That is the message of the historical record of the past sixty years. Since the Army lost the tradition of relief in the Korean War, each conflict has instead been marked by the firing of top commanders by civilians: MacArthur in that war, Harkins and Westmoreland in Vietnam, Woerner before Panama, Dugan during the Gulf War, Wesley Clark after Kosovo, Casey in Iraq, McKiernan and McChrystal in Afghanistan. These ousters are necessarily clumsier and tardier than internal military moves would be, because they are less like routine maintenance and more like blowing the safety valve on a boiler. But, as with a boiler under pressure, even a late move generally is better than the alternative of doing nothing.

ACKNOWLEDGMENTS

This book was written at the Center for a New American Security, a small and collegial refuge in the middle of Washington, D.C. I am indebted to its recent leaders, Nate Fick, John Nagl, and Richard Fontaine, as well as its founders, Kurt Campbell and Michèle Flournoy. Other colleagues there have helped me with various aspects of this book, among them Kristin Lord, Shannon O'Reilly, Dana Stuster, Tiffany Sirc, David Barno, Andrew Exum, and Nora Bensahel. At a time when I felt I was at a dead end, Richard Danzig, a former secretary of the Navy and now the chairman of CNAS, wrote a particularly incisive critique of my second draft that helped me see the way forward. Robert Killebrew was in many ways the mentor for this book, beginning with his admonition several years ago that I should learn more about George Marshall. All were generous in sharing their thinking, but, in keeping with CNAS's policy of not taking corporate positions, none necessarily agree with the arguments made nor the conclusions reached in this book.

I am especially indebted to the squad of first-class researchers provided by CNAS: Michael Zubrow, Peter Henry, Kyle Flynn,

Matthew Irvine, Jessica Glover, Gregory McGowan, Brendon Mills, and J. Dana Stuster. Without their energetic and thoughtful help and their long hours in archives and libraries, this book would be less than it is and also would have taken years longer to produce. I did not realize as I began this project what a sprawling effort it would be. Their help was essential. Dana Stuster in particular did a wonderful job in the long and difficult task of assembling the photo insert.

I will forever appreciate the people who gave the first draft of this book a critical review: Vernon Loeb and Mary Kay Ricks worked mightily to help me restructure the first one hundred pages of the book. Rick Atkinson gave the chapters on World War II a good wire-brushing. Andrew Wylie, Tom Donnelly, Eliot Cohen, Roger Cirillo, Conrad Crane, Richard Kohn, John Cushman, Henry Gole, Volney Warner, Michael Bayer, T. X. Hammes, and David Fuhrman also brought their many areas of expertise and experience to a critical reading of the manuscript. Mark Stoler read the entire manuscript twice without even being asked to do so, making helpful comments both times. Robert Killebrew and Robert Goldich also deserve special notice for endurance as two-time reviewers of my drafts. I was especially impressed by the comments of two retired Army officers—Col. Stuart Herrington, who, by serving in the Army for thirty years, might have missed a great career as a book editor, and Lt. Gen. James Dubik, whose thirty-seven-page critique of the first draft spurred me to make major revisions in my manuscript and who then reviewed the second draft incisively.

I am deeply indebted to four military archives that welcomed me and even made suggestions for additional research. I remember particularly one day when an Army archivist said, while handing me the files of an obscure general, "If you're interested in this general, you also need to read the papers of Dandridge Malone—heard of him?" I spent several weeks working at the U.S. Army

Military History Institute, in Carlisle, Pennsylvania, and am grateful to Conrad Crane and his colleagues there—Richard Sommers, Robert Mages (formerly), Rich Baker, Rodney Foytik, Guy Nasuti, Gary Johnson, Terry Foster, Tom Buffenbarger, Steve Bye, Monica Duke, Shannon Schwaller, Carol Funck, and Martin Andresen. Erik Villard, at the U.S. Army Center of Military History, Fort McNair, Washington, D.C., was especially generous in sharing his research files with me. I also appreciate the assistance given me by Brian Shaw and his colleagues Paul Barron and Jeffrey Kozak at the George C. Marshall Research Library, in Lexington, Virginia. Mark Stoler went the extra mile in policing my work on Marshall. My thanks as well to the archivists and librarians of the Marine Corps University library, in Quantico, Virginia. Timothy Nenninger, chief of modern military records at the National Archives, pointed me to some particularly helpful files on the management of general officers in World War II.

Lt. Gen. John Cushman (U.S. Army, Ret.) not only served as a critical reader but also shared his privately published memoirs and a variety of documents. In addition, he showed a good deal of patience in dealing with my questions. Col. Henry Gole (U.S. Army, Ret.) was generous in helping me to understand William DePuy. Brig. Gen. John Johns (U.S. Army, Ret.) aided my research on the history of operational effectiveness in the Army and provided supporting documentation. Robert Goldich and Donald Vandergriff were repeatedly helpful in explaining the intricacies of personnel and promotion policies. I owe thanks also to Wade Markel of the RAND Corporation for generously sharing his insightful work on Army promotion policies and their relationship to risk averseness in the post–World War II officer corps— and thanks, too, to RAND's David Johnson for sending me to Markel.

I also appreciate the weekly encouragement given me by the Dow Road Choir.

In publishing this book, I feel I once again have the best team in the business: Scott Moyers, Andrew Wylie, and the wonderful gang at The Penguin Press—Ann Godoff, Elisabeth Calamari, Tracy Locke, and Mally Anderson.

And, as always, I am deeply grateful to my wife. Without her, this all would mean nothing.

The mistakes are of course my own.

NOTES

PROLOGUE: CAPTAIN WILLIAM DEPUY AND THE 90TH DIVISION IN NORMANDY, SUMMER 1944

1 **"We could locate no regimental or battalion headquarters":** J. Lawton Collins, *Lightning Joe* (Louisiana State University Press, 1979), 208–9.

1 **"Goddammit, General, you can't lead this division":** John Colby, *War from the Ground Up: The 90th Division in WWII* (Nortex, 1991), 29.

2 **"Orders may have been issued":** Lt. Col. Romie Brownlee and Lt. Col. William Mullen, *Changing an Army: An Oral History of General William E. DePuy, USA Retired* (U.S. Army Military History Institute, Carlisle Barracks, PA, 1985), 38. Hereafter: DePuy Oral History.

2 **Its battalion commander walked around:** Henry Gole, *General William E. DePuy: Preparing the Army for Modern War* (University Press of Kentucky, 2008), 35.

2 **Later that summer in Normandy:** Colby, *War from the Ground Up,* 149.

2 **In six weeks of small advances:** Martin Blumenson, *Breakout and Pursuit* (U.S. Army Center of Military History, 2005), 201.

2 **The average term of service:** William DePuy, "Battle Participation and Leadership," remarks to the TRADOC Commanders Conference, Fort Leavenworth, KS, March 1989; quoted in Paul Gorman, *The Secret of Future Victories* (U.S. Army Combat Studies Institute, Fort Leavenworth, KS, 1992).

2 **"a killing machine":** DePuy Oral History, 202.

2 **Gen. Collins wrote:** Harold Meyer, *Hanging Sam: A Military Biography of General Samuel T. Williams* (University of North Texas, 1990), 72. However, the official Army historian Martin Blumenson disagrees, concluding on page 76 of *Breakout and Pursuit* that during the course of the summer, the 90th "met enemy forces at least numerically equal in strength who occupied excellent defenses." For the 90th Division's combat performance in Normandy, see also Gordon Harrison, *Cross-Channel Attack* (U.S. Army Center of Military History, 1951), 400–405.

2 **"a horse's ass of the worst order":** Gole, *DePuy,* 306.

2 **"almost constantly made the wrong decisions":** John McManus, *The Americans at Normandy: The Summer of 1944—The American War from the Normandy Beaches to Falaise* (Forge, 2005), 98.

3 **he was placed under arrest:** Meyer, *Hanging Sam,* 77.

3 **His successor, Col. John Sheehy:** Maj. Charles Ronan, "The Operations of the 3rd Battalion, 357th Infantry (90th Infantry Division) in the Hedgerow Battle of Normandy, 8–11 June 1944" (U.S. Army Infantry School, Fort Benning, GA, 1948), 7.

3 **"had never before experienced":** Meyer, *Hanging Sam,* 81.

3 **judged to be wanting:** J. D. Morelock, *Generals of the Ardennes: American Leadership in the Battle of the Bulge* (National Defense University Press, 1994), 145.

3 **"I feel that a general officer":** Meyer, *Hanging Sam,* 91.

4 **the pop singer Eddie Fisher:** "Extra Added," *Billboard,* October 4, 1952, 20.

4 **In 1963, Ginder retired:** Wade Markel, "Winning Our Own Hearts and Minds: Promotion in Wartime," *Military Review,* November–December 2004, 27.

4 **"Hanging Sam Williams was the assistant division commander":** DePuy Oral History, 31.

5 **"You are fired":** Meyer, *Hanging Sam,* 162.

5 **Creighton Abrams, the future American commander:** Lewis Sorley, *Thunderbolt: From the Battle of the Bulge to Vietnam and Beyond: General Creighton Abrams and the Army of His Times* (Simon & Schuster, 1992), 131 and 136.

5 **giving him a list of sixteen field-grade officers:** Omar Bradley, *A Soldier's Story* (Modern Library, 1999), 298.

6 **During the war he was awarded:** Gole, *DePuy,* ix.

6 **"one of the most outstanding":** Bradley, *A Soldier's Story,* 297.

6 **"Because incompetent commanders were fired":** Henry Gole, "General William DePuy: His Relief of Subordinates in Combat," VMI Cold War essay contest, 2006–7, 20.

6 **"The brutality and stupidity":** DePuy Oral History, 38.

6 **"The Army owes him a great debt":** "Life and Career of General Donn A. Starry," interviews by Lt. Col. Matthias Spruill and Lt. Col. Edwin Vernon, February 15–18, 1986, in Lewis Sorley, ed., *Press On!: Selected Works of General Donn A. Starry,* vol. 2 (Combat Studies Institute, Fort Leavenworth, KS, 2009), 1163.

7 **At least five corps commanders:** Gary Wade, "World War II Division Commanders," Combat Studies Institute, Fort Leavenworth, KS, n.d., 2. Also, Robert Berlin, "U.S. Army World War II Corps Commanders: A Composite Biography," Combat Studies Institute, Fort Leavenworth, KS, 1989, 16. For a discussion of the relief of corps commanders in World War II, see Stephen Taaffe, *Marshall and His Generals: U.S. Army Commanders in World War II* (University Press of Kansas, 2011), 322.

7 **"the critical level of professional competence":** Henry Stimson and McGeorge Bundy, *On Active Service in Peace & War* (Harper & Brothers, 1948), 659.

8 **a private who lost his rifle:** Lt. Col. Paul Yingling, "A Failure of Generalship," *Armed Forces Journal,* May 2007, accessed online.

9 **"Personality plays a tremendous part":** Martin Blumenson, *The Patton Papers, 1940–1945* (Houghton Mifflin, 1974), 572.

12 **more Army troops have been sent:** This fact is mentioned in Leonard Wong, "Where Have All the Army Generals Gone?," Strategic Studies Institute, U.S. Army War College, November 15, 2011, accessed online.

PART I: WORLD WAR II

15 **"not even a third-rate military power":** *The War Reports of General of the Army George C. Marshall, General of the Army H. H. Arnold, Fleet Admiral Ernest J. King* (Lippincott, 1947), 290.

15 **Of the nine infantry divisions:** Russell Weigley, *History of the United States Army* (Indiana University Press, 1984), 419.

15 **By September 1944:** Richard Stewart, ed., *American Military History*, vol. 2, *The United States Army in a Global Era, 1917–2003* (U.S. Army Center of Military History, 2005), 123.

1. GENERAL GEORGE C. MARSHALL: THE LEADER

17 **Less than two weeks after the attack:** Gordon Prange, *At Dawn We Slept: The Untold Story of Pearl Harbor* (Penguin, 2001), 39–44.

17 **When Lt. Gen. George Kenney arrived:** Thomas Griffith Jr., *MacArthur's Airman: General George C. Kenney and the War in the Southwest Pacific* (University Press of Kansas, 1998), 50–56.

18 **One-third of the Navy's submarine captains:** Allan Millett and Peter Maslowski, *For the Common Defense: A Military History of the United States of America* (Free Press, 1984), 455.

18 **"I hate to think that fifty years":** Robert Sherwood, *Roosevelt and Hopkins: An Intimate History* (Harper, 1948), 770.

18 **this "coolly impersonal" man:** Albert Wedemeyer, *Wedemeyer Reports!* (Henry Holt, 1958), 212.

18 **"Things look very disturbing":** George C. Marshall to Mrs. George Patton, September 1, 1939, in Larry I. Bland, Sharon Ritenour Stevens, and Clarence E. Wunderlin Jr., eds., *The Papers of George Catlett Marshall*, electronic version based on *The Papers of George Catlett Marshall*, vol. 2, *"We Cannot Delay," July 1, 1939–December 6, 1941* (Johns Hopkins University Press, 1986), 47–48.

19 **"stubborn, pompous, occasionally ignorant":** Robert Payne, *The Marshall Story* (Prentice-Hall, 1951), 167.

19 **"Yes, but I would prefer to serve":** Forrest Pogue, *George C. Marshall*, vol. 1, *Education of a General, 1889–1939* (Viking Press, 1963), 138. Hereafter: Pogue, *Marshall*, vol. 1.

20 **"foreign leaders still considered":** Conrad Crane, "Beware of Boldness," *Parameters*, Summer 2006, 92.

20 **first large groups of draftees:** Weigley, *History of the United States Army*, 372.

20 **The initial American casualties:** Maurice Matloff, ed., *American Military History* (U.S. Army Center of Military History, 1985), 382.

20 **"He didn't give General Sibert a chance":** Larry Bland, Joellen Bland, and Sharon Ritenour Stevens, *George C. Marshall: Interviews and Reminiscences for Forrest C. Pogue* (George C. Marshall Foundation, 1991), 197. Hereafter: Bland, *Marshall Interviews*.

21 **Pershing's opinion of Sibert:** Donald Smythe, *Pershing: General of the Armies* (Indiana University Press, 1986), 55.

21 **By the end of the year:** "General Sibert, Pershing Aid, [*sic*] Relieved of Duty and Assigned to Command Department at Home," *New York Times*, January 3, 1918.

21 **"telling them they'd be 'relieved'":** Robert Bullard, *Personalities and Reminiscences of the War* (Doubleday, Page, 1925), 95.

21 **Pershing was "looking for results":** Edward Coffman, *The War to End All Wars: The American Military Experience in World War I* (Oxford, 1968), 142.

21 **Maj. Gen. Clarence Edwards:** Frank Palmer Sibley, *With the Yankee Division in France* (Little, Brown, 1919), 311. Also, Bullard, *Personalities,* 175, and Anne Cipriano Venzon, *The United States in the First World War: An Encyclopedia* (Routledge, 1995), 213–14.

22 **he survived the war:** James Cooke, *Pershing and His Generals: Command and Staff in the AEF* (Praeger, 1997), 67–68, 133.

22 **Pershing relieved at least six . . . American soldiers often pronounced:** Timothy Nenninger, "John J. Pershing and Relief for Cause in the American Expeditionary Forces, 1917–1918," *Army History,* Spring 2005, 22, 23.

22 **President Lincoln also relieved a series:** This sentence is more or less lifted from the writing of my friend Eliot Cohen on page 21 of his *Supreme Command: Soldiers, Statesman and Leadership in Wartime* (Free Press, 2002).

23 **"These changes weeded out":** Joseph Joffre, *The Personal Memoirs of Joffre,* vol. 1 (Harper, 1932), 276.

23 **Pershing kept an eye on Marshall:** Pogue, *Marshall,* vol. 1, 153.

23 **"the combat division":** George C. Marshall, *Memoirs of My Services in the World War, 1917–1918* (Houghton Mifflin, 1976), vii.

23 **That unit later became the 1st Infantry Division:** Mark Stoler, *George C. Marshall: Soldier-Statesman of the American Century* (Twayne, 1989), 39.

23 **"Colonel Marshall's greatest attribute":** Benjamin Caffey, "General George C. Marshall as a Staff Officer in WWI," in "Reminiscences About George C. Marshall," box 1, folder 23, George C. Marshall Research Library, Lexington, VA, 4. Note: In the library's files, Caffey's surname is misspelled as "Coffey."

23 **reputation as a "brilliant planner":** General James A. Van Fleet, interviews by Col. Bruce Williams, 1973, Van Fleet Papers, box 1, U.S. Army Military History Institute, Carlisle Barracks, PA (hereafter: USAMHI), 26.

24 **The Germans were resurgent:** John Keegan, *The First World War* (Vintage, 2000), 375.

24 **"The French and British had no reserves":** Marshall lecture on World War I, April 9, 1919, Marshall-Winn papers, box 2, World War I, Marshall Library, 2.

24 **"In the midst of a profound depression":** Marshall, *Memoirs,* 79. Marshall supposedly had asked that the manuscript of that memoir be burned but had lost track of a second copy, which was published after his death.

24 **maintained a "little black book":** Paul Barron, archivist, George C. Marshall Library, e-mail message to author, December 12, 2011. There was a moment in 2012 when it was thought that the famous notebook was among a newly found batch of Marshall papers. Marshall's 1929 appointment diary contained notations of "1," "2," and "3" after the names of officers, suggesting some kind of system for ranking them. Further investigation revealed that these actually were notes for dinner parties, with the figures in parentheses representing the number of guests each officer was expected to bring. Additional e-mail messages to author from Barron, May 7, 2012, and from his colleague Jeffrey Kozak, May 8, 2012.

25 **he listed the qualities of the successful leader:** George Marshall to Brig. Gen. John Mallory, November 5, 1920, Letter 1-176, in Larry I. Bland and Sharon Ritenour Stevens, eds., *The Papers of George Catlett Marshall,* vol. 1, *"The Soldierly Spirit," December 1880–June 1939* (Johns Hopkins University Press, 1981), 202–3. See also Marshall letter of March 15, 1944, in Larry I. Bland and Sharon Ritenour Stevens, eds., *The Papers of George Catlett Marshall,* vol. 4, *"Aggressive and Determined Leadership," June 1, 1933–December 31, 1944* (Johns Hopkins University Press, 1996), 345–46.

25 **a "policy of unpreparedness":** Bland, *Marshall Interviews,* 420.

25 **"optimistic and resourceful type":** Marshall, *Memoirs,* 172.

26 **units led by these "calamity howlers":** Marshall, *Memoirs,* 175.

26 **"You may not be in proper uniform":** Pogue, *Marshall,* vol. 1, 279.

26 **"You can sometimes win a great victory":** Bland, *Marshall Interviews,* 387.

26 **whom Marshall had studied "religiously":** Forrest Pogue, *George C. Marshall,* vol. 3, *Organizer of Victory, 1943–1945* (Viking, 1973), 257. Hereafter: Pogue, *Marshall,* vol. 3.

27 **"We cannot understand the difference":** Peter Schifferle, *America's School for War: Fort Leavenworth, Officer Education, and Victory in World War II* (University Press of Kansas, 2010), 195. I also have relied on Schifferle's discussion of the competence of senior American officers in World War II, on page 185.

27 **the Army Air Corps possessed:** Forrest Pogue, *George C. Marshall,* vol. 2, *Ordeal and Hope, 1939–1942* (Viking Press, 1966), 50. Hereafter: Pogue, *Marshall,* vol. 2.

28 **"the president gave me":** Bland, *Marshall Interviews,* 109.

28 **he pledged in a "fireside chat":** David Kennedy, *Freedom from Fear: The American People in Depression and War, 1929–1945* (Oxford, 1999), 396, 427.

29 **he promised not to send American boys:** Steven Gillon, *Pearl Harbor: FDR Leads the Nation into War* (Basic, 2011), 13.

29 **French troops were running from the battlefield:** William Shirer, *The Collapse of the Third Republic: An Inquiry into the Fall of France in 1940* (Simon & Schuster, 1969), 641ff.

29 **"was not desirous of seeing us":** Bland, *Marshall Interviews,* 329.

30 **Marshall's two civilian overseers:** John Nelsen, "General George C. Marshall: Strategic Leadership and the Challenges of Reconstituting the Army, 1939–41," Strategic Studies Institute, U.S. Army War College, 1993, 31.

30 **"Of course, General Marshall":** Bland, *Marshall Interviews,* 516.

30 **"If you don't do something":** Bland, *Marshall Interviews,* 306.

30 **"We are in a situation now":** Bland, *Marshall Interviews,* 517.

30 **"stood right up to the president":** John Morton Blum, *From the Morgenthau Diaries: Years of Urgency, 1938–1941* (Houghton Mifflin, 1965), 141.

31 **"I found informal conversation with the president":** Pogue, *Marshall,* vol. 1, 324.

32 **they discussed the future of the Army:** "Conversations Between General Matthew B. Ridgway, USA, Ret., and Colonel John Blair, USA, AWC 1971–72," box 89, Matthew Ridgway Papers, USAMHI, 13, 43.

32 **"He knew from his own experience":** Matthew Ridgway, "My Recollections of General of the Army George C. Marshall," October 3, 1980, in "Reminiscences about George C. Marshall," box 1, folder 24, Marshall Library, 6.

32   **"The present general officers"**: Eric Larrabee, *Commander in Chief: Franklin Delano Roosevelt, His Lieutenants, and Their War* (Harper & Row, 1987), 101.

33   **At Marshall's behest**: Mark Skinner Watson, *Chief of Staff: Prewar Plans and Preparations* (U.S. Army Center of Military History, 1950), 242–45.

33   **"I was accused right away"**: Bland, *Marshall Interviews*, 534.

33   **"I'm sorry, then you are relieved"**: Bland, *Marshall Interviews*, 306.

33   **While on the march in the Shenandoah**: Henry Kyd Douglas, *I Rode With Stonewall* (Fawcett, 1961), 78.

34   **"I am not going to leave him in command"**: Bland, *Marshall Interviews*, 456.

34   **"most of our senior officers"**: Watson, *Chief of Staff*, 247.

34   **"some officers . . . had of necessity"**: Dwight Eisenhower, *Crusade in Europe* (Da Capo, 1977), 13.

34   **Only eleven of the forty-two generals**: Morelock, *Generals of the Ardennes*, 90.

34   **"a whole group of people"**: Dwight D. Eisenhower, interview by Forrest Pogue, OH-10, Dwight D. Eisenhower Library, Abilene, KS, 21–22.

35   **"I was the youngest of the people"**: Eisenhower, interview by Pogue, Eisenhower Library, 22.

35   **He took over an Army of just**: *The War Reports of General of the Army George C. Marshall, General of the Army H. H. Arnold, Fleet Admiral Ernest J. King* (Lippincott, 1947), 16, 28, 65. Also, Weigley, *History of the United States Army*, 599.

35   **"I'm going to put these men"**: Larrabee, *Commander in Chief*, 101–2. My italics.

35   **At one point Marshall, irked by the erratic quality**: Bland, *Marshall Interviews*, 437–39.

35   **The unprecedented mobility that the Americans**: See Weigley, *History of the United States Army*, 477.

36   **"If there was a justification"**: Weigley, *History of the United States Army*, 479.

36   **"Was that a fact?" Marshall recalled asking**: Bland, *Marshall Interviews*, 534. The reluctant officer apparently was Maj. Gen. Robert H. Lewis: See "Marshall to Eisenhower," October 31, 1944, *The Papers of George Catlett Marshall*, vol. 4, 646, footnote 1.

36   **found Chaney "completely at a loss"**: Eisenhower, *Crusade*, 50.

36   **Chaney and his staff were working**: D. K. R. Crosswell, *Beetle: The Life of General Walter Bedell Smith* (The University Press of Kentucky, 2010), 260.

37   **"I deem it of urgent importance"**: Alfred Chandler, *The Papers of Dwight David Eisenhower*, vol. 1, *The War Years* (Johns Hopkins University Press, 1970), 338.

37   **Marshall declined to meet with him**: General Charles Bolte, interviews by Maclyn Burg, 1973–1975, Eisenhower Library, 62–63, 104.

37   **"Well, you better go along, too"**: Bolte, interviews by Burg, Eisenhower Library, 134.

38   **In August 1942, Buckner unaccountably chose**: Pogue, *Marshall*, vol. 3, 152.

38   **"fear . . . that his habit of talking"**: George C. Marshall to John Lejeune, November 24, 1931, Marshall-Winn Papers, box 3, folder 32, Marshall Library.

38   **the Navy sacked Theobald**: Thomas Buell, *Master of Sea Power: A Biography of Fleet Admiral Ernest J. King* (Little, Brown, 1980), 320. See also Richard Frank, "Picking Winners?," *Navy History*, June 2011, accessed online.

38   **"The interesting question"**: Wade Markel, "The Organization Man at War: Promotion Policies and Military Leadership, 1929–1992," unpublished paper, 2003, 125, xi.

38 **at the front line in June 1945:** Nicholas Evan Sarantakes, *Seven Stars: The Okinawa Battle Diaries of Simon Bolivar Buckner Jr. and Joseph Stilwell* (Texas A&M, 2004), 83.

39 **"A flexible system of personnel management" . . . "replaced by the capable":** First part of quote from Wade Markel, "Winning Our Own Hearts and Minds: Promotion in Wartime," *Military Review,* November–December 2004, 25. Second part is from Markel, "Organization Man at War," xi.

2. DWIGHT EISENHOWER: HOW THE MARSHALL SYSTEM WORKED

41 **"The chief says for you to hop a plane":** Eisenhower, interview by Pogue, June 28, 1962, OH-10, Eisenhower Library, xi.

41 **"Had Drum or another officer":** Crosswell, *Beetle,* 206.

42 **"I suppose it's too much to hope":** Blumenson, *The Patton Papers, 1940–1945,* 14.

42 **went out of his way to note:** Dwight Eisenhower, *At Ease: Stories I Tell to Friends* (Doubleday, 1967), 186.

42 **a friend asked him why:** Larrabee, *Commander in Chief,* 415.

42 **after an article by him appeared:** Robert Berlin, "Dwight David Eisenhower and the Duties of Generalship," *Military Review,* October 1990, 16.

43 **"Particularly, I was not to publish anything":** Eisenhower, *At Ease,* 173.

43 **"There's nothing so profound":** Bland, *Marshall Interviews,* 527.

43 **"was nervous as a girl":** "Interview with Frank McCarthy," January 7, 1981, Ed Cray Collection, box 1, Marshall Library, 27.

44 **"This message was a hard blow":** Eisenhower, *Crusade,* 14.

44 **He had missed the last passenger train:** This account is largely based on Eisenhower, *Crusade,* 14. Information about Richardson's role that weekend is from Mrs. Mamie Doud Eisenhower, interviews by Maclyn Burg and John Wichman, 1972, Eisenhower Library, 86, and also from Bryan Burrough, *The Big Rich: The Rise and Fall of the Greatest Texas Oil Fortunes* (Penguin, 2009), 144–45, 217. A slightly different account of Eisenhower's rail journey is given on page 146 of Geoffrey Perret, *Eisenhower* (Random House, 1999). Eisenhower confirmed Kittrell's role in a letter to Kittrell, in Eisenhower papers, Document 1191, December 7, 1954, "To William H. Kittrell," Series: EM, WHCF, President's Personal File 1301, *The Papers of Dwight David Eisenhower,* vol. 15, *The Presidency: The Middle Way, Part VI,* Eisenhower Library, online.

45 **He didn't know the Army chief well:** Eisenhower, *Crusade,* 16.

45 **Marshall clearly had heard good reports:** Eisenhower, interview by Pogue, OH-10, Eisenhower Library, 2.

45 **"I walked into his office":** Eisenhower, interview by Pogue, Eisenhower Library, 20.

45 **"I loved to do that kind of work":** Eisenhower, *At Ease,* 201.

46 **"The question before me":** Eisenhower, *Crusade,* 19.

46 **"I agree with you":** Eisenhower, *Crusade,* 22.

46 **In the early 1920s, the Navy's War Plan Orange:** Brian Linn, "*The American Way of War* Revisited," *Journal of Military History,* April 2002, 528. However, there may be an additional reason for Marshall's inquiry to Eisenhower: According to Henry Stimson, secretary of war at the time, in mid-1941, spurred by what Stimson called "the contagious optimism" of Douglas MacArthur, there was a spate of talk among military planners that the Philippine Islands might

indeed be defensible; see Stimson and Bundy, *On Active Service in Peace &
War,* 388.

46 **"we cannot, even as conditions are today":** Henry Gole, *The Road to Rainbow:
Army Planning for the Global War, 1934–1940* (Naval Institute Press, 2003), 97.

47 **The Navy's "Rainbow 5" global war plan:** Chief of Naval Operations, "Promul-
gation of Navy Basic War Plan–Rainbow No. 5 (WPL-46)," printed as Exhibit
No. 4, *Joint Committee on the Investigation of the Pearl Harbor Attack* (U.S. Government Printing Office, 1946), 965.

47 **MacArthur had put aside Ike:** Paul Rogers, *The Good Years: MacArthur and
Sutherland* (Praeger, 1990), 39–40. See also Matthew Holland, *Eisenhower
Between the Wars: The Making of a General and Statesman* (Praeger, 2001), 196, and
Carlo D'Este, *Eisenhower: A Soldier's Life* (Henry Holt, 2002), 248–49.

47 **"Eisenhower," Marshall said, "the department":** Dwight Eisenhower, "George
Catlett Marshall," *The Atlantic,* August 1964, accessed online.

48 **"the security of England":** Chandler, *Papers of Eisenhower,* vol. 1, *The War Years,*
205. See also Eisenhower memorandum to Marshall titled "Strategic Concep-
tions and their application to Southwest Pacific," February 28, 1942, record
group 165, box 43, book 4, National Archives, 1–2.

48 **In his memoirs, he recalled making the decision:** Eisenhower, *Crusade,* 30.

49 **he could envision "launching a decisive blow":** Joseph Hobbs, *Dear General:
Eisenhower's Wartime Letters to Marshall* (Johns Hopkins University Press,
1999), 54.

49 **"Some men reach the top" . . . "He is, in fact, a great democrat":** Maj. Gen.
Sir Francis de Guingand, *Generals at War* (Hodder and Stoughton, 1964),
192–93.

50 **"Here was somebody" . . . "most natable":** Maj. Gen. Sir Kenneth Strong, *Intelligence at the Top: The Recollections of an Intelligence Officer* (Cassell, 1968), 79, 113.

50 **minor aristocrats and country gentlemen:** In 1912, 9 percent of new British
officers "came from titled families and 32 percent from country landowning
families," observed John Lewis-Stempel in *Six Weeks: The Short and Gallant Life of
the British Officer in the First World War* (Orion, 2010), 59–60. Almost all the rest,
he added, were from the upper middle class. But by 1918, so many British officers had been killed that about 40 percent of officers came from "working and
lower middle class backgrounds" and so were given the status of "Temporary
Gentlemen."

50 **One officer who shot to prominence:** Clarence Huebner, "Leadership in World
War II," *Coast Artillery Journal,* November–December 1946, 42.

51 **"At any moment, it is possible":** David Eisenhower, *Eisenhower at War, 1943–
1945* (Random House, 1986), 63.

52 **"He was not one of those in whom":** Hobbs, *Dear General,* 51.

52 **"Patton I think comes closest to meeting":** Alfred Chandler Jr., *The Papers of
Dwight David Eisenhower,* vol. 2, *The War Years* (Johns Hopkins University Press,
1970), 824–25.

52 **On February 4, 1943, Eisenhower even recommended:** Hobbs, *Dear General,* 66.

52 **"Generals are expendable":** Chandler, *Papers of Eisenhower,* vol. 2, *The War
Years;* quoted in Rick Atkinson, *An Army at Dawn* (Henry Holt, 2002), 317.

52 **Two hundred Army engineers:** The number two hundred is from Gerald Astor, *Terrible Terry Allen* (Presidio, 2003), 148.

52 **"It was the only time":** Eisenhower, *Crusade*, 141.

53 **Ike was shaken by the lackadaisical attitude:** Eisenhower, *At Ease*, 262.

53 **the worst defeat of American ground forces:** For this judgment, see Peter Mansoor, *The GI Offensive in Europe: The Triumph of American Infantry Divisions, 1941–1945* (University Press of Kansas, 1999), 89.

53 **In about a week, Allied losses:** Antulio Echevarria, "American Operational Art, 1917–2008," in John Andreas Olsen and Martin Van Creveld, eds., *The Evolution of Operational Art: From Napoleon to the Present* (Oxford University Press, 2011), 147.

53 **"The proud and cocky Americans today":** Harry Butcher, *My Three Years with Eisenhower: The Personal Diary of Captain Harry C. Butcher, USNR, Naval Aide to General Eisenhower, 1942 to 1945* (Simon & Schuster, 1946), 268.

53 **One of the few bright spots at Kasserine:** Roger Spiller, ed., *American Military Leaders* (Praeger, 1989), 345.

53 **"Our people from the very highest":** Pogue, *Marshall*, vol. 3, 185.

53 **"bedraggled . . . tired . . . down":** Eisenhower, "Speech in New York, NY, December 3, 1946," in Rudolph Treuenfels, ed., *Eisenhower Speaks* (Farrar, Straus, 1948), 168.

53 **"the black reminders":** Eisenhower, *Crusade*, 96.

53 **he wrote to his old friend Leonard "Gee" Gerow:** D'Este, *Eisenhower*, 393.

54 **Ike's intelligence officer had to be British:** Hobbs, *Dear General*, 102–3.

54 **the American forces were "complete amateurs":** Nigel Hamilton, *Master of the Battlefield: Monty's War Years, 1942–1944* (McGraw-Hill, 1983), 206.

54 **"Believe me, the British have nothing to learn":** Kenneth Macksey, *The Tank Pioneers* (Jane's, 1981), 187; quoted in Douglas Delaney, "A Quiet Man of Influence: General Sir John Crocker," *Journal of the Society for Army Historical Research*, Autumn 2007, 196.

54 **"The s.o.b. publicly called our troops cowards":** Blumenson, *Patton Papers*, 222. In a sign of how pervasive cross-ally unhappiness could be in World War II, just over a year later, Canadian Gen. Harry Crerar tried in turn to fire Crocker. See John English, *Patton's Peers: The Forgotten Allied Field Commanders of the Western Front, 1944–45* (Stackpole, 2009), xxviii.

54 **"peculiar apathy":** Hobbs, *Dear General*, 67, 105.

54 **He already had received internal reports:** Crosswell, *Beetle*, 390.

54 **"My own real worry":** Hobbs, *Dear General*, 105.

55 **"to be cold-blooded about removal":** Butcher, *Three Years*, 273.

55 **"if I thought anyone was not making the grade":** Strong, *Intelligence at the Top*, 83.

55 **"Patton would parade around":** "General William C. Westmoreland, USA Retired," interview by Col. Duane Cameron and Lt. Col. Raymond Funderburk, 1978, William Westmoreland Papers, box 69, USAMHI, 94.

55 **"a Wild West cowboy":** James Polk, "Patton: 'You Might As Well Die a Hero,'" *Army Magazine*, December 1975, 42.

55 **"I think Fredendall is either a little nuts":** Blumenson, *Patton Papers*, 181.

55 **"Ward lacks force":** Blumenson, *Patton Papers*, 199.

56 **"the impression of a degree of pessimism"**: Russell A. Gugeler, *Major General Orlando Ward: Life of a Leader* (Red Anvil Press, 2007), 205.

56 **"In my opinion General Ward"**: Gugeler, *Ward*, 201.

56 **"the troops had to be picked up quickly"**: Eisenhower, *Crusade*, 150.

56 **Ward was permitted to see Marshall**: Bland, *Marshall Interviews*, 617.

56 **Ward was forgiven his indiscretion**: Maj. Gen. Orlando Ward, interview by Forrest Pogue, Denver, Colorado, May 5, 1957, 183N, Copy 2, Forrest C. Pogue Oral History Collection, George C. Marshall Research Library, Lexington, VA. Hereafter: Pogue Oral History Collection, Marshall Library.

56 **Ernest Harmon was instructed by Patton**: Ernest Harmon, *Combat Commander: Autobiography of a Soldier* (Prentice-Hall, 1970), 123.

57 **"Among all the figures of antiquity"**: Eisenhower, *At Ease*, 40.

57 **"Immediate and continuous loyalty"**: Eisenhower, *Crusade*, 158.

57 **"men who have measured up"**: *The War Reports*, 125.

58 **"if results obtained by the field commander"**: Eisenhower, *Crusade*, 369.

3. GEORGE PATTON: THE SPECIALIST

59 **"You have no balance at all"**: Bland, *Marshall Interviews*, 582.

59 **"strange, brilliant, moody"**: Harmon, *Combat Commander*, 69.

59 **Marshall concluded that Patton**: Bland, *Marshall Interviews*, 547.

59 **"General Patton has . . . approached"**: Hobbs, *Dear General*, 37.

60 **"The General immediately flared up"**: This and subsequent quotations from Blumenson, *Patton Papers*, 330–33.

61 **"not more than one in ten"**: Douglas MacArthur, *Reminiscences* (McGraw-Hill, 1964), 94.

61 **when he informed MacArthur**: D. Clayton James, "Eisenhower's Relationship with MacArthur in the 1930s: An Interview," August 29, 1967, OH-501, Eisenhower Library, 3. For a more sympathetic account of MacArthur's actions that day that also relies on Eisenhower but does not reflect Eisenhower's account that MacArthur said he did not want to see the orders, see Geoffrey Perret, *Old Soldiers Never Die: The Life of Douglas MacArthur* (Random House, 1996), 159.

62 **"George Patton continues to exhibit"**: Hobbs, *Dear General*, 121. See also Eisenhower to Marshall, August 24, 1943, in record group 185, box 44, document 116, National Archives.

62 **"respected their positions as fighting soldiers"**: Eisenhower, *Crusade*, 181. Eisenhower would later justify relieving another officer, Maj. Gen. Ernest Dawley, in precisely democratic terms: "Lives of thousands are involved—the question is not one of academic justice for the leader, it is that of concern for the many and the objective of victory"; Eisenhower, *Crusade*, 188.

62 **"the evident destiny of the British and Americans"**: Pogue, *Marshall*, vol. 3, 384.

62 **"apparently he is unable to use reasonably good sense"**: Pogue, *Marshall*, vol. 3, 385.

62 **"I am thoroughly weary of your failure"**: Pogue, *Marshall*, vol. 3, 385.

62 **"frankly I am exceedingly weary"**: Hobbs, *Dear General*, 160.

63 **"admittedly unbalanced but nevertheless aggressive"**: Pogue, *Marshall*, vol. 3, 385.

63 **"but he couldn't spare him":** "Reminiscences of James M. Gavin," interview by Ed Edwin, Columbia Center for Oral History, Columbia University, 1967, 7.

63 **When the war began, it had been Patton:** Eisenhower, *At Ease*, 237; Blumenson, *Patton Papers*, 15.

63 **"Hell, get on to yourself, Ike":** Blumenson, *Patton Papers*, 432.

63 **Patton also told Eisenhower:** Blumenson, *Patton Papers*, 55, 168.

63 **"He is the most modern general":** Blumenson, *Patton Papers*, 654. See also B. H. Liddell Hart, *The German Generals Talk* (Berkley, 1958), 215.

63 **"a master of fast" . . . "United States Army has known":** Eisenhower, *At Ease*, 172–73.

4. MARK CLARK: THE MAN IN THE MIDDLE

65 **"It makes my flesh creep" . . . "Clark is always in danger":** Blumenson, *Patton Papers*, 157, 361.

65 **the assault was a "near disaster":** General Mark W. Clark, *Calculated Risk* (Enigma, 2007), 152.

66 **"Mark, leave enough ammunition":** Frank James Price, *Troy H. Middleton: A Biography* (Louisiana State University Press, 1974), 169.

66 **British Gen. Harold Alexander:** Rick Atkinson, *The Day of Battle: The War in Sicily and Italy, 1943–1944* (Henry Holt, 2007), 231.

66 **But Clark needed to settle blame:** Clark, *Calculated Risk*, 164.

66 **"I do not want to interfere":** Brian Reid, "The Italian Campaign, 1943–45: A Reappraisal of Allied Generalship," *Journal of Strategic Studies* 13, no. 1 (1990), 140.

67 **"For God's sake, Mike":** Atkinson, *Day of Battle*, 234.

67 **"handled his job as well":** Fred Walker, *From Texas to Rome* (Taylor Publishing, 1969), 258. By 1944 Walker did not much like Clark, especially after Clark ordered him to fire his assistant division commander, Brig. Gen. William Wilbur, despite Wilbur having received a somewhat political Medal of Honor a year earlier. Walker wrote in his diary that Clark had said that "Wilbur was a bad influence in the Division." Walker disagreed: "Wilbur knows his business. Back at Salerno, Wilbur . . . was highly praised by Clark when he urged me to accept him as my Assistant Division Commander." See *From Texas to Rome*, 322.

67 **"It seems that when the going is really tough":** Hobbs, *Dear General*, 128. See also Eisenhower to Marshall, September 20, 1943, record group 165, box 44, folder 2, National Archives, 1.

67 **At first Marshall had some "misgivings":** Sidney T. Matthews, Howard Smyth, Maj. Roy Lemson, and Maj. David Hamilton, Office of the Chief of Military History, "Interview with General George C. Marshall, Part One," July 25, 1949, reel 322, Marshall Library, 8.

67 **"His concern for personal publicity":** General Lucian Truscott, March 21, 1959, Pogue Oral History Collection, Marshall Library, 6.

67 **"I have sometimes thought":** Lucian Truscott, *Command Missions: A Personal Story* (Dutton, 1954), 547.

67 **"I always had a feeling that":** Gavin to Ridgway, September 1, 1978, in Matthew Ridgway Papers, series 2, Correspondence 1960–1991, box 36, USAMHI.

67 **To his opponents:** Atkinson, *Day of Battle,* 223.

68 **"a sensitive and compassionate man":** Julian Thompson, "John Lucas and Anzio, 1944," in Brian Bond, ed., *Fallen Stars: Eleven Studies of Twentieth Century Military Disasters* (Brassey's, 1991), 189.

68 **"I felt like a lamb"** . . . **"certainly prolong the war":** Lucas typed diary, box 6, John P. Lucas Papers, USAMHI, 285, 295. See also Martin Blumenson, "General Lucas at Anzio," in Kent Roberts Greenfield, ed., *Command Decisions* (U.S. Army Center of Military History, 2000), 333.

69 **"The strain of a thing like this":** Lucas diary, 328. See also Thompson, "John Lucas and Anzio," 199.

69 **the "draining sore" of Gallipoli:** Eisenhower, *Crusade,* 264.

69 **"But in Italy the situation was quite the other way":** Sidney T. Matthews, Howard Smyth, Maj. Roy Lemson, and Maj. David Hamilton, Office of the Chief of Military History, "Interview with General George C. Marshall, Part II," July 25, 1949, reel 322, 2–3, Marshall Library.

69 **Confronted with the mess at Anzio:** This paraphrases pages 152–53 of Lloyd Clark, *Anzio: Italy and the Battle for Rome—1944* (Atlantic Monthly, 2006). See also Carlo D'Este, *Fatal Decision: Anzio and the Battle for Rome* (HarperCollins, 1991), 159.

69 **"That ended the matter":** Truscott, *Command Missions,* 314.

70 **"He arrives today with eight generals":** Lucas diary, 394.

70 **"In one paragraph the commander of VI Corps":** Lloyd Clark, *Anzio,* 198.

70 **"My own feeling was that Johnny Lucas":** Clark, *Calculated Risk,* 244.

70 **"was one of my saddest experiences":** Truscott, *Command Missions,* 328.

70 **"his removal was both necessary and timely":** Thompson, "John Lucas and Anzio," 206.

71 **"Unlike Lucas, who had not often ventured":** Martin Blumenson, *Anzio: The Gamble That Failed* (Cooper Square, 2001), 146.

71 **"He thinks he is God Almighty":** Atkinson, *Day of Battle,* 506.

72 **"Clark proved one of the more disappointing U.S. commanders":** Williamson Murray and Allan Millett, *A War to Be Won: Fighting the Second World War* (Belknap, 2000), 379.

5. "TERRIBLE TERRY" ALLEN: CONFLICT BETWEEN MARSHALL AND HIS PROTÉGÉS

73 **"Terrible Terry" Allen was as Old Army as they came:** A. J. Liebling, "Find 'Em, Fix 'Em, and Fight 'Em," part 1, *The New Yorker,* April 24, 1943, 23.

73 **In 1920, he represented the Army:** Astor, *Terrible Terry Allen,* 70–71. See also Atkinson, *Army at Dawn,* 81.

73 **Allen was in the same class:** Liebling, "Find 'Em," 25.

74 **he had made bathtub gin:** On the gin, see Carlo D'Este, *Patton: A Genius for War* (New York: HarperCollins, 1995), 291; on the polka, see John S. D. Eisenhower, *General Ike: A Personal Reminiscence* (Free Press, 2003), 39.

74 **Allen, who could become so staggeringly drunk:** Astor, *Terrible Terry Allen,* 276.

74 **"of that unusual type":** *The Papers of George Catlett Marshall,* vol. 2, 172.

74 **"Terry Allen, nobody wanted to give a star to":** "Telephone interview with H. Merrill Pasco, November 4, 1986," Ed Cray Collection, box 1, Marshall Library, 12.

74 **Lt. Col. Allen was being chewed out:** Thomas Dixon, "Terry Allen," *Army Magazine,* April 1978, 59.

74 **"I must explain to you":** *The Papers of George Catlett Marshall,* vol. 3, *"The Right Man for the Job," December 7, 1941–May 31, 1943* (Johns Hopkins University Press, 1991), 285. See also Astor, *Terrible Terry Allen,* 171.

75 **"It is the most honorable place":** A. J. Liebling, "Find 'Em, Fix 'Em, and Fight 'Em," part 2, *The New Yorker,* May 1, 1943, 30.

75 **Early on the morning of March 17, 1943:** Maj. R. J. Rogers, "A Study of the Leadership of the First Infantry Division During World War II: Terry de la Mesa Allen and Clarence Ralph Huebner" (quoting a 1964 interview of Allen by Capt. E. W. Martin), U.S. Army Command and General Staff College, 1965, 23–24.

75 **"I think the division has done fairly well today" . . . "motor trouble," he sneered:** Liebling, "Find 'Em," part 2, 28.

76 **Gen. Allen's finest day of the war:** Terry Allen, "A Summary of the Sicily Campaign, During World War II," n.d., Terry Allen Papers, box 6, USAMHI, 8.

77 **"I question whether any other U.S. division":** Bradley, *Soldier's Story,* 130. I generally have tried to avoid quoting Bradley's two memoirs in his book, because of questions about how much of them he actually wrote, especially the second one, *A General's Life,* which was published two years after his death. I made an exception here in part because the phrasing is consistent with other statements made by Bradley. Similarly, I have not relied on Stephen Ambrose's extensive writings about Eisenhower because of questions about the veracity of his work, including about quotations he attributed to the general. In my years of research for this book, I became familiar with both Eisenhower's written voice and his conversational one (in oral history interviews) and was struck that some of the phrases Ambrose attributes to him do not sound to me like Eisenhower. The historian Jean Edward Smith concludes in his new biography, *Eisenhower in War and Peace* (Random House, 2012), 730, that some of Ambrose's assertions about Eisenhower are not credible and simply were fabricated. For more, see especially Richard Rayner, "Channeling Ike," *The New Yorker,* April 26, 2010, and Russell Goldman, "Did Historian Stephen Ambrose Lie About Interviews with Dwight D. Eisenhower?," ABCNews.com, April 27, 2010.

77 **Westmoreland, whose artillery battalion was attached:** Westmoreland oral history with Cameron and Funderburk, Westmoreland Papers, USAMHI, 104.

77 **"the hardest battle":** Blumenson, *Patton Papers,* 304.

77 **toughest of the war to that point:** Atkinson, *Day of Battle,* 158.

77 **"they had been ordered to hold Troina":** Allen, "Summary of the Sicily Campaign," 13.

77 **Bradley removed Allen as commander:** Blumenson, *Patton Papers,* 301; see also Albert Garland and Howard Smyth, *Sicily and the Surrender of Italy* (U.S. Army Center of Military History, 1993), 56.

78 **"it was painful to see Terry break down":** Rogers, "Study of the Leadership," 49.

78 **He had been "shanghaied":** Astor, *Terrible Terry Allen,* 238.

78 **the puzzled notes Allen wrote in pencil to his wife:** Allen to his wife, August 5, 1943, Terry Allen Papers, correspondence, box 2, USAMHI.

78 **"inconsistent and confusing":** Maj. Richard Johnson, "Investigation into the Reliefs of Generals Orlando Ward and Terry Allen," School of Advanced Military Studies, Fort Leavenworth, 2009, 30.

78 **"Allen had become too much of an individualist":** Bradley, *Soldier's Story*, 155. For another analysis of Bradley's conflicting accounts, see Astor, *Terrible Terry Allen*, 222–24.

79 **"won the respect and admiration":** *The Papers of George Catlett Marshall*, vol. 4, 45.

79 **By the end of September:** On September 23, 1943, Maj. Gen. M. G. White wrote a note of response to Marshall about what division Allen might command; record group 165, entry 13, box 54, folder 210, file 311, National Archives.

79 **"Terry was nothing but a tramp":** General Wade Haislip, interview by Forrest Pogue, January 19, 1959, Pogue Oral History Collection, Marshall Library, 45. Note that transcript has a typographical error saying "have" when Haislip clearly meant "gave." J. Lawton Collins discusses the Allen situation in his own interview with Pogue, January 23, 1958, Pogue Oral History Collection, Marshall Library.

79 **Joe Collins, his corps commander:** "J. Lawton Collins, General, USA, Retired," interview by Lt. Col. Charles Sperow, 1972, Collins Papers, box 1, USAMHI, vol. 1, 242–43.

79 **Allen was especially impressive:** Collins, *Lightning Joe*, 274–77.

79 **"The whole artillery section functions beautifully":** Charles MacDonald, *The Siegfried Line Campaign* (U.S. Army Center of Military History, 1963), 621.

80 **"Misfits defeat the purpose of the command":** Eisenhower, *Crusade*, 75.

6. EISENHOWER MANAGES MONTGOMERY

81 **"Certainly I can say":** Bernard Law Montgomery, *The Memoirs of Field-Marshal the Viscount Montgomery of Alamein* (K.G. World, 1958), 17.

81 **"I know well that I am regarded":** Montgomery, *Memoirs*, 160.

82 **"not permit smoking in his office":** Clark, *Calculated Risk*, 18.

82 **Even after leaving the meeting:** Kay Summersby, *Past Forgetting* (Simon & Schuster, 1976), 28.

82 **"in their dealings with people":** Chester Wilmot, *The Struggle for Europe* (Harper, 1952), 427.

82 **"The characteristic American resentment":** Wilmot, *Struggle for Europe*, 463.

82 **"demanded a degree of patience":** Wilmot, *Struggle for Europe*, 596.

82 **Montgomery lost as many as four hundred tanks:** Jonathan Jordan, *Brothers, Rivals, Victors: Eisenhower, Patton, Bradley and the Partnership That Drove the Allied Conquest in Europe* (New American Library, 2011), 346.

83 **Marshall ordered Eisenhower to transfer:** Bland, *Marshall Interviews*, 540.

83 **On September 1, Eisenhower formally became:** Cornelius Ryan, *A Bridge Too Far* (Simon & Schuster, 1974), 64–65.

83 **"The British, who had uninterruptedly fought":** Norman Gelb, *Ike and Monty: Generals at War* (William Morrow, 1994), 338.

84 **Patton wanted 400,000 . . . German aviation fuel:** Robert Allen, *Lucky Forward: Patton's Third U.S. Army* (Manor, 1974), 103, 107.

84 **"Ike was very pontifical":** Blumenson, *Patton Papers*, 537.

85 **"Ike is drinking too much":** Blumenson, *Patton Papers*, 420.

85 **Eisenhower hobbled a mile:** This account is drawn mainly from Butcher, *Three Years*, 658–59, but also from D'Este, *Eisenhower*, 604–5. The quotation about "a

miserable walk" is from Eisenhower, *Crusade*, 305. The story of the engine malfunction is mainly from Laurence Hansen, *What It Was Like Flying for Ike* (Aero-Medical Consultants, 1983), 38–39. The information on Eisenhower's coffee consumption is from David Eisenhower, *Eisenhower at War*, 218. The description of his arrival at his villa that evening is from Summersby, *Past Forgetting*, 239.

85 **"arrogant, hawk-like loner"**: Russell Weigley, *Eisenhower's Lieutenants: The Campaign of France and Germany, 1944–1945* (Indiana University Press, 1990), 146.

85 **Eisenhower found Churchill's preference**: Eisenhower, *Crusade*, 211.

85 **"just at present" . . . "at lunch tomorrow"**: Montgomery, *Memoirs*, 244.

86 **he was mocked by some American officers**: Butcher, *Three Years*, 667.

86 **"I explained my situation fully"**: Montgomery, *Memoirs*, 246–47.

86 **"ignorance as to how to run a war"**: Alistair Horne with David Montgomery, *The Lonely Leader: Monty, 1944–1945* (Macmillan, 1994), 267.

86 **Montgomery opened the discussion**: The details in this paragraph rely mainly on the account given in Weigley, *Eisenhower's Lieutenants*, 279, but also in Wilmot, *Struggle for Europe*, 488–89; in Gelb, *Ike and Monty*, 360; and in D'Este, *Eisenhower*, 606.

87 **"Well, they're balls"**: Larrabee, *Commander in Chief*, 479. In a footnote, Larrabee stated that this was the first time this contemptuous remark had been published. His source was "Interview with Major General Sir Miles Graham," who was chief administrative officer to Montgomery and attended the meeting, with the interview conducted on January 19, 1949, and now located in the Wilmot Papers, Liddell Hart Centre for Military Archives, Kings College, London.

87 **"I not only approved Market Garden"**: David Eisenhower, *Eisenhower at War*, 465.

87 **"Almost every feature of Operation Market Garden"**: John Ellis, *Brute Force: Allies Strategy and Tactics in the Second World War* (Andre Deutsch, 1990), 414.

88 **It was indeed a powerful demonstration**: This paraphrases Ellis, *Brute Force*, 419.

88 **"got driven back and he was still talking"**: Dwight D. Eisenhower, interview by Forrest Pogue, Gettysbury, PA, June 28, 1962, Pogue Oral History Collection, Marshall Library, 11.

88 **Montgomery, for his part, muttered**: Terry Brighton, *Patton, Rommel, Montgomery: Masters of War* (Crown, 2009), 354. See also Montgomery, *Memoirs*, 298.

88 **"The American generals did not understand"**: Montgomery, *Memoirs*, 243.

88 **Montgomery had put him on notice**: Butcher, *Three Years*, 737.

89 **"The speed of our movements"**: Blumenson, *Patton Papers*, 607.

89 **"Joe, you can't supply a corps"**: Collins, *Lightning Joe*, 292.

89 **"One was that they were unteachable"**: Bernard Lewis, "Second Acts," *The Atlantic Monthly*, November 2007, 25. My italics.

90 **When British Gen. Harold Alexander made a crack**: Matthews, Smyth, et al., Marshall interview, 20.

90 **"What was astonishing was the speed"**: B. H. Liddell Hart, ed., *The Rommel Papers* (Easton Press, 1953), 521–23.

90 **"I don't think the British ever solved"**: Friedrich von Mellenthin, *Panzer Battles* (Ballantine, 1984), 179.

91 **In a series of battlefield studies**: Mansoor, *The GI Offensive in Europe*, 263.

91 **In a recent analysis, Meir Finkel:** Meir Finkel, *On Flexibility: Recovery from Technological and Doctrinal Surprise on the Battlefield* (Stanford University Press, 2011), 181–82.

91 **"really tired and worried":** De Guingand, *Generals at War,* 108.

91 **Early in 1944, Churchill had pledged:** Dwight Eisenhower, "Command in War," lecture, National War College, October 30, 1950, text on file at USAMHI, 9. Eisenhower recalled in that lecture that Churchill told him, "There is no possibility of any British commander staying with you if you will express . . . any dissatisfaction."

91 **"He is going to do what I order":** Eisenhower, interview by Pogue, June 28, 1962, Pogue Oral History Collection, Marshall Library, 11.

91 **"Since the Americans were the stronger":** De Guingand, *Generals at War,* 109.

92 **"It's on the cards":** De Guingand, *Generals at War,* 111.

92 **"the situation began to deteriorate":** Weigley, *Eisenhower's Lieutenants,* 565.

93 **"What I did not say":** Montgomery, *Memoirs,* 282.

93 **"I think probably the great generalship":** "Oral History of Bruce C. Clarke," interview by Jerry Hess, January 14, 1970, Harry S. Truman Library, 23.

93 **"most satisfying" . . . "let me completely free":** General Matthew Ridgway, interview by Forrest Pogue, February 26, 1959, Pogue Oral History Collection, Marshall Library, 28.

93 **However, Lt. Gen. William Simpson:** Forrest Pogue, notes from interview with Lt. Gen. William H. Simpson at Alamo National Bank, San Antonio, Texas, April 12, 1952, Pogue Oral History Collection, Marshall Library.

93 **"The incident caused me more distress":** Eisenhower, *Crusade,* 356.

93 **Even Simpson:** Weigley, *Eisenhower's Lieutenants,* 615.

94 **"overwhelming egotism":** Pogue, *Marshall,* vol. 3, 475.

94 **"his full dislike and antipathy":** Pogue, *Marshall,* vol. 3, 516.

94 **"unwilling to be a member of the team":** Pogue, *Marshall,* vol. 3, 517.

94 **"I was just not interested":** Ryan, *A Bridge Too Far,* 76.

94 **"Commanders and staff officers" . . . "then he must go":** Montgomery, *Memoirs,* 66–67, 79.

95 **"today, fifteen years ago":** Robert Ferrell, ed., *The Eisenhower Diaries* (W. W. Norton, 1981), 366.

7. DOUGLAS MACARTHUR: THE GENERAL AS PRESIDENTIAL ASPIRANT

97 **"MacArthur's sense of duty":** Berlin, "Duties of Generalship," 18.

97 **"General MacArthur kept General Marshall":** Transcript of Tape 25, Omar N. Bradley, interviews by Forrest Pogue, May 27, 1957, and July 19, 1957, Pogue Oral History Collection, Marshall Library.

97 **"Marshall is the exact antithesis" . . . "all the credit for himself":** General Matthew Ridgway, interview by John Toland, December 4, 1986, box 88, Matthew Ridgway Papers, USAMHI, 13.

97 **In August 1942, Marshall:** George Marshall to Douglas MacArthur, August 10, 1942, *The Papers of George Catlett Marshall,* vol. 3, 296–98.

98 **"a message was received from you":** Marshall to MacArthur, February 15, 1943, *The Papers of George Catlett Marshall,* vol. 3, 551–52.

98 **"as a matter of fact keeping his hand":** Pogue, *Marshall,* vol. 3, 405.

98 **"I heard both of them talk":** General A. C. Wedemeyer, Friends Advice, interview by Forrest Pogue, Boyds, Maryland, February 1, 1958, Pogue Oral History Collection, Marshall Library.

99 **"After our entry into the war":** Larrabee, *Commander in Chief,* 12.

99 **Marshall pushed to give him a Medal of Honor:** Eisenhower, interview by Pogue, June 28, 1962, Pogue Oral History Collection, Marshall Library, 4. For Eisenhower arguing against it, see James, "Eisenhower's Relationship with MacArthur," 6.

99 **"I wanted to do anything I could":** Bland, *Marshall Interviews,* 244. This was not the only time the nation's highest citation for valor was used during the war by the administration for political ends. In 1943, Brig. Gen. William Wilbur was given the medal for his efforts to arrange the Vichy French surrender in North Africa. "The President gave a Medal of Honor to General Wilbur, and that was ground out for the benefit of the American people," presidential aide Harry Hopkins dictated to a notetaker. Sherwood, *Roosevelt and Hopkins,* 687.

100 **"No other crew member":** H. R. McMaster, *Dereliction of Duty: Lyndon Johnson, Robert McNamara, the Joint Chiefs of Staff, and the Lies That Led to Vietnam* (HarperCollins, 1997), 51.

100 **"because he knew of a man":** Jay Luvaas, ed., *Dear Miss Em: General Eichelberger's War in the Pacific, 1942–1945* (Greenwood, 1972), 76. In James, "Eisenhower's Relationship with MacArthur," 6, Eisenhower confirmed that he had told Marshall he would refuse a Medal of Honor for the North African landings. Elliott Roosevelt, the president's son, wrote in his memoir *As He Saw It* (Duell, Sloan and Pearce, 1946), 145, that FDR told him, "At the same time MacArthur was given the Medal of Honor, it was offered to Ike, and he turned it down. Said it was given for valor, and he hadn't done anything valorous."

100 **during the war he had thwarted efforts:** John Shortal, *Forged by Fire: General Robert L. Eichelberger and the Pacific War* (University of South Carolina Press, 1987), 66. On July 30, 1942, Marshall sent a message to Douglas MacArthur recommending that Wainwright be "awarded" the Medal of Honor. The next day, MacArthur responded, stating that he was "nonconcurring." The recommendation was shelved with a note written on it by one of Marshall's aides, Maj. Gen. Joseph McNarney, stating, "Personally, I question Gen. MacArthur's motives. . . . I also question Gen. MacArthur's judgment where matters of personal prestige are concerned." Personal file on Gen. J. M. Wainwright, record group 165, entry 15, box 2, National Archives.

100 **MacArthur also turned down:** Taaffe, *Marshall and His Generals,* 170.

100 **"Eisenhower raised his officers' profiles":** Taaffe, *Marshall and His Generals,* 52.

100 **"one of the two most dangerous men"** . . . **"make them useful to us":** Rexford Tugwell, *The Democratic Roosevelt* (Doubleday, 1957), 349–50. Similar accounts are in Larrabee, *Commander in Chief,* 305; and T. Harry Williams, *Huey Long* (Knopf, 1969), 640.

101 **FDR was confronted by MacArthur:** MacArthur, *Reminiscences,* 101.

101 **"Most of the senior officers I had known":** Eisenhower, *At Ease,* 213.

102 **"The general has been following":** Ferrell, *Eisenhower Diaries,* "September 26, 1936," 21–22. See also Kerry Irish, "Dwight Eisenhower and Douglas MacArthur

in the Philippines: There Must Be a Day of Reckoning," *Journal of Military History*, April 2010, 454.

102 **Eisenhower turned down a similar gift:** Larrabee, *Commander in Chief*, 315. See also Ferrell, *Eisenhower Diaries*, 63; and Carol Petillo, *Douglas MacArthur: The Philippine Years* (Indiana University Press, 1981), 211–13.

102 **"pompous and rather ridiculous" . . . "virtually nonexisting":** James, "Eisenhower's Relationship with MacArthur," 2.

103 **"What he had to say":** Eisenhower, interview by Pogue, June 28, 1962, Pogue Oral History Collection, Marshall Library, 3.

103 **"My Chief talked of the Republican nomination":** Luvaas, *Dear Miss Em*, 71.

103 **Vandenberg, an influential Republican:** D. Clayton James, *The Years of MacArthur*, vol. 2, *1941–45* (Houghton Mifflin, 1975), 410. See also Michael Schaller, *Douglas MacArthur: The Far Eastern General* (Oxford University Press, 1989), chapter 6.

103 **"I am certain that" . . . "our next president":** *Time*, April 24, 1944; quoted in Pogue, *Marshall*, vol. 3, 445.

103 **MacArthur had responded:** Pogue, *Marshall*, vol. 3, 445.

104 **At the Republican National Convention:** James, *Years of MacArthur*, vol. 2, 440.

104 **"I dare to say that the American people":** Courtney Whitney, *MacArthur: His Rendezvous with History* (Knopf, 1956), 125.

104 **"General Eisenhower broke off his recital":** Joseph Alsop, *I've Seen the Best of It* (W. W. Norton, 1992), 338. See also James, "Eisenhower's Relationship with MacArthur," 4.

104 **"accepting any public duty":** Charles Willoughby and John Chamberlain, *MacArthur 1941–1951* (McGraw-Hill, 1954), 519.

8. WILLIAM SIMPSON: THE MARSHALL SYSTEM AND THE NEW MODEL AMERICAN GENERAL

106 **"in battles of this kind":** Eisenhower, *Crusade*, 354.

107 **"Well, I think from what we have here":** General William H. Simpson, interview by Maclyn Burg, March 15, 1972, Eisenhower Library, 90.

107 **"Simpson actually got more Ninth Army units":** Morelock, *Generals of the Ardennes*, 206.

107 **"Simpson was smart, adaptive, and aggressive":** MacDonald, *Siegfried Line Campaign*, 379.

107 **"Simpson, though little known":** Harmon, *Combat Commander*, 211–12, 216.

107 **"Even-tempered and composed":** Thomas Stone, "General William Hood Simpson: Unsung Commander of the U.S. Ninth Army," *Parameters* 11, no. 2 (1981), 44–45, 48.

108 **"Simpson could think ahead":** General Jacob Devers, interview by Maclyn Burg, August 19, 1974, Eisenhower Library, 43.

108 **"Our chins are up":** Butcher, *Three Years*, 737.

108 **"a very pompous guy" who was overly cautious:** Simpson oral history, Eisenhower Library, 72, 94–95.

109 **"If Simpson ever made a mistake":** Eisenhower, *Crusade*, 376.

109 **"uncommonly normal":** Bradley, *Soldier's Story*, 422.

109 **"the most forgotten American field army commander"**: English, *Patton's Peers,* 250.

109 **"had to get results"**: Gavin, interview by Edwin, Columbia Center for Oral History, 23.

109 **"that he did not feel well"** . . . **"in charge of the battalion"**: Gavin, *On to Berlin,* 128.

110 **"Summarily relieving those who"**: Gavin, *On to Berlin,* 259.

110 **"unwarranted if not altogether unjustified"**: Martin Blumenson, "Relieved of Command," *Army Magazine,* August 1971, 36–37.

111 **"a typical infantryman's operation"**: Harmon, *Combat Commander,* 208.

111 **Some 59 percent**: Edward Meyer and R. Manning Ancell with Jane Mahaffey, *Who Will Lead?: Senior Leadership in the United States Army* (Praeger, 1995), 223.

111 **"in contrast to the Eastern theater"**: Ellis, *Brute Force,* 380–81.

111 **"The mission of this Allied Force"**: Berlin, "Duties of Generalship," 24.

112 **"a New Deal war"**: Larrabee, *Commander in Chief,* 3.

112 **"The only basis upon which"** . . . **"are of minor importance"**: *Marshall Papers,* vol. 3, 594–95.

113 **"In all these matters"**: *The War Reports,* 33.

113 **"democratic theory"**: *The War Reports,* 125.

113 **Two-thirds of the Army's combat officers**: Of the 872,000 men who became commissioned officers between Pearl Harbor and the end of the war, some 72,000 were doctors and chaplains. "Of the remaining 800,000, some 531,000, or 66.37 percent, were commissioned after serving as enlisted men in this war," noted Lt. Gen. Clarence Huebner, who, before becoming an officer, had himself served in the enlisted ranks for seven years, including time as a mess sergeant. Huebner, "Leadership in World War II," 42.

113 **"never was the strength"**: *The War Reports,* 143.

113 **"Those of us who had spent"** . . . **"to be so as well"**: Paul Nitze, "Recollections of George C. Marshall," June 23, 1987, in "Reminiscences About George C. Marshall," box 1, folder 25, Marshall Library, 3.

114 **"They were embittered"**: Bland, *Marshall Interviews,* 536–37.

114 **"you must remember that man"**: Frank Hayne to Edgar Puryear, March 7, 1963, in "Reminiscences About George C. Marshall," Marshall Library, 3.

114 **When Middleton's commander, George Patton**: Price, *Troy H. Middleton,* 160.

115 **Early in 1963, he was slightly wounded**: Eric Pace, "Edwin Walker, Controversial General, Dies at 83," *New York Times,* November 2, 1993.

116 **a reputation for "irritable suspiciousness"**: Russell Weigley, *Eisenhower's Lieutenants: The Campaign of France and Germany 1944–1945* (Indiana University Press, 1990), 131.

116 **"merely competent"**: Weigley, *Eisenhower's Lieutenants,* 216.

116 **"forward observers would bring down"**: Weigley, *Eisenhower's Lieutenants,* 360.

117 **Despite his advantages**: This sentence summarizes Weigley, *Eisenhower's Lieutenants,* 356.

117 **"a disturbing number of botched battles"**: Daniel Bolger, "Zero Defects," *Military Review,* May 1991, 62.

117 **"I wish he had a little daring"**: Blumenson, *Patton Papers,* 566.

118 **"unimaginative caution":** Weigley, *Eisenhower's Lieutenants,* 729.

118 **"is essentially bland and plodding":** Martin Blumenson, "America's World War II Leaders in Europe: Some Thoughts," *Parameters,* December 1989, 3.

118 **"at considerably less cost":** Gavin, interview by Edwin, Columbia Center for Oral History, 9.

118 **"one avoids losing":** Bolger, "Zero Defects," 62.

PART II: THE KOREAN WAR

119 **It had 555,000 soldiers:** Weigley, *History of the United States Army,* 501.

119 **About half of its soldiers:** Stewart, *American Military History,* vol. 2, 204.

9. WILLIAM DEAN AND DOUGLAS MACARTHUR: TWO GENERALS SELF-DESTRUCT

122 **"not prepared mentally, physically":** Clay Blair, *The Forgotten War: America in Korea, 1950–1953* (Times Books, 1987), xi.

122 **The first American in Japan:** Alexander Haig Jr., *Inner Circles: How America Changed the World* (Warner, 1992), 19. Over the next three decades, Haig would continue to display a knack for showing up in the middle of interesting situations, from the wars in Korea and Vietnam to the White House staff during the Watergate crisis and then again during the hectic aftermath of the near assassination of Ronald Reagan in 1981.

123 **"one man who could read my thoughts":** William Dean with William Worden, *General Dean's Story* (Viking, 1954), 25.

123 **"You have to remember":** Dean, *General Dean's Story,* 145.

123 **"I didn't see any generals":** Lewis Sorley, *Honorable Warrior: General Harold K. Johnson and the Ethics of Command* (University Press of Kansas, 1998), 97.

124 **"There were heroes in Korea":** Dean, *General Dean's Story,* 3.

124 **"I didn't recognize him":** Lieutenant General Henry E. Emerson, interview by Lt. Col. Jonathan Jackson, Senior Officer Oral History Program, December 17 and 23, 2003, USAMHI, 21–22.

125 **"Unknown to either Harriman or Ridgway":** Blair, *Forgotten War,* 187.

125 **MacArthur wondered aloud:** Blair, *Forgotten War,* 287.

125 **Consider the case of Lt. Col. Melvin Blair:** Blair, *Forgotten War,* 474–76. See also William Bowers, William Hammond, and George MacGarrigle, *Black Soldier, White Army: The 24th Infantry Regiment in Korea* (U.S. Army Center of Military History, 1996), 176ff. Also see chronology of Bing Crosby's life at Bing Magazine.co.uk.

125 **Vain and mendacious, MacArthur was always:** James Schnabel, *United States Army in the Korean War: Policy and Direction, The First Year* (Office of the Chief of Military History, U.S. Army, 1972), 77, footnote 51; 218.

126 **resulting in the loss of almost all:** Murray and Millett, *A War to Be Won,* 182.

126 **"General, you don't have a staff":** Dean Acheson, *Present at the Creation: My Years in the State Department* (Norton, 1969), 424.

127 **The Chinese force, for example, had few trucks:** F. M. Berger et al., *Combat Studies Institute Battle Book: Chosin Reservoir* (Combat Studies Institute, Fort Leavenworth, KS, 1983), 13.

127 **he had a "far better feel":** Collins, interview by Sperow, USAMHI, vol. 2, 332.

127 **Perhaps most damaging of all:** Larrabee, *Commander in Chief,* 333.

127 **He encouraged sycophantism:** Blair, *Forgotten War,* 434, and Allan Millett, *The War for Korea, 1950–1951: They Came From the North* (University Press of Kansas, 2010), 316.

128 **When questioned by the White House:** MacArthur, *Reminiscences,* 342.

128 **"The result was a reaction":** Blair, *Forgotten War,* 234.

128 **When MacArthur greeted Truman:** Joseph Goulden, *Korea: The Untold Story of the War* (McGraw-Hill, 1983), 265.

129 **"Listen, you know I'm president":** "Oral History Interview with Frank M. Boring," September 21, 1988, Harry S. Truman Library and Museum, Independence, MO, 25. Two weeks after the Wake Island session, Boring would be one of the agents who fired his weapon in defense of Truman during an assassination attempt by Puerto Rican nationalists. The incident, which occurred outside Blair House—where the president was living while the White House, just across the street, was being refurbished—left a police officer dead, along with one of the assailants. Neither Truman nor Boring was harmed.

129 **"I believe that formal resistance":** This and subsequent quotations from the Wake Island conference are from "Substance of Statements Made at Wake Island Conference on 15 October 1950, Top Secret, Compiled by General of the Army Omar N. Bradley, Chairman of the Joint Chiefs of Staff, From Notes Kept by the Conferees from Washington," in *Foreign Relations of the United States* [*FRUS*], *1950,* vol. 7, *Korea* (U.S. Government Printing Office, 1976), 948–60. Hereafter: *FRUS 1950,* vol. 7.

129 **the CIA had just issued an analysis:** For an illuminating discussion of how American officials were fooled by Chinese efforts to cloak their movement of troops into Korea, see Patrick Roe, *The Dragon Strikes: China and the Korean War: June–December 1950* (Presidio, 2000), 404–7.

129 **MacArthur later would bitterly deny:** "Texts of Accounts by Lucas and Considine on Interviews with MacArthur in 1954," *New York Times,* April 9, 1964, 16. In one of those birthday interviews, MacArthur would call President Eisenhower "a naïve and honest man," while in the other he denounced him as "once a man of integrity."

130 **in a 1961 interview:** Douglas MacArthur, interview by Forrest Pogue, January 3, 1961, Tape 75, Pogue Oral History Collection, Marshall Library. The "transcript" is actually Pogue's thorough notes; the interview with MacArthur was not recorded.

130 **"seemed to take great pride" . . . "he knew little":** MacArthur, *Reminiscences,* 361.

130 **"a curious, and sinister, change":** MacArthur, *Reminiscences,* 363.

130 **But with MacArthur, it was too late:** I am indebted to Lt. Gen. (Ret.) James Dubik, one of the critical readers of an early draft of this book, for this observation, and for related ones about the strained civil-military discourse during the wars in Vietnam and Iraq. See also James Dubik, "Prudence, War and Civil-Military Relations," *Army Magazine,* September 2010.

130 **"the war is very definitely":** Schnabel, *The First Year,* 216.

130 **We now know that by this point, Peng Dehuai:** Peng Dehuai, *Memoirs of a Chinese Marshal: The Autobiographical Notes of Peng Dehuai* (Foreign Languages Press, 1984), 474.

131 **"if successful, . . . for all practical purposes":** Lynn Montross and Nicholas Canzona, *U.S. Marine Operations in Korea, 1950–53*, vol. 3, *The Chosin Reservoir Campaign* (U.S. Marine Corps, 1957), 144.

131 **a sizable "reconnaissance in force":** For an example of the "reconnaissance in force" argument, see Willoughby and Chamberlain, *MacArthur 1941–1951*, 388. For a discussion of the Joint Chiefs' directive, see Schnabel, *The First Year*, 218.

131 **"the final destruction":** Schnabel, *The First Year*, 282.

132 **"For the first time in military history":** Blair, *Forgotten War*, 394.

132 **"any program short of this":** "The Commander in Chief, Far East [MacArthur] to the Joint Chiefs of Staff, Top Secret / Emergency, Tokyo, November 9, 1950," *FRUS 1950*, vol. 7, 1108.

132 **"immoral . . . proposition" . . . "in recent times":** *FRUS 1950*, vol. 7, 1109.

132 **addressed him as "son":** "Oral Reminiscences of General Oliver P. Smith, USMC," interviews by D. Clayton James, August 25, 1971, U.S. Marine Corps University Library Archives, Quantico, VA, 200.

132 **"the worst working relationship":** Shelby Stanton, *America's Tenth Legion: X Corps in Korea, 1950* (Presidio, 1989), 52.

132 **"the disposition of those troops":** Schnabel, *The First Year*, 278.

133 **"absolute falsehood":** Ridgway, interviews by John Blair, USAMHI, 74.

133 **"the Eighth Army":** Schnabel, *The First Year*, 278.

133 **"I don't have pneumonia" . . . "You tell General Walker":** S. L. A. Marshall, *Bringing Up the Rear* (Presidio, 1979), 181–83.

134 **"I can only brace myself":** Marshall, *Bringing Up the Rear*, 188.

134 **One of his first orders:** Julian Burns Jr., "The Education of Matthew Ridgway in Generalship," U.S. Army War College, 1989, 31.

10. ARMY GENERALS FAIL AT CHOSIN

135 **The Marines were on the west:** S. L. A. Marshall, "A Study Based on the Operations of the 1st Marine Division in the Koto-ri, Hagaru-ri, Yudamn-ni Area, 20 November–10 December 1950," 23; part 2 of "CCF in the Attack," staff memorandum, January 27, 1951, on file at USAMHI. Also reprinted as an appendix to William Hopkins, *One Bugle No Drums: The Marines at Chosin Reservoir* (Avon, 1988).

135 **Col. Gregon Williams:** "Oral Reminiscences of General Oliver P. Smith," 254.

135 **"I can still see the icicles":** Martin Russ, *Breakout: The Chosin Reservoir Campaign, Korea 1950* (Fromm, 1999), 321.

135 **one peculiarity of Chosin:** Goulden, *Korea*, 365.

135 **The cold was a lethal curse:** Charles Holloway Jr., *Escape from Hell: A Navy Surgeon Remembers Pusan, Inchon, and Chosin,* unpublished manuscript on file at Learning Resource Center, Uniformed Services University of the Health Sciences, Bethesda, MD, 95–96, 102.

136 **"I was in the Bulge":** Roy Appleman, *East of Chosin: Entrapment and Breakout in Korea, 1950* (Texas A&M, 1987), 328–29.

136 **When Lt. Col. Don Faith Jr.'s 1st Battalion:** Appleman, *East of Chosin,* 31.

138 **"Now, look, don't go out on a limb":** "Oral Reminiscences of General Oliver P. Smith," 219.

138 **Brig. Gen. "Hammerin' Hank" Hodes:** Paul Berquist, "Organizational Leadership in Crisis: The 31st Regimental Combat Team at Chosin Reservoir, Korea, 24 November–2 December 1950," U.S. Army Command and General Staff College, Fort Leavenworth, KS, 2007, 34–35.

138 **he had set the stage for a defeat:** In his own history of the Korean War, Gen. Ridgway twice compares MacArthur's handling of Chosin to Custer's Last Stand. Matthew Ridgway, *The Korean War* (Da Capo, 1967), 63, 76.

138 **The 31st was commanded:** Blair, *Forgotten War,* 389; Edwin Simmons, *Frozen Chosin: U.S. Marines at the Changjin Reservoir* (U.S. Marine Corps Historical Center, 2002), 49.

138 **"The sum total of the 1/32 IN":** Berquist, "Organizational Leadership in Crisis," 19.

139 **The first ominous sign:** Russ, *Breakout,* 106.

139 **"were going to take back" . . . "couldn't take it from us":** "Interview with Captain Edward P. Stamford, Former Air Controller (ANGLICO Team) Attached to 1st Battalion, 32nd Infantry Regiment, 7th Infantry Division, USA," March 16, 1951, Historical Division, Headquarters, U.S. Marine Corps, 71.

139 **"I already know all this" . . . "Chinamen in those mountains":** Russ, *Breakout,* 108.

139 **"the G-2 of 1st Marine Division":** Edward Almond, "Reflections on the Hungnam Evacuation, Korea, December 1950," Edward Almond Papers, box 70, USAMHI, 108.

139 **the record is clear that the Marines:** Marshall, "CCF in the Attack, Part II," staff memorandum, January 27, 1951, on file at USAMHI.

140 **"Those aren't Chinese soldiers" . . . "That's a Marine lie":** "Oral Reminiscences of General Oliver P. Smith," 3.

140 **By 1951, Willoughby had served MacArthur:** James, *Years of MacArthur,* vol. 2, 80.

140 **He persisted in this even after Omar Bradley:** Omar Bradley to Charles Willoughby, May 21, 1948, Charles Willoughby Papers, box 6, Gettysburg College, Gettysburg, PA.

140 **The same year, Robert McCormick:** McCormick to Willoughby, July 30, 1948, Willoughby Papers, box 8, Gettysburg College.

140 **"to congratulate you and the able GOP" . . . "Far Eastern policy":** Willoughby to Brewster, November 21, 1950, Willoughby Papers, box 6, Gettysburg College.

140 **"a lone voice":** Willoughby to McCarthy, January 28, 1951, Willoughby Papers, box 8, Gettysburg College.

141 **"to the second greatest military genius":** Willoughby to Francisco del Castillo, Spanish ambassador to Japan, March 9, 1951, Willoughby Papers, box 6, Gettysburg College.

141 **"my pet fascist":** Andrew Gordon, *A Modern History of Japan: From Tokugawa Times to the Present* (Oxford, 2009), 237.

141 **"One minute we were planning":** Appleman, *East of Chosin,* 71.

141   **In the middle of the night:** "Interview with Captain Edward P. Stamford," 74.

141   **"We're still attacking":** "Chosin Reservoir," chap. 6 in Russell Gugeler, ed., *Combat Actions in Korea,* rev. ed. (U.S. Army, 1970).

142   **"there weren't two Chinese divisions":** Berquist, "Organizational Leadership in Crisis," 46.

142   **The only opposition Faith was facing:** Appleman, *East of Chosin,* 71.

142   **Almond also told Faith:** Almond to Appleman, May 22, 1978, "Military Correspondence, 1960–1977," Edward Almond Papers, box 129, USAMHI.

142   **"After the helicopter carrying General Almond":** Donald Knox, *The Korean War, Pusan to Chosin: An Oral History* (Harcourt Brace Jovanovich, 1985), 549.

142   **"While geographically his elements":** "The Commander in Chief, United Nations Command (MacArthur) to the Joint Chiefs of Staff, Top Secret/Flash, Tokyo, 30 November 1950," *FRUS 1950,* vol. 7, 1260.

143   **"The situation was much more serious":** Maj. Gen. David Barr, lecture at Army War College, February 21, 1951, in "Lectures, AY 1950–51," USAMHI.

143   **"that MG Barr did not coordinate":** Berquist, "Organizational Leadership in Crisis," 70.

143   **"Nothing was working out":** Knox, *The Korean War,* 551.

144   **"They had been fighting":** Berquist, "Organizational Leadership in Crisis," 66.

144   **The dead performed a final posthumous service:** Appleman, *East of Chosin,* 194.

144   **"We had proceeded only a short way":** Appleman, *East of Chosin,* 208.

144   **"Looking back up I could see":** Appleman, *East of Chosin,* 212.

145   **"It was terrible":** Knox, *The Korean War,* 552.

146   **"by yelling, shouting":** Appleman, *East of Chosin,* 253.

146   **"It was a sad and outrageous":** Russ, *Breakout,* 279. Faith's killing of the South Korean soldiers is also discussed in Appleman, *East of Chosin,* 379.

146   **"After Colonel Faith was killed":** Knox, *The Korean War,* 553.

147   **"Wounded men inside were spilled":** Chap. 6 in Gugeler, *Combat Actions in Korea,* accessed online.

147   **That was the end of the convoy:** Appleman, *East of Chosin,* 274.

147   **A Marine pilot who flew low:** Stanton, *America's Tenth Legion,* 243.

147   **"some of these men were dragging":** "Oral Reminiscences of General Oliver P. Smith," 220.

147   **Marine Lt. Col. Olin Beall, the crusty commander:** Details of Beall's background are from Appleman Papers, box 7, USAMHI, and from Simmons, *Frozen Chosin,* 78. Details of the rescue are from Hopkins, *One Bugle No Drums,* 138, 253.

148   **The Marines fed the survivors hot soup:** Appleman, *East of Chosin,* 285.

11. O. P. SMITH SUCCEEDS AT CHOSIN

150   **"was a MacArthur man":** "Oral Reminiscences of General Oliver P. Smith," 215.

151   **"Colonel Marshall was pretty definite":** "Oral Reminiscences of General Oliver P. Smith," 41–47. Marines seemed to like Marshall. At about the same time Smith was a student at Fort Benning, Maj. Gen. John Lejeune, the retired Marine commandant, offered Marshall the position of commandant at Virginia Military Institute. Lejeune to Marshall, November 20, 1932 (referred to in

Marshall letter of response, November 24, 1932), box 3, folder 32, in Marshall-Winn Papers, Marshall Library.

151 **"But when you run down":** "Oral Reminiscences of General Oliver P. Smith," 52.

151 **As a general, the quiet, pipe-smoking:** Biographical data, "Oral Reminiscences of General Oliver P. Smith."

151 **Peleliu proved to be a bloodbath:** James, *Years of MacArthur,* vol. 2, 491.

152 **"Hagaru-ri had to be held":** Gail Shisler, *For Country and Corps: The Life of General Oliver P. Smith* (Naval Institute Press, 2009), 197.

153 **"Infantry literally dissolved":** Pogue, *Marshall,* vol. 3, 538.

153 **"unsatisfactory," Almond blamed:** Elliott Converse et al., *The Exclusion of Black Soldiers from the Medal of Honor in World War II: The Study Commissioned by the United States Army to Investigate Racial Bias in the Awarding of the Nation's Highest Military Decoration* (McFarland, 1997), 126.

153 **"People think that being from the South":** Atkinson, *Day of Battle,* 383.

153 **"a slave unit for white masters":** Converse et al., *The Exclusion,* 96–98.

154 **Almond manned his corps headquarters:** Stanton, *America's Tenth Legion,* 51.

154 **"there was nothing wrong with him":** D. Clayton James with Anne Sharp Wells, *Refighting the Last War: Command and Crisis in Korea, 1950–1953* (Free Press, 1993), 77.

154 **"when it pays to be aggressive":** Spiller, *American Military Leaders,* 6.

154 **"We've got to go barreling" . . . "the airfield built":** Russ, *Breakout,* 71.

154 **"Our left flank is wide open":** Russ, *Breakout,* 72.

154 **At one point in mid-November 1950:** Stanton, *America's Tenth Legion,* 194.

154 **"We went cautiously":** "Oral Reminiscences of General Oliver P. Smith," 4.

155 **"In effect, 1st Mar Div stood" . . . "the upper hand":** Marshall, "A Study Based on the Operations of the 1st Marine Division in the Koto-ri, Hagaru-ri, Yudamn-ni Area, 20 November–10 December 1950," 6–7.

155 **"Instead of going to positions":** Marshall, "A Study Based on the Operations," 254.

155 **"The airstrip was 'ordered prepared'":** Almond to Roy Appleman, October 29, 1975, Edward Almond Papers, box 100, USAMHI.

156 **"Almond seems to have remained optimistic":** Matthew Ridgway, *The Korean War, Issues and Policies, June 1950 to June 1951,* undated manuscript filed in 1963 with Office of the Chief of Military History, U.S. Army Center of Military History, Fort McNair, Washington, DC, 324.

156 **Smith, in a letter:** Shisler, *For Country and Corps,* 184.

156 **when Smith asked for the help:** Clifton La Bree, *The Gentle Warrior: General Oliver Prince Smith, USMC* (Kent State University Press, 2001), 142.

156 **"The [X] corps at the time":** "Oral Reminiscences of General Oliver P. Smith," 226.

156 **"I talked to him and said, 'O. P.'":** Oral history of Gen. Lemuel Shepherd, Marine Corps Historical Center, Quantico, VA, accessed online.

157 **"Having been a schoolmate":** Oral history of Shepherd.

157 **But Smith saw mounting reasons:** Russ, *Breakout,* 104.

157 **When Smith learned that the Chinese:** Shisler, *For Country and Corps,* 185.

157 **"We will employ a strategy":** Shu Guang Zhang, *Mao's Military Romanticism: Chinese and the Korean War, 1950–1953* (University Press of Kansas, 1995), 109. Smith

most likely was aided by the expertise of his division G-2, or intelligence chief, Col. Bankson Holcomb, who had grown up in Beijing, served in China and Japan, and even led Chinese guerrillas during World War II. Millett, *The War for Korea,* 302.

157 **"encircle and exterminate":** Russell Spurr, *Enter the Dragon: China's Undeclared War Against the U.S. in Korea, 1950–51* (Newmarket, 1988), 169.

158 **"was to slow down the advance":** "Oral Reminiscences of General Oliver P. Smith," 210.

158 **"We spent the night shooting":** Russ, *Breakout,* 181.

158 **"Their buglers sounding some kind of battle call":** "General Raymond G. Davis, Oral History Transcript," interview by Benis Frank, Headquarters, U.S. Marine Corps, 1978, 162.

158 **When Smith asked Col. Lewis "Chesty" Puller:** Hopkins, *One Bugle No Drums,* 140–41.

159 **"The Army figured we were finished":** "Oral Reminiscences of General Oliver P. Smith," 7.

159 **Unlike Faith and those around him:** Russ, *Breakout,* 122, 134, 148.

159 **"Word had been passed to kill":** Knox, *The Korean War,* 514.

160 **recalled another member of the company, PFC Robert Ezell:** Knox, *The Korean War,* 474.

160 **Another Marine, Cpl. Robert Kelly:** Knox, *The Korean War,* 607.

160 **"we had to climb on our hands and knees":** Davis, "Oral History," 166.

160 **"we could smell the garlic":** Charles McKellar, interview by J. D. Eanett, March 2, 2006, Archives of Virginia Military Institute, 7.

161 **"probably twenty feet high" . . . "burned into my brain":** McKellar interview, 8.

161 **All of Fox's survivors:** T. R. Fehrenbach, *This Kind of War* (Bantam, 1991), 350.

161 **A total of fourteen Marines:** Stanton, *America's Tenth Legion,* 299.

161 **Over four days and three nights:** Fehrenbach, *This Kind of War,* 352.

161 **"The dead were stacked in trucks":** Knox, *The Korean War,* 532.

161 **"No one ever doubted the troops":** Roe, *The Dragon Strikes,* 343.

162 **"singing in the midst of this" . . . "We've got it made":** "Oral History Transcript: Lieutenant General Alpha L. Bowser, U.S. Marine Corps (Retired)," Headquarters, U.S. Marine Corps, Washington, DC, 1970, 243.

162 **"We had so many patients lying":** Holloway, *Escape from Hell,* 107.

162 **The aerial supply and evacuation:** La Bree, *The Gentle Warrior,* 170.

163 **"I considered that the critical part":** O. P. Smith, "Letter of 17 December 1950 from the Commanding General, 1st Marine Division, to the Commandant of the Marine Corps," O. P. Smith Collection, box 57, Marine Corps Historical Center, Quantico, VA, 6.

163 **"dig in and be prepared":** Appendix A-1 in Paul McCloskey Jr., *The Taking of Hill 610* (Eaglet Books, 1992).

163 **"This was a very powerful force":** O. P. Smith, "Looking Back at Chosin," *Marine Corps Gazette,* November 2000 (reprinted from December 1960 issue), 63.

163 **Gen. Almond flew over the convoy:** Stanton, *America's Tenth Legion,* 282.

164 **"Found most of them":** Knox, *The Korean War,* 580.

164 **"The tracers were weird streaks":** Joseph Owen, *Colder Than Hell: A Marine Rifle Company at Chosin Reservoir* (Naval Institute Press, 1996), 222.

164 Chinese soldiers, ill-clad: Roe, *The Dragon Strikes*, 389.

164 "like gravel being thrown": Holloway, *Escape from Hell*, 122.

164 "To leave them was unthinkable": Knox, *The Korean War*, 593.

165 "He was kind of a grouchy guy" . . . "I'll get you a bridge": "Oral Reminiscences of General Oliver P. Smith," 250.

165 An officer in his 1st Battalion: Russ, *Breakout*, 157.

165 "Is that you, Pearl?": Russ, *Breakout*, 419.

165 "five or six of these great large Tootsie Rolls": Davis, "Oral History," 182.

165 One of Davis's Marines, Charles McKellar: McKellar interview, 10.

166 had mauled the Chinese divisions: Simmons, *Frozen Chosin*, 122.

166 "came down off the mountain": "Personal-Confidential," O. P. Smith to Clifton Cates, December 17, 1950, O. P. Smith Collection, box 57, Marine Corps Archives, Quantico, VA.

166 the Chinese commander in Korea, Marshal Peng Dehuai: Spurr, *Enter the Dragon*, 266.

166 Twenty-three years later: Spurr, *Enter the Dragon*, 315.

166 The Chinese divisions that attacked: Eliot Cohen and John Gooch, *Military Misfortunes: The Anatomy of Failure in War* (Vintage, 1990), 186.

166 the campaign was a strategic victory: F. M. Berger et al., *CSI Battlebook: Chosin Reservoir* (Combat Studies Institute, Fort Leavenworth, KS, 1983), 79.

166 "Communist China—until then considered": Roe, *The Dragon Strikes*, 412.

167 "If it wasn't for his tremendous leadership": General Matthew B. Ridgway, interview by Maj. Matthew Caulfield and Lt. Col. Robert Elton, August 26, 1969, in box 88, Matthew Ridgway Papers, USAMHI, 26.

167 "perhaps the most brilliant divisional feat": Shisler, *For Country and Corps*, 232.

167 Smith is not much remembered . . . "Regimental commanders spoke": This omission and its causes are discussed in Shisler, *For Country and Corps*, 263.

167 The exhibit on the Chosin campaign: Author visit, February 3, 2012.

168 "Marine commanders at Chosin": Faris Kirkland, "Soldiers and Marines at Chosin Reservoir: Criteria for Assignment to Combat Command," *Armed Forces & Society* 22, no. 2 (Winter 1995–96), 264.

169 "On the battlefield, Faith was a clone": Blair, *Forgotten War*, 292.

169 "[He] had not mastered the fundamentals": Kirkland, "Soldiers and Marines at Chosin," 266.

169 "There is no evidence that any effort": Appleman, *East of Chosin*, 178.

170 "both the beneficiary and the victim": Kirkland, "Soldiers and Marines at Chosin," 266.

170 "About Faith, I have not placed": Appleman to Hugh May, November 9, 1981, in Roy Appleman Collection, box 6, "Correspondence with Chosin Survivors," USAMHI. Emphasis in original.

170 "Of the six generals initially assigned": Kirkland, "Soldiers and Marines at Chosin," 258.

170 "The communications breakdown": Stanton, *America's Tenth Legion*, 250.

171 This extended even to the chief of staff: Blair, *Forgotten War*, 289.

171 They produced a thick report: "Report of First OCAFF Observer Team to the Far East Command," page 4 of main report, page 7 of appendix C-4, page 2 of

first enclosure, August 16, 1950, included as enclosure, Gen. Mark Clark to Gen. J. Lawton Collins, August 28, 1950, file 350.07, Far East, box 128, Army Intelligence Project, decimal file 1949–50, record group 319, National Archives and Records Administration, College Park, MD. See also William Donnelly, "Bilko's Army: A Crisis in Command," unpublished paper, U.S. Army Center of Military History, 7. A version of this paper subsequently was published as William M. Donnelly, "Bilko's Army: A Crisis in Command?," *Journal of Military History,* October 2011.

172 **"officers considered by their seniors":** Donnelly, "Bilko's Army," 9.

172 **If World War III came, the Army's plan:** David Fautua, "An Army for the 'American Century': The Origins of the Cold War U.S. Army, 1949–1959," unpublished doctoral dissertation, University of North Carolina at Chapel Hill, 2006, 14.

173 **"I gave him the 7th Regiment":** "Oral Reminiscences of General Oliver P. Smith," 30.

173 **Lt. Col. Raymond Murray:** Ray Davis, *The Story of Ray Davis: General of Marines* (Research Triangle Publishing, 1995), 67.

173 **"I spent many a moment standing atop":** Davis, "Oral History," 122.

173 **Davis led a battalion at Tarawa:** Davis, *The Story of Ray Davis,* 66.

173 **"perhaps the most famous Marine":** Berger et al., *CSI Battlebook,* 43.

173 **As a battalion commander at Guadalcanal:** Simmons, *Frozen Chosin,* 9, 12, 50.

174 **But Kirkland said that the Army:** Faris Kirkland, interview by author at time of his article's publication in *Armed Forces & Society.*

174 **"in an uncoordinated rush toward the border":** Roe, *The Dragon Strikes,* 411.

174 **he told *U.S. News & World Report:*** Blair, *Forgotten War,* 524.

175 **"What good would that do?" . . . "both puzzled and amazed":** Ridgway, *Korean War,* 62.

175 **"I regard General MacArthur's insistence":** Ridgway to Appleman, March 6, 1978, Edward Almond Papers, "Military Correspondence, 1960–1977," box 129, USAMHI, 1.

175 **"could well choose this operation":** Ridgway, *The Korean War, Issues and Policies,* 331.

12. RIDGWAY TURNS THE WAR AROUND

176 **"for days a whisper had run through":** Fehrenbach, *This Kind of War,* 364.

176 **Ridgway was sipping a highball:** Ridgway, *Korean War,* 79.

177 **He had worked under MacArthur:** Ridgway, notes in preparation for an interview about Marshall, March 20, 1989, Matthew Ridgway Papers, box 43, USAMHI.

177 **"There was hardly a tactical exercise":** General Matthew Ridgway, interview by Forrest Pogue, February 26, 1959, in Pogue Oral History Collection, Marshall Library, 2–4.

178 **Marshall was staying at Maj. Ridgway's house:** Ridgway, interviews by John Blair, USAMHI, 40. Also see additional detail in Ridgway, "Reminiscences About George C. Marshall," Marshall Library, 5.

178 **He began the war as a colonel:** Ridgway, "Reminiscences About George C. Marshall," Marshall Library, 7.

178 **From there he went on to be assistant commander:** Harold R. Winton, *Corps Commanders of the Bulge: Six American Generals and Victory in the Ardennes* (University Press of Kansas, 2007), 41.

178 **lost fourteen battalion commanders:** Ridgway, interview by Caulfield and Elton, 8.

178 **"No one knew where anyone else was":** Ridgway, interview by Caulfield and Elton, 24.

178 **"the best of troops will fail":** Ridgway, interview by Caulfield and Elton, 20.

179 **"I always disliked standing above people":** Ridgway, interview by Caulfield and Elton, 22–23.

179 **He left Washington determined:** Ridgway, interviews by John Blair, USAMHI, 73.

179 **"Everybody in life has their fallibilities":** General Matthew B. Ridgway, interview by Harold Hitchens and Frederick Hetzel, March 5, 1982, Matthew Ridgway Papers, box 88, USAMHI, 2, 4.

180 **"beginning in 1950":** Ridgway, *The Korean War, Issues and Policies*, 211.

180 **"I thought the president had made it":** General Matthew B. Ridgway, interview by Maurice Matloff, April 18, 1984, Matthew Ridgway Papers, box 88, USAMHI, 14–15.

180 **"You will have my utmost":** Ridgway, *Korean War*, 262.

180 **"The granite peaks rose to six thousand feet":** Matthew Ridgway, *Soldier: The Memoirs of Matthew B. Ridgway* (Greenwood, 1974), 203–4.

181 **visiting South Korean president Syngman Rhee:** Matthew Ridgway Papers, log, series 3, Official Papers, Eighth U.S. Army Special Files, December 1950–April 1951, box 68, USAMHI.

181 **"I intend to stay":** Ridgway, interview by Toland, 15.

181 **"Is he confident, does he know":** Matthew Ridgway and Walter Winton Jr., "Troop Leadership at the Operational Level: The Eighth Army in Korea," *Military Review*, April 1990, 59. This article is an edited transcript of a talk Ridgway and Winton gave to the School of Advanced Military Studies, at Fort Leavenworth, KS, on May 9, 1984.

181 **"These division commanders did not know":** Ridgway and Winton, "Troop Leadership," 60.

181 **"roadbound" . . . "conducting operations here":** Ridgway and Winton, "Troop Leadership," 62.

181 **"The troops were confused":** Ridgway and Winton, "Troop Leadership," 61.

181 **"I could sense it":** Ridgway, *Soldier*, 205.

182 **"The consensus from private to general":** Ridgway, interview by Caulfield and Elton, 26.

182 **"Weather terrible, Chinese ferocious":** Ridgway and Winton, "Troop Leadership," 67.

182 **Eighth Army's staff "very mediocre":** Ridgway, interview by Toland, 10.

182 **"I told him frankly that we had been put":** "Oral Reminiscences of General Oliver P. Smith," 260.

182 **He told them to begin patrolling:** Ridgway, *The Korean War, Issues and Policies*, 380.

183 **"Ridgway was such a breath of fresh air":** Blair, *Forgotten War*, 605.

183 **"What was perfectly, clearly apparent":** Ridgway and Winton, "Troop Leadership," 59.

183 **"The leadership I found":** Ridgway, *Korean War,* 88.

183 **"you can't relieve them right way":** Ridgway, interview by Toland, 11.

183 **"Everything is going fine":** Ridgway to Collins, January 3, 1951, Matthew Ridgway Papers, box 9, USAMHI.

184 **"be ruthless with our general officers":** Ridgway to Collins, January 8, 1951, Matthew Ridgway Papers, box 68, USAMHI.

184 **"young, vigorous, mentally flexible":** Ridgway to Collins, January 8, 1951, Matthew Ridgway Papers, box 9, USAMHI.

184 **that was item six on his agenda:** Ridgway, notes for meeting with corps commanders, January 8, 1951, Matthew Ridgway Papers, box 68, USAMHI.

184 **"Can't execute my future plans":** Ridgway, agenda for meeting with Hickey, January 11, 1951, Matthew Ridgway Papers, box 68, USAMHI; Ridgway, message to Collins, January 15, 1951, Matthew Ridgway Papers, box 68, USAMHI.

184 **"What are your attack plans?":** Blair, *Forgotten War,* 574.

185 **the second snap relief of Jeter's career:** MacDonald, *Siegfried Line Campaign,* 446–47.

185 **Over the following three months:** Millett, *The War for Korea,* 392; Markel, "The Organization Man at War," 168.

185 **On January 14, Maj. Gen. Robert McClure was fired:** Almond to Appleman, October 29, 1975, Edward Almond Papers, box 100, USAMHI. See also Almond to McClure, January 13, 1951, Matthew Ridgway Papers, box 68, USAMHI.

186 **"Press here has played up relief":** "Personal for Ridgway Secret," January 16, 1951, "Matthew Ridgway Papers," box 10, USAMHI.

186 **"We are still very much concerned" . . . "unconvincing such an answer will be":** Haislip to Ridgway, February 14, 1951, Matthew Ridgway Papers, box 68, USAMHI.

186 **"Dear Ham," Ridgway wrote back:** Ridgway to Haislip, February 24, 1951, Matthew Ridgway Papers, box 68, USAMHI.

187 **Of the ousted generals:** "The New Command Team in Korea," *Time,* March 5, 1951, 30.

187 **"Try to find good men":** James Michener, "A Tough Man for a Tough Job," *Life,* May 12, 1952, 111.

187 **"Dear Matt," Collins, the Army chief of staff, wrote:** Collins to Ridgway, May 24, 1951, Matthew Ridgway Papers, USAMHI.

188 **Ridgway also requested the removal:** Thomas Thayer, *War Without Fronts: The American Experience in Vietnam* (Westview, 1985), 60. See also Ridgway, interview by Caulfield and Elton, 60.

188 **"Almond was a very able officer" . . . "could be cutting and intolerant":** Ridgway, interviews by John Blair, USAMHI, 76.

188 **"the most unpopular war in United States history":** Mark Clark, *From the Danube to the Yalu* (repr., Tab Books, 1988), 230.

188 **"He [Ridgway] told me he had a hell of a time":** Roger Cirillo, e-mail message to author, September 8, 2010.

189 **"he had increasing difficulty":** Dean Acheson, *Sketches from Life of Men I Have Known* (Harper, 1960), 165.

189 **At the end of January 1951:** Blair, *Forgotten War,* 668.

189 **With the same number of troops:** This thought is drawn from William Hopkins, a Marine veteran of Korea, in his *One Bugle No Drums,* 224.

189 **"it was a disintegrating army":** "Oral History of Harold K. Johnson," interview by Col. Richard Jensen and Lt. Col. Rupert Glover, Section II, February 7, 1972, Harold K. Johnson Papers, box 201, USAMHI, 33.

189 **"as mean-spirited an American officer":** Allan Millett, "The Korean War: A 50-Year Critical Historiography," *Journal of Strategic Studies* 24, no. 1 (March 2001), 215.

190 **"had a short temper and made snap judgments":** Millett, *The War for Korea,* 372.

190 **"He didn't come to visit me":** Ridgway, interview by John Toland, USAMHI, 14.

190 **"It appears from all estimates":** "Personal From: Joint Chiefs of Staff / Personal For: General MacArthur / JCS 99935," December 29, 1950, Matthew Ridgway Papers, box 68, USAMHI.

191 **"blockade the coast of China":** Douglas MacArthur, "Personal for JCS," December 30, 1950, Matthew Ridgway Papers, box 68, USAMHI.

191 **MacArthur's cables were "pretty frantic":** Collins, interview by Sperow, USAMHI, vol. 2, 341.

191 **"it can be accepted as basic fact":** Schnabel, *The First Year,* 338.

13. MACARTHUR'S LAST STAND

192 **"incurably recalcitrant":** Acheson, *Present at the Creation,* 515.

192 **"every means at his disposal":** Benjamin Persons, *Relieved of Command* (Sunflower University Press, 1997), x.

193 **"wrote back a very insulting telegram":** Transcript of Tape 25, Omar N. Bradley, interviews by Forrest Pogue, May 27, 1957, and July 19, 1957, Pogue Oral History Collection, Marshall Library.

193 **"The concept advanced":** Edward Imparato, ed., *General MacArthur Speeches and Reports, 1908–1964* (Turner Publishing, 2000), 161.

194 **"freedom of action":** Blair, *Forgotten War,* 737.

194 **"Assuming no diminution"** . . . **"abnormal military inhibitions":** Robert Leckie, *Conflict: The History of the Korean War, 1950–53* (G. P. Putnam's, 1962), 265.

194 **"We didn't set out to conquer":** Leckie, *Conflict,* 266–67.

194 **"The seizure of the land":** Ridgway, *Soldier,* 220.

195 **"painfully aware":** "The Secretary of State to Certain Diplomatic Offices, Secret, Washington, March 23, 1951," *Foreign Relations of the United States, 1951,* vol. 7, *Korea and China* (U.S. Government Printing Office, 1983), 266.

195 **"I got the impression":** "Oral Reminiscences of General Oliver P. Smith," 13.

195 **"If we are not in Korea"** . . . **"There is no substitute for victory":** William Manchester, *American Caesar: Douglas MacArthur, 1880–1964* (Dell, 1978), 763.

196 **"With deep regret I have concluded":** Blair, *Forgotten War,* 796.

196 **"No office boy, no charwoman":** MacArthur, *Reminiscences,* 395.

196 **an "infamous purge":** Willoughby and Chamberlain, *MacArthur 1941–1951,* 472.

196 **"mental illness":** Ridgway, interviews by John Blair, USAMHI, 81.

196 **"out of his head":** Merle Miller, *Plain Speaking: An Oral Biography of Harry S. Truman* (Berkley, 1974), 291.

196 **"defeatism":** Douglas MacArthur, address to Congress, April 19, 1951, Library of Congress, accessed online.

197 **One afternoon in 1947:** A. E. Schanze, *This Was the Army,* unpublished manuscript, "Col. A. E. Schanze Papers," box 1, USAMHI, 55.

197 **He retired:** Shortal, *Forged by Fire,* 128.

198 **"Frankly," he stated:** "Testimony of General of the Army Omar Bradley Before the Senate Committees on Armed Services and Foreign Relations, May 15, 1951, Military Situation in the Far East," 82nd Congress, 1st session, part 2, 732.

198 **"no more subordinate soldier":** James, *Refighting the Last War,* 212.

198 **on the "direct order":** Interview with George Elsey, April 9, 1970, Harry S. Truman Library and Museum, 285.

198 **At first, mail to the White House:** James, *Refighting the Last War,* 214.

198 **His travels were bankrolled:** Information about MacArthur's financial backing is from D. Clayton James, *The Years of MacArthur,* vol. 3, *Triumph and Disaster, 1945–1964* (Houghton Mifflin, 1985), 642–43. See also Burrough, *The Big Rich,* 218.

199 **"deputy commander-in-chief":** Willoughby and Chamberlain, *MacArthur 1941–1951,* 524.

199 **"A tremendous demonstration" . . . "cooked his own goose":** C. L. Sulzberger, *A Long Row of Candles* (Macmillan, 1969), 769.

199 **By the time MacArthur finished:** Walter Karp, "Truman vs. MacArthur," *American Heritage,* April/May 1984, 769.

199 **In his presidential memoirs:** Dwight Eisenhower, *Mandate for Change, 1953–1956* (Doubleday, 1963), 70.

199 **"in many ways":** Ferrell, *Eisenhower Diaries,* "January 19, 1942," 44.

199 **"that traitor Eisenhower":** D'Este, *Eisenhower,* 295.

200 **MacArthur, meeting with journalists:** James, *Years of MacArthur,* vol. 2, 587.

200 **"I'll have to see":** Mark W. Clark, interview by John Luter, January 4, 1970, Eisenhower Administration Project, Columbia Center for Oral History, Columbia University, 15–16. Clark does not mention his own interest in high office, but according to Clark Lee, a war correspondent, it was said in Clark's headquarters that "the youngish, tall, and handsome Clark had his heart set on becoming President of the United States, and these rumors were never denied by his highest officers." Clark Lee, *One Last Look Around* (Duell, Sloan and Pearce, 1947), 281.

200 **Ike was so persuasive:** Harry C. Butcher to Robert D. Heinl, July 13, 1948, in "Reminiscences About George C. Marshall," box 1, folder 17, Marshall Library, 2. President Truman, whose dislike of Eisenhower might have colored his memories, stated that Eisenhower "swore up and down to me he would never run for any political office." Miller, *Plain Speaking,* 319. See also pages 338–39.

200 **"Dear Pete," he wrote:** Dwight D. Eisenhower to Charles Corlett, December 22, 1949, in Corlett Papers, box 1, USAMHI. It is worth noting that the two men were sufficiently close that, three years later, Eisenhower, as the new president, took time to reach out to him, writing to Corlett, "I haven't heard from you in a long time. . . . Please write to me when you have a chance and bring me up to date." Eisenhower to Corlett, February 25, 1953, also in Corlett Papers, box 1, USAMHI.

201 **"haunted Eisenhower":** Stoler, *George C. Marshall,* 192.

201 **Ike would argue:** Eisenhower, interview by Pogue, June, 28, 1962, Pogue Oral History Collection, Marshall Library.

201 **In January 1954, he boasted:** "Texts of . . . Interview with MacArthur in 1954," *New York Times*, April 9, 1964, 16.

201 **"a shell of tarnished magnificence":** Larrabee, *Commander in Chief*, 336.

202 **"MacArthur was guilty of contumacy":** Bruce Clarke oral history, Truman Library, 30.

202 **"Didn't MacArthur say the same":** Robert McNamara, *In Retrospect: The Tragedy and Lessons of Vietnam* (Random House, 1995), 163.

202 **"I have a lot riding on you":** William C. Westmoreland, *A Soldier Reports* (Doubleday, 1976), 193. For a slightly different account, see Douglas Kinnard, *The War Managers: American Generals Reflect on Vietnam* (Da Capo, 1991), 21.

14. THE ORGANIZATION MAN'S ARMY

203 **As Whyte wrote:** William Whyte, *The Organization Man* (Doubleday Anchor, 1957), 149–51.

204 **"a rather automatic":** Whyte, *Organization Man*, 169.

204 **"a personal identity":** William Henry, "Executive Personality," in *The Emergent American Society: Large-Scale Organizations* (Yale University Press, 1967), 247.

204 **"To his paratroopers":** Ernest Ferguson, *Westmoreland: The Inevitable General* (Little, Brown, 1968), 208.

204 **"I remember":** Lewis Sorley, *Westmoreland: The General Who Lost Vietnam* (Houghton Mifflin Harcourt, 2011), 36.

205 **"There is more than a semantic":** Thomas Schelling, "Economic Reasoning and Military Science," *The American Economist*, May 1960, 4.

205 **"Today's strategy" . . . "currently militarily capable":** Schelling, "Economic Reasoning and Military Science," 7.

206 **"would be precisely":** Robert Osgood, *Limited War: The Challenge to American Strategy* (University of Chicago Press, 1957), 271–72.

206 **"If the early 1960s":** Robert Osgood, *Limited War Revisited* (Westview, 1979), 33.

206 **"the Army was feeling sorry":** Henry Gole, "The Relevance of Gen. William E. DePuy," *Army Magazine*, March 2008, 68.

206 **"the decade of doctrinal chaos":** Robert Doughty, "The Evolution of US Army Tactical Doctrine, 1946–76," Combat Studies Institute, Fort Leavenworth, KS, August 1979, 29.

206 **The Air Force was rapidly expanding:** Millett and Maslowski, *For the Common Defense*, 515–17.

207 **ground combat had begun to seem:** Roger Spiller, "Six Propositions," in Matthew Moten, ed., *Between War and Peace: How America Ends Its Wars* (Free Press, 2011), 33.

207 **the U.S. Army's size was reduced:** McMaster, *Dereliction of Duty*, 10.

207 **"a man," as historian Adrian Lewis put it:** Adrian Lewis, *The American Culture of War: The History of U.S. Military Force from World War II to Operation Iraqi Freedom* (Routledge, 2007), 152.

207 **"has left them somewhat unsatisfied":** Andrew Goodpaster, "Memorandum of Conference with the President," April 18, 1956, box 15, 4/56, Eisenhower Library, 3.

207 **Reporting to Fort Dix:** John Collins, *Military Professional*, unpublished memoir, 6.

207 **"The ones who were still"** . . . **"before seven o'clock":** H. Norman Schwarz-kopf, *It Doesn't Take a Hero* (Bantam, 1993), 91–92.

208 **"in many ways":** Schwarzkopf, *It Doesn't Take a Hero*, x.

208 **"When I came back to Washington":** "Address by General Maxwell D. Taylor, Chief of Staff, United States Army, at the First Annual Meeting of the Associa-tion of the United States Army, Fort Benning, Georgia, Saturday, October 22, 1955," Maxwell Taylor Papers, online archives, special collections, National Defense University, 20.

208 **"period of Babylonian captivity":** Maxwell Taylor, *The Uncertain Trumpet* (Harper, 1959), 198.

208 **"The Army [was]":** "Coordination Group," interviews with Lt. Gen. John Cushman, U.S. Army (Retired), unpublished, USAMHI, shared with author by General Cushman; chap. 10, page 1.

208 the **"Pentomic Army":** A. J. Bacevich, *The Pentomic Era: The U.S. Army Between Korea and Vietnam* (National Defense University Press, 1986), 96. See also "The Nuclear Revolution, 1945–1960," chap. 1 in Thomas Mahnken, *Technology and the American Way of War* (Columbia University Press, 2008).

209 **Nevertheless, by 1957:** Brian Linn, *The Echo of Battle: The Army's Way of War* (Harvard, 2007), 170.

209 **In 1959, Taylor lamented:** Taylor, *Uncertain Trumpet*, 66.

209 **"We must be able to deter":** Maxwell Taylor, letter to retired generals, Novem-ber 28, 1955, copy in Andrew Goodpaster Papers, box 18, folder 12, "White House 1954–1961," Marshall Library.

209 **an article for *Military Review*:** Raymond Shoemaker et al., "Readiness for the Little War—Optimum Integrated Strategy," *Military Review,* April 1957, 24.

209 **Also in 1957, Taylor established:** Weigley, *History of the United States Army,* 534, 543.

210 **"From corporals to colonels":** George Fielding Eliot, "Has the Army Lost Its Soul?," *Military Review,* November 1953, 8 (repr. from *Ordnance Magazine,* July–August 1953).

210 **"The noncoms who receive":** Eliot, "Has the Army Lost Its Soul?," 9.

211 **"The leader is often rewarded":** Col. Steven M. Jones, "Improving Account-ability for Effective Command Climate: A Strategic Imperative," U.S. Army War College, Carlisle, PA, April 2003, 8.

211 **"like the mass society":** Roger Little, "Solidarity Is the Key to the Mass Army," *The Army Combat Forces Journal,* February 1955, 27–28.

211 **A full 81 percent:** Donnelly, "Bilko's Army," 34.

211 **"to reward caution and conformity":** Donnelly, "Bilko's Army," 35.

212 **"Over-supervision stifles initiative":** Donnelly, "Bilko's Army," 36–38.

212 **"Why do so many generals":** Aubrey Newman, *What Are Generals Made Of?* (Presidio, 1987), 121.

212 **"command and management":** David Ramsey Jr., "Management or Com-mand," *Military Review,* September 1961, 39.

212 **"It can be said"** . . . **"World War II or Korea":** Charles J. V. Murphy, "A New Multi-Purpose U.S. Army," *Fortune,* May 1966, 124.

213 **"Officers were doing the tasks":** Henry Gole, "The U.S. Army in the After-math of Conflict," unpublished notes, 2010, 7.

213 **"The ideal almost seems to be":** Peter Dawkins, "Freedom to Fail," *Infantry,* September–October 1965, 9.

PART III: THE VIETNAM WAR
15. MAXWELL TAYLOR: ARCHITECT OF DEFEAT

217 **"All the way from Westmoreland":** "General William DePuy," interview by Michael Perlman, part 2, May 16, 1987, DePuy Papers, box 2, USAMHI, 24–25.

217 **"We never had very much":** "General Water T. Kerwin Jr., USA Retired," interview by D. A. Doehle, 1980, Walter Kerwin Papers, USAMHI, 2.

218 **Kerwin, for example:** Truscott, *Command Missions,* 325–26.

218 **"brigadier generals":** Kerwin, interview by Doehle, 74–75.

218 **"It was the strangest thing":** "General Bruce Palmer Jr.," interviews by James Shelton and Edward Smith, 1975–1976, Bruce Palmer Papers, USAMHI, 235.

219 **The first draft of the book:** John Cushman interviews, unpublished, USAMHI, chap. 10, page 3.

219 **"We had been affected":** Ronald Carpenter, "General Maxwell D. Taylor and the Joint Chiefs of Staff During the Cuban Missile Crisis," in *Rhetoric in Martial Deliberations and Decision Making* (University of South Carolina Press, 2004), 70.

219 **"may have influenced the United States":** Dave Richard Palmer, *Summons of the Trumpet: A History of the Vietnam War from a Military Man's Perspective* (Presidio, 1978), 271.

219 **Taylor would become almost the opposite:** This thought is from an e-mail message from Henry Gole to the author, November 25, 2011.

220 **"Those sons of bitches":** Carpenter, *Rhetoric in Martial Deliberations,* 73. See also "Maxwell D. Taylor Oral History," interview no. 1a, by Dorothy Pierce, January 9, 1969, Lyndon Baines Johnson Library, Austin, TX (hereafter: LBJ Library), 8–9.

220 **"I would often see him":** Taylor Oral History, LBJ Library, 11.

220 **"General Taylor had an influence":** "Oral History Interview with Earle Wheeler," interview by Chester Clifton, 1964, John F. Kennedy Library, Boston, MA (hereafter: JFK Library), 67.

220 **the first issue Taylor took up:** Wheeler Oral History, JFK Library, 28.

220 **He was regarded warily:** Douglas Kinnard, *The Certain Trumpet: Maxwell Taylor and the American Experience in Vietnam* (Brassey's, 1991), 212–13.

221 **"bears as much responsibility":** Bernard Brodie, *War and Politics* (Macmillan, 1973), 191.

221 **"He is largely responsible":** "Interview with General Nathan F. Twining," interview by John T. Mason Jr., June 5, 1967, Columbia Center for Oral History, Columbia University, 146, 225–26.

222 **"My answer is a qualified 'yes,'":** Nathan Twining, "Memorandum for Admiral Radford," April 2, 1954, Matthew Ridgway Papers, box 78, USAMHI. The "three A-bombs" quotation is from Twining, interview by Mason, Columbia University, 148.

222 **Two American aircraft carriers:** Osgood, *Limited War,* 217–18.

222 **"My answer is an emphatic and immediate 'NO,'":** Matthew Ridgway, "Memorandum for the Joint Chiefs of Staff," April 6, 1954, Matthew Ridgway Papers, box 78, USAMHI, 1–2.

222 **Nor, he stated in another document:** "Army Position on NSC Action No. 1074-A," n.d., document 31, *The Pentagon Papers*, "Gravel Edition" (Beacon Press, 1971), vol. 1.

222 **Over Radford's objections:** Maj. Jay Parker, "The Colonels' Revolt: Eisenhower, the Army, and the Politics of National Security," Naval War College, June 17, 1994, 38.

223 **"I'm convinced that no military victory":** Ferrell, *Eisenhower Diaries*, "March 17, 1951," 190.

223 **"As long as I'm president":** "Douglas MacArthur II," interview by Mack Teasley, April 6, 1990, Eisenhower Library, 29.

223 **"we would not":** Andrew Goodpaster, "Memorandum of Conference with the President, May 24, 1956; 10:30 AM," Andrew Goodpaster Papers, box 18, folder 12, "White House 1954–1961," Marshall Library, 2.

223 **"American advisers in the 1950s":** William Westmoreland, "A Military War of Attrition," in W. Scott Thompson and Donaldson Frizzell, eds., *The Lessons of Vietnam* (Crane, Russak, 1977), 70.

224 **Williams and his comrades tried:** Andrew Krepinevich Jr., *The Army and Vietnam* (Johns Hopkins University Press, 1986), 24–25.

224 **"was convinced that that was the way":** Ronald Spector, *The United States Army in Vietnam: Advice and Support, The Early Years, 1941–1960* (U.S. Army Center of Military History, 1983), 273. Another subordinate, Lt. Col. Bergen Hovell, recalled, "People were scared to death of General Williams. . . . People were afraid to speak"; Spector, *Advice and Support*, 295.

224 **"Hell," Williams responded:** Meyer, *Hanging Sam*, 140.

224 **"tact, judgment on other than military matters":** Meyer, *Hanging Sam*, 143.

225 **"precisely the areas":** Cao Van Vien, "Reflections on the Vietnam War," in Lewis Sorley, ed., *The Vietnam War: An Assessment by South Vietnam's Generals* (Texas Tech University Press, 2010), 833.

225 **"When fighting finally broke out":** Ngo Quang Truong, "Territorial Forces," in Sorley, *Vietnam War: An Assessment*, 183, 187. For the quality of Lt. Gen. Truong, see, among other material, Kinnard, *The War Managers*, 86: "By a wide margin, he was considered the best combat commander in the South Vietnamese Army."

225 **"hasty, ill-conceived":** Spector, *Advice and Support*, 350.

226 **"a long and valuable time":** Truong, "Territorial Forces," in *Vietnam War: An Assessment*, 210.

226 **"From 1954–61":** Office of the Deputy Chief of Staff for Military Operations, "PROVN: A Program for the Pacification and Long-Term Development of South Vietnam," U.S. Army, March 1966, 102.

226 **He made a habit in Saigon:** Krepinevich, *Army and Vietnam*, 56; "Oral History of Paul Harkins," November 10, 1981, LBJ Library, 8.

226 **"General McGarr was not an adept change agent":** John Cushman, *Fort Leavenworth—A Memoir*, vol. 1, unpublished manuscript, September 2001, on file at USAMHI, 17.

226 **"made himself thoroughly unpopular"**: Graham Cosmas, *MACV: The Joint Command in the Years of Escalation, 1962–1967* (U.S. Army Center of Military History, 2005), 24. The nickname, which refers to his hair being parted in the middle, is referenced in "Samuel T. Williams Oral History," interview 2, conducted by Ted Gittinger, March 16, 1981, LBJ Library, 35.

226 **undercut the "offensive spirit"**: Krepinevich, *Army and Vietnam*, 67.

226 **only "lukewarm interest"**: Tran Dinh Tho, "Pacification," in *Vietnam War: An Assessment*, 262.

227 **intense "mirror imaging"**: "Interview with Robert Montague," August 26, 1982, for *Vietnam: A Television History* (WGBH, 1983).

227 **"I never got the feeling"**: John Dabrowski, ed., "An Oral History of General Gordon R. Sullivan," USAMHI, 2008, 38–39.

227 **"discontinuity between the mixed counterinsurgency strategy"**: R. W. Komer, *Bureaucracy Does Its Thing: Institutional Constraints on U.S.-GVN Performance in Vietnam* (RAND Corporation, 1972), v–vi.

227 **The attitude of the Joint Chiefs**: Leslie Gelb and Richard Betts, *The Irony of Vietnam: The System Worked* (Brookings, 1979), 231.

227 **"Kennedy's preferred battleground"**: Parker, "The Colonels' Revolt," 84.

227 **"The risks of backing into a major Asian war"**: Taylor, "Memorandum for the President, November 11, 1961," in *Pentagon Papers* (Gravel), vol. 2, 100.

228 **"a carefully orchestrated bombing attack"**: *Pentagon Papers* (Gravel), vol. 3, 369.

228 **"we cannot win a conventional war"**: Senate Committee on Foreign Relations, *The U.S. Government and the Vietnam War: Executive and Legislative Roles and Relationships, Part II, 1961–1964* (U.S. Government Printing Office, 1985), accessed online.

228 **"When he found it expedient"**: McMaster, *Dereliction of Duty*, 106.

229 **"Taylor . . . had sort of adopted me"**: Harkins oral history, LBJ Library, 3.

229 **"I think General Harkins was"**: "John Michael Dunn," interview by Ted Gittinger, July 25, 1984, LBJ Library Oral History Collection, Austin, 12–13.

229 **"I do not know anyone" . . . "Harkins should be replaced"**: McGeorge Bundy, "Eyes Only" memo to President Johnson, "The U.S. Military Command in Saigon," January 9, 1964, LBJ Library, national security files, MP, 1/33, 1–2.

230 **"wasn't worth a damn" . . . "You need intelligent people"**: Henry Graff, *The Tuesday Cabinet: Deliberation and Decision on Peace and War Under Lyndon B. Johnson* (Prentice-Hall, 1970), 35–36.

230 **"a good friend" . . . "When they relieved General Harkins"**: Interview by Spruill and Vernon, in Sorley, ed., *Press On!*, 1094.

230 **in May 1964 the general "abruptly"**: Cosmas, *MACV: The Joint Command*, 123.

16. WILLIAM WESTMORELAND: THE ORGANIZATION MAN IN COMMAND

231 **Twelve years later**: McMaster, *Dereliction of Duty*, 66.

232 **"Lombardi was too tough"**: Phillip Davidson, *Vietnam at War: The History, 1946–1975* (Presidio, 1988), 376.

232 **his aide calling a captain**: Sorley, *Westmoreland*, 59. It is not clear whether the aide was acting on his own.

232 **"I felt at the time"**: Gen. Harold K. Johnson, interview by Lt. Col. James Agnew, May 21, 1974, Harold K. Johnson Papers, box 201, USAMHI, 19, 21.
232 **"He is spit and polish"**: Sorley, *Westmoreland*, 67.
233 **"He simply doesn't have any interests"**: Sorley, *Westmoreland*, 264.
233 **"General Westmoreland was intellectually very shallow"**: Sorley, *Westmoreland*, 212.
233 **"the crossover point"** . . . **"in no way accurate"**: Sorley, *Westmoreland*, 155.
234 **"the fact remains"**: Sorley, *Westmoreland*, 228.
234 **"not only false, but reckless"**: Sorley, *Westmoreland*, 176.
234 **he sued CBS News for libel**: Sorley, *Westmoreland*, 289.
234 **"General Westmoreland's capacity"**: Sorley, *Westmoreland*, 118.
234 **"platitudes of squad leading"**: Sorley, *Westmoreland*, 119.
234 **"He seemed rather stupid"**: Sorley, *Westmoreland*, 212.
235 **"no capable war president"**: Russell Weigley, review of "Supreme Command: Soldiers, Statesmen, and Leadership in Wartime," *Journal of Military History*, October 2002, 1276.
235 **"he was not interested in theory"**: Kinnard, telephone interview by author, May 26, 2011.
235 **had attended only two Army schools**: S. L. A. Marshall, *The Armed Forces Officer* (Department of Defense, 1960), 50.
235 **"He was uniquely unschooled"**: Davidson, *Vietnam at War*, 373.
235 **the first Army officer to attend**: Becca Horan, Harvard Business School executive education section, e-mail message to author, January 6, 2011.
235 **"Westy was a corporation executive in uniform"**: Stanley Karnow, *Vietnam: A History* (Viking, 1983), 345.
236 **"The U.S. involvement in the Vietnam war"** . . . **"that ever took to the field"**: Andrew O'Meara Jr., "Who Commands Today's Army? Managers or Leaders?," *Army Magazine*, August 1975, 16–17.
237 **"The Chairman of the Joint Chiefs"**: Westmoreland, *A Soldier Reports*, 432.
237 **"I realized that the airfields"**: "Interview with William C. (William Childs) Westmoreland," April 27, 1981, for *Vietnam: A Television History*.
238 **"The cut-and-run people"**: Westmoreland, *A Soldier Reports*, 433.
238 **"Since I had no intention of crossing him in any way"**: Westmoreland, *A Soldier Reports*, 193.
238 **"It is always the basic objective"**: Westmoreland, *A Soldier Reports*, 99.
239 **"We don't serve Vietnamese"**: Schwarzkopf, *It Doesn't Take a Hero*, 145.
239 **"I, of course, was not at all happy"**: "General Frederick Weyand," interview by Lewis Sorley, November 9–15, 1999, Weyand Papers, box 1, USAMHI, 273.
239 **"Vietnam seemed to be a war fought by committee"**: John Gates, "American Military Leadership in Vietnam," in *Military Leadership and Command: The John Biggs Cincinnati Lectures, 1987* (VMI Foundation, 1987), 186–87.

17. WILLIAM DEPUY: WORLD WAR II–STYLE GENERALSHIP IN VIETNAM

241 **"We went to war with incompetents"**: DePuy Oral History, 90.
242 **"banty rooster"**: Gole, *DePuy*, photo insert caption.
242 **"I wanted people who were flexibly minded"**: DePuy Oral History, 140.

242 **In his one year of leading:** Interview by Spruill and Vernon, in Sorley, ed. *Press On!,* 1055–56.

242 **"If every division commander relieved people":** Gole, *DePuy,* 189.

243 **"Many a division commander has failed":** Bradley, *Soldier's Story,* 65.

243 **"he was not getting his share" . . . "with the resources he has":** Gen. Jonathan Seaman, interview by Charles MacDonald, June 16, 1973, historians' files, U.S. Army Center of Military History, Fort McNair, Washington, DC, 4.

243 **DePuy and his assistant division commander:** Haig, *Inner Circles,* 157.

243 **"You are relieving too many" . . . "save soldiers' lives":** Gole, *DePuy,* 191.

244 **"I'm not here to run a training ground":** Recollection of then-Maj. Eugene Cocke, quoted in Lewis Sorley, *Honorable Warrior: General Harold K. Johnson and the Ethics of Command* (University Press of Kansas, 1998), 257.

244 **"I fought in Normandy":** William DePuy, interview by Ted Gittinger, October 28, 1985, LBJ Library, 42.

244 **"I either would have to be removed":** DePuy Oral History, 153.

244 **"I can't have you be the filter":** Gole, "DePuy: His Relief of Subordinates in Combat," 12.

245 **"The chief of staff just left":** Sorley, *Honorable Warrior,* 257.

245 **"a. LTC Simpson, William J." . . . "with command of soldiers in combat":** William DePuy to Harold K. Johnson, December 29, 1966, William E. DePuy Papers, box 4, Correspondence 1966, USAMHI.

245 **"I can tell if a commander is competent":** Gole, quoting Gen. William Tuttle's account of DePuy in "DePuy: His Relief of Subordinates in Combat," 28–29.

246 **"When it came to the tactics":** Haig, *Inner Circles,* 159.

246 **"was an ideal commander":** Paul Gorman, *Cardinal Point: An Oral History— Training Soldiers and Becoming a Strategist in Peace and War* (Combat Studies Institute, Fort Leavenworth, KS, 2011), 34.

246 **"There was no question of brilliance" . . . "to those who worked for him":** Brown, e-mail messages to author, July 29, 2008, and June 16, 2010.

246 **"Bill would not accept officers":** Weyand oral history, Weyand Papers, USAMHI, 43.

247 **he became the special assistant to the chairman:** Westmoreland, *A Soldier Reports,* 429.

248 **"We are going to stomp them to death":** Neil Sheehan, *A Bright Shining Lie* (Random House, 1988), 568.

248 **CIA veteran Robert Komer:** Tim Weiner, "Robert Komer, 78, Figure in Vietnam, Dies," *New York Times,* April 12, 2000.

248 **"firepower alone was not the answer":** Sheehan, *Bright Shining Lie,* 21.

248 **"firepower became the dominant characteristic":** Doughty, "Evolution of US Army Tactical Doctrine," 38.

248 **when one Vietnamese sniper:** Charles Krohn, *The Lost Battalion of Tet: Breakout of the 2/12th Cavalry at Hue* (Pocket Star, 2008), 149.

248 **saw a battalion commander call in air strikes:** Michael Lee Lanning and Dan Cragg, *Inside the VC and the NVA: The Real Story of North Vietnam's Armed Forces* (Fawcett Columbine, 1992), 221.

248 **On one day alone:** George MacGarrigle, *Taking the Offensive: October 1966 to October 1967* (U.S. Army Center of Military History, 1998), 56.

249 **"With one salvo" . . . "they could not control":** Stuart Herrington, e-mail message to author, November 21, 2011; see also Stuart Herrington, *Silence Was a Weapon: The Vietnam War in the Villages* (Ballantine, 1987), 43.

249 **"over 675 sightings":** Harry Maurer, *Strange Ground: An Oral History of Americans in Vietnam, 1945–1975* (Avon, 1990), 457.

249 **"That the Army never could determine":** Gregory Daddis, *No Sure Victory: Measuring U.S. Army Effectiveness and Progress in the Vietnam War* (Oxford,2011), 18.

250 **"You only see the things":** *Selected Papers of General William E. DePuy*, 441.

250 **"I was deficient at the next level up":** DePuy, interview by Perlman (Combat Studies Institute, Fort Leavenworth, KS, 1994), DePuy Papers, USAMHI, 24–25.

250 **"We got into a firepower war":** Harold Johnson, interview by Agnew, USAMHI, 20.

250 **"The time gap between when the infantry":** Interview by Spruill and Vernon, in Sorley, ed., *Press On!*, 1070.

250 **"I have looked over your training guides":** DePuy to Terry Allen, March 13, 1967, DePuy Papers, box 4, Correspondence 1967, USAMHI.

251 **Allen's son and namesake:** MacGarrigle, *Taking the Offensive*, 359. The encounter in which the younger Allen died is discussed extensively by David Maraniss in *They Marched Into Sunlight: War and Peace, Vietnam and America, October 1967* (Simon & Schuster, 2003).

251 **"It is the duty of the executive" . . . "if found less than outstanding":** Peter Drucker, *The Effective Executive* (HarperCollins, 1993), 89.

18. THE COLLAPSE OF GENERALSHIP IN THE 1960s

252 **"That's why I am suspicious":** Doris Kearns Goodwin, *Lyndon Johnson and the American Dream* (Harper & Row, 1976), 252.

253 **"The campaign of escalating pressure":** Westmoreland, "A Military War of Attrition," 61.

253 **"It just seemed ridiculous" . . . "I didn't like any of them":** Weyand oral history, Weyand Papers, USAMHI, 108.

254 **Kinnard surveyed Army generals:** Kinnard, *The War Managers*, 45.

254 **"We . . . didn't know":** *Selected Papers of General William E. DePuy*, 441.

254 **"We were searching and destroying":** "Interview #2 with General Bruce Palmer Jr.," interview by Lt. Col. James Shelton and Lt. Col. Edward Smith, January 6, 1976, in historians' files, USAMHI.

255 **"One reason they [Hanoi] could not read our signal":** Westmoreland, "A Military War of Attrition," 61.

255 **On May 30 of that year, they met without him present:** McMaster, *Dereliction of Duty*, 100–102. This paragraph relies heavily on his chapters 4 and 5, as does this entire chapter.

256 **"Taylor gave misleading answers":** McMaster, *Dereliction of Duty*, 152.

256 **Later in 1964, the Chiefs again made a run:** McMaster, *Dereliction of Duty*, 175–76.

256 **McNamara omitted a key phrase:** McMaster, *Dereliction of Duty*, 192.

256 **"the assumptions that underlay the president's policy":** McMaster, *Dereliction of Duty*, 178.

256 **"You're my team":** McMaster, *Dereliction of Duty*, 265.

257 **they would behave as his minions:** McMaster, *Dereliction of Duty*, 309–11.

257 **Finally, in November 1965, Wheeler and the other members:** These three paragraphs combine two accounts provided by Cooper: Charles Cooper, "The Day It Became the Longest War," *Proceedings of the Naval Institute*, May 1996, 80; and Christian Appy, *Patriots: The Vietnam War Remembered from All Sides* (Viking, 2003), 122. Historians have tended to keep Cooper's account at arm's length, in part because no corroborating evidence has been provided by other attendees, but I am not aware of any evidence that has surfaced to cast doubt on his account.

258 **"a wary beagle":** Henry Kissinger, *White House Years* (Little, Brown, 1979), 34.

258 **"And then on the way to the White House":** As told by retired Army Col. Harry Summers in David Anderson, ed., *Facing My Lai: Moving Beyond the Massacre* (University Press of Kansas, 1998), 158.

258 **"I acquired the feeling":** Charles W. Jones and R. Manning Ancell, eds., *Four-Star Leadership for Leaders* (Executive Books, 1997), 62.

258 **"The president was lying":** McMaster, *Dereliction of Duty*, 331.

258 **"his patron, exemplar":** Goodwin, *Lyndon Johnson*, 90.

259 **"At no time that I was aware":** Alsop, *I've Seen the Best of It*, 466.

259 **American involvement in combat in Vietnam:** This useful summary of the Vietnam War by years was stated to me in March 2011 by Erik Villard, a historian at the U.S. Army Center of Military History.

259 **"We met with very strong enemy units":** David Elliott and W. A. Stewart, "Pacification and the Viet Cong System in Dinh Tuong: 1966–1967," RAND Corporation, January 1969, 67.

259 **"The Tam Hiep villagers' confidence":** Elliott and Stewart, "Pacification and the Viet Cong System," 73.

260 **"the situation has never been as favorable":** MacGarrigle, *Taking the Offensive*, 439.

260 **"The officer corps of the 1960s":** Krohn, *The Lost Battalion of Tet*, 82.

260 **"its standard operational repertoire" . . . "long-term patrolling of a small area":** Krepinevich, *Army and Vietnam*, 49, 53.

261 **Pentagon analyst Thomas Thayer recalled:** Thayer, *War Without Fronts*, 18.

261 **"Our direction was you organized":** Kim Willenson, *The Bad War: An Oral History of the Vietnam War* (New American Library, 1987), 105.

261 **they were misused:** Krepinevich, *Army and Vietnam*, 69–73.

262 **Truong Nhu Tang, then a Viet Cong official:** Truong Nhu Tang, *A Vietcong Memoir* (Harcourt Brace Jovanovich, 1985), 160.

262 **"The rationale that ceaseless U.S. operations" . . . "and their dedicated commitment":** F. J. West, "Area Security," RAND Corporation, August 1968, 4, 10. See also Krepinevich, *Army and Vietnam*, 59–61.

262 **When advisers in the field:** Krepinevich, *Army and Vietnam*, 76.

262 **"accentuate the positive":** Sorley, *Westmoreland*, 74.

262 **Lt. Col. John Paul Vann, effectively demanded a hearing:** Krepinevich, *Army and Vietnam*, 83; see also Sheehan, *Bright Shining Lie*, 340–42.

262 **A similarly skeptical State Department report:** Krepinevich, *Army and Vietnam*, 89, and Appy, *Patriots*, 84.

263 **"noted the absence of an overall counterinsurgency plan":** Krepinevich, *Army and Vietnam*, 85.

263 **In March 1966, a lengthy report:** The background of the authors of the report is discussed in Komer, *Bureaucracy Does Its Thing*, 137.

263 **The report found that:** "PROVN," 24, 31, 52, 53, 48–49, 70.

264 **"the South Vietnamese were virtually shunted aside":** James Willbanks, *Abandoning Vietnam: How America Left and South Vietnam Lost Its War* (University Press of Kansas, 2008), 280.

264 **"The study deserved more mature consideration":** Davidson, *Vietnam at War*, 410–11.

264 **which is how bureaucracies act:** This last clause is the formulation of retired Army Lt. Gen. James Dubik, one of the critical readers of two drafts of this book.

264 **"We went and fought the Vietnam War":** "Interview with R. W. Komer," January 25, 1982, for *Vietnam: A Television History*.

265 **"all that was needed":** Krepinevich, *Army and Vietnam*, 165.

265 **"Firepower":** Krepinevich, *Army and Vietnam*, 197.

265 **by one measure, financial expenditures:** Thayer, *War Without Fronts*, 25–26, 79.

265 **"They [the Americans] didn't want to pacify":** Willenson, *The Bad War*, 137.

265 **"The military battlefield":** Truong, *Vietcong Memoir*, 212.

266 **In a poll of 976 teachers and students:** John Moellering, "Future Civil-Military Relations: The Army Turns Inward?," *Military Review*, July 1973, 79.

266 **"the American Army fought magnificently":** Anthony Wermuth, "A Critique of Savage and Gabriel," *Armed Forces and Society*, May 1977, 490.

266 **"The war was not lost on the battlefield":** Appy, *Patriots*, 400.

266 **"our American leadership":** Taylor interview no. 1b, by Dorothy Pierce, February 10, 1969, LBJ Library, 7.

266 **"By the second decade after World War II":** Sheehan, *Bright Shining Lie*, 285.

267 **"If an officer progresses":** Westmoreland, *A Soldier Reports*, 335.

267 **"No reaction, no questions":** John Cushman, e-mail to author, January 1, 2012.

268 **"The Vietnamese people are the prize":** Sheehan, *Bright Shining Lie*, 631.

268 **President Johnson read a copy of Krulak's memo:** Sheehan, *Bright Shining Lie*, 633.

268 **"I am deeply concerned":** Cover note to "Top Secret/SPECAT exclusive for Lt. Gen. Walt from Lt. Gen. Krulak," October 7, 1966, Victor Krulak Papers, Marine Corps Archives, Quantico, VA.

268 **Combined Action Platoons:** James Donovan, "Combined Action Program: Marines' Alternative to Search and Destroy," *Vietnam Magazine*, August 2004, 7.

269 **"In the process of operating":** Michael Hennessy, *Strategy in Vietnam: The Marines and Revolutionary Warfare in I Corps, 1965–1972* (Praeger, 1997), 80.

269 **One CAP that was almost entirely surrounded:** West, "Area Security," 15.

269 **Marines in the program accounted for just 1.5 percent:** Ronald Spector, *After Tet: The Bloodiest Year in Vietnam* (Free Press, 1993), 192–93.

269 **"absolutely disgusted" . . . "the deliberate, mild sort":** Both Kinnard and DePuy quoted in Krepinevich, *Army and Vietnam*, 175.

269 **"I detect a tendency for the Marine chain of command":** Cosmas, *MACV: The Joint Command*, 333.

269 **urged him to order the Marines:** Gates, "American Military Leadership in Vietnam," 194.

270 **Lt. Gen. Phillip Davidson:** "Oral History of Gen. Phillip Davidson," part 1, March 30, 1982, LBJ Library, 2, 28.

270 **The cost of bringing in a Communist defector:** Thayer, *War Without Fronts,* 202.

270 **"The solution in Vietnam is more bombs":** Sheehan, *Bright Shining Lie,* 619.

270 **"It turned out to be infelicitous":** *Selected Papers of General William E. DePuy,* 439.

270 **In one two-month operation:** Krepinevich, *Army and Vietnam,* 191.

271 **"I soon figured out how Westy liked to operate":** Jack Shumlinson et al., *U.S. Marines in Vietnam: The Defining Year, 1968* (U.S. Marine Corps Headquarters, 1997), 13.

271 **"I thought it was the most unpardonable thing":** Shumlinson et al., *U.S. Marines in Vietnam,* 238.

271 **"Westmoreland never understood it":** Victor Krulak, "Interview by John Mason Jr., U.S. Naval Academy, 8 Dec 1969," appendix to "Oral History, Lieutenant General Victor Krulak," Benis Frank, interviewer, Historical Division, U.S. Marine Corps Headquarters, 1973, 53.

271 **some 8,500 sorties:** Thayer, *War Without Fronts,* 84.

271 **"The allies had enormous firepower":** Thayer, *War Without Fronts,* 27.

271 **Another view, heard more often outside the military:** This paragraph reflects the analysis of historian George Herring, especially as presented in his article "American Strategy in Vietnam: The Postwar Debate," *Military Affairs,* April 1982.

272 **"Given the iron determination of the communists":** Richard Hunt, *Pacification: The American Struggle for Vietnam's Hearts and Minds* (Westview, 1995), 279.

272 **"Tactics employed" . . . "break the enemy infrastructure":** Ngo Quang Truong, "RVNAF and US Operational Cooperation," in *Vietnam War: An Assessment,* 158–59.

273 **"Had it been fully developed":** Dong Van Khuyen, "The RVNAF," in *Vietnam War: An Assessment,* 78.

273 **"a protracted war of attrition":** Westmoreland, "A Military War of Attrition," 60.

273 **"It turned out they controlled the tempo":** *Selected Papers of General William E. DePuy,* 441. See also Krepinevich, *Army and Vietnam,* 190.

274 **the entire strategy of attrition:** Here I am borrowing the terms used in Thayer, *War Without Fronts,* 91. See also Keith Nolan, *House to House: Playing the Enemy's Game in Saigon, May 1968* (Zenith, 2006), 19.

274 **"As long as they could control their losses":** DePuy interview, LBJ Library, 28.

274 **A strategy of attrition might possibly have succeeded:** See Stephen Young, "How North Vietnam Won the War: An Interview with Bui Tin," *Wall Street Journal,* August 3, 1995.

274 **"If you attempted to run a business":** Edward Coffman, "Commentary," in John Schlight, ed., *The Second Indochina War* (U.S. Army Center of Military History, 1986), 187.

275 **"It's the stupidest damn thing":** Starry, interview by Spruill and Vernon, in Sorley, ed., *Press On!,* 1157.

275 **The Army began a policy:** Weigley, *History of the United States Army,* 510.

275 **"little or no acquaintance with the battlefield" . . . "had to start all over again":** Walter G. Hermes, *Truce Tent and Fighting Front: United States Army in the Korean War* (University Press of the Pacific, 2005), 186, 350–51.

276 **"patrol leaders had learned to lie":** Marshall, *Bringing Up the Rear,* 218.

276 **"Stripped of its experienced leadership":** Blair, *Forgotten War,* 923.

276 **smoking marijuana "every night":** Gorman, *Cardinal Point,* 19.

276 **the 3,500-man unit:** Gilberto N. Villahermosa, *Honor and Fidelity: The 65th Infantry in Korea, 1950–1953* (U.S. Army Center of Military History, 2009), 205, 232.

276 **under a system devised in 1964:** Donald Vandergriff, *The Path to Victory: America's Army and the Revolution in Human Affairs* (Presidio, 2002), 99, 302.

276 **"few units were in sustained combat":** Lewis, *The American Culture of War,* 272.

277 **a survey of officers:** "Cincinnatus" (pseudonym for Cecil Currey), *Self-Destruction: The Disintegration and Decay of the United States Army during the Vietnam Era* (Norton, 1981), 158, 277.

277 **"the problem with six-month or twelve-month command tours":** "Lieutenant General Walter F. Ulmer Jr., USA Retired," interview by Lt. Col. Rick Lynch, 1996, Walter Ulmer Papers, box 1, USAMHI, 120.

278 **"cast an amateurish quality":** Keith Nolan, *Ripcord: Screaming Eagles Under Siege, Vietnam 1970* (Presidio, 2000), 42.

278 **"With regard to having six months in command":** DePuy Oral History, 154.

279 **more than twice as likely to die:** Thayer, *War Without Fronts,* 113–14.

279 **"Major offensives or waves":** Thayer, *War Without Fronts,* 16.

279 **"This inquiry found that":** William Peers, "Report of the Department of the Army Review of the Preliminary Investigations into the My Lai Incident, Volume 1: The Report of the Investigation," March 14, 1970, B-4. Hereafter: Peers Report.

280 **"The relatively rapid turnover":** Truong, "RVNAF and US Operational Cooperation," in *Vietnam War: An Assessment,* 173.

280 **tactical commanders in the South Vietnamese military:** Ngo Quang Truong, "ARVN Battalion to the Corps and the Tactical Advisor," in Cao Van Vien et al., "The U.S. Advisor," in *Vietnam War: An Assessment,* 687.

280 **Lt. Col. David Holmes charged:** David Holmes, "Some Tentative Thoughts After Indochina," *Military Review,* August 1977, 86.

280 **"culture of insecurity":** Markel, "Organization Man at War," iv–v, xiv.

280 **tended toward "excessive caution":** Doughty, "Evolution of US Army Tactical Doctrine," 37.

281 **"The great majority of all ground battles":** Guenter Lewy, *America in Vietnam* (Oxford, 1978), 83.

281 **"Pursuit became a forgotten art":** Palmer, *Summons,* 145.

281 **"Our ground, naval and air forces":** George Keegan, "Dissatisfaction with the Air War," in W. Scott Thompson and Donaldson Frizzell, eds., *The Lessons of Vietnam* (Crane, Russak, 1977), 143.

281 **"atrocious" . . . "indications of American operations":** Davidson oral history, part 1, LBJ Library, 15.

281 **"We placed our own girls" . . . "never hit the ordinary American targets":** "Interview with Nguyen Thi Dinh," February 16, 1981, for *Vietnam: A Television History.*

282 **"The U.S. soldier is very poor":** Albert Garland, *A Distant Challenge: The U.S. Infantryman in Vietnam, 1967–1972* (Jove, 1985), 170.

282 **"An American unit cannot take or destroy":** Garland, *A Distant Challenge*, 170. See also Lanning and Cragg, *Inside the VC and the NVA*, 236.

282 **"Their idea was to surround us":** David Chanoff and Doan Van Toai, *Portrait of the Enemy* (Random House, 1986), 155.

282 **"They had a lot of bombs" . . . "they reacted very slowly":** "Interview with Nguyen Van Nghi," February 10, 1981, for *Vietnam: A Television History*.

283 **"When the American soldiers fell down":** "Interview with Nguyen Thi Hoa," March 1, 1981, for *Vietnam: A Television History*.

283 **"The puppet troops were also Vietnamese":** "Interview with Dang Xuan Teo," March 10, 1981, for *Vietnam: A Television History*.

283 **"All the U.S. defensive positions":** Garland, *A Distant Challenge*, 168.

283 **"We know we cannot defeat the Americans":** Garland, *A Distant Challenge*, 173.

284 **"The stubborn commitment of the high command":** Gates, "American Military Leadership in Vietnam," 198. This chapter is influenced by his analysis in that article.

284 **"The battalion commander was almost forced":** From "Company Command in Vietnam Collection," USAMHI Oral History Collection, quoted in Spector, *After Tet*, 219.

284 **"squad leaders in the sky":** Kinnard, *The War Managers*, 59.

19. TET '68: THE END OF WESTMORELAND AND THE TURNING POINT OF THE WAR

285 **"We have reached an important point":** Don Oberdorfer, *Tet!: The Turning Point in the Vietnam War* (Johns Hopkins University Press, 2001), 105.

286 **"The majority of them clearly was killed":** "Interview with Ngo Minh Khoi," July 26, 1981, for *Vietnam: A Television History*.

286 **Some were almost successful:** Oberdorfer, *Tet*, 145. This paragraph and the ones preceding and following it rely heavily on Oberdorfer's account and on James Willbanks, *The Tet Offensive: A Concise History* (Columbia University Press, 2007).

287 **The Communist tapes:** "Dang Xuan Teo," *Vietnam: A Television History*.

287 **"This small squad of VC sappers":** Willbanks, *Tet Offensive*, 35.

287 **executed a Viet Cong guerrilla:** One author has contended that the dead guerrilla had operated under the nom de guerre Bay Lop and was the leader of one of the assassination squads and had been captured shortly after killing thirty members of families of police officers and pushing them into a ditch. See James Robbins, *This Time We Win: Revisiting the Tet Offensive* (Encounter Books, 2010), 154–56. But Erik Villard, author of a forthcoming official U.S. Army history of the Tet Offensive, concluded after studying documents from both sides that the executed man was "definitely not" Bay Lop and instead was probably a member of the T4 section of Sub-Region 6 (Saigon Party Committee), the Viet Cong headquarters for political affairs in the city. The T4 section's mission was to assassinate South Vietnamese and American officials. Villard, e-mail message to author, March 17, 2011.

287 **"They killed many Americans":** Willbanks, *Tet Offensive*, 36.

288 **on December 15, 1967:** Oberdorfer, *Tet*, 137.

288 **"'Hey, something is going on here'"**: Weyand, interview by Sorley, Weyand Papers, USAMHI, 123–34.

288 **This move, commented Lt. Gen. Dave Richard Palmer:** Palmer, *Summons,* 184.

288 **Westmoreland would fudge the facts:** See discussion in Sorley, *Westmoreland,* 180.

288 **When it was over, between 45,000:** The lower number is from Cao Van Vien, "Leadership," in *Vietnam War: An Assessment,* 296. The higher one is from Oberdorfer, *Tet,* vii.

288 **"We saw the Germans do this":** "Interview with William C. (William Childs) Westmoreland," April 27, 1981, for *Vietnam: A Television History.*

289 **"Our soldiers' morale had been very high":** Military History Institute of Vietnam, *Victory in Vietnam: The Official History of the People's Army of Vietnam, 1954–1975* (University Press of Kansas, 2002), 224.

289 **When the people of South Vietnam did not rise up:** Konrad Kellen, "Conversations with Enemy Soldiers in Late 1968/Early 1969: A Study of Motivation and Morale," RAND Corporation, September 1970, 70–71.

289 **"The president's tax proposal":** William Conrad Gibbons, *The U.S. Government and the Vietnam War: Executive and Legislative Roles and Relationships,* part 4: *July 1965–January 1968* (Princeton University Press, 1995), 907.

289 **"the American imperialist will" . . . "the American ruling clique":** Military History Institute of Vietnam, *Victory in Vietnam,* 221, 223.

289 **"Washington panicked":** Willenson, *The Bad War,* 95–96.

290 **"they were all in a state of shock":** Willenson, *The Bad War,* 150.

290 **"Nobody believed anything":** DePuy interview, LBJ Library, 46.

290 **50 percent of Americans interviewed:** Oberdorfer, *Tet,* 246.

290 **"He told me some stories":** Kent Sieg, ed., *Foreign Relations of the United States, 1963–1968,* vol. 6, *Vietnam, January–August 1968* (U.S. Government Printing Office, 1992), 226. Also accessed online as *FRUS, Vietnam: Jan–August 1968,* vol. 6, Document 80, "Notes of Meeting, Washington, February 20, 1968, 1:05–2:50 pm." Hereafter: *FRUS 1963–1968,* vol. 6.

290 **Brandon spoke with Johnson a few days later:** Henry Brandon, *Anatomy of Error: The Inside Story of the Asian War on the Potomac, 1954–1969* (Gambit, 1969), 130.

290 **Johnson sent a telegram:** *FRUS 1963–1968,* vol. 6, 45.

291 **"in virtually ignoring pacification":** Sorley, *Westmoreland,* 107.

291 **"Every night when I fell asleep":** Goodwin, *Lyndon Johnson,* 253.

292 **"Even before assuming office":** Henry Kissinger, *Years of Upheaval* (Little, Brown, 1982), 83.

292 **"In any area where the grass was green":** "Interview with Nguyen Cong Minh," n.d., for *Vietnam: A Television History.*

292 **Some had been buried alive:** Nguyen Ngoc Bich, "The Battle of Hue 1968 as Seen from the Perspective of Its NVA Commander," April 15, 2010, *Viet Thuc,* 5.

292 **In the city, many more corpses:** Oberdorfer, *Tet,* 201, 214–15, 232.

292 **"You had this horrible smell":** "Interview with Myron Harrington," December 8, 1981, for *Vietnam: A Television History.*

20. MY LAI: GENERAL KOSTER'S COVER-UP AND GENERAL PEERS'S INVESTIGATION

293 **"The Americal Division strives":** "Senior Officer Debriefing Report, Major General S. W. Koster," June 2, 1968, Defense Technical Information Center, 10.

294 **"a collective nervous breakdown":** Ronald Spector, "The Vietnam War and the Army's Self-Image," in *The Second Indochina War* (U.S. Army Center of Military History, 1986), 170.

294 **Charlie Company was not a unit driven around the bend:** Peers Report, 4/8. See also commentary by a former Army platoon leader in Vietnam, Philip Beidler, "Calley's Ghost," in *Late Thoughts on an Old War: The Legacy of Vietnam* (University of Georgia Press, 2004), 157.

294 **"They had received casualties":** "Lecture by Hugh Thompson," in *Moral Courage in Combat: The My Lai Story* (U.S. Naval Academy, 2003), 15.

295 **"The people we received at mid-level":** "Interview with BG Koster, Samuel W., Retired," notes taken by George McGarrigle, August 26, 1982, in historians' files, U.S. Army Center of Military History, Fort McNair, Washington, DC, 2.

295 **"It was the most unhappy group":** Seymour Hersh, *Cover-up: The Army's Secret Investigation of the Massacre at My Lai 4* (Random House, 1972), 29.

295 **"He was a protégé":** "Oral History of General William A. Knowlton, USA Retired," interview by Lt. Col. David Hazen, USA, 1982, Senior Officer Oral History Collection, USAMHI, 461. See also a similar account in "Interview #2 with General Bruce Palmer Jr.," USAMHI, 214.

296 **"Terribly difficult command and control problem" . . . "least qualified to be a division commander":** "Interview #2 with General Bruce Palmer Jr," USAMHI, 239–40.

296 **"When I was assigned to Charlie Company":** Appy, *Patriots,* 350.

296 **Army investigators later would determine:** Peers Report, 8/14.

296 **He would later testify:** William Eckhardt, "My Lai: An American Tragedy," accessed from the Web site of the law faculty of the University of Missouri at Kansas City, http://law2.umkc.edu/faculty/projects/ftrials/mylai/ecktragedy .html, 8.

296 **"When we left the briefing":** Peers Report, 5/14.

297 **"Waste them":** William Calley, "Testimony at Court-Martial," excerpted in James Olson and Randy Roberts, *My Lai: A Brief History with Documents* (Bedford, 1998), 112.

297 **"I was ordered to go in there":** Excerpt from direct examination by George Latimer of Lt. William Calley, Calley court-martial transcript, accessed at http://law2.umkc.edu/faculty/projects/ftrials/mylai/myl_Calltest.html.

297 **"There are many versions of what happened":** Anderson, ed., *Facing My Lai,* 21.

297 **At around eight the following morning:** Richard Hammer, *The Court-Martial of Lt. Calley* (Coward, McCann & Geoghegan, 1971), 4, 57–59.

297 **"As the 1st Platoon moved":** Peers Report, 6/7.

297 **"Kill everybody":** Herbert Carter, "Testimony to U.S. Army CID," excerpted in Olson and Roberts, *My Lai: A Brief History,* 79.

298 **"I walked over to the ditch":** Dennis Conti, "Testimony to the Peers Commission," excerpted in Olson and Roberts, *My Lai: A Brief History,* 78.

298 **"at least one gang-rape":** Peers Report, 6/10.

298 **"I killed about eight people":** Varnado Simpson, "Testimony to U.S. Army CID," excerpted in Olson and Roberts, *My Lai: A Brief History*, 88–89.

298 **Lt. Col. Frank Barker:** Peers Report, 6/9.

298 **"This was an operation":** Anderson, ed., *Facing My Lai*, 56.

299 **"It was our guys doing all the killing":** Appy, *Patriots*, 347.

299 **"I was brought up in the country":** Thompson, Naval Academy lecture, 26.

299 **When the soldiers of Charlie Company finished:** Peers Report, 6/17.

299 **The nearby dead totaled:** Trent Angers, *The Forgotten Hero of My Lai: The Hugh Thompson Story* (Acadian House, 1999), 223.

299 **some 120 were children:** Appy, *Patriots*, 347.

299 **Of about twenty females raped:** "Summary of Rapes," CID Deposition Files, excerpted in Olson and Roberts, *My Lai: A Brief History*, 99–102.

299 **"There's a ditch full of dead women and children":** Angers, *The Forgotten Hero of My Lai*, 132.

300 **"a result of justifiable situations":** Quoted in Peers Report, 10/13.

300 **That afternoon, Gen. Koster:** Testimony of Maj. Gen. Samuel W. Koster before the Peers Commission, December 15–16, 1969, 35–36.

300 **"as their goal the suppression":** "Summary Report," Peers Report, 2/6 and 7.

301 **"he felt the pilot had been confused":** Koster testimony, Peers Commission, 188.

301 **"This operation was well planned":** Quoted in "Suppression and Withholding of Information," Peers Report, 11/7.

301 **Col. Henderson wrote a document:** Oran Henderson, "Report of Investigation," April 24, 1968, reproduced in Peers Report, 10/57, 58.

302 **"Lieutenant Kally":** "Letter of Mr. Ronald L. Ridenhour to Secretary of Defense, March 29, 1969," Peers Report, 1/8.

302 **"But if the Pinkville incident":** William Wilson, "I Had Prayed to God That This Thing Was Fiction," *American Heritage*, February 1990, reproduced in Olson and Roberts, *My Lai: A Brief History*, 153ff.

302 **"a repugnant picture was forming":** Wilson, "I Had Prayed to God," 156.

302 **"We just moved on in" . . . "I was just following orders?":** "Testimony of Paul D. Meadlo," July 16, 1969, taken during the investigation by Col. William V. Wilson, Office of the Inspector General, U.S. Army, 1010–13, accessed at Clemson.edu.

303 **"Something in me died":** Wilson, "I Had Prayed to God," 162.

303 **"We investigated this thing fully":** "William C. Westmoreland," vol. 2, interview by Lt. Col. Martin Ganderson, 1982, William Westmoreland Papers, box 70, USAMHI, 237.

303 **"I have been getting pressure":** "William C. Westmoreland," vol. 1, interview by Lt. Col. Martin Ganderson, 1982, William Westmoreland Papers, box 69, USAMHI, 76.

304 **"There was no use":** Quoted by a Peers investigator, Koster testimony, Peers Commission, 186.

304 **"We have not only searched":** Question during Koster testimony, Peers Commission, 225.

305 **Peers had known Koster:** W. R. Peers, *The My Lai Inquiry* (W. W. Norton, 1979), 113, 117.

305 **"They made no statements"** . . . **"I can't explain that":** Koster testimony, Peers Commission, 151.

305 **"Efforts were made at every level":** Summary, Peers Report, 6/7, 9.

306 **"I threw the files against the wall":** Anderson, ed., *Facing My Lai,* 42.

306 **"This prosecutorial record was abysmal":** Eckhardt, "My Lai: An American Tragedy," 7.

307 **"Poor Sam Koster":** "Oral History of General William A. Knowlton, USA Retired," interview by Lt. Col. David Hazen, 1982, Senior Officer Oral History Collection, USAMHI, 461, 465.

307 **"My opinion was that":** "Interview with Gen. Jonathan Seaman," 1.

307 **"unfair and unjust":** David Stout, "Gen. S. W. Koster, 86, Who Was Demoted After My Lai, Dies," *New York Times,* February 11, 2006.

307 **"a travesty of justice":** Peers, *The My Lai Inquiry,* 223.

308 **In his official oral history:** "Conversations Between Major General Kenneth J. Hodson and Lieutenant Colonel Robert E. Boyer," vol. 2, section 6, side 1, January 12, 1971, Kenneth J. Hodson Papers, box 1, USAMHI, 2, 11, 14, and 16.

308 **When he appeared before a congressional committee:** House Armed Services Investigatory Subcommittee, "Investigation of the My Lai Incident," 91st Congress, April 17, 1970, 234–35, 246.

308 **"death threats at three o'clock":** Thompson, Naval Academy lecture, 12.

309 **"It appeared to the Inquiry":** Peers, *The My Lai Inquiry,* 232.

309 **"Thus," Peers wrote:** Peers, *The My Lai Inquiry,* 254.

310 **"so many people in command positions":** Peers, *The My Lai Inquiry,* 209.

310 **"Because men's lives are at stake":** Peers, *The My Lai Inquiry,* 247. My italics.

311 **"The memo shook Westy":** Stuart Loory, *Defeated: Inside America's Military Machine* (Random House, 1973), 28.

311 **"moral and professional climate":** *Study on Military Professionalism,* U.S. Army War College, June 30, 1970, 53.

311 **"He said that we should use it":** Ulmer, interview by Lynch, USAMHI, 114–15.

311 **"The traditional standards of the American Army officer":** *Study on Military Professionalism,* iii.

311 **"Duty, honor and country":** D. M. Malone, "The Trailwatcher," *Army,* May 1981, 186, collected in D. M. Malone, *The Trailwatcher: A Collection of Colonel Mike Malone's Writings* (U.S. Army, 1982).

311 **"an ambitious, transitory commander":** *Study on Military Professionalism,* iv.

312 **Close to half the officers surveyed:** *Study on Military Professionalism,* B-31–B-34.

312 **"Nobody out there believes the body count":** *Study on Military Professionalism,* B-1-10.

312 **"so that if they did kill someone":** *Study on Military Professionalism,* B-1-14.

312 **"that there will be no AWOLs":** *Study on Military Professionalism,* B-1-10.

312 **"to accept mediocrity":** *Study on Military Professionalism,* B-1-1.

312 **Senior officers, "including generals":** *Study on Military Professionalism,* B-1-2.

312 **"The honest commander who reports":** *Study on Military Professionalism,* B-1-5.

313 **"led by fear, would double-cross":** *Study on Military Professionalism,* B-1-2.

313 **"Unless you are willing to compromise":** *Study on Military Professionalism,* B-1-19.

313 **"it's necessary today to lie":** *Study on Military Professionalism,* B-1-28.

313 **"isolated, perhaps willingly"**: *Study on Military Professionalism,* v.
313 **"Senior officers appear to be deluding themselves"**: *Study on Military Professionalism,* B-1-13.
313 **Senior leaders were portrayed**: *Study on Military Professionalism,* 19.
313 **" 'bleed' his troops dry"**: *Study on Military Professionalism,* 17.
313 **"cover your ass" . . . "endless CYA exercises create suspicion"**: *Study on Military Professionalism,* 14–15.
313 **"True loyalty among men"**: *Study on Military Professionalism,* 23.
313 **"the leaders of the future"**: *Study on Military Professionalism,* 29.
314 **"winners in the system"**: Gole, "U.S. Army in the Aftermath of Conflict," 9.
314 **"he kept shaking his head"**: Malone, "The Trailwatcher," 186.
314 **"I mean close"**: Malone, "The Trailwatcher," 187.
314 **"We put a couple of hundred copies"**: Ulmer, interview by Lynch, USAMHI, 115.

21. THE END OF A WAR, THE END OF AN ARMY

316 **In 1965, Communist forces**: Lewis Sorley, ed., *Vietnam Chronicles: The Abrams Tapes, 1968–1972* (Texas Tech University Press, 2004), 347.
316 **"to minimize the role of local forces"**: Peter Brush, "The Significance of Local Communist Forces in Post-Tet Vietnam," *Journal of Third World Studies* 15, no. 2 (1998), 198, collected in Walter Hixson, ed., *The United States and the Vietnam War: Significant Scholarly Articles* (Garland, 2000).
316 **"By winter of 1969"**: Lt. Gen. Julian Ewell, oral history, LBJ Library, 4.
316 **"The NVA were tenacious"**: Lanning and Cragg, *Inside the VC and the NVA,* 221–22.
316 **"was pleading with the units"**: Maurer, *Strange Ground,* 509.
317 **In mid-1965, the Army**: Spector, "The Vietnam War and the Army's Self-Image," 175.
317 **"concluded that it is not essential"**: Lyndon B. Johnson, news conference, July 28, 1965, John Woolley and Gerhard Peters, "The American Presidency Project," University of California, Santa Barbara, 2.
317 **The Army was not designed to go to war**: Weigley, *History of the United States Army,* 534.
317 **The president's refusal to activate**: Lewis Sorley, *A Better War: The Unexamined Victories and Final Tragedy of America's Last Years in Vietnam* (Harcourt, 1999), 294.
318 **"I didn't have the NCOs"**: Gorman, *Cardinal Point,* 55.
318 **By 1969, draftees made up 88 percent**: Sorley, *A Better War,* 288.
318 **"After only two months in Vietnam"**: Spector, "The Vietnam War and the Army's Self-Image," 179–80.
318 **"appalling" . . . "There would be a lieutenant"**: Starry, interview by Spruill and Vernon, in Sorley, ed., *Press On!,* 1002.
319 **"Individual personnel redeployments"**: Donn Starry, "New Abrams Biography: 'A Life So Full,' " *Armor,* September–October 1992, 51.
320 **"The way Westy ran the organization"**: Kerwin, interview by Doehle, 351–52.
320 **"In the whole picture" . . . "how many losses he takes"**: Sorley, *A Better War,* 59, 124.

320 **"Hanoi had pushed most of the best":** "R. W. Komer," *Vietnam: A Television History.*

321 **"When Johnson rolled out":** Al Santoli, *Everything We Had* (Ballantine, 1981), 149.

321 **By the end of 1971:** Robert Komer, "Was There Another Way?," in Thompson and Frizzell, eds., *The Lessons of Vietnam,* 220.

321 **"During late 1968 the enemy" . . . "new plots and schemes":** Military History Institute of Vietnam, *Victory in Vietnam,* 237.

322 **"The political and military struggle":** Military History Institute of Vietnam, *Victory in Vietnam,* 238–39.

322 **the Communists lost all but three:** Military History Institute of Vietnam, *Victory in Vietnam,* 250, 468.

322 **"The enemy's horrible, insidious":** Military History Institute of Vietnam, *Victory in Vietnam,* 240.

323 **"the population of our liberated areas":** Military History Institute of Vietnam, *Victory in Vietnam,* 246–47.

323 **"we recruited only 100 new soldiers":** Military History Institute of Vietnam, *Victory in Vietnam,* 247.

323 **"There's no doubt that 1969":** Chanoff and Toai, *Portrait of the Enemy,* 109.

323 **"When the Tet campaign was over":** Chanoff and Toai, *Portrait of the Enemy,* 157.

324 **"COSVN Resolution 9":** See Sorley, *A Better War,* 155–56. See also "A Preliminary Report on Activities During the 1969 Autumn Campaign, 30 October 1969," Douglas Pike Collection: Unit 06—Democratic Republic of Vietnam, box 12, folder 13, the Vietnam Archive, Texas Tech University.

324 **"The Communists are simply avoiding":** Daddis, *No Sure Victory,* 183.

324 **From 1965 to 1968:** Andrew Birtle, *U.S. Army Counterinsurgency and Contingency Operations Doctrine, 1942–1976* (U.S. Army Center of Military History, 2007), 367.

324 **Smaller and fewer operations:** Daddis, *No Sure Victory,* 156.

324 **"In some locations" . . . "virtually eliminated":** Truong, *Vietcong Memoir,* 201.

324 **"because they were able to infiltrate":** "Interview with Nguyen Thi Dinh," February 16, 1981, for *Vietnam: A Television History.*

325 **"The problem was that it came too late":** *Selected Papers of General William E. DePuy,* 439.

325 **"the United States could not have prevented":** Jeffrey Record, "Vietnam in Retrospect: Could We Have Won?," *Parameters,* Winter 1996–97, 63.

325 **"By '69, it was just a joke":** Santoli, *Everything We Had,* 88.

326 **"Things were going to hell":** Appy, *Patriots,* 445.

326 **"It was very difficult":** General William R. Richardson, interview by Lt. Col. Michael Ackerman, 1987, USAMHI, 202.

326 **"When I hear people say":** Appy, *Patriots,* 408.

326 **losing a soldier a day:** William Hauser, *America's Army in Crisis: A Study in Civil-Military Relations* (Johns Hopkins University Press, 1973), 119.

326 **Desertions and AWOL incidents:** Lewy, *America in Vietnam,* 154–57.

326 **According to a statement:** Richard Gabriel and Paul Savage, *Crisis in Command: Mismanagement in the Army* (Hill and Wang, 1978), 45.

326 **In at least two instances:** Shelby Stanton, *The Rise and Fall of an American Army: U.S. Ground Forces in Vietnam, 1965–1973* (Presidio, 1985), 357.

327 **"a bogus combat-veteran culture":** Schwarzkopf, *It Doesn't Take a Hero*, 181–83.

327 **In 1968, a year in which there were 14,592 Americans:** Hauser, *America's Army in Crisis*, 175.

327 **the Army seemed to be putting:** For a more sympathetic account of the Army of the late Vietnam War, see William Shkurti, *Soldiering On in a Dying War: The True Story of the Firebase Pace Incidents and the Vietnam Drawdown* (University Press of Kansas, 2011). The essence of Shkurti's argument, especially on pages 85–95, is that while the Army of that time was frayed, it was not as bad as people think. He argues, for example, that some combat refusals were justified. He also notes that in 1971 "only 4.5 percent of Vietnam GIs were hard-core heroin users." What this argument leaves out is that a unit can go bad when only a small percentage of its soldiers are ill-disciplined, criminally inclined, extremely demoralized, or simply poorly led and trained.

327 **There were 120,000 Army personnel:** Thayer, *War Without Fronts*, 36–37.

328 **"These guys would work stoned":** Santoli, *Everything We Had*, 128.

328 **"In my units, the majority":** "Interview with George Cantero," May 12, 1981, for *Vietnam: A Television History.*

328 **almost half the Army enlisted men:** Lee Robins, Darlene Davis, and Donald Goodwin, "Drug Use by U.S. Army Enlisted Men in Vietnam: A Follow-Up on Their Return Home," *American Journal of Epidemiology*, April 1974, 240.

328 **Even more were using marijuana:** Moskos, "The American Combat Soldier in Vietnam," 33.

328 **"the person that got fragged":** "George Cantero," *Vietnam: A Television History.*

328 **between 1969 and 1971:** Robert Scales Jr., *Certain Victory: United States Army in the Gulf War* (U.S. Army Office of the Chief of Staff, 1993), 6.

328 **one infantry company that went through:** Keith William Nolan, *Sappers in the Wire: The Life and Death of Firebase Mary Ann* (Pocket Books, 1996), 85. Nolan does not indicate whether the rapid turnover was caused by casualties, reliefs, promotions, or some other cause.

328 **"There were times I was very frightened":** Nolan, *Sappers*, 104.

328 **When one platoon refused to move:** Nolan, *Sappers*, 114.

329 **In 1965, the Army's rate of court-martials:** George Lepre, *Fragging: Why U.S. Soldiers Assaulted Their Officers in Vietnam* (Texas Tech University Press, 2011), 10, 113, 162.

329 **At 2:40 A.M. on March 28, 1971:** Stanton, *Rise and Fall of an American Army*, 359–60.

329 **"They were just walking":** Nolan, *Sappers*, 232.

330 **"It was a mistake":** Richardson, interview by Ackerman, USAMHI, 194.

330 **Baldwin was replaced:** Information on the removal of Maj. Gen. Baldwin is from Nolan, *Sappers*, 253–59; Frederick Kroesen, *General Thoughts: Seventy Years with the Army* (Association of the United States Army, 2003), 21–22; and Richardson, interview by Ackerman, USAMHI.

330 **"the atmosphere was somewhat poisonous":** *Selected Papers of General William E. DePuy*, 427.

330 **In a public opinion poll:** D. M. Malone, "Leadership at the General Officer Level," 1975, in Malone, *The Trailwatcher*, 217.

331 **"the senior officer corps":** Both the Westmoreland speech information and the quotation are from Roger Spiller, "In the Shadow of the Dragon: Doctrine and the U.S. Army After Vietnam," originally published in the *RUSI Journal* in 1997 and reprinted in James Willbanks, ed., *The Vietnam War* (Ashgate, 2006), 421. In a footnote in his biography of Westmoreland, Lewis Sorley says that Kevin Crow, an Army historian, has cast doubt on whether these booings of Westmoreland actually occurred (Sorley, *Westmoreland*, 348). But in his oral history, General Paul Gorman, who was there, recalls that Westmoreland's speech at Fort Benning's Infantry School "nearly created a mutiny" (Gorman, *Cardinal Point*, 64).

331 **"We reached a condition":** Frederick Kroesen, "Korean War Lessons," *Army* magazine, August 2010, 18.

332 **"Those were the dog days":** From online version of Montgomery Meigs, "Generalship: Qualities, Instincts and Character," *Parameters*, Summer 2001.

332 **"The Army was really on the edge":** Barry McCaffrey, interview by Lt. Col. Conrad Munster, U.S. Army War College, April 2004, 24.

332 **"An entire American army was sacrificed":** Stanton, *Rise and Fall of an American Army*, 368.

332 **"As a young officer, I watched":** "Colonel (Ret.) Richard Sinnreich," interviews by Lt. Col. Steven Fox, 2001, in Sinnreich Papers, box 1, USAMHI, 81.

PART IV: INTERWAR

22. DEPUY'S GREAT REBUILDING

335 **President Nixon did not like Abrams:** H. R. Haldeman, *The Haldeman Diaries: Inside the Nixon White House* (Berkley, 1995), 313, 531.

336 **"I had no doubt":** Haig, *Inner Circles*, 275.

336 **the discussions about who would succeed:** Sorley, *Thunderbolt*, 334–35.

336 **"Your Army is on its ass":** Gole, *DePuy*, 213.

336 **The Grant-like Abrams:** For the Grant-Abrams comparison, see Davidson oral history, part 1, LBJ Library, 14.

336 **"expeditious discharge program":** Scales, *Certain Victory*, 8.

336 **"the full battalion would cheer":** McCaffrey, interview by Munster, USAMHI, 38.

337 **"In 1973, I was present":** Interview with person requesting anonymity, October 2007, 2.

337 **That year the Army War College:** Linn, *Echo of Batle*, 213.

337 **"arguably, the most important general"** . . . **"likely the most important figure":** Spiller, "In the Shadow of the Dragon," 44, and Richard Swain, introduction to *Selected Papers of General William E. DePuy*, vii.

337 **"What DePuy did was take a broken Army":** Gole, interview by author, Carlisle, PA, December 14, 2010.

337 **a fast-rising young officer:** James Kitfield, *Prodigal Soldiers: How the Generation of Officers Born of Vietnam Revolutionized the American Style of War* (Simon & Schuster, 1995), 127.

338 **"The soldier moved to the next sequential task":** Gole, *DePuy*, 249.

338 **DePuy and his subordinates:** Kitfield, *Prodigal Soldiers*, 162.

339 **"We cannot have the best man":** Gole, "Relevance of DePuy," 70.

340 **He threw his institutional weight behind:** Kitfield, *Prodigal Soldiers*, 216.

340 **"It not only ensured that the best"**: David Barno, "Military Adaptation in Complex Operations," *Prism* 1, no. 1 (December 2009), 29–30.

340 **Cushman had grown up in the interwar Army:** John Cushman, e-mail message to author, March 5, 2011. In the 1930s, Cushman's father worked again for Marshall, in Illinois, and introduced his fifteen-year-old son to him, but that personal connection did not keep Maj. Gen. Troy Middleton and George Patton from relieving the father, then a brigadier general, as an assistant commander of the 45th Division in Sicily in 1943. Author interview with the younger Cushman, November 12, 2011.

341 **"basic questions such as honesty":** Cushman, *Fort Leavenworth—A Memoir,* vol. 1, 58.

341 **"It was tough, direct"** . . . **"Lock your heels":** Malone, "The Trailwatcher," 189. A somewhat different account is given in Kitfield, *Prodigal Soldiers,* 147.

342 **"the more senior an officer is":** Morris Brady, "Memorandum for MG Cushman," April 2, 1974, 1–2, included in John Cushman, *Fort Leavenworth—A Memoir,* vol. 2.

342 **"What the hell happened out there":** Malone, "The Trailwatcher," 189. Abrams had long harbored suspicions about Army intellectuals. John Wickham, who would become Army chief of staff eleven years after Abrams did, recalled being at an officers' bar in Saigon as a lieutenant colonel and being loudly told by Abrams, "Wickham, the Army needs fighters like Hollingsworth [Gen. DePuy's old assistant], it doesn't need eggheads like you." Wickham had plenty of time to ponder this crack after he was almost killed in Vietnam and then spent five months hospitalized, believing he would never walk again. "General John A. Wickham Jr.," interview by Jose Alvarez, 1991, John Wickham Papers, USAMHI, 13, 26.

342 **"did not want a dialogue":** Paul Herbert, "Deciding What Has to Be Done: General William E. DePuy and the 1976 Edition of FM 100-5, Operations," Combat Studies Institute, Fort Leavenworth, KS, 1988, 42.

342 **"In 1964–67 I had taken exception":** Cushman, *Fort Leavenworth—A Memoir,* vol. 1, 28.

343 **"the Army War College":** "Remarks by General William E. DePuy, TRADOC Commanders' Conference, 25 May 1977," in *Selected Papers of General William E. DePuy,* 245.

343 **"All I want from this class":** Cushman, *Fort Leavenworth—A Memoir,* vol. 1, 47.

343 **"They said that DePuy":** "Remarks by General William E. DePuy, TRADOC Commanders' Conference, 25 May 1977," in *Selected Papers of General William E. DePuy,* 241.

343 **"Nice warm human relationships":** "TRADOC Leadership Conference, 22 May 1971, at Fort Benning, Georgia," in *Selected Papers of General William E. DePuy,* 113.

343 **"be examples of the soldierly virtues"** . . . **"out of here":** Cushman, *Fort Leavenworth—A Memoir,* vol. 1, 63–64.

344 **"Major General Cushman believed":** Herbert, "Deciding What Has to Be Done," 54.

344 **"General Jack Cushman at Leavenworth":** Starry, interview by Spruill and Vernon, in Sorley, ed., *Press On!,* 1111.

345 **"Don't get too lofty":** Herbert, "Deciding What Has to Be Done," 87.

345 **In 1976, DePuy published the edition of the manual:** Spiller, "In the Shadow of the Dragon," 429.

345 **DePuy made the drafting of doctrine:** This group of sentences paraphrases Spiller, "In the Shadow of the Dragon," 430.

346 **"doctrine became one device":** Hew Strachan, "Strategy or Alibi? Obama, McChrystal and the Operational Level of War," *Survival,* October–November 2010, 160.

346 **"the molasses in the system":** Gole, "Relevance of DePuy," 73.

346 **"DePuy wanted USACGSC":** Herbert, "Deciding What Has to Be Done," 54.

346 **"We were tactical guys":** Gole, *DePuy,* 261.

347 **"servicing targets" . . . "clear and broadly accepted":** Donald Bletz, "The 'Modern Major General' (Vintage 1980)," *Parameters,* vol. 4, 1974.

347 **"courted the dangers of oversimplification":** Herbert, "Deciding What Has to Be Done," 58.

347 **"Dear Jack," DePuy wrote to Cushman:** DePuy to Cushman, October 22, 1975, Correspondence, DePuy Papers, box 35, USAMHI.

348 **In its twenty-first-century wars:** The terms used in this sentence borrow from those used by Gary Klein in his wonderful book *Sources of Power: How People Make Decisions* (MIT, 2001).

348 **DePuy told Starry:** Starry, interview by Spruill and Vernon, in Sorley, ed., *Press On!,* 1128.

348 **"General Cushman is a very strong minded individual":** Cushman, *Fort Leavenworth—A Memoir,* vol. 1, 44.

349 **"From 1982 on, the National Training Center":** Paul Yingling, interview by author, Baghdad, June 7, 2008.

349 **"The fixation on winning day-long battles":** Linn, *Echo of Battle,* 216.

350 **"right now, . . . we have":** "National Defense Funding Levels for Fiscal Year 1981," Hearing of Investigations Subcommittee of the House Armed Services Committee, May 29, 1980, 9, 18.

350 **"Meyer felt that lack of essential honesty":** Kitfield, *Prodigal Soldiers,* 200.

350 **after returning to the Pentagon from Capitol Hill:** Kitfield, *Prodigal Soldiers,* 202–3.

351 **"He can be counted on":** Malone, "Leadership at the General Officer Level," 222.

351 **"potentially creative managerial type":** Bletz, "The 'Modern Major General,'" 50.

351 **personality and intelligence tests:** David Campbell, "The Psychological Test Profiles of Brigadier Generals: Warmongers or Decisive Warriors?," address to the American Psychological Association Convention, New York, August 30, 1987, 13.

352 **"on the flexibility scale":** Campbell, "Test Profiles of Brigadier Generals," 10.

352 **"a maladaptive Army senior officer corps":** Lloyd Matthews, "Anti-Intellectualism and the Army Profession," in Lloyd Matthews, ed., *The Future of the Army Profession,* rev. ed. (McGraw-Hill, 2005), 83.

352 **In 1983, an Army survey:** Tilden Reid, "Performance of Successful Brigade Commanders Who Were Selected to BG as Viewed by Their Former Battalion Commanders," U.S. Army War College, June 5, 1983, 21, 24, 26, 29, 56.

352 **In 1975, the Army established:** C. M. Dick Deaner, "The U.S. Army Organizational Effectiveness Program: A Eulogy and Critique," *PAQ: Public Administration Quarterly,* Spring 1991, 22–23.

353 **"While organizational effectiveness":** John Marsh and John Wickham Jr., "Personal for General Rogers, . . . Subject: Organizational Effectiveness Program," June 7, 1985, in author's files.

353 **"that could easily be measured":** Peter Varljen, "Leadership: More Than Mission Accomplishment," *Military Review,* March–April 2003, 78.

23. "HOW TO TEACH JUDGMENT"

354 **"was confined to the science" . . . "you're trying to do?":** Brig. Gen. (Ret.) Huba Wass de Czege, unpublished interview by Col. (Ret.) Kevin Benson, January 14, 2009, files of Col. Benson, 9, 11.

355 **In June 1981, Wass de Czege buttonholed Richardson:** Huba Wass de Czege, "The School of Advanced Military Studies: An Accident of History," *Military Review,* July–August 2009, 3. See also Kevin Benson, "School of Advanced Military Studies [SAMS] Commemorative History, 1984–2009," U.S. Army Command and General Staff College, Fort Leavenworth, KS, 2009, 4–5.

355 **"A system of officer education":** Col. Huba Wass de Czege, "Army Staff College Level Training Study," U.S. Army War College, June 13, 1983, 3. Italics in original.

355 **"marginally qualified" . . . "what to think about war":** Wass de Czege, "Army Staff College Level Training Study," 29–30, 51–52. Italics in original.

355 **"better military judgment":** Wass de Czege, "Army Staff College Level Training Study," 4.

356 **"The Army gave them the opportunity":** "Lieutenant Colonel Harold R. Winton, USA, Retired," interview by Lt. Col. Richard Mustion, 2001, Winton Papers, box 1, USAMHI, 46.

356 **For example, its second director:** Benson, "SAMS Commemorative History," 24.

356 **"I came out of that war" . . . "but what about the war?":** Sinnreich, interviews by Fox, 14–16.

357 **"When you get to the unit":** Wass de Czege, interview by Benson, 16.

357 **"Getting these guys was like gold" . . . "around the Army than anybody":** Robert Killebrew, e-mail message to author, June 14, 2011.

357 **Gen. Richardson, who had approved the idea:** General William R. Richardson, interview by Lt. Col. Michael Ackerman, 1987, USAMHI, 336.

357 **"would make a tremendous impact":** Wass de Czege, "Army Staff College Level Training Study," 10.

358 **"just seemed to approach the issues":** Huba Wass de Czege, e-mail message to author, June 20, 2011.

358 **"War is much more than a tactical battle":** Quoted in Benson, "SAMS Commemorative History," 33.

358 **"For nearly ten years":** Wass de Czege, "Army Staff College Level Training Study," Appendix B, 21.

359 **a plan developed by "SAMSters":** Benson, "SAMS Commemorative History," 49.

359 **"are innovative leaders":** "Converting Intellectual Power into Combat Power," SAMS brochure, 2009, 2.

359 **In 1984, an Army survey:** Lt. Col. Duane Lempke, "Command Climate: The Rise and Decline of a Military Concept," U.S. Army War College, April 29, 1988, 8.

359 **An internal survey conducted:** Linn, *Echo of Battle*, 219.

359 **In 1987, a survey of 141:** Lt. Col. Thomas Baker, "Leadership: Does the Officer Corps Truly Care for the Enlisted Soldier?," U.S. Army War College, April 20, 1987, 15, 16, 24, 26, 27, 32, 37, 49.

360 **"Not trusting people":** Walter Ulmer, "Leaders, Managers and Command Climate," *Armed Forces Journal*, July 1986, 58.

360 **according to another 1987 survey:** Lt. Col. Bruce Malson, "Tarnished Armor: Erosion of Military Ethics," Army War College, Carlisle, PA, March 23, 1988, 27.

360 **"As a rule . . . general officers":** Clay Buckingham, "Ethics and the Senior Officer: Institutional Tensions," *Parameters*, Autumn 1985, 26.

361 **"It would be much better" . . . "beyond our scope":** Starry, interview by Spruill and Vernon, in Sorley, ed., *Press On!*, 1043.

361 **"The Army gained tactical":** Suzanne Nielsen, "An Army Transformed: The U.S. Army's Post-Vietnam Recovery and the Dynamics of Change in Military Organizations," Strategic Studies Institute, U.S. Army War College, September 2010, viii.

362 **"We were trying to change the Army":** Sinnreich, interviews by Fox, 47, 51.

362 **William DePuy's legacy lived on:** Kitfield, *Prodigal Soldiers*, 209–14.

362 **"I figured it was my obligation":** "Oral History: Richard Cheney," *Frontline: The Gulf War*, Public Broadcasting System, WGBH, III-4.

362 **"Let me use the example first":** "Statement of Gen. William E. DePuy, USA (Ret.)," *Crisis in the Persian Gulf: Sanctions: Diplomacy and War*, Hearings Before the Committee on Armed Services, House of Representatives, December 1990, 461–62.

PART V: IRAQ AND THE HIDDEN COSTS OF REBUILDING

24. COLIN POWELL, NORMAN SCHWARZKOPF, AND THE EMPTY TRIUMPH OF THE 1991 WAR

368 **"We were confident":** Schwarzkopf, *It Doesn't Take a Hero*, 221.

368 **"Eighteen months of hard work":** Schwarzkopf, *It Doesn't Take a Hero*, 222.

369 **"Democracy did not always function well":** Colin Powell with Joseph Persico, *My American Journey* (Random House, 1995), 173.

369 **"always felt a special affinity":** Powell, *My American Journey*, 312.

369 **"perpetual optimism":** Powell, *My American Journey*, 347.

370 **"If it hadn't been for Iran-Contra":** Henry Louis Gates Jr., *Thirteen Ways of Looking at a Black Man* (Random House, 1997), 78.

370 **"Cars, unlike people":** Powell, *My American Journey*, 219.

370 **"DePuy alumnus":** Powell, *My American Journey*, 240.

371 **"I had long since learned" . . . "considered vital":** Powell, *My American Journey*, 220.

371 **"the higher you rise":** David Barno, interview by author, November 2010.

372 **"And that," Powell stated:** Powell, *My American Journey*, 383.

372 **"fighting the war in Vietnam"** . . . **"stick to military matters":** Powell, *My American Journey*, 464–66.

373 **According to a staff log he quotes:** Frank Schubert and Theresa Kraus, eds., *The Whirlwind War: The United States Army in Operations Desert Shield and Desert Storm* (U.S. Army Center of Military History, 1995), 99.

373 **But Cheney decided:** Schwarzkopf, *It Doesn't Take a Hero*, 419, 437.

373 **"For the benefit of the Vietnam vets":** Schwarzkopf, *It Doesn't Take a Hero*, 444.

373 **Schwarzkopf would begin his counteroffensive:** Rick Atkinson, *Crusade: The Untold Story of the Persian Gulf War* (Houghton Mifflin, 1993), 59.

373 **"It will be massive":** State Department transcript of meeting of Secretary of State James Baker and Iraqi Foreign Minister Tariq Aziz, Geneva, Switzerland, January 9, 1991, archives of the James A. Baker III Institute for Public Policy, Rice University, Houston, 5.

374 **"I found the plan unimaginative":** Dick Cheney interview, "The Gulf War," *Frontline*, WGBH, January 9, 1996, I-3.

374 **"the charge of the light brigade":** Michael R. Gordon and Bernard E. Trainor, *The Generals' War: The Inside Story of the Conflict in the Gulf* (Little, Brown, 1995), 144.

374 **"hey diddle diddle":** Atkinson, *Crusade*, 111.

374 **"I was pretty appalled":** Brent Scowcroft interview, "The Gulf War," III-4.

374 **"sent the signal to everybody":** Cheney interview, "The Gulf War," I-4.

374 **"In a single story, Dugan made":** Powell, *My American Journey*, 478.

375 **"I don't give a damn":** Atkinson, *Crusade*, 15.

375 **"We assumed with respect to the air war":** Cheney interview, "The Gulf War," I-7.

375 **"fully understood the importance":** Dick Cheney, *In My Time: A Personal and Political Memoir* (Threshold, 2011), 215.

375 **"The guy supposedly has read Clausewitz":** Atkinson, *Crusade*, 119.

376 **"I needed to be able to say":** Cheney interview, "The Gulf War," II-7 and III-2.

376 **in order to find and destroy Scud launchers:** This point is made in Gordon and Trainor, *The Generals' War*, 247.

376 **"designed to humiliate the Saudi army":** Gordon and Trainor, *The Generals' War*, 288.

377 **One rattled member of Iraq's 5th Mechanized Division:** Paul Westermeyer, "The Battle of al-Khafji," Marine Corps History Division, Washington, DC, 2008, 32.

377 **"After the operations of al Khafji":** Kevin Woods, David Palkki, and Mark Stout, eds., *The Saddam Tapes: The Inner Workings of a Tyrant's Regime, 1978–2001* (Cambridge University Press, 2011), 215.

377 **"about as significant as a mosquito":** John Newell III, "Airpower and the Battle of Khafji: Setting the Record Straight," School of Advanced Airpower Studies, Maxwell Air Force Base, Alabama, June 1998, iii.

377 **a failure of generalship:** This paragraph relies heavily on the conclusions of Gordon and Trainor, *The Generals' War*, 288–89.

378 **"My responsibility is the lives":** Atkinson, *Crusade*, 345.

378 **a remarkably revealing exchange:** Most of this account of their conversation is drawn from Powell, *My American Journey*, 515–16; Schwarzkopf's final comment comes from Atkinson's *Crusade*, which largely agrees with Powell's account.

25. THE GROUND WAR: SCHWARZKOPF VS. FREDERICK FRANKS

379 **destroyed roughly 30 Iraqi tanks:** Estimate of Capt. H. R. McMaster, quoted in Tom Clancy with General Fred Franks Jr., *Into the Storm: On the Ground in Iraq* (Berkley, 1998), 357–58.

379 **"a brilliant slaughter":** Atkinson, *Crusade,* 467.

380 **"What the hell's going on with VII Corps?":** Schwarzkopf, *It Doesn't Take a Hero,* 527.

380 **"I was thinking forty-eight hours ahead":** Frederick Franks interview, "The Gulf War," II-4.

380 **In his memoir, Franks would criticize:** Clancy and Franks, *Into the Storm,* 367, 380. See also pages 294, 339, 367–68, 440–42, 455, and 522 for additional comments about Schwarzkopf's misapprehension of the movements and performance of VII Corps.

380 **"overly elaborate plan":** Gordon and Trainor, *The Generals' War,* 380.

381 **"more like he belonged in a morgue":** Atkinson, *Crusade,* 392.

381 **In fact, Gordon and Trainor concluded:** Gordon and Trainor, *The Generals' War,* 380, 431, 464.

381 **"Schwarzkopf's great shortcoming":** Richard Swain, *"Lucky War": Third Army in Desert Storm* (U.S. Army Command and General Staff College Press, 1994), 340–41.

382 **He misleadingly told the world:** This paragraph relies heavily on "The Gate Is Closed," chap. 19 of Gordon and Trainor's *The Generals' War,* 400–432. The second Schwarzkopf quotation, about "surrender or destruction," is from Atkinson, *Crusade,* 470.

382 **"As long as it is not over the part"** . . . **"where we are not located":** Gordon and Trainor, *The Generals' War,* 446.

383 **"They fell down on their job":** Robert Goldich, e-mail message to author, February 26, 2012.

383 **"the U.S. war effort split open":** Gideon Rose, *How Wars End* (Simon & Schuster, 2010), 223.

384 **They viewed it through the prism of the Vietnam War:** Scales, *Certain Victory,* 383.

384 **Powell and Schwarzkopf even discussed the feasibility:** Schwarzkopf, *It Doesn't Take a Hero,* 548.

384 **"in case they ever wanted to recreate":** Schwarzkopf, *It Doesn't Take a Hero,* 560.

384 **"We were fighting a limited war":** Powell, *My American Journey,* 519.

384 **"For once," he concluded:** Schwarzkopf, *It Doesn't Take a Hero,* 580.

385 **"Its underlying concepts":** Antulio Echevarria, "Toward an American Way of War," Strategic Studies Institute, U.S. Army War College, March 2004, 16.

385 **"The confusion surrounding the termination":** Justin Kelly and Mike Brennan, "Alien: How Operational Art Devoured Strategy," Strategic Studies Institute, U.S. Army War College, September 2009, 69.

386 **"The assumption was that Saddam":** Cheney interview, "The Gulf War," II-4.

386 **Saddam Hussein's view of the ending of the war:** Woods, Palkki, and Stout, eds., *The Saddam Tapes,* 39, 43, 211.

386 **"As a mechanism to advance the cause":** Andrew Bacevich, "The United States in Iraq: Terminating an Interminable War," in Moten, ed., *Between War and Peace,* 415.

386 **the effect of the 1991 campaign:** Andrew Bacevich, "The Revisionist Imperative: Rethinking Twentieth Century Wars," 2012 George C. Marshall Lecture
of the American Historical Association, American Historical Association
Annual Meeting, Chicago, January 7, 2012, 7. On the issue of the effects of the
1991 war, one question about which surprisingly little is known even now is
whether the way in which the war ended gave Iran entrée into Iraqi affairs,
with its Revolutionary Guards also encouraging Iraqi Shiites to rise against
Saddam. On the captured tapes of his meetings, Saddam complains that the
Iranians "imposed on our land" after the 1991 war, especially in Diyala Province. Woods, Palkki, and Stout, *The Saddam Tapes,* 206.

387 **the United States imposed a no-fly zone:** Michael Knights, "The Long View of
No-Fly and No-Augmentation Zones," in Michael Knights, ed., *Operation Iraqi
Freedom and the New Iraq: Insights and Forecasts* (Washington Institute for Near
East Policy, 2004), 41.

26. THE POST–GULF WAR MILITARY

388 **"above average":** Linn, *Echo of Battle,* 229.

388 **"Basking in the glow of victory":** Maj. Chad Foster, comment posted on
author's *Best Defense* blog, October 16, 2009.

388 **"The thing that killed us":** Gen. Jack Keane, interview by author, January 16,
2008.

389 **"shallow 'bumper sticker' concepts":** Huba Wass de Czege, "Lessons from the
Past: Making the Army's Doctrine 'Right Enough' Today," Institute of Land
Warfare, Association of the U.S. Army, September 2006, 21.

389 **intellectually oriented programs:** Harold R. Winton, interview by Mustion, 52.
See also 47, Sinnreich oral history.

389 **"defense conversion":** Bill Clinton and Al Gore, *Putting People First: How We
Can All Change America* (Times Books, 1992), 10, 75, 148.

389 **the size of the Army was cut:** Priscilla Offenhauer, "General and Flag Officer
Authorizations for the Active and Reserve Components: A Comparative and
Historical Analysis," Federal Research Division, The Library of Congress,
December 2007, 49–50.

390 **"Not all went right":** James Dubik, e-mail message to the author, December 6,
2011.

390 **"It only took one boss"** . . . **"in the decade of war":** Col. John Ferrari, interview by author, October 25, 2009, and e-mail message to author, September 23,
2011.

390 **"The overcontrolling leader":** Lloyd Matthews, "The Overcontrolling Leader,"
Army Magazine, April 1996, 33.

391 **Maj. Gen. John Faith wrote:** John Faith, "The Overcontrolling Leader: The
Issue Is Trust," *Army Magazine,* June 1997, 7.

391 **A study done at West Point:** Don Snider, "The U.S. Army as Profession," in
Matthews, *The Future of the Army Profession,* 22–27.

391 **"Departing from the tried and proven"** . . . **"immature, reckless":** Michael
Cody, "Selecting and Developing the Best Leaders," in Lloyd Matthews, ed.,

Building and Maintaining Healthy Organizations: The Key to Future Success (U.S. Army War College, October 2000), 96.

392 **"felt that there was a high degree":** Lee Staab, "Transforming Army Leadership—The Key to Officer Retention," U.S. Army War College, Carlisle, PA, April 2001, 8.

392 **"relationships between junior and senior leaders":** Anneliese Steele, "Are the Relationships Between Junior and Senior Leaders in the U.S. Army Officer Corps Dysfunctional?," School of Advanced Military Studies, U.S. Army Command and General Staff College, Fort Leavenworth, KS, April 2001, 48.

392 **"self-serving, short-sighted":** Varljen, "Leadership: More Than Mission Accomplishment," 75.

392 **"short-term mission accomplishment":** Jones, "Improving Accountability for Effective Command Climate," 18.

392 **essays about generalship in *Parameters:*** Walter Ulmer Jr., "Military Leadership into the 21st Century: Another 'Bridge Too Far'?," *Parameters,* Spring 1998; Montgomery Meigs, "Generalship," *Parameters,* Summer 2001.

393 **"When war is reduced to fighting"** . . . **"enemy who fights smarter":** Colin Gray, *Fighting Talk: Forty Maxims on War, Peace and Strategy* (Potomac, 2009), 33.

394 **the nature and extent of his isolation:** My language here is similar to that on page 334 of Karen DeYoung's *Soldier: The Life of Colin Powell* (Knopf, 2006).

395 **"My colleagues, every statement":** Ricks, *Fiasco,* 90.

396 **"Who went to the United Nations":** Colin Powell, interview by Bob Shieffer, *Face the Nation,* CBS, August 28, 2011.

396 **"I will forever be known":** "Colin Powell: 'I'm very sore,'" London *Daily Telegraph,* February 26, 2005. For a more sympathetic account of Powell's role in this matter, see Bob Drogin's *Curveball* (Random House, 2007), which essentially argues that the CIA's Tenet actively sought to mislead Powell.

396 **"presented not opinions":** "Secretary Rumsfeld Address to the Munich Conference on European Security Policy," Defense Department, February 8, 2003.

396 **"But Tommy was confident":** "Remarks by General Colin Powell (Ret.)," Fort Leavenworth, KS, April 29, 2008, transcript by Federal News Service, 18.

27. TOMMY R. FRANKS: TWO-TIME LOSER

397 **"During the Vietnam War":** Tommy Franks, *American Soldier* (Regan, 2004), 441. Italics in original.

398 **"His development approached":** Cushman, e-mail message to author, November 12, 2011.

398 **"The American military is simply uncomfortable":** William Taylor, "Spin Machine," *Armed Forces Journal,* August 2011.

398 **The warning signs about Franks:** Peter Bergen, *The Longest War: America and al-Qaeda Since 9/11* (Free Press, 2011), 74.

399 **certain he had bin Laden cornered:** Bergen, *Longest War,* 72. For chronology and presence of bin Laden at Tora Bora, see also Special Operations Command, *USSOCOM History, 1987–2007* (U.S. Special Operations Command, 2007), 93–97. For a notably more sympathetic account of Franks's handling of

Tora Bora, see Lester Grau and Dodge Billingsley, *Operation Anaconda: America's First Major Battle in Afghanistan* (University Press of Kansas, 2011), 75–81.

399 **"I thought it was a very successful operation":** Tommy Franks, transcript of *Meet the Press*, NBC News, March 24, 2002.

400 **"That's a great question":** Thomas E. Ricks, *Fiasco: The American Military Adventure in Iraq* (Penguin Press, 2006), 127.

400 **A document prepared for public release:** Army War College staff, " 'Operation Enduring Freedom/Noble Eagle' Initial Impressions Conference Report," 1.

402 **"the fifty-pound brains":** Franks, *American Soldier*, 362.

402 **"this is the ultimate consequence":** Franks, *American Soldier*, 8.

402 **"actually was going as I had expected":** Franks, *American Soldier*, 531.

402 **"most tribesmen, including Sunni loyalists":** United States Central Command, notes from "Phase IV 'Rule of Law' Logical Line of Operation Operational Planning Team," March 9, 2003, 59.

402 **Franks had told him in June 2003:** Ricardo Sanchez, *Wiser in Battle: A Soldier's Story* (Harper, 2008), 212.

403 **depicted himself as a maverick:** Franks, *American Soldier*, 203, 367.

403 **"The treatment of Army General Eric Shinseki":** "Voices from the Stars? America's Generals and Public Debate," *American Bar Association National Security Report* 28, no. 4 (November 2006), 9.

403 **"didn't provide anything":** Franks, teleconference with journalists, August 2, 2004, 18.

403 **the variety of ways he had devised:** Franks, *American Soldier*, 410.

403 **"basic grand strategy":** Franks, *American Soldier*, 340–41.

404 **"The October 2002 Centcom war plan":** "Final Report of the Independent Panel to Review DoD Detention Operations," August 24, 2004, 11.

404 **"post conflict stabilization":** RAND Corporation, "Iraq: Translating Lessons into Future DoD Policies," attachment to letter from James Thompson, president and chief executive officer, RAND Corporation, to Defense Secretary Donald Rumsfeld, February 7, 2005, 6.

404 **"There's never been a combat operation":** Franks, *American Soldier*, 524.

404 **"I just think it's interesting":** Franks teleconference, August 2, 2004, 16.

405 **"The guys who did well":** Telephone interview with American civilian official in Kabul who requested anonymity, December 2007.

405 **"This was real leadership":** Nathaniel Fick, *One Bullet Away: The Making of a Marine Officer* (Houghton Mifflin, 2005), 118.

405 **"We're doing it in the Marines":** James Mattis, interview by author at Pentagon, August 12, 2009.

406 **"Are you attacking?":** This and subsequent quotations are from Col. Joe D. Dowdy, interview by Gary Solis, Marine Corps History Division, January 24, 2004.

406 **"Maybe General Mattis won't do it":** This is the sole quotation in this account that is not from Dowdy's oral history. It is from Christopher Cooper, "How a Marine Lost His Command in Race to Baghdad," *Wall Street Journal*, April 5, 2004, 1.

409 **"If we are to keep this great big experiment"** . . . **"then you have won":** James Mattis, "Ethical Challenges in Contemporary Conflict: The Afghanistan and Iraq Cases," 2004 William C. Stutt Ethics Lecture, Alumni Hall, U.S. Naval Academy, Annapolis, MD, November 8, 2004, 7 and 19.

28. RICARDO SANCHEZ: OVER HIS HEAD

410 **One dissent to this narrative:** Philip Zelikow, interviews by author, April and May 2007, and e-mail message to author, June 6, 2011.

411 **"I came away from my first meeting":** The quotations in this paragraph and the next are from interviews done by the author in 2007 and 2008 for Thomas E. Ricks, *The Gamble: General David Petraeus and the American Military Adventure in Iraq, 2006–2008* (Penguin, 2009).

411 **Bremer believed he outranked him:** L. Paul Bremer III, *My Year in Iraq: The Struggle to Build a Future of Hope* (Simon & Schuster, 2006), 186.

411 **"I'm not going to do it":** Sanchez, *Wiser in Battle*, 361.

413 **"Some observers feel":** Jeffrey White, "Eyewitness Perspectives Assessing Progress in Iraq: Security and Extremism," in Knights, ed., *Operation Iraqi Freedom and the New Iraq*, 125.

414 **"The efforts of 1-124" . . . "having learned nothing":** Army intelligence officer who asked not to be identified, e-mail message to author, December 27, 2010.

414 **"In the summer of '03":** "Interview with LTC Russell Godsil," Operational Leadership Experiences, Combat Studies Institute, Fort Leavenworth, KS, 2009, 8.

415 **An Army intelligence expert later estimated:** Maj. Gen. George Fay, investigating officer, "AR 15-6 Investigation of the Abu Ghraib Detention Facility and 205th Military Intelligence Brigade," U.S. Army, August 2004, 37.

415 **"bark like a dog":** Ricks, *Fiasco*, 292. Several other quotations in this section are from that book.

415 **he was contemplating relieving:** Sanchez, *Wiser in Battle*, 274.

416 **In a privately circulated essay:** John Cushman, "An Added Input to the Profession of Arms Discussion," privately circulated essay, June 11, 2011, 1.

417 **"When Lieutenant General Ricardo S. Sanchez":** Andrew Bacevich, "A Modern Major General," *New Left Review*, September–October 2004, 1.

417 **"You all have betrayed me":** Sanchez, *Wiser in Battle*, 435.

418 **"Boy, am I glad to be leaving":** Sanchez, *Wiser in Battle*, 397–98.

418 **"Perhaps most unforgivably" . . . "answer is that simple":** Douglas Pryer, *The Fight for the High Ground: The U.S. Army and Interrogation Training During Operation Iraqi Freedom, May 2003–April 2004* (CGSC Foundation Press, Fort Leavenworth, KS, 2009), 7, 49, 121.

418 **Franks made news in 2008:** Brian Ross, *ABC World News,* January 17, 2008.

418 **"I speak to you today":** "Sanchez Delivers Democratic Party Weekly Address," *Small Wars Journal,* November 27, 2007.

419 **In 2011, Sanchez announced:** Josh Lederman, "Lone Democrat Drops Out of Senate Race in Texas," *The Hill*, December 16, 2011.

420 **"The troops were good":** This and the following quotations are from a series of e-mail exchanges between the author and Robert Killebrew, 2007–2011.

420 **"A system of officer education":** Huba Wass de Czege, "How to Change an Army," *Military Review,* November 1984, accessed online.

421 **That is the way it always goes:** I am indebted to Robert Killebrew for the observations in these three sentences.

421 **"One of the reasons we were able":** Sean MacFarland, "U.S. Army Leader Development: Past, Present and Future," in *Cultivating Army Leaders: Historical*

Perspectives, the Proceedings of the Combat Studies Institute 2010 Military History Symposium (U.S. Army Combined Arms Center, Fort Leavenworth, KS, 2011), 226.

421 **In 2005, a RAND Corporation study:** Margaret Harrell, Harry Thie, Peter Schirmer, and Kevin Brancato, "Developing and Using Army General Officers," in Matthews, ed., *The Future of the Army Profession,* 563.

421 **"If the behavior does not change":** George Reed, "Toxic Leadership," *Military Review,* July–August 2004, 71.

422 **a study done at the Army War College:** Jones, "Improving Accountability for Effective Command Climate."

422 **"I was with Nate":** Conrad Crane, interview by author, December 14, 2011.

422 **"In person, the ruggedly handsome commander":** Vivian Gembara, *Drowning in the Desert: A JAG's Search for Justice in Iraq* (Zenith, 2008), 71.

423 **"With a heavy dose of fear":** Dexter Filkins, "A Region Inflamed: Tough New Tactics by U.S. Tighten Grip on Iraq Towns," *New York Times,* December 7, 2003, 18.

423 **"The simple, somewhat barbaric truth":** Nathan Sassaman, *Warrior King: The Triumph and Betrayal of an American Commander in Iraq* (St. Martin's, 2008), 99.

423 **"I neither trusted nor respected him":** Sassaman, *Warrior King,* 117.

423 **"Screw brigade"** . . . **"I couldn't do that":** Sassaman, *Warrior King,* 160–61.

424 **"First Battalion, 8th Infantry Regiment":** Gembara, *Drowning in the Desert,* 284.

424 **This time Gen. Odierno gave Sassaman:** Ricks, *The Gamble,* 108–9.

29. GEORGE CASEY: TRYING BUT TREADING WATER

426 **"oblivious to the inefficacy":** Ricks, *The Gamble,* 25.

427 **"Because the Army won't change itself":** Ricks, *The Gamble,* 12.

427 **"The potential second- and third-order effects":** Ricks, *Fiasco,* 418.

427 **"By and large":** Francis "Bing" West, *The Strongest Tribe: War, Politics, and the Endgame in Iraq* (Random House, 2009), 107.

428 **"There was no downtime":** Jim Frederick, *Black Hearts: One Platoon's Descent Into Madness in Iraq's Triangle of Death* (Harmony, 2010), 185.

428 **"shitbags" who constantly "fucked up":** Frederick, *Black Hearts,* 109.

429 **"I did everything by the book":** Frederick, *Black Hearts,* 205–6.

429 **Cushman faulted the chain of command:** John Cushman, "Chain of Command Performance of Duty, 2nd Brigade Combat Team, 101st Airborne Division, 2005–06: A Case Study Offered to the Center for the Army Professional Ethic," unpublished paper, June 2, 2011, 1, 30.

430 **there were fifty insurgent attacks:** Seth Jones, *Hunting in the Shadows: The Search for al Qa'ida Since 9/11* (W. W. Norton, 2012), 247.

430 **"Jack, I just came out of Iraq":** Ricks, *The Gamble,* 82.

430 **"I didn't see that at the time":** This and other quotations from Casey in this and following paragraphs are from author interview with Gen. George Casey, October 13, 2008.

431 **"I respected General Casey":** Cheney, *In My Time,* 439.

30. DAVID PETRAEUS: AN OUTLIER MOVES IN, THEN LEAVES

432 **"Not a single general has been removed":** Ricks, *The Gamble,* 99.

434 **"We feel—the Chiefs feel":** Bob Woodward, *The War Within* (Simon & Schuster, 2008), 371.

434 **"I always felt that as a professional":** George Casey, interview by author, October 13, 2008.

435 **"It is not possible to fire all former Baathists":** David Petraeus, "Lessons of the Iraq War and Its Aftermath," in Knights, ed., *Operation Iraqi Freedom and the New Iraq,* 225.

436 **"By the beginning of the surge":** Peter Mansoor, "The Softer Side of War," *Foreign Affairs,* January–February 2011, accessed online.

436 **"Our mindset was not to kill":** Quoted in *Armor,* July–August 2008.

437 **"I don't think it was something":** Ricks, *The Gamble,* 202.

437 **"he basically inherited a strategic void":** Philip Zelikow, interview by author, April 2007.

437 **"almost an excruciating period":** Quotations from Petraeus in this paragraph and the following one are from an interview by the author, October 15, 2008.

437 **"I think he had one shot":** U.S. Army colonel in Iraq who asked not to be identified, interview by author, June 30, 2007.

439 **"We were really an orphan headquarters":** Christopher Koontz, ed., *Enduring Voices: Oral Histories of the U.S. Army Experience in Afghanistan, 2003–2005* (U.S. Army Center of Military History, 2008), 42, 47, 49.

439 **the number of reported security problems:** Joseph Collins, *Understanding War in Afghanistan* (National Defense University Press, 2011), 72.

439 **The turning point in the war:** Army Lt. Gen. (Ret.) David Barno, interview by author, February 28, 2012. Barno commanded in Afghanistan in 2004–5. See also Seth Jones, *In the Graveyard of Empires: America's War in Afghanistan* (W. W. Norton, 2009), 245–46.

439 **a number of incidents:** Jones, *In the Graveyard of Empires,* 257.

439 **its officials grew unhappy:** David Isby, *Afghanistan, Graveyard of Empires: A New History of the Borderlands* (Pegasus, 2010), 284.

440 **"The replacement of McKiernan":** Lt. Col. Donald Drechler and retired Army Col. Charles Allen, "Why Senior Military Leaders Fail," *Armed Forces Journal,* July/August 2009.

440 **"You have ten commanders":** Barno, interview by author, February 28, 2012.

441 **"America's generals have failed":** This and subsequent quotations are from Yingling, "A Failure of Generalship."

442 **"which," Nagl recalled:** Nagl, interview by author, October 3, 2011.

443 **"I believe in our generals":** This account and the quotations from Gen. Hammond are from Greg Jaffe, "Critiques of Iraq War Reveal Rifts Among Army Officers," *Wall Street Journal,* June 29, 2007, 1.

443 **he gave Yingling a mediocre performance evaluation:** Yingling, e-mail messages to author, January 31 and February 1, 2012.

443 **"I think we've got great general officers":** The account of Gen. Cody's exchanges with captains at Fort Knox is from Fred Kaplan, "Challenging the Generals," *New York Times,* August 26, 2007, accessed online.

443 **"guilty of three important failures":** Paul Yingling, "The Evolution of American Civil-Military Relations," lecture at George C. Marshall European Center for Security Studies, May 4, 2011, 11–12.

444 **"I would say most of the current GO":** Maj. Neil Smith, e-mail message to author, January 2011.

445 **"They have somewhat abdicated their role":** "Interview with Col. (Ret.) Dale Eikmeier," Operational Leadership Experiences, Combat Studies Institute, Fort Leavenworth, KS, March 10, 2011, 11.

445 **"With Gates, it is not to destroy people":** James Mattis, interview by author, August 12, 2009.

446 **Dempsey stated early in 2012:** "A Conversation with General Martin Dempsey," Carnegie Endowment for International Peace, May 1, 2012. Transcript accessed online.

446 **"We're going to go back":** Chinn was quoted in Michelle Tan, "Training Gets a Reboot," *Army Times,* April 16, 2012, accessed online.

EPILOGUE: RESTORING AMERICAN MILITARY LEADERSHIP

448 **"Generals are, or should be":** Cohen, *Supreme Command,* 215.

449 **"For a number of my officers":** Army officer who asked not to be identified, e-mail messages to author, 2011.

449 **"rings loudly of institutionalizing mediocrity":** Brig. Gen. Mark Arnold, "Don't Promote Mediocrity," *Armed Forces Journal,* May 2012, accessed online.

450 **"In 1914 every army of all the belligerent powers":** Michael Howard, "Military Science in an Age of Peace," *RUSI Journal,* March 1974, 6–7.

451 **"Accountability provides the motivation":** Jones, "Improving Accountability for Effective Command Climate," 25.

452 **"the first thing that a commander":** Jones and Ancell, eds., *Four-Star Leadership,* 13.

453 **"There's no way to tell":** Donn Starry, interview by Charles Cavanaugh Jr., October 1985, in Sorley, ed., *Press On!,* 1221.

453 **A 2011 study at Harvard's Kennedy School:** Sayce Falk and Sasha Rogers, "Junior Office Military Retention: Challenges and Opportunities," Policy Analysis Exercise, Kennedy School of Government, Harvard University, March 2011, 2–4 of executive summary and 1, 11, 13, 19.

454 **"will have minimal impact":** Michelle Tan, "Army Looks to Make MSAF More Random," *Army Times,* October 10, 2011, 25.

458 **"We don't educate [our officers]":** Barak Salmoni, Jessica Hart, Renny McPherson, and Aidan Kirby Winn, "Growing Strategic Leaders for Future Conflict," *Parameters,* Spring 2010, 77.

459 **"It is depressing how so many":** Komer, *Bureaucracy Does Its Thing,* 155.

460 **"In the absence of orders and guidance":** Petraeus, in videotaped interview at WashingtonPost.com, February 9, 2010.

460 **"Intellectuals are most valued":** Yingling, e-mail message to author, April 14, 2011.

461 **In 1969, there were 398 military veterans:** Jennifer Manning, "Membership of the 112th Congress: A Profile," Congressional Research Service, August 4, 2011, 7–8.

INDEX

Page numbers in *italics* refer to the map.

PHOTOGRAPH CREDITS

14 (bottom): Scott Olson / Getty Images

15 (top): Chris Hondros / Getty Images

15 (bottom): Photo by the 447th Air Expeditionary Group Public Affairs. Permission granted by DVIDS (Defense Video & Imagery Distribution System), photo 18988

16: Photo by Cameron Boyd, Joint Combat Camera Afghanistan. Permission granted by DVIDS, photo 389967